SOCIAL-SPATIAL SEGREGATION

Concepts, processes and outcomes

Edited by
Christopher D. Lloyd
Ian G. Shuttleworth
David W.S. Wong

First published in Great Britain in 2015 by

Policy Press   North America office:
University of Bristol   Policy Press
1-9 Old Park Hill   c/o The University of Chicago Press
Bristol   1427 East 60th Street
BS2 8BB   Chicago, IL 60637, USA
UK   t: +1 773 702 7700
t: +44 (0)117 954 5940   f: +1 773-702-9756
pp-info@bristol.ac.uk   sales@press.uchicago.edu
www.policypress.co.uk   www.press.uchicago.edu

British Library Cataloguing in Publication Data
A catalogue record for this book is available from the British Library.

Library of Congress Cataloging-in-Publication Data
A catalog record for this book has been requested.

ISBN 978-1-4473-0134-9 paperback
ISBN 978-1-4473-2082-1 ePub
ISBN 978-1-4473-2930-5 Kindle

The rights of Christopher D. Lloyd, Ian G. Shuttleworth and David W.S. Wong to be identified as editors of this work has been asserted by them in accordance with the Copyright, Designs and Patents Act 1988.

The statements and opinions contained within this publication are solely those of the editors and not of the University of Bristol or Policy Press. The University of Bristol and Policy Press disclaim responsibility for any injury to persons or property resulting from any material published in this publication.

Policy Press works to counter discrimination on grounds of gender, race, disability, age and sexuality.

Cover design by Andrew Corbett.
Front cover: images kindly supplied by Melody T. Wong (top) and
Andrey Bayda/Shutterstock (bottom).
Printed and bound in Great Britain by Marston Book Services, Oxford

Contents

Outcomes

List of tables, figures and maps

Tables

Figures

Maps

Notes on contributors

Eva K. Andersson is associate professor in the Department of Human Geography, Stockholm University, Sweden. Her research interests include urban geography, neighbourhood effects, residential/school segregation, social justice, socioeconomic career, rural gentrification, residential mobility and the elderly.

Paul Barr is a postdoctoral research fellow at Dartmouth College, USA. In 2008 he received the Margaret Kenwright Young Scientist of the Year Award.

Gemma Catney is a lecturer in the School of Environmental Sciences at the University of Liverpool, UK. She is a population geographer with research interests in internal migration with an ethnic group dimension, and in residential segregation and integration in Britain.

Danny Dorling is the Halford Mackinder Professor of Geography at the University of Oxford, UK. His research interests include data visualisation and social inequality.

Mark Ellis is professor of geography and director of the Center for Studies in Demography and Ecology, University of Washington, USA. He studies immigration, migration and labour markets.

Nissa Finney's research focuses on internal migration (including ethnicity and life course perspectives), migrant settlement and ethnic inequalities, particularly spatial dimensions. She uses a mixture of qualitative and quantitative methods in her research. Nissa's background is in geography and she now works at the University of Manchester (UK) as lecturer in social statistics. She is a member of the Cathie Marsh Institute for Social Research and a member of the ESRC Centre on Dynamics of Ethnicity.

James Forrest is associate professor in the Department of Environment and Geography at Macquarie University, Australia. His research interests are mainly in the social and electoral areas, focusing on geographies of advantage and disadvantage, most recently on ethnic group disadvantage.

Kenneth N. French is a lecturer at the University of Nebraska, USA. His research interests include ethnicity geography and the geography of rap.

Richard Harris is a reader in quantitative geography in the School of Geographical Sciences, University of Bristol (UK), with interests in spatial statistics, geodemographics and education.

Myles Gould is a lecturer in human geography at the University of Leeds, UK. His research interests include multilevel modelling and health geography.

Steven R. Holloway is professor of geography at the University of Georgia, USA. His research interests centre on residential segregation, racial mixing and housing.

Sungsoon Hwang is associate professor of geography at DePaul University, USA. Her research has been focused on the spatial analysis of housing markets, residential segregation, sustainable transportation, GIS for sustainability education and spatial data mining.

Ron Johnston is a professor in the School of Geographical Sciences at the University of Bristol (UK), where he specialises in electoral studies and urban social geography.

Christopher D. Lloyd (editor) works in the School of Environmental Sciences, University of Liverpool, UK. His research interests focus on spatial data analysis, and in particular on local spatial statistics and the exploration of spatial scale.

John Logan is professor of sociology and director of the S4 initiative at Brown University, USA. His research interests include urban sociology, race and ethnicity, migration and immigration, family and political sociology.

Fernando A. López Hernández is professor in the Department of Quantitative Methods and Computing, Polytechnic University of Cartagena, Spain. His research interests are in spatial econometrics, economic geography, spatio–temporal statistics and quantitative spatial processes.

Bo Malmberg is professor in the Department of Human Geography, Stockholm University, Sweden. His research interests are in human, urban and economic geography.

David Manley is lecturer in the School of Geographical Sciences, University of Bristol, UK. He is interested in trying to better understand how the places in which individuals live interact with the outcomes that they experience over their life course.

Pablo Mateos is lecturer in human geography at the Department of Geography, University College London, UK. His research interests lie within population and urban geography and his work focuses on investigating ethnicity, identity, migration and segregation in contemporary cities.

John Östh is senior lecturer in human geography in the Department of Social and Economic Geography, Uppsala University, Sweden. His research interest is oriented towards software development and quantitative analysis in population and economic geography with a special focus on demography and migration, school choice and labour market opportunities, and more recently, the geography of human interaction on the internet.

Antonio Páez is associate professor in the School of Geography and Earth Sciences, McMaster University, Canada. His recent work includes studies on accessibility, spatial filtering, ageing and mobility, spatial analysis of qualitative variables, transportation and social exclusion, the influence of the built and social environments on travel behaviour, social networks and decision making, telework adoption, and blood donor behaviour and trends.

Michael Poulsen is associate professor in the Department of Environment and Geography at Macquarie University, Australia. His academic career has focused on quantitative methods of information extraction from spatial data.

Manuel Ruiz is associate professor in Department of Quantitative Methods and Computing at the Technical University of Cartagena, Spain. His fields of expertise include spatial econometrics, nonparametric statistics and symbolic analysis.

Albert Sabater is currently research fellow in the Department of Geography and Sustainable Development at the University of St Andrews, UK. He has an interest in social and demographic issues with a background in quantitative analysis, including the long-term implications of immigration and the (re)production of inequalities through diverse processes such as segregation.

Ian G. Shuttleworth (editor) is senior lecturer in human geography at Queen's University Belfast, UK. He has research interests in population mobility as well as segregation.

Maarten van Ham is professor of urban renewal and head of the Neighbourhood Change and Housing Research Group at Delft University of Technology, the Netherlands. He is a population geographer with a background in economic and urban geography.

David W.S. Wong (editor), professor of geography, University of Hong Kong, and George Mason University, USA, has a research focus on segregation.

Richard Wright holds the Orvil E. Dryfoos Chair in Public Affairs and is professor of geography at Dartmouth College, USA. He researches immigration and racial mixing.

ONE

Introduction

*Christopher D. Lloyd, Ian G. Shuttleworth
and David W.S. Wong*

Segregation is a key theme for academic research and is also of major policy and political interest (see, for example, Ouseley, 2005; Finney and Simpson, 2009). Questions often asked include what the segregation level is, whether segregation has increased or decreased and how, whether it is greater or less in one country or city than in another, and whether it is socially harmful. These questions are eminently sensible and are easy to ask, but their answers are not simple to provide despite the weight of academic research on segregation dating back to the 1950s, and earlier. These questions remain hard to answer (and may indeed always be problematic), because they involve method and interpretation, themes about which there is considerable discussion. In the UK context, for instance, there was much debate as to how far residential segregation had grown by the time of the 2001 Census, and about the mechanisms that underpinned changes in the distribution of populations (Simpson, 2004, 2005; Johnston et al, 2005; Carling, 2008). However, the academic community is probably nearer now to dealing with these and similar questions than it has ever been before. This book aims to show how and why this is the case by showcasing some recent international research on segregation that highlights how new methods and new data can offer fresh insights into the measurement of segregation and understandings of some of the mechanisms that lead to (or away from) segregation.

This volume's initial beginnings lay in conversations between the editors about global and local measures of residential segregation. These interchanges rapidly expanded to debates about how population is structured across space and how to deal most effectively with the complex and difficult phenomenon of spatial scale. As the discussions broadened out, and individual research agendas developed, attention also started to be given to the population processes that shape residential segregation and, following the growing academic and policy interest in neighbourhood research (van Ham et al, 2012), on some of the social outcomes of segregation across a variety of domains. It also seemed that segregation research was at an interesting juncture for several reasons that lay on the intersection between data and methods.

First, new census data are becoming available as the results of the 2011 UK and 2010 US Censuses were being released at the time the book was being prepared. These will provide a valuable major resource for segregation researchers in the UK and the US for the foreseeable future and will be the focus for much future analysis. It is therefore important to consider how these data can be used and how some of the problems inherent in the analysis of geographical data might be overcome. Besides this, there are emerging general trends across several countries, towards greater access to individual-level micro-data for academic researchers in secure settings. This has arisen because of changing data provision by national statistical agencies, the demands of researchers and changes in political and legal attitudes towards data. It is likely that these trends will continue and accelerate since the nature and range of population data collection strategies in many national contexts are changing. In the UK, for instance, the 2011 Census may well be the last in traditional form, and could be superseded by a combination of administrative data and surveys taking the UK some of the way towards countries like Sweden, Denmark and Finland in the ways in which population data are collected and disseminated. This could help to avoid the problem of a 'data glut' of statistics that rapidly become outdated in the years just after a census, since it may well be possible to provide useful information more frequently. In the US, the traditional long form used in the census every decade to collect detailed socioeconomic and housing data from a sample of the US population has already been replaced by the rolling American Community Survey (ACS). The likely contours of the emerging 'data landscape' mean that segregation researchers will have to work in new ways to access data and to conduct analyses, and that there will be benefits as well as costs. Some of the methods and approaches, for instance, that were possible, may no longer be so in a decade's time, but alternatively, it may well be possible to do things that are completely new. In this context, there may be lessons and experiences that could be usefully shared internationally.

Second, new methods have been developed and are being applied in segregation research. These reach far beyond the calculation of global, 'one size fits all' indices of segregation that formerly characterised this research field to a concern with local and spatial indices that measure more effectively geographical variations. Beyond this, there is a growing academic interest in investigating the geographical scales over which residential segregation can be most appropriately measured, and this has adapted work by spatial econometricians and geostatisticians to allow more sensitive approaches to the analysis of the spatial structure of populations. The greater understanding of population and social phenomena that have developed over the past decade have also extended to the realisation that many standard approaches to segregation analysis, whether through the use of census data or other data sources, essentially deal with a 'night-time' population that is residentially fixed, whereas, in reality, people have diverse daily experiences across a variety of domains of activity such as work, education and play. This realisation has led to a developing academic and policy interest in understanding '24/7 populations' or 'ambient populations' in an expansion of the space-time geography of Hägerstrand (1970), and new ways to conceptualise segregation (Wong and Shaw, 2011).

These developments, challenges and opportunities led the editors to convene sessions on segregation at the 2010 'Ashcloud' Association of American Geographers Conference in Washington, DC. These sessions were international, bringing together researchers from the UK and the US, but the book is not restricted to these national perspectives, with several other countries, such as Sweden, represented. The aim was to take a broad overview of segregation studies, primarily with a methodological focus, and to bring together different national perspectives on this fast-changing field. This edited volume draws on these contributions. It has a threefold structure, starting with *concepts*, then moving on to *processes* and ending with a consideration of some of the *outcomes* of segregation to show some of the ways in which segregation could have implications for lives 'on the ground'. The themes of new data and new methods crosscut this structure and, as we introduce the book in the following pages, we try to tease out how these themes combine across the various sections and chapters.

Concepts

The first section of the book is conceptual in its primary focus although, of course, other chapters in later sections also deal with concepts and reflect and amplify some of the ideas started here. 'Concepts' is a broad area. In this book it covers material ranging from general theoretical debates about how segregation can be thought about as a social phenomenon to much more detailed methodological questions of data and method. It starts with Johnston et al (Chapter Two), who make the point that 'segregation matters, measurement matters' by reflecting on conceptual issues in thinking about, and measuring, residential segregation in multicultural cities. They also usefully comment on the influence of segregation on life chances – a theme to which the book returns in its third section where its potentially positive and negative effects are discussed. The central contribution of this chapter lies in its illustration of a typology that incorporates unevenness, inequality and concentration in a multigroup framework that is suited to many cosmopolitan cities across the world. Chapter Six, by Wright et al, is closely related to these arguments since it examines how segregation in US cities is not best characterised by a Black/White dichotomy that dominated earlier research, but by the analysis of mixing and multiethnic diversity instead. A typology is constructed that leads away from thinking about segregation to neighbourhood dominance and diversity, and the ways that White people fit into this pattern with regard to social status and income. The approaches in Chapters Two and Six can be generalised to other multiethnic cities, and this push towards meaningful cross-city and cross-country comparisons surfaces elsewhere in the volume. In Chapter Three Wong makes a case for considering the spatiality of segregation using either physical distance or attribute difference as a measure of separation between places and groups, exploring the relationship between the concepts of clustering and segregation in an approach that permits statistical significance testing and the use of individual-level data (see also Páez et al in Chapter Five).

Chapter Four (Lloyd et al) develops these ideas from a different perspective. Its concern is in defining appropriate spatial units for the measurement and study of residential segregation, and it considers what 'appropriate' might mean. Usually, quantitative analyses of residential segregation, in particular, are tied to census or other official statistical output geographies, but the main problem is that these units are not always designed to be socially meaningful as neighbourhoods. In fact, they might not even be suitable for statistical analysis because of uneven population distribution across them (Cockings and Martin, 2005). Moreover, the modifiable areal unit problem (MAUP) (Openshaw, 1984) also rears its head. In essence, MAUP means that the size and shape of the geographical units used to represent spatial data shapes the outcome of the analysis – the results obtained are a function of the output geography. This limits the extent to which it is possible to make segregation comparisons between different times and places – after all, if the spatial units used to represent population in Country A differ from those in Country B, how is it possible to tell if differing levels of segregation are (a) real or (b) purely a result of the output geographies that are used? These and similar concerns run across

–

several chapters, but one answer, put forward by Lloyd et al using a Northern Ireland example, is to use information on flows between spatial units to measure their interaction and thereby to construct neighbourhoods that are more meaningful. In the same way as Wong, the authors of Chapter Four also consider attribute difference (in this case, the difference between places in terms of their religious composition) to give additional information on whether places are the same or different and whether they can be grouped together. The questions of the 'correct' spatial scale and of the 'neighbourhood' are tricky and not susceptible to easy answers, but they run, in a variety of forms, either explicitly or implicitly, through most of the chapters of the book, and they are issues that will be returned to in the book's Conclusion.

While many chapters in the book have used spatially aggregated or ecological data (as have most segregation studies since the 1950s), Páez et al (Chapter Five) take a very different approach. They use historical US Census data from the 19th century to showcase a method that offers an escape from MAUP by the use of individual-level data, and demonstrate how a new spatial association measure for categorical data can be used to measure segregation at individual and very small spatial scales. Although historical in focus, this contribution opens avenues for future research given that the current greater availability of individual population data, and the population data systems of some countries, mean that segregation measures will have to accommodate data formats that go beyond standard spatially aggregated census data. Östh et al (Chapter Seven) use finely geocoded Swedish population register data to construct bespoke population neighbourhoods to assess segregation levels and population concentrations across user-selected geographical scales. This draws on new methods and data – the Swedish Population Register – that are likely to be of interest in the English-speaking world by describing and analysing the relationship between the concentration of foreign-born children and poor educational outcomes across a set of Swedish cities. Their analysis demonstrates that there are poorer outcomes for those who live in areas with high concentrations of foreign-born – a conclusion that is likely to be replicated in other national contexts but one that remains of concern given the intractability of these outcomes. Returning directly to the theme of data, these chapters (and likewise that of van Ham and Manley in Chapter Eleven) show how non-standard datasets (likely to increase in importance, for example, in the UK *if* the traditional census is downgraded or replaced) can be used in segregation analysis. Furthermore, methodologically, by dodging the restrictions imposed by fixed spatial units to represent population data, they avoid some of the effects of MAUP, and illustrate how segregation comparisons may be made between different places and different times by using data capable of more flexible aggregation. However, cross-country comparisons face other problems, and these are clearly illustrated in the chapter by Mateos (Chapter Eight). This compares population data across 20 countries spanning America (Canada, Mexico and the US), East Asia (Japan and Korea), Oceania (Australia and New Zealand) and a variety of European states to consider the conceptual and ideological considerations that underlie the collection and release of data on ethnicity. As pointed out by Johnston et al and Mateos, international segregation comparisons are a challenging but desirable goal, and one that is perhaps nearer to being attained now than it was previously.

Processes

Many previous segregation studies have tended to be cross-sectional, not least because they have relied on standard census geographical outputs in the UK and the US. However, the insight that segregation is not just a *pattern* but also a *dynamic process* is not new. Highly influential and much-cited work by Schelling (1969) (see, for example, Clark, 1991, 1992) has considered how small differences in residential preferences can lead to 'tipping points' where the demographic composition of neighbourhoods suddenly shifts. There has also been a growing recent literature on neighbourhoods, and the population sifting effects of migration, with regard to race, health and wider aspects of social deprivation. These, and similar themes, are explored in the five chapters in this section, using non-census data sources that are capable of capturing population dynamics often on quite a fine temporal resolution. Shuttleworth et al (Chapter Nine) begin the section, using individual-level longitudinal data from Northern Ireland, to explore how internal migration has reshaped population distributions by religion since 2001, and how and why historically segregation levels have been stable for long periods only to increase rapidly over very short time periods. This experience is compared and contrasted with expectations taken from the Schelling Model. Harris (Chapter Ten) focuses on ethnic segregation in British schools and how this has changed over time using administrative data. This chapter is not only noteworthy for using administrative data (as we have seen, a possible harbinger for future developments), but also for showing how to analyse such data to extract maximum value from them, and for its findings that are a useful antidote to demographic scare stories that British society is inexorably fragmenting on ethnic lines (such stories are countered by Finney and Simpson, 2009). Van Ham and Manley (Chapter Eleven) build on the extensive literature on neighbourhood choice and population dynamics, dating back to Schelling, by looking at the residential moves of minority ethnic groups in Britain. It is interesting to note that again, administrative data, used with data from the census, is a powerful combination, with census data bringing information on neighbourhood/area contexts and the administrative data escaping the shackles of cross-sectional census data by enabling dynamic change through time to be evaluated.

Sabater and Finney (Chapter Twelve) use traditional census sources to discuss ethnic residential segregation in England and Wales. They make the interesting contribution that residential segregation is a dynamic process with a significant life cycle component with a greater general evenness in the geographical distribution of young adults from minority ethnic groups through time because of patterns of internal migration that tend to mean that young adults from all urban backgrounds move to major diverse urban centres. This is a powerful finding, not least because, as they age, these young adults may have experienced more ethnic diversity than older members of their respective groups. The section concludes with Hwang's contribution (Chapter Thirteen). This considers the socioeconomic background to ethnic residential segregation in two US cities where there are powerful drivers in the housing market that have shaped where different groups live. The notion that population is spatially sorted across different housing submarkets is the fundamental process creating residential segregation.

Outcomes

Johnston et al make a powerful case at the start of the book that 'segregation matters', and it is to this theme that the book returns in its final section that considers the outcomes of segregation, although it is by no means clear what these outcomes are. It is possible to make an argument that segregation and inequality are harmful but, equally, a plausible case can also be made that segregation can, in some circumstances, be beneficial. The case for segregation being harmful can be more easily made than the one that it is beneficial. The negative case is that segregation at small spatial scales may lead to social exclusion, an inability to access the full range of social and economic opportunities (White, 1987), and the spatial concentration of social disadvantage that is cumulative over and above individual problems. The geographical concentration of minority ethnic groups, for instance, can lead to the formation of what have been termed 'ghettos' – spatial focuses for marginalised populations isolated from the social mainstream of the host society where social capital (Putnam, 2002) is internalised within communities but does not reach outside. However, there is also a case that local segregation can be beneficial for some groups. Bonding social capital may lead to tightly knit mutually supportive social networks that help outcomes for members of these groups across a variety of life domains, and it offers economies of scale that allow for the maintenance of specific shops and services that are particular to those ethnic groups. This sense of security, it is argued, may well have beneficial outcomes for minority group members.

This interchange is played out in various ways in the chapters in this section. There is a strong argument (Wilkinson and Pickett, 2010) that social inequality is deeply harmful, not only for people at the bottom end of the scale, but also for *all* members of society. Catney (Chapter Fourteen) examines the health outcomes of Catholics and Protestants in small areas in Northern Ireland using individual-level microdata similar to the Shuttleworth et al contribution. She shows that in Northern Ireland there are paradoxical features perhaps reflecting the unique features of that society since Catholics in areas where they are a large majority have poorer health outcomes than in those where they are a minority, whereas Protestants have poorer outcomes where they are in a minority (for example, in Catholic areas). This perhaps reflects the social geography of Northern Ireland where majority Catholic areas remain less socially advantaged. Dorling (Chapter Fifteen) takes up some of these arguments with reference to macro-level social changes and the ways in which socioeconomic restructuring have manifested across the advanced world in terms of socio-spatial polarisation. This restricts the life chances and set of opportunities that are open to those in weaker disadvantaged positions with regard to health, education and social mobility. Furthermore, these inequalities *within* countries cannot be separated from large and growing *international* inequalities, themes that resonate with the broader argument of Wilkinson and Pickett (2010). The central question of concern is the extent to which the concentration of minority populations in socially disadvantaged areas can have a negative effect on health outcomes, as noted on occasion in the US, or the degree to which spatial concentration can lead to greater social cohesion, bonding social capital and more positive health outcomes. French (Chapter Sixteen) takes another perspective and explores the

–

impacts of living in segregated neighbourhoods for those living in Milwaukee, Wisconsin in the US. This identifies social inequalities between neighbourhoods with different ethnic compositions. For example, Whites living in the 'White' neighbourhoods tended to have higher levels of educational attainment and higher income levels, while African Americans and Hispanics living in their respective neighbourhoods had lower educational attainment and income levels. In contrast, Hispanics in Milwaukee considered the development of ethnic business enclaves to be a positive outcome of their population concentration.

Conclusion

This book brings together new data sources, methods and perspectives in an attempt to sketch out future directions for segregation research. This is not an easy task – the old questions about spatial scale and measurement remain, for instance, and new ones about data and social change have arisen – but it is hoped that the contributions will start to show fresh ways to approach them. Particular issues to which it is hoped the book will contribute are discussions about how new sources of data can be effectively used for social science research, how segregation studies can move beyond its hitherto main focus of *residential* segregation to incorporate analysis across other activity domains, how segregation studies can move beyond cross-sectional analyses that deal with specific segregation dimensions (for example, exposure, unevenness and clustering) to deal better with population dynamics and segregation as a process, and how and why segregation matters. This is an ambitious agenda, but we hope that the book will mark the first step towards tackling these and related questions.

References

Carling, A. (2008) 'The curious case of the mis-claimed myth claims: Ethnic segregation, polarisation, and the future of Bradford', *Urban Studies*, vol 45, pp 553-89.

Clark, W.A.V. (1991) 'Residential preferences and neighborhood racial segregation: a test of the Schelling segregation model', *Demography*, vol 28, pp 1-19.

Clark, W.A.V. (1992) 'Residential preferences and residential choices in a multiethnic context', *Demography*, vol 29, no 3, 451-66.

Cockings, S. and Martin, D. (2005) 'Zone design for environment and health studies using pre-aggregated data', *Social Science & Medicine*, vol 60, no 12, pp 2729-42.

Finney, N. and Simpson, L. (2009) *'Sleepwalking to segregation'? Challenging myths about race and migration*, Bristol: Policy Press.

Hägerstrand, T. (1970) 'What about people in regional science?', *Papers of the Regional Science Association*, vol 24, pp 1-12.

Johnston, R., Poulsen, M. and Forrest, J. (2005) 'On the measurement and meaning of residential segregation: A response to Simpson', *Urban Studies*, vol 42, pp 1121-227.

Openshaw, S. (1984) *The modifiable areal unit problem*, Concepts and Techniques in Modern Geography 38, Norwich: Geobooks.

Ouseley, H. (2001) *Community pride not prejudice: Making diversity work in Bradford*, Bradford: Bradford Vision.

Putnam, R.D. (ed) (2002) *Democracies in flux: the evolution of social capital in contemporary society*, Oxford: Oxford University Press.

Schelling, T. (1969) 'Models of segregation', *The American Economic Review*, vol 59, pp 488-93.

Simpson, L. (2004) 'Statistics of racial segregation: Measures, evidence and policy', *Urban Studies*, vol 41, pp 661-81.

Simpson, L. (2005) 'On the measurement and meaning of residential segregation: A reply to Johnston, Poulsen and Forrest', *Urban Studies*, vol 42, pp 1229-30.

van Ham, M., Manley, D., Bailey, N., Simpson, L., Duncan Maclennan, D. (2012) *Neighbourhood effects research: New perspectives*, Springer, Dordrecht.

White, M. (1987) *American neighborhoods and residential differentiation*, New York: Russell Sage Foundation.

Wilkinson, R. and Pickett, K. (2010) *The spirit level: why equality is better for everyone*, London: Penguin.

Wong, D.W.S. and Shaw, S.-L. (2011) 'Measuring segregation: an activity-space approach', *Journal of Geographical Systems*, vol 13, no 2, 127-45.

CONCEPTS

TWO

Segregation matters, measurement matters[1]

Ron Johnston, Michael Poulsen and James Forrest

> There's many a difference quickly found
> Between the different races.
> But the only essential differential
> Is living in different places.
> (Ogden Nash)[2]

Introduction

Segregation across neighbourhoods, schools and workplaces, by ethnicity, age, socioeconomic class and gender, for example, provides frequent material for political and social commentators – especially at times of social unrest when it (in particular residential and school segregation by ethnicity – school segregation is the focus of Richard Harris in Chapter Ten – and/or socioeconomic class – see Danny Dorling, Chapter Fifteen) is often presented as a causal factor underpinning that situation.[3] It has also attracted a great deal of academic attention, across the social sciences and beyond, for many decades (Nightingale, 2012). Much of that attention has focused on the measurement of segregation, and the volume of work is not diminishing, more than half a century after the pioneering studies that established how segregated North American cities were. New ways of measuring this key concept are regularly proposed, capitalising on the increased availability of small-area data, developments in spatial statistics and rapid advances in computer power.

Despite that wealth of literature, in 1998 we inaugurated research that was to add to it, proposing new ways of measuring (ethnic) residential segregation in a range of societies where some form of multiculturalism was established. The work focused on two linked arguments. The first was that the commonly deployed methods of measuring segregation are of limited value and disclose little of the detailed patterning that characterises contemporary urban residential mosaics – where diversity of neighbourhood ethnic composition is the norm. The second was that the idealised pattern that underpinned so much writing on this topic – the experience of African Americans and, to a lesser extent, other immigrant groups to US cities in the early to mid-20th century (on which see, for example, Peach, 2005; Johnston et al, 2006a) – is of only marginal relevance to the study of contemporary situations, within as well as beyond US cities (Johnston et al, 2002). It was clear that future research should focus on the degree and nature of ethnic mix not in a city as a whole, but in its various parts, as Johnston et al (2010a) emphasised.[4] By looking at alternative ways of measuring segregation we could better appreciate those contemporary patterns, in the context of alternative paradigms/typologies of the processes by which members of ethnic groups select different types of residential neighbourhoods and the diversity of milieux that result from those choices. Indeed, our work suggests that there is a strong case – although we have not proposed it, and given the long history of the term's use it is unlikely to get much support – for the concept of segregation to be replaced by concentration; segregation implies a pattern imposed by others, through the exercise of economic, social, cultural and political power, whereas concentration – probably now the dominant process – implies choice by most of those involved. Many residents of multiethnic districts are not choosing to live in areas where one group predominates, so that the outcomes are neighbourhoods of varying ethnic diversity. The core argument of the research summarised here – and the measurement issues that it addresses – is the need for methods that identify that diversity rather than conceal it by using measures that just focus on average situations.

Segregation matters

Measuring residential segregation only matters because residential segregation matters – as many claim and show (for a recent, extensive and much applauded example, see Sampson, 2012; see also Uslaner, 2012).[5] It matters to people's life chances – in their neighbourhoods and schools, and their local labour markets; in the delivery of public services to their homes and districts; and in the provision of facilities by both the private and the voluntary sector. Where you live matters to your future (as shown, for example, in analyses of minority ethnic groups' experiences in the UK labour market – see Khattab et al, 2010a, 2010b; Johnston et al, 2010b – and in the educational attainment of English school and university students – see Johnston et al., 2005; Hoare and Johnston, 2011).

It also matters with regard to lifestyle and development of the ideologies and attitudes that underpin how people behave. Much of their learned attitudes and behaviour patterns derive from socialisation and mobilisation processes operating through social networks, many of which (especially at certain life stages and for some groups more than others) are spatially structured with a clear focus on local neighbourhoods (Verwoort et al, 2011). Where you live matters because it influences with whom you come into contact, whether you trust your neighbours (Bécares et al, 2011; Sampson, 2012) and, following their models, how you choose to live your life. (Bowyer, 2009, is a good example of such work, which has a long history; see also Wright, 1977.)

Segregation matters, too, because it is frequently a source – or at least an exacerbation – of individual and, especially, group identity and difference within society that can generate tensions and occasional conflict, especially where the differences are linked with economic, social and political disadvantage. As societies become increasingly multiethnic, multicultural and unequal, with ethnicity a major source of identity in an increasingly mobile and potentially anomic world, segregation's role in many aspects of identity formation – not least the 'us-and-them' images often associated with such divided societies – is an important topic of public and political as well as academic debate.

The literature about these claims regarding the role of segregation in the development of life chances (see Chapter Sixteen, this volume), lifestyles, personal and group identity and inter-group relations is massive, and growing rapidly. So is that on how the negative consequences might be countered (Hewstone, 2009). The relationships adduced are not deterministic: every situation is in some way unique (some, such as apartheid South Africa, were undoubtedly singular), and local contingency as well as individual characteristics is crucial. In addition, greater mobility – and ease of contact via mobile telephony and the internet – means that proximity is not a necessary prerequisite for sustaining friendship ties and links to cultural institutions (Zelinsky and Lee, 1998; Johnston and Pattie, 2011).

As well as a constraint, segregation also offers opportunities with positive potential impacts – in business development, for example; in providing employment opportunities for local co-ethnic residents; and in sustaining cultural distinctions (even if those opportunities are not realised by all; see Zhou, 1997; Zhou et al, 2008). But these advantages are usually seen as minor relative to the disadvantages that characterise segregated societies, which is why many governments have programmes that seek either to counter those disadvantages (through various forms of spatially targeted positive discrimination, for example) or to desegregate, to create more mixed environments which, it is believed, will alleviate if not remove them.[6] It is also why governments and others react to claims that a society is 'sleepwalking towards segregation' with all the negative potential consequences that such a situation – if true – implies.[7]

Measurement matters

That segregation matters is the axiom underpinning our work. But to know in detail how it matters, a prerequisite is the ability to measure it well – hence the programme of work that we summarise here. Most segregation measures – certainly those commonly deployed, such as the indices of dissimilarity and segregation and, less frequently, those of isolation and exposure – suffer from a major defect. As single-number indices they indicate the average situation within the territory being studied without any indication of variation around that situation or the range of contexts – areas with different ethnic mixes – where individual members of various groups experience the contacts and events that structure their daily lives. Indeed, given the *Oxford English Dictionary* (OED) definition of segregation as

> The separation or isolation of a portion of a community or a body of persons from the rest

(which implies both a condition – separation, or isolation – and an associated process) it can be reasonably claimed that they are at best only weak surrogate measures of the concept. Such measures may have descriptive value and can be used to identify general trends, but not to uncover the spatial contexts – the mechanisms – within which segregation matters.

Probably the most commonly used indices are those popularised by Otis Dudley Duncan and his collaborators at Chicago in the 1950s – the index of dissimilarity and the index of segregation (Duncan and Duncan, 1955).[8] As Massey and Denton (1988) recognised in their classic study, these are measures of unevenness, of the difference between two maps; their use assumes that unevenness is a good surrogate for segregation, that an unevenly distributed group is also a segregated group. Ranging between 0 and 100, the index is usually interpreted as the share of a group's population that would have to be moved to achieve an even pair of distributions – two maps with the same relative relief (although not absolute relief if the groups are of different sizes). An index of dissimilarity between groups x and y of 30 indicates that at least 30 per cent of either group (the index is symmetrical) would have to be redistributed across the city's areal units (census tracts, say) for the two to have the same distribution; an index of segregation of 30 for group x would indicate that at least 30 per cent of its members would have to be redistributed for it to have the same distribution – the same share of each area's population – as the rest of the population (that is, $\Sigma - x$).

Is unevenness the same as segregation? When the index of segregation is very high (more than 80, say) it almost certainly indicates not only that group x's distribution is very different from that of the rest of the population, but also that a large proportion of group x probably live in areas where they predominate. The main exception to this occurs with small groups. Take a city of 100,000 people divided into 50 areas with 2,000 residents each. Group x comprises 4,500 people, with 500 of them in each nine of those 50 areas and none in the remainder. Its distribution is very uneven but its members are not isolated: they do not even form a majority in any of the nine areas where they live. They are clustered and concentrated, but they are not isolated – so are they segregated?

That example may be an extreme case, but it points up the problem – as do a myriad empirical studies. A high index of segregation is a rarity in the contemporary world – certainly in the cities of the five countries we have been studying (Australia, Canada, New Zealand, the UK and the US – with the, now only partial, example of African Americans and Hispanics in the last of those five; see Johnston et al, 2007a). How do we interpret indices of between 40 and 60? The index of segregation for Koreans in Auckland, New Zealand, in 2006 (using the smallest spatial scale available for studying that group: 333 census areal units), was 51, which many would consider moderately high. But Koreans did not form even 20 per cent of the local population in any area. Their distribution was uneven, they were clustered and (relatively) concentrated into certain parts of the city – but they were not isolated in any absolute sense.

Some studies use other measures of unevenness, notably those based on the entropy concept developed in information theory (see, for example, Wright et al, 2011; Holloway et al, 2012). These suffer the same disadvantage as the other single-number indices in depicting the average situation only, and they also generate interpretative difficulties: an area whose population is 20 per cent group x and 80 per cent group y would have the same entropy value as one where the percentages are reversed – so any number of indices of diversity would say the areas are the same when in fact they are very different.

If segregation is equated with isolation, with living apart, why not use the index of exposure for the comparison of two groups, x and y, and the index of isolation for comparing one group with the remainder of the population? These were popularised by Lieberson (1981), with an important standardisation component being later added to facilitate comparative studies where groups differed in their relative size (without it, between-group and between-city comparisons can be very misleading; see Cutler et al, 1999; Noden, 2000). Ranging between 0.0 and 1.0, the index of isolation for group x can be interpreted as the probability that if one member of group x is selected at random, another person selected at random from the same area will also belong to that group; the index of exposure between x and y is the probability that the second individual will be from group y. The index of isolation for Koreans in Auckland in 2006 was 0.07: they may have been unevenly distributed across the city, but they were certainly not isolated. So were they segregated?

The overriding problem – which includes the indices of exposure and isolation – remains that single-number indices depict the average situation only, and thereby waste much of the available information on who lives where and in what situations. An average may be meaningful, but rarely so without some associated measure of variation. It may be, for example, that although the average index of isolation for Auckland's Koreans was 0.07, for some it was 0.9 – that is, a small proportion of them lived in areas where they predominated, whereas the remainder were randomly distributed through the rest of the city (with an index perhaps of only 0.005). In other words, are some members of a group relatively isolated but others not – something that cannot be assessed by any of the single-number indices because they look at relative distributions only and provide very little insight into the varying nature of local milieux?

This is a key question in addressing many of the issues raised in our discussion of why 'segregation matters'. If neighbourhood context is a crucial influence on attitude formation and life chances, then if various members of group x live in different types of milieu (that is, areas with different ethnic mixtures) within the same city, they will face different sets of influences – or the same sets, but at different intensities. To study those influences, we need to investigate individuals' particular situations, not just the average. The latter characterises a number of recent studies; for example, Fieldhouse and Cutts (2010), following Putnam's (2007) lead, have regressed inter-ethnic trust in a city against its ethnic fragmentation (another single-number index). But the attitudes of members of group *x* towards group *y* living in a district where *x* form only 20 per cent of the population is likely to be very different from those members of *x* living in areas where *x* form 80 per cent of the total and *y* only 20 – and yet the index of fragmentation would be the same for both areas.[9] So if the contemporary reality is variation around the city-wide average, we need to reconsider how we measure segregation as well as how we conceptualise it, focusing on the variation in district characteristics, on the different types of milieux according to the mix of residents from different ethnic backgrounds within which life chances and attitudes are moulded, rather than on the average situation which may apply to nobody there.[10]

Moving forward

Our analysis concluded that the single-number indices provide poor representations of segregation as the OED defines it – although those of isolation and exposure are better than those of dissimilarity and segregation[11] – and that by focusing on the average situation, we get no insight into the proportions of the population who live in very different types of neighbourhood milieux.[12] We need measures that draw attention to differences between neighbourhoods in their ethnic composition. Reibel (2011) has developed a similar argument, noting that few studies have deployed classification approaches to studying neighbourhood characteristics – including their ethnic mixture – and he has promoted a particular form of cluster analysis (Reibel and Regelson, 2007, 2011). This, however, like many other cluster analysis algorithms, defines the inter-cluster boundaries pragmatically (reflecting the empirical structure being analysed) rather than normatively.

Our proposed classification of neighbourhood types according to their ethnic composition (starting in Poulsen et al, 2001; for the updated version, see Johnston et al, 2007a) takes a normative approach, using pre-determined boundaries for the typology's membership, which allows for comparability across time and space that is precluded in more inductive classifications. Areas, such as census tracts, are classified along two main dimensions (an approach stimulated by both Boal, 1999, and Philpott, 1978; the latter's work was also taken up by Peach, 1996, although he continues to favour the single-number indices; see Peach, 2009):

1. The share of their population drawn from the dominant group (usually, but not always, the majority – often termed the 'host society', although we use the less pejorative term 'charter group' here); and
2. The share of the remaining population (that is, the ethnic 'minorities') drawn from a single ethnic group only.[13]

This produced six basic types (Figure 2.1), although one (which we originally termed ghetto[14]) was extremely rare outwith the US:

I.   Areas where members of the charter group predominate, forming more than 80 per cent of the total population.
II. Areas where members of the charter group dominate, forming 50–80 per cent of the total population, but members of other ethnic groups form a substantial minority.
III. Areas where members of ethnic groups dominate, forming 50–70 per cent of the total population, but members of the majority group form a substantial minority.
IV. Areas where members of ethnic groups predominate, forming 70 per cent or more of the total, but no one group dominates the others.

Figure 2.1: The typology of areas according to their ethnic composition

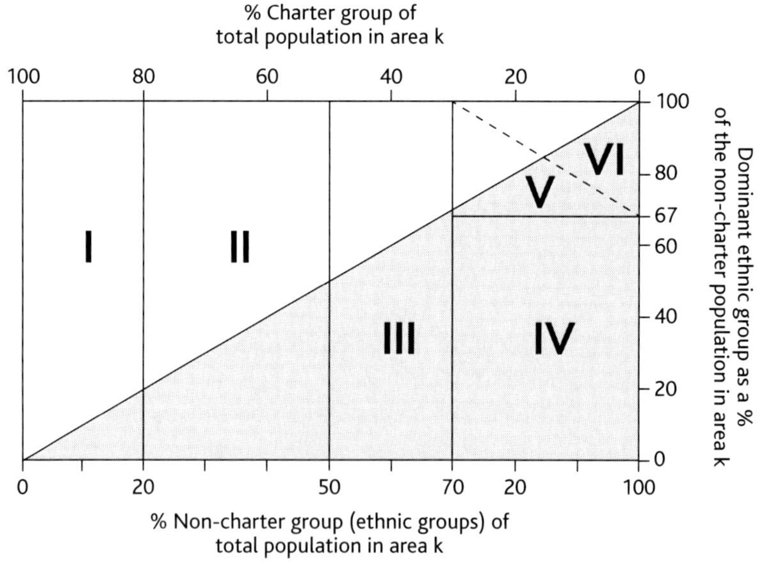

Note: for a full description of the six types, see text

V. Areas where members of ethnic groups y and z predominate, forming 70 per cent or more of the total, and one group is at least twice as large as the other.

VI. Areas where members of ethnic groups predominate, forming 70 per cent or more of the total, one group is at least twice as large as any other, and at least 30 per cent of that group's total population in the city live in those areas.

Type I tracts are areas of extreme segregation, where members of the majority group live in relatively exclusive separation from minority ethnic groups (what Marcuse, 1997, terms 'white citadels'). Types IV–VI are similarly highly segregated areas where minority ethnic groups live largely isolated from the majority group: within those three, type V areas are typical ethnic enclaves where one group predominates, whereas type VI areas are characteristic of ghetto-like situations. Type II and III areas are relatively mixed in their ethnic composition. Subtypes are identified within type V and VI areas to distinguish those where group x predominates, for example, from those where type y predominates.

Most of the boundary lines between the types are based on a simple majority–minority division: those between types I-II on the one hand and types III-IV on the other are relatively arbitrary, but were based on inspection of a large number of datasets. Exploration suggests that moving them slightly – for example, that between types I and II from 80 to 75 per cent – would change the absolute patterns although not the relative situation. Recently, Wright et al (2011) have suggested an alternative, but very similar, approach based on an entropy measure of the ethnic diversity in each area (see also Sandoval, 2011; Sharma, 2012). They place areas into three types – low, moderately and highly diverse – and further categorise the former two according to which group forms the majority. Such a classification can be used for a very similar methodology to that described here, except that there is no formal analysis of clustering of the types. (One benefit of our approach rather than theirs, however, is that our category boundaries are fixed so that comparisons over time and space are more meaningful than those based on changing situations.)

This typology identifies the share of each ethnic group's population living in different types of residential area; rather than concentrating on the average, it illustrates the range of different milieux comprising an individual city (which could be widened, as Brimicombe, 2007, and Brama, 2008, showed, and Peach, 2009, has argued should be the case). If segregation is equated with separation or isolation, this approach shows how many members of group *x* are very isolated, how many are somewhat isolated, and so forth.

Auckland's Asian population illustrates this approach; it grew by 358 per cent over just 15 years (see Table 2.1), but the indices of segregation suggest very little change in its relative distribution across the city's census meshblocks (whose populations averaged around 100 at each of the four censuses); about 40 per cent of them would have to be redistributed for each area to have the same proportions of all Asian residents as well as the remaining population. The indices of isolation suggest considerable change, however. The raw indices indicate that the probability of two Asians being selected at random in the same meshblock almost tripled – from 0.13 to 0.34. When standardised for the changing size of the Asian population (5.6 per cent of Auckland's total in 1996 and 16.8 per cent in 2006), the modified indices suggest a similar amount of change – although the index of 0.21 for 2006 suggests only a one-in-five chance of two people selected at random in the same meshblock being Asian. (If there was a random allocation of Asians across meshblocks, that index would be 0.168, given their share of the total population.)

The index of segregation suggests no change in the residential patterning of Asians in Auckland over those 15 years, therefore, whereas the index of isolation suggests considerable change. Each index is, of course, correct within its own terms, but their production leaves considerable confusion for those wanting a description of the changing

Table 2.1: The distribution and segregation of Auckland's Asian population, 1991-2006

	1991	1996	2001	2006
Asian population	50,295	100,101	148,886	230,514
Indices	**1991**	**1996**	**2001**	**2006**
Segregation	0.43	0.38	0.39	0.41
Isolation	0.13	0.20	0.26	0.34
Modified isolation	0.08	0.11	0.15	0.21

Percentage distribution by neighbourhood type

Year	I	II	III	IV	VM	VP	VA
1991	31.2	46.1	15.3	5.5	0.1	1.7	0.2
1996	12.8	59.0	19.3	6.3	0.0	1.8	0.9
2001	7.9	52.9	25.8	9.1	0.0	2.1	2.3
2006	3.4	40.4	35.1	9.4	0.0	1.7	10.0

Key to types: VA – VM – Type V with Maori dominant; VP – Type V with Pacific Islanders dominant; Type V with Asians dominant.

geography and some appreciation of the types of neighbourhood within which Auckland's Asians lived. The final block of data in Table 2.1, based on our classification of the meshblocks at each date, provides much fuller information. Asians comprised only a small proportion of Auckland's population in 1991 and most lived in type I-II neighbourhoods where New Zealand Europeans formed the majority[15] – almost one-third of Asians in areas where the charter group formed 80 per cent or more of the total population. Over the next 15 years these shares fell – the percentage of Asians in type I areas from 31 to 3 – although still in 2006 almost half of them lived in areas with New Zealand European majorities. Complementing that change, the percentage of Asians living in relative isolation (in type V areas) increased, but nevertheless, by 2006, only 10 per cent were in areas where New Zealand Europeans formed a small minority and Asians dominated within the minority ethnic population (the type VA areas); most Asians lived in the relatively mixed type II and III areas. Even in the parts of the city where Asians were most common, most were living in relatively mixed areas where they were in a minority; their spatial separation from the charter population had increased somewhat (with a much smaller proportion living in type I areas), but mixed neighbourhoods were the norm for Auckland's Asians throughout the period.

Bringing more geography in

One criticism of early applications of this neighbourhood classification was that, like most of the index-based approaches, it is largely aspatial, taking no account of where different types of neighbourhood are located within the city.[16] Are all type V neighbourhoods clustered together, for example, or are they scattered throughout the residential fabric? In the index literature centralisation, clustering and concentration were treated separately from unevenness and isolation (Massey and Denton, 1988; Johnston et al, 2007b). A number of efforts have been made to combine measures of two dimensions – usually unevenness and clustering (see Reardon and O'Sullivan, 2004) – but these composite indices are difficult to interpret, as well as suffering from the general problem of depicting the average situation only, with no indication of variation around it.

To address this issue of the spatiality of segregation – to bring geography back into its study (Johnston et al, 2009; see also Chapter Four, this volume, for an application of the local index of dissimilarity) – we followed and extended pioneering work by Logan, Zhang and Alba (2002) and Brown and Chung (2006). We first identified areas within which members of the different ethnic groups were concentrated, and then established the ethnic mix therein. We applied spatial econometric measures developed by Luc Anselin and others from Moran's classic work on spatial autocorrelation (Anselin, 1995; Anselin et al, 2007) to identify the areas where a minority group's members were clustered and (in the Logan et al (2002, 2011) case) their socioeconomic and socio-demographic characteristics.[17] We prefer the Getis-Ord $G*$ measure for exploratory analyses (Getis and Ord, 1992; Ord and Getis, 2001) as it enables clusters of small values (small values of $G*$) to be distinguished from clusters of large values (large values of $G*$), while Anselin's local I would be large in both of these cases (although clusters of small or large values can be identified using the Moran scatterplot; see Lloyd, 2010, for an example). Here, $G*$ is based on the characteristics of all areas (meshblocks in the Auckland case) within a given distance of each meshblock in turn. This rigorous, statistically based procedure maps those parts of a city where a group is over-represented not just in one area but in neighbouring areas too, as well as those parts where it is similarly under-represented and those where there is no clustering of either under- or over-represented areas. (It is therefore important that the areal unit is small, relative to the group's size. There are other technical issues – how significant should the difference from the average be, what scale should be deployed, how should edge effects be handled, what distance band around each area should be used, and should it be a constant or vary by, for example, population density? Our analyses of Auckland show that the wider the band the coarser the clusters and the less their internal homogeneity; see Poulsen et al, 2010.[18] For the studies of Auckland and London discussed here, we used unweighted distance bands of 1,000m; see Poulsen et al, 2011; Johnston et al, 2011.)

Figure 2.2 illustrates Auckland's Asian clusters in 2006, showing where Asians are most and least likely to be found in substantial numbers, but revealing nothing about the intensity of the segregation there. Unless a group's distribution is either uniform across all of the meshblocks or random, the procedure is almost certain to identify clusters. It is therefore important to study the clusters' characteristics. Figure 2.3 illustrates this for two of the main clusters identified in Figure 2.2, using the neighbourhood classification to characterise each meshblock within them. That in the north – where Koreans predominate (Johnston et al, 2011) – is comprised almost entirely of type II areas: it represents a significant clustering of Asians in suburbs where they nevertheless form only a minority of the total population. The southern cluster is internally structured, comprising a core of

Figure 2.2: Spatial clusters of Asians in Auckland, 2006

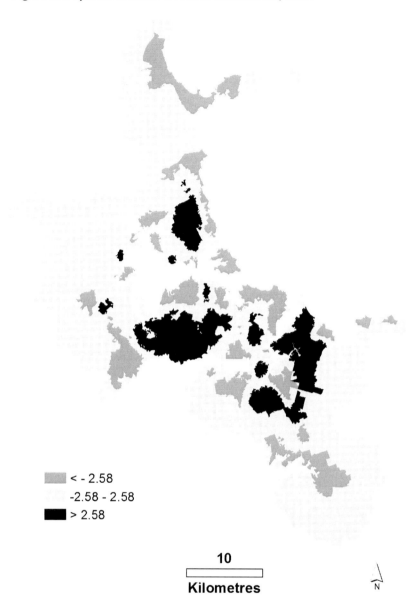

 < - 2.58
-2.58 - 2.58
 > 2.58

10

Kilometres

N

Note: The areas with G^* values exceeding 2.58 comprise the clusters where neighbouring areas have significantly larger percentages of Asian residents than average for the city as a whole; those with indices smaller than –2.58 are those clusters where neighbouring areas have significantly smaller percentages than average for the city as a whole; and the remaining areas (with indices between +2.58 and –2.58) are areas where there is no significant clustering of meshbocks with either above or below average percentages of Asians.

Figure 2.3: The classification of meshblocks within two of the positive clusters of Asians in Auckland in 2006 identified in Figure 2.2, **using the classification scheme in** Figure 2.1.

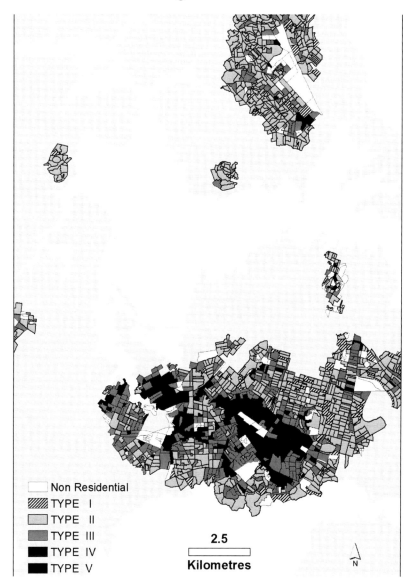

Non Residential
TYPE I
TYPE II
TYPE III
TYPE IV
TYPE V

2.5
Kilometres
N

type III-V areas where minority groups form a majority of the local population and a periphery of type II areas where they form a minority – and into which, if the classic invasion–succession models of ethnic enclaves still have validity, future expansion of the type III-V areas might be anticipated.

After exploratory analyses of Auckland and of Māori in Sydney (Forrest et al, 2009), we developed a full methodology using output area (OA) data for London as the example (Poulsen et al, 2011; OAs averaged some 300 residents in London in 2001). Each of the main minority ethnic groups was clustered in different parts of the city. Figure 2.4 shows the Bangladeshi clusters – in the inner eastern area north of the river – and the small block of territory further west, where their numbers were much smaller than average. Across most of

Figure 2.4: Spatial clusters of Bangladeshis in London, 2006

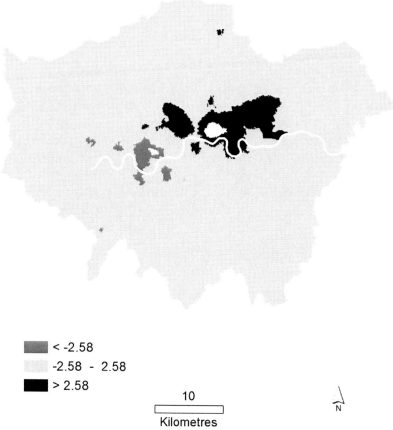

■ < -2.58
▨ -2.58 - 2.58
■ > 2.58

10
Kilometres

N

Note: The areas with G* values exceeding 2.58 comprise the clusters where neighbouring areas have significantly larger percentages of Bangladeshi residents than average for the city as a whole; those with indices smaller than –2.58 are those clusters where neighbouring areas have significantly smaller percentages than average for the city as a whole; and the remaining areas (with indices between +2.58 and –2.58) are areas where there is no significant clustering of meshbocks with either above or below average percentages of Bangladeshis.

London, however, there was neither significant over-representation nor under-representation of Bangladeshis in clusters of adjacent OAs.[19]

The first block of data in Table 2.2 shows the percentages of each of the five main minority ethnic groups identified by the UK census, as well as the White population, who lived in each group's positive, negative and intermediate clusters. For the minority groups, around two-thirds lived within their respective positive clusters; for the majority White population, just under half. This indicates considerable concentration of each group within different parts of the city, but how segregated were they there and to what extent did they share those spaces with members of the other groups? The second block of data in Table 2.2 shows the percentages of the total population within each group's positive cluster who lived in different neighbourhood types: thus, of the 695,000 people living in the Bangladeshi positive clusters (Figure 2.4), for example, well over half (63 per cent) lived in type I and II areas where Whites formed the majority and less than one-fifth (17 per cent) lived in the type IV and V areas where non-whites predominated. Similar distributions are recorded for the Indian and Pakistani clusters and an even greater concentration in type I and II areas for the Black Caribbean and Black African clusters. Almost all residents in the White clusters not surprisingly lived in type I areas

Table 2.2: The segregation of ethnic groups in London, 2001

Ethnic group	B	I	P	BC	BA	W
Percentage living within						
Positive cluster	68	61	62	60	66	49
Intermediate area	32	26	29	29	22	25
Negative cluster	1	13	10	11	12	26
Percentage of total population within each of the positive clusters living in neighbourhood types						
I	21	14	9	18	20	95
II	42	48	49	60	60	5
III	21	25	28	17	16	0
IV	11	8	8	5	4	0
V	6	5	5	1	0	0
Percentage of each ethnic group population within each of the Bangladeshi positive clusters living in neighbourhood types						
I	4	7	2	8	8	32
II	32	19	18	48	48	47
III	29	26	38	30	28	15
IV	10	47	40	12	13	4
V	25	1	1	2	2	2

Key to ethnic groups: B – Bangladeshi; I – Indian; P – Pakistani; BC – Black Caribbean; BA – Black African; W – White.

where Whites predominated; they were, in effect, the most segregated group within London.

Although neighbourhoods where members of minority ethnic groups dominated the local population were thus a minority of all of the OAs within each of the clusters where they were concentrated, was this the same for members of each group? The final block of data in Table 2.2 indicates that this was not the case for the Bangladeshi positive cluster. Of the 695,000 living there, 104,000 were Bangladeshis, one-quarter of whom lived in type V areas; less than 40 per cent lived in the areas with White majorities (types I-II), compared to the 63 per cent of the total population as shown in the previous block. That cluster also contained 43,000 Indians and 28,000 Pakistanis; almost one-half of them lived in areas where Whites were in a small minority, virtually all of them in type IV areas where there was a mixed, predominantly non-White population. Most of the Whites living in the cluster, on the other hand, lived in the type I-II areas. As with Asians in Auckland, the cluster where Bangladeshis were concentrated within London was internally structured into: a core, where Bangladeshis predominated; an inner periphery, where Bangladeshis, Indians and Pakistanis occupied mixed, predominantly non-White neighbourhoods; and an outer periphery, where the Bangladeshi percentage of the total was on average much larger than it was across London as a whole, but where that residential space was shared with a White majority.

This approach provides much more information about the residential patterning of each ethnic group than a single index number, and its output can readily be summarised. Table 2.3's first block gives the number of members of each ethnic group living in London in 2001. The next gives the total population of the positive clusters defined for each group using the G* statistics and the population of the relevant ethnic group for which the clusters were defined living there. These allow calculation of the next block of statistics, which show the percentage of each group living within its own positive clusters, and their percentage of the total population there. The first of these replicates the top row of Table 2.2, re-emphasising the difference between the five minority groups on the one hand, and the White population on the other; many more of the latter live outwith the clusters where they are concentrated, to the relative exclusion of members of the other groups. The second row in that block shows the group as a percentage of the total population in its positive clusters. With the exception of the Whites – who form the great majority of the total population in their clusters – these figures are small; no group forms even one-quarter of the population in the

Table 2.3: Segregation in London, 2001 – a summary

Ethnic group	B	I	P	BC	BA	W
Group population	153,849	437,305	142,763	343,699	378,976	5,116,932
Positive clusters						
Total population	695,240	1,301,192	1,231,284	1,908,144	2,080,745	2,906,967
Group population	104,073	268,005	88,006	226,457	227,253	2,543,476
Group						
% in cluster	68	61	62	66	60	50
% of cluster	15	21	7	12	11	88
% of total population in cluster living in neighbourhoods of						
Types I-II	62	62	59	78	80	99
Types III-IV	33	33	37	21	20	1
Type V	6	5	5	0	1	0
% of cluster group population living in neighbourhoods of						
Types I-II	36	42	42	69	75	100
Types III-IV	39	43	52	30	25	0
Type V	25	15	6	1	0	0

Key to ethnic groups: B – Bangladeshi; I – Indian; P – Pakistani; BC – Black Caribbean; BA – Black African; W – White.

parts of London where it is concentrated, and for Pakistanis, that figure is only 7 per cent. So, although members of London's minority groups are concentrated into particular clusters within the city's residential fabric, they do not predominate there: they are, in many ways, much less segregated than the majority White population, over half of whom live in clusters of neighbourhoods that contain very few non-Whites.

This clear spatial pattern – of concentration but not of segregation as generally understood – is emphasised by the next two blocks of data in Table 2.3. The first shows that OAs in which Whites form the majority of the population (types I-II) dominate not only in those parts of London where Whites are concentrated, but also in those where members of the five main minority ethnic groups are too. In the clusters where Black Caribbeans and Africans are concentrated, only one-fifth of the constituent OAs has a non-White majority. Finally, the last block shows that even for the group whose geography was the basis for identifying the clusters, only a small percentage of its members live in areas (type V) where they predominate – 25 and 15 per cent respectively for Bangladeshis and Indians, but only 6 per cent for Pakistanis and virtually none for the two Black groups.

For each of London's main ethnic groups recognised by the census – which is far from comprehensive – there is thus one or more core areas where its members are clustered together, but they rarely predominate, even in small parts of those clusters. Many of the group's members live outside them, probably having moved there away from the cluster (as studies of migration suggest; see Stillwell, 2010), reflecting social mobility aspirations. There is considerable spatial concentration, but little spatial isolation.

These applications of the methodology facilitate a much more nuanced description of the city's residential fabric than single-number indices even approach, providing details of the extent of concentration, clustering and isolation that those indices obscure – and its application over a sequence of censuses (especially if, as with Auckland, they use constant areal units) can illuminate changing patterns of concentration. But it is much more than a descriptive tool. If, as we have argued here, segregation matters, hypotheses regarding how it matters can be tested using the classification approach as the sampling frame: people who live in different types of neighbourhood, set in different types of clusters of neighbourhoods, will experience different local contexts, and should respond accordingly (as illustrated in Sampson, 2012).

Ethnoburbs

Residential segregation of minority ethnic groups is normally causally associated with one or more of three main processes: discrimination, disadvantage and choice. With discrimination there is no choice – group members can only live in their prescribed areas. With disadvantage there is some choice – the less the disadvantage (in most cases, the greater the income) the greater the choice. And with the third process, concentration and clustering only occurs because members want to live among their co-ethnics. Most studies of segregation have focused on discrimination and disadvantage, linking declines in segregation as discrimination evaporates and disadvantages are removed through economic and social mobility. Clustering by choice is then treated as a residual category, as the decision-making of a minority who prefer to remain in relative concentrations even though a much wider choice set is available to them.

Li (1998, 2006) has identified a further settlement pattern, however – of ethnoburbs, suburban clusters of high socioeconomic status and income ethnic groups who have much of the housing market available to them but who choose to concentrate in low-density concentrations, mainly in cities of the Pacific Rim. Auckland provides a good example. Its Asian population, treated as a single block in our earlier examples, is culturally very heterogeneous; the largest groups in 2006 were Chinese, Indian, Korean, Filipino, Japanese and Sri Lankan, with each clustered in different parts of the city (see Xue et al, 2012). Using larger areal units we used a zonal system to map expansion of those ethnoburbs across the four censuses (Johnston et al, 2011): an inner core where the group's members were clustered in 1991 (zone 1) and additions as the clusters grew over the next three censuses (zones 2-4); zone 0 comprises the rest of the city. This is illustrated for the Indian population (which grew from 16,650 in 1991 to 68,409 in 2006) in Figure 2.5.

Figure 2.5: The zonal structure of Auckland's Indian ethnoburbs, 1991–2006

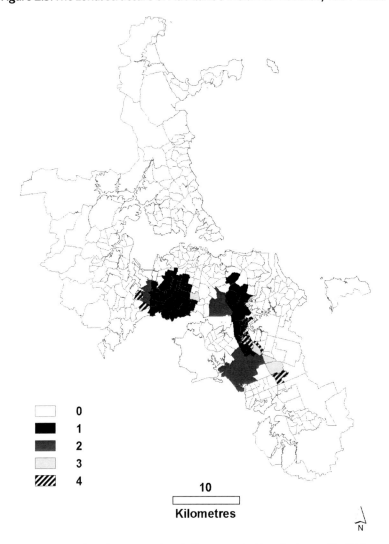

Note: Zone 1 comprises those areas where Indians were significantly clustered in 1991; Zone 2 is the additional areas where they were clustered in 1996; Zone 3 the additional areas in 2001; and Zone 4 the additional areas in 2006. Zone 0 is the remainder of the city.

Although the maps identified clear clusters, these were not only low density (that is, the relevant group's members formed only a relatively small proportion of the total population), but also a majority of each group's members lived outwith the defined clusters. Table 2.4 illustrates their characteristics for the Indians and the two other largest groups. Of Auckland's Indians in 2006, 21 per cent lived in zone 1 – the cluster in place at the time of the 1991 Census – but only 6.6, 6.2 and 4.0 per cent respectively lived in zones 2-4, the extensions established by 1996, 2001 and 2006; fully 62 per cent of Indians lived outside the clusters, indicating that it was very much a minority choice to live there. Further, those ethnoburbs were not dominated by Indians – on average, as the second row of data shows, they formed only 15 per cent of the meshblock population in zone 1, 21 per cent in zone 2 and 16 and 11 per cent respectively in the outer two zones. Beyond the clusters, however, they formed on average only 4.1 per cent of the local population in zone 0. Similar patterns are shown for the other two groups, although the Chinese comprise similar shares of the local population across the four zones of their clusters and there is no Korean zone 1 – there were only 543 Koreans in Auckland in 1991 and a clear cluster (on the North Shore; see Figure 2.3) only formed in time for the 1996 Census, when their numbers had increased to 8,910.

The traditional indices tell us very little about these nascent settlement patterns. As already suggested for the Koreans, the indices of segregation over-state the degree of clustering. The indices of isolation provide a more accurate indication of the very low intensity of these clusters – even for the largest group (the Chinese) it was only 0.14 in 2006 – but give very little feel for the geographical detail.

Table 2.4: Auckland's ethnoburb populations, 2006

Zone	1	2	3	4	0
Indian					
% of group	21.0	6.6	6.2	4.0	62.2
Group mean %	15.0	20.9	16.3	10.9	4.1
Chinese					
% of group	18.1	8.4	8.4	7.4	57.7
Group mean %	19.1	17.5	15.8	16.3	5.2
Korean					
% of group	–	26.1	5.8	1.3	66.7
Group mean %	–	6.3	9.4	2.7	2.4

Key to zones: 1 – clusters formed in 1991; 2 – 1996 additions to clusters; 3 – 2001 additions to clusters; 4 – 2006 additions to clusters; 0 – remainder of the city outwith the clusters.

Conclusion

Measurement of (ethnic residential) segregation matters because (ethnic residential) segregation matters. Because it matters, we need to measure it in ways that fulfil two main functions. The first is descriptive, to indicate just how segregated a city or an ethnic group is, as part of a general statement on a society's condition. The second is analytic, providing measures that can be used in explorations of the impacts (negative and positive) that segregation has on individuals (see Chapters Fourteen and Fifteen, this volume). In the societies that we have concentrated on here, where neoliberal economic and associated social policies have generated greater inequalities in recent decades, where individuals live – including the characteristics of their neighbourhood milieux (and, argues Sampson, 2012, adjacent neighbourhoods too) – is a crucial influence on their life chances and choices. To understand that influence, we need to measure segregation meaningfully.

But the nature of ethnic residential segregation has changed considerably over recent decades, making the models developed on the early and mid-20th century North American experience increasingly redundant (although perhaps not in some of the country's older cities; Sandoval, 2011, for example, reports that Chicago was not characterised by growing neighbourhood diversity between 1980 and 2000). It is changing again now and rethinking its measurement is only part of coming to terms with those changes – with moving away from what Gilbert (2010; see also Goldberg, 1998) has termed the 'homogeneous ghetto' towards a continuum of situations, ranging from:

- locked-in segregation, with group members confined to particular areas only – where they are allowed to live and most others will choose not to; through
- locked-out segregation, with group members precluded from living in certain areas because they do not qualify for housing there, in most cases through either market price mechanisms or social allocation procedures; to
- congregation, with group members choosing to live in relative proximity even though they have a wide range of choice of areas.

The first of these processes is largely a consequence of discrimination; the second reflects disadvantage combined with cultural choice; and the third represents choice alone. In the first, most of a group's members are necessarily concentrated into prescribed areas (ghettos?); in the second, the less disadvantaged members of a group are less likely to live in the areas where the more disadvantaged are concentrated; and in the third only those who prefer to live in relative proximity to their co-ethnics are found in the clusters.

The first of these tends to be the model against which we evaluate all of the patterns we explore, and for which our measurement techniques are calibrated. But it was extremely rare in the late 20th century, let alone the early 21st (Denton, 1994). The second scenario has been the most common and the degree of 'locking out' has varied according to two factors – success in the labour market and the degree to which group members prefer to live in relative proximity to their co-ethnics when they could live elsewhere. (In other words, locking-out is in part an exogenous constraint and in part endogenous choice.) As a group's members become more like the wider population in their socioeconomic characteristics, and as the cultural and other ties leading to congregation weaken, so a smaller proportion of a group chooses to live in enclave-like situations – and, as we have seen with the Auckland example, where they do choose to congregate, it is usually only at low intensities.

Indices of dissimilarity and segregation are, at best, only weak measures of these altered processes and patterns of segregation. The indices of exposure (isolation and interaction) are slightly better, because they can be directly linked to the OED definition of segregation. But these are only averages. If some members of group x live in relatively homogeneous areas and others live in more heterogeneous districts, the index is a weighted average of the two and so we lose information: we cannot know from the single index number how much segregation (according to our definition) there is.

And so we need a different approach, one that not only provides a better descriptive portrait of how segregated a group is within a city – what types of neighbourhood of differing ethnic diversity they live in – but also a template within which studies of the impact of segregation on individual life chances and behaviour can be set. We have suggested one, and illustrated its potential, recognising that it can be either modified further or replaced by something better. It reflects the contemporary situation in most cities where segregation does not involve concentration of members of ethnic and/or cultural minorities into districts where few members of other groups are to be found. What we have instead is people living in a great variety of milieux that differ in the ethnic/cultural mix of their populations. Our goal is to identify those different types of area, as a preliminary to exploring whether the variation they describe is as important an influence on life chances, lifestyles and inter-group contacts as the more extreme segregation of decades ago.

Notes

[1] This is a revised version of the text of Ron Johnston's Distinguished Scholar Lecture delivered to the Ethnic Geography Speciality Group, Association of American Geographers Annual Meeting, Washington DC, April 2010. It reported on a large collaborative programme of research to which all three members of the group contributed equally, hence the joint authorship here. That research programme developed serendipitously when Ron was a Visiting Fellow at Macquarie University, Australia, for a month in 1998. He had originally gone there to work with Jim on some electoral projects, but discussions with him and Mike about other work on immigration to Australia and on the measurement of segregation stimulated us to develop the work, part of which is reviewed here. Much of it has been supported by grants from the Australian Research Commission, the British Academy and Macquarie University, whose support is gratefully acknowledged.

[2] With thanks to Miles Hewstone who brought this to our attention.

[3] See, for example, www.ft.com/cms/s/0/236110aa-d716-11e0-bc73-00144feabdc0.html#axzz1XFvHFFmk on the homes of those charged after the London riots of August 2011.

[4] Wong (1996) had earlier argued for studying segregation at the local scale, but using the single-number indices that we criticise here.

[5] See http://chronicle.com/article/The-Neighborhood-Effect/135492 for a discussion of the impact of socio-spatial isolation on life chances.

[6] Some seek to ignore the situation, of course – as with the unwillingness of successive French governments to collect census data on ethnicity despite substantial circumstantial evidence of segregation there that has exacerbated inequalities and tensions across ethnic groups, on the grounds that all French citizens are equal under the Republican constitution that provides (or should provide) the predominant source of identity.

[7] Our experience on this can be traced in Poulsen and Johnston (2006) and Johnston et al (2010a).

[8] This is an assertion; we have never actually tried to count them.

[9] A similar difficulty arises with the approach taken in a recent paper by Brown and Sharma (2010), in which average diversity across a city's tracts is measured.

[10] All of this work measuring segregation is, of course, subject to the well-known modifiable areal unit problem (MAUP), to which Kwan (2012) has recently added the uncertain geographic context problem (UGCP).

[11] And we were certainly not the first to realise that; see Trlin (1984).

[12] We ignore here the other three types of segregation measure identified by Massey and Denton (1988) as both conceptually and empirically distinct from the other two (although our own research doubted the empirical claim; see Johnston et al, 2007b). Alongside unevenness and isolation/exposure they placed indices of concentration (the degree to which members of a group were concentrated in the higher density parts of a city), of centralisation (the degree to which the areas where they predominate are in or close to the city centre) and of clustering (the degree to which the areas where they predominate are clustered together). To some considerable extent these were especially relevant to studying the situation of African Americans, and few have used the indices in those groups.

[13] Throughout this work we have focused on individuals who report membership of a single ethnic group only. Increasing numbers in the societies we have analysed report membership of two groups, and future work building on this approach will need to take that into consideration (for an initial analysis of this phenomenon, see Johnston et al, 2006b). A change in the ethnic groupings used in the typology – for example, looking at Indian, Chinese, Korean groupings and so on separately rather than the Asian grouping as a single category – will not alter its fundamentals, since they are based on the distribution of the charter group. However, the nature of the type IV and V areas (and type VI if there are any) will alter. The results of applying the typology are also scale-specific: the larger the unit area used, the smaller the likelihood of identifying type V and VI areas.

[14] We later dropped use of the term 'ghetto' to describe type VI because of its very limited relevance outside the US, and we are not going to re-open the debate about whether the UK has ghettos. Slater and Anderson (2012) have recently argued that whatever the statistical situation regarding an area's ethnic population, it may attract the stigma of a ghetto.

[15] 'New Zealand Europeans' is the official term for those of – mainly UK – descent, the majority of whom were born in New Zealand and have no loyalty to a European country; the Māori term for them is *pakeha*.

[16] This was by far the most cogent of Watts' (2008) comments; see also Johnston et al (2008).

[17] Lee et al (2008) have proposed an alternative approach to the spatiality of segregation issue (see also Reardon et al, 2008). They use an unevenness

measure (Reardon and O'Sullivan, 2004) which looks at pairwise segregation only (for example, Black-White, Black-Hispanic etc) rather than the diversity of an area's ethnic population across all ethnic groups. (However, Reardon and Firebaugh, 2002, have proposed measures of multigroup segregation that could be used.) For a further approach see Logan et al (2011). See also Paez et al's (2011, and also Chapter Five of this volume) pioneering use of Q-analysis for analysing clustering at the individual scale.

[18] On neighbourhood size, homogeneity and segregation, see Wong (1997).

[19] Significance levels are readily deployed in these analyses because G* has the same distribution as the Z-statistic. We used a Z-value of +/−2.58 in these analyses, which means that any clusters identified were only likely to occur at random in less than 1 in 100 applications.

References

Anselin, L. (1995) 'Local indicators of spatial association – LISA', *Geographical Analysis*, vol 27, pp 93-115.

Anselin, L., Sridharan, S. and Gholston, S. (2007) 'Using exploratory spatial data analysis to leverage social indicator databases: the discovery of interesting patterns', *Social Indicators Research*, vol 82, pp 287-309.

Bécares, L., Stafford, M., Laurence, M. and Nazroo, J. (2011) 'Composition, concentration and deprivation: exploring their association with social cohesion among different ethnic groups in the UK', *Urban Studies*, vol 48, pp 2771-87.

Boal, F.W. (1999) 'From undivided cities to undivided cities: assimilation to ethnic cleansing', *Housing Studies*, vol 14, pp 585-600.

Bowyer, B.T. (2009) 'The contextual determinants of whites' racial attitudes in England', *British Journal of Political Science*, vol 39, pp 559-86.

Brama, A. (2008) 'Dynamics of ethnic residential segregation in Göteborg, Sweden, 1995-2000', *Population, Space and Place*, vol 14, pp 101-17.

Brimicombe A. (2007) 'Ethnicity, religion and residential segregation in London: evidence from a computational typology of minority communities', *Environment and Planning B: Planning and Design*, vol 34, pp 884-904.

Brown, L.A. and Chung, S.-Y. (2006) 'Spatial segregation, segregation indices and the geographical perspective', *Population, Space and Place*, vol 12, pp 125-43.

Brown, L.A. and Sharma, M. (2010) 'Metropolitan context and racial/ ethnic intermixing in residential space: US metropolitan statistical areas, 1990-2000', *Urban Geography*, vol 31, pp 1-28.

Cutler, D.M, Glaeser, E.L. and Vigdor, J.L. (1999) 'The rise and decline of the American ghetto', *Journal of Political Economy*, vol 107, pp 456-506.

Denton, N.A. (1994) 'Are African-Americans still hypersegregated?', in R.D. Bullard, J.E. Grigsby and C. Lee (eds) *Residential apartheid: the American legacy*, Los Angeles, CA: CAAS Publications, pp 49-81.

Duncan, O.D. and Duncan, B. (1955) 'Occupational stratification and residential distribution', *American Journal of Sociology*, vol 64, pp 364-74.

Fieldhouse, E. and Cutts, D. (2010) 'Does diversity damage social capital? A comparative study of neighbourhood diversity and social capital in the US and Britain', *Canadian Journal of Political Science*, vol 43, pp 289-318.

Forrest, J., Poulsen, M.F. and Johnston, R.J. (2009) 'Temporary and disadvantaged? The economic and spatial assimilation of New Zealand Maori in Sydney', *Population, Space and Place*, vol 15, pp 475-92.

Getis, A. and Ord, J.K. (1992) 'The analysis of spatial association by use of distance statistics', *Geographical Analysis*, vol 24, pp 189-206.

Gilbert, M.R. (2010) 'Place, space and agency: moving beyond the homogenous "ghetto"', *Urban Geography*, vol 31, pp 148-52.

Goldberg, D.T. (1998) 'The new segregation', *Race and Society*, vol 1, pp 15-32.

Hewstone, M. (2009) 'Living apart, living together? The role of intergroup contact in social integration', *Proceedings of the British Academy, 162*, Oxford: Oxford University Press for the British Academy, pp 243-300.

Holloway, S.R., Wright, R. and Ellis, M. (2012) 'The racially fragmented city? Neighborhood racial segregation and diversity jointly considered', *The Professional Geographer*, vol 64, pp 63-82.

Hoare, A.G. and Johnston, R.J. (2011) 'Widening participation through admissions policy – a British case study of school and university performance', *Studies in Higher Education*, vol 36, pp 21-41.

Johnston, R.J. and Pattie, C.J. (2011) 'Social networks, geography and neighbourhood effects', in J. Scott and P. Carrington (eds) *The Sage handbook of social network analysis*, London: Sage Publications, pp 301-11

Johnston, R.J., Poulsen, M.F. and Forrest, J. (2002) 'The ethnic geography of EthnicCities: the "American model" and residential concentration in London', *Ethnicities*, vol 2, pp 209-35.

Johnston, R.J., Poulsen, M.F. and Forrest, J. (2006a) 'Blacks and Hispanics in urban America: similar patterns of residential segregation?', *Population, Space and Place*, vol 12, pp 389-406.

Johnston, R.J., Poulsen, M.F. and Forrest, J. (2006b) 'Ethnic residential segregation and assimilation in British towns and cities: a comparison of those claiming single and dual ethnic identities', *Migration Letters*, vol 3, pp 11-30.

Johnston, R.J., Poulsen, M.F. and Forrest, J. (2007a) 'The geography of ethnic residential segregation: a comparative study of five countries', *Annals of the Association of American Geographers*, vol 97, pp 713-38.

Johnston, R.J., Poulsen, M.F. and Forrest, J. (2007b) 'Ethnic and racial segregation in US metropolitan areas, 1980-2000: the dimensions of segregation revisited', *Urban Affairs Review*, vol 42, pp 479-504.

Johnston, R.J., Poulsen, M.F. and Forrest, J. (2008) 'Back to basics: a reply to Watts', *Environment and Planning A*, vol 40, pp 2037-41.

Johnston, R.J., Poulsen, M.F. and Forrest, J. (2009) 'Measuring ethnic residential segregation: putting some more geography in', *Urban Geography*, vol 30, pp 91-109.

Johnston, R.J., Poulsen, M.F. and Forrest, J. (2010a) 'Moving on from indices, refocusing on mix: on measuring and understanding ethnic patterns of residential segregation', *Journal of Ethnic and Migration Studies*, vol 36, pp 697-706.

Johnston, R.J., Poulsen, M.F. and Forrest, J. (2011) 'Using spatial statistics to identify and characterise ethnoburbs: establishing a methodology using the example of Auckland, New Zealand', *GeoJournal*, vol 76, pp 447-67.

Johnston, R.J., Wilson, D. and Burgess, S. (2005) 'England's multi-ethnic educational system? A classification of secondary schools', *Environment and Planning A*, vol 37, pp 45-62.

Johnston, R.J., Sirkeci, I., Khattab, N. and Modood, T. (2010b) 'Ethno-religious categories and measuring occupational attainment in relation to education in England and Wales: a multi-level analysis', *Environment and Planning A*, vol 42, pp 578-91.

Khattab, N., Johnston, R.J., Sirkeci, I. and Modood, T. (2010a) 'The impact of spatial segregation on the employment outcomes amongst Bangladeshi men and women in England and Wales', *Sociological Research Online*, vol 15, no 1, pp 1-16.

Khattab, N., Johnston, R.J., Sirkeci, I. and Modood, T. (2010b) 'Ethnicity, religion, residential segregation and life chances', in T. Modood and J. Salt (eds) *Global migration, ethnicity and Britishness*, Basingstoke: Palgrave Macmillan, pp 153-76.

Kwan, M.-P. (2012) 'The uncertain geographic context problem', *Annals of the Association of American Geographers*, vol 102, pp 958-68.

Lee, B.A., Reardon, S.F., Firebaugh, G., Farrell, C.R., Matthews, S.A. and O'Sullivan, D. (2008) 'Beyond the census tract: patterns and determinants of racial segregation at multiple geographic scales', *American Sociological Review*, vol 73, pp 766-91.

Li, W. (1998) 'Anatomy of a new ethnic settlement: the Chinese Ethnoburb in Los Angeles', *Urban Studies*, vol 35, 479-501.

Li, W. (ed) (2006) *From urban enclave to ethnic suburb: new Asian communities in Pacific Rim countries*, Honolulu: University of Hawaii Press.

Lieberson, S. (1981) 'An asymmetrical approach to segregation', in C. Peach, V. Robinson and S.J. Smith (eds) *Ethnic segregation in cities*, London: Croom Helm, pp 61-83.

Lloyd, C.D. (2010) 'Exploring population spatial concentrations in Northern Ireland by community background and other characteristics: an application of geographically weighted spatial statistics', *International Journal of Geographical Information Science*, vol 24, pp 1193-221.

Logan, J.R., Zhang, W. and Alba, R.D. (2002) 'Immigrant enclaves and ethnic communities in New York and Los Angeles', *American Sociological Review*, vol 67, pp 279-302.

Logan, J.R., Spielman, S., Xu, H. and Klein, P.N. (2011) 'Identifying and bounding ethnic neighborhoods', *Urban Geography*, vol 32, pp 334-59.

Marcuse, P. (2007) 'The enclave, the citadel and the ghetto: what has changed in the post-Fordist US city?', *Urban Affairs Review*, vol 33, pp 228-64.

Massey, D.S. and Denton, N.A. (1988) 'The dimensions of residential segregation', *Social Forces*, vol 67, pp 281-315.

Nightingale, C.H. (2012) *Segregation: a global history of divided cities*, Chicago, IL: University of Chicago Press.

Noden, P. (2000) 'Rediscovering the impact of marketisation: dimensions of social segregation in England's schools', *British Journal of Sociology of Education*, vol 21, pp 372-90.

Ord, J.K. and Getis, A. (2001) 'Testing for local spatial autocorrelation in the presence of global autocorrelation', *Journal of Regional Science*, vol 41, pp 411-32.

Paez, A., Ruiz, M., Lopez, F. and Logan, J.R. (2011) 'Measuring ethnic clustering and exposure using the Q statistic: an exploratory analysis of Irish, Germans and Yankees in 1880 Newark', *Annals of the Association of American Geographers*, vol 102, pp 84-102.

Peach, C. (1996) 'Does Britain have ghettos?', *Transactions of the Institute of British Geographers*, vol NS22, pp 216-35.

Peach, C. (2005) 'The mosaic versus the melting pot: Canada and the USA', *Scottish Geographical Journal*, vol 121, pp 3-27.

Peach, C. (2009) 'Slippery segregation: discovering or manufacturing ghettos?', *Journal of Ethnic and Migration Studies*, vol 35, pp 1381-95.

Philpott, T.L. (1978) *The slum and the ghetto: neighborhood deterioration and middle class reform*, Chicago, IL: University of Chicago Press.

Poulsen, M.F. and Johnston, R.J. (2006) 'Ethnic residential segregation in England: getting the right message across', *Environment and Planning A*, vol 38, pp 2195-9.

Poulsen, M.F., Johnston, R.J. and Forrest, J. (2001) 'Intraurban ethnic enclaves: introducing a knowledge-based classification method', *Environment and Planning A*, vol 33, pp 2071-82.

Poulsen, M.F., Johnston, R.J. and Forrest, J. (2010) 'The intensity of ethnic residential clustering: exploring scale effects using local indicators of spatial association', *Environment and Planning A*, vol 42, pp 874-94.

Poulsen, M.F., Johnston, R.J. and Forrest, J. (2011) 'Using local statistics and neighbourhood classifications to portray ethnic residential segregation: a London example', *Environment and Planning B: Planning and Design*, vol 38, pp 636-58.

Putnam, R. (2007) '*E pluribus unum*: diversity and community in the twenty-first century. The 2006 Johann Skytte Prize Lecture', *Scandinavian Political Studies*, vol 30, pp 137-74.

Reardon, S. F. and Firebaugh, G. (2002) 'Measures of multigroup segregation', *Sociological Methodology*, vol 33, pp 33-67.

Reardon, S.F. and O'Suillivan, D. (2004) 'Measures of spatial segregation', *Sociological Methodology*, vol 34, pp 121-62.

Reardon, S.F., Matthews, S.A., O'Sullivan, D., Lee, B.A., Firebaugh, G., Farrell, C.R. and Bischoff, K. (2008) 'The geographical scale of metropolitan racial segregation', *Demography*, vol 45, pp 489-514.

Reibel, M. (2011) 'Classification approaches in neighborhood research: introduction and review', *Urban Geography*, vol 32, pp 305-16.

Reibel, M. and Regelson, M. (2007) 'Quantifying neighborhood racial and ethnic transition clusters in multiethnic cities', *Urban Geography*, vol 28, pp 361-76.

Reibel, M. and Regelson, M. (2011) 'Neighborhood racial and ethnic change: the time dimension in segregation', *Urban Geography*, vol 32, pp 360-82.

Sampson, R.J. (2012) *Great American city: Chicago and the enduring neighborhood effect*, Chicago, IL: University of Chicago Press.

Sandoval, J.S.O. (2011) 'Neighborhood diversity and segregation in the Chicago metropolitan region, 1980-2000', *Urban Geography*, vol 32, pp 609-40.

Sharma, M. (2012) 'A geographic perspective in intra–urban racial/ethnic diversity, segregation and clustering in Knoxville, Tennessee: 1990-2000', *Applied Geography*, vol 32, pp 310-23.

Slater, T. and Anderson, N. (2012) 'The reputational ghetto: territorial stigmatisation in St Paul's, Bristol', *Transactions of the Institute of British Geographers*, vol NS37, pp 530-46.

Stillwell, J.C.H. (2010) 'Internal migration propensities and patterns of London's ethnic groups', in J.C.H. Stillwell, O.W. Duke-Williams, and A. Dennett (eds) *Technologies for migration and commuting analysis: spatial interaction data applications*, Hershey, PA: IGI Global, pp 175-95.

Trlin, A.D. (1984) 'Changing ethnic residential distribution and segregation in Auckland', in P. Spoonley, C. Macpherson, D. Pearson and C. Sedgwick (eds) *Tauiwi: racism and ethnicity in New Zealand*, Palmerston North: Dunmore Press, pp 172-98.

Uslaner, E.M. (2012) *Segregation and mistrust: diversity, isolation and social cohesion*, Cambridge: Cambridge University Press.

Verwoort, M., Flap, H. and Dagevos, J. (2011) 'The ethnic composition of the neighbourhood and ethnic minorities' social contacts: three unresolved issues', *European Sociological Review*, vol 27, pp 586-605.

Watts, M.J. (2008) 'Ethnic residential segregation: some comments on a commentary', *Environment and Planning A*, vol 40, pp 2031-36.

Wong, D.W.S. (1996) 'Enhancing segregation studies through GIS', *Computers, Environment and Urban Systems*, vol 20, pp 99-109.

Wong, D.W.S. (1997) 'Spatial dependency of segregation indices', *The Canadian Geographer*, vol 41, pp 128-36.

Wright, G.C. Jr (1977) 'Contextual models of voting behavior: the southern Wallace vote', *American Political Science Review*, vol 71, pp 497-508.

Wright, R., Holloway, S. and Ellis, M. (2011) 'Reconsidering both diversity and segregation: a reply to Poulsen, Johnston and Forrest, and to Peach', *Journal of Ethnic and Migration Studies*, vol 37, pp 167-76.

Xue, J., Friesen, W. and O'Sullivan, D. (2012) 'Diversity in Chinese Auckland: hypothesising multiple ethnoburbs', *Population, Space and Place*, vol 18, pp 579-95.

Zelinsky, W. and Lee, B.A. (1998) 'Heterolocalism: an alternative model of the sociospatial behaviour of immigrant ethnic communities', *International Journal of Population Geography*, vol 4, pp 281-98.

Zhou, M. (1997) 'Segmented assimilation: issues, controversies, and recent research on the new second generation', *International Migration Review*, vol 31, pp 975-1008.

Zhou, M., Tseng, Y.-F. and Kim, R.Y. (2008) 'Rethinking residential assimilation: the case of a Chinese ethnoburb in the San Gabriel Valley, California', *Amerasia Journal*, vol 34, pp 55-83.

THREE

Using a general spatial pattern statistic to evaluate spatial segregation

David W.S. Wong

Introduction

Many indices proposed by social scientists to measure segregation have been criticised for their aspatial nature, failing to distinguish different spatial patterns of population effectively. During the past two decades, a series of spatial measures have been proposed to address this deficiency. However, most of these measures adopt the 'smoothing' approach by including populations in the neighbouring units when comparing racial–ethnic mix across areal units. The actual separations among populations over space are not considered. In this chapter, a newly proposed general measure of spatial patterns based on proximity was modified to measure racial–ethnic segregation. To demonstrate the utility of this measure, it was used to evaluate the spatial separations between population groups in hypothetical landscapes and Washington, DC, based on the 2000 and 2010 Census data. While the proposed measure shares some conceptual similarities with the proximity index proposed several decades ago, it has a statistical foundation that its value can be tested for significance. However, the current testing procedure is not highly robust. This chapter also discusses several conceptual issues in measuring segregation, including the nature of segregation and its relations to clustering.

As pointed out by Johnston et al in Chapter Two of this volume, to be able to measure segregation level accurately is critical in determining if segregation matters. However, how segregation can be and should be measured is very much dependent on our conceptualisations of segregation. Numerous segregation indices or methods for assessing the level of segregation have been introduced. Each of them, either implicitly or explicitly, adopts specific or multiple conceptualisations of segregation. In other words, segregation is multidimensional (Massey and Denton, 1988) and multifaceted (Peach, 1996). Thus, results from different measures may complement each other, but they may not be comparable, as they likely reflect different aspects of segregation. Several scholars have assessed the number of 'effective' dimensions of segregation (see, for example, Reardon and O'Sullivan, 2004; Brown and Chung, 2006). While thoroughly assessing this topic is beyond the scope of this chapter, and the focus here is on improving segregation measurement along the spatial dimension, only the clustering dimension of segregation will be dealt with as it is more spatial than other dimensions of segregation. Specifically, the objective of this chapter is to evaluate how different population groups are spatially separated.

Although spatial separation may not be the only criterion in determining segregation, it is definitely a logical and important one (Newby, 1982). Many existing measures of segregation evaluate group heterogeneity within enumeration or administrative units, and the degrees of spatial separation among groups are not considered. Such limitations are partly attributable to the traditional ways that population data were made available to the public. Data gathered from individuals are aggregated according to units at different levels of the census geography. Therefore, ecological or aggregated data derived from censuses reporting the population composition within areal units are often used in segregation studies. The nature of these data, to a large degree, has constrained our conceptualisations of segregation. These data were often collected at a particular time point (such as the census day), and told us who these people were within the specific geographical areas or regions. Our understanding of the population seems to be bounded by the ecological nature of these data reflecting the condition of the population on those given days.

Recently, individual-level population data have been used to facilitate new approaches to measure segregation (see, for example, Wong and Shaw, 2011, Páez et al 2012, and Chapter Five, this volume). Developments of these approaches are partly reactions to the convenient but overly simplistic ways often used to define neighbourhoods. Numerous studies across disciplinary boundaries, including geography and public health, have customarily used census tracts as proxies of neighbourhoods in the US. Data on population and housing characteristics reported at census tracts are widely available. Recognising the potential heterogeneous nature within tracts due to their relatively large sizes and the scale effect under the modifiable areal unit problem (MAUP), recent studies used smaller and thus more homogeneous areas (see, for example, Hewko et al, 2002; Taylor et al,

2003). Effects of ecological fallacy may still be significant, however (Wong, 2009). Lloyd et al (in Chapter Four, this volume) address this and related issues of defining neighbourhoods.

On the other hand, the increasing availability of disaggregated data not only enables researchers to exploit the utility of activity space in modelling human interaction beyond the residential space, especially in studies on public health and environmental epidemiology (see, for example, Cummins et al, 2007; Kwan, 2009), but also encourages the development of new approaches to measure segregation (see, for example, Schnell and Yoav, 2001; Schönfelder and Axhausen, 2003; Wong and Shaw, 2011). Nevertheless, the availability of individual-level data is still quite limited, and using these data is also subject to many pragmatic restrictions and conceptual difficulties. Therefore, we still have to live with using aggregated data in measuring segregation in many situations.

In this chapter, I demonstrate how a recently introduced general statistic on measuring spatial patterns can be used to evaluate the spatial separation among population groups. The statistic carries many possible forms, with the extreme cases for measuring spatial autocorrelation and spatial proximity. The spatial proximity version is used in this chapter to demonstrate how population groups are spatially separated. In the next section, I briefly review some aspects of the spatial dimension of measuring segregation. Then I briefly describe the general spatial pattern statistic, focusing on the spatial proximity version. To demonstrate the utilities of this measure, I analyse hypothetical landscapes and population data for Washington, DC, over two decades.

Spatiality of segregation indices

Numerous measures have been proposed in the more than half a century of segregation research. Front-runners of these measures are probably the index of dissimilarity and the entropy-based diversity index (White, 1986; Massey and Denton, 1988; Reardon and Firebaugh, 2002). Some geographers and sociologists have been quite critical of the aspatial nature of these and other popular segregation measures. The aspatial nature of these traditional segregation indices involves at least two aspects. Since the early 1990s, much of the work on measuring segregation introduced by geographers (see, for example, Morrill, 1991; Wong, 1993) has been focusing on spatialising segregation measures that were originally introduced mostly by sociologists. The primary argument for such efforts was that traditional segregation indices were aspatial in nature because their formulations assume that people across enumeration unit boundaries, regardless of the nature of the boundaries, cannot and do not interact. This implicit assumption is embedded in those indices partly because they rely on population data tabulated by areal units, such as census enumeration units or political-administrative entities. Locations of individuals within these reporting units are not provided. As a result, assessing segregation levels using measures such as the diversity index has been limited to measuring intra-unit population heterogeneity. Measures comparing inter-unit population compositions assume populations between units do not mix or interact. Thus, most spatial segregation measures were introduced with the objective to 'remove' the artificial boundary effect of separating populations between areal units.

Two major approaches have been proposed to tackle the boundary issue. Morrill (1991) and Wong (1993) introduced additional terms to the original index of dissimilarity to capture the gradients of racial-ethnic mixes across areal units, implicitly accounting for the interaction across unit boundaries. This approach creates some complications in the index formulations and the interpretations of index values. The second approach to remove the separation effect of the artificial boundaries is to define neighbourhoods in a 'spatially fuzzy' manner such that populations on the other side of a unit boundary may be included, implicitly accounting for the potential interaction across boundaries. This idea was first introduced through the concept of composite population counts, which was implemented by including all populations in the neighbouring units for a reference unit (Wong, 1988). A more sophisticated version of this idea was implemented through a spatial kernel such that population counts in surrounding units were weighted by the kernel's distance decay function with respect to the unit when they were counted toward the unit (see, for example, Reardon and O'Sullivan, 2004).

When the neighbourhood definition is extended or becomes fuzzy, the population counts are smoothed spatially across areal unit boundaries to derive the composite population counts for the reference units. To a large degree, counting populations beyond the boundaries of a reference unit implies that the 'neighbourhood' of the reference unit goes beyond its own boundaries. Then the question is how far the spatial extent of the 'neighbourhood' is. As reviewed above, existing methods in defining these neighbourhoods have been very simplistic, and these methods are not grounded in theory. Recent attempts employed sophisticated spatial statistical methods (see, for example, Logan et al, 2011). Chapter Four by Lloyd et al addresses this issue partially. Different definitions of neighbourhood will provide different results in the analysis, part of the MAUP problem (Wieczorek et al, 2012).

Another aspatial aspect of traditional segregation measures is that when inter-unit population compositions are compared, the spatial relationships between units are not considered in the evaluation of segregation. Massey and Denton (1988) proposed that segregation has five dimensions captured by different measures. These dimensions are evenness, exposure, concentration, centralisation and clustering. Reardon and O'Sullivan (2004), and later Brown and Chung (2006), argued that the five dimensions could be reduced to fewer dimensions. Regardless of the actual number of segregation dimensions, the dimensions that are intrinsically spatial are centralisation and clustering, but centralisation loses its appeals as the urban structure related to minority populations evolves over time. The clustering dimension can be represented by two general types of measures: spatial autocorrelation measures, which evaluate the levels of attribute similarity across areal units; and distance-based measures, that include some metrics representing distances between population groups. Examples of the former type can be Moran's I and the latter one can be the spatial proximity index (White, 1983). The former type uses some forms of distance to determine the spatial relationships between areal unit, while the second type uses distance explicitly. Thus, distance should be a critical component in capturing the clustering dimension of segregation.

Clustering is a frequently used concept in geography. But when the term is used, especially in segregation studies, it is often applied in a very imprecise and even confusing manner. Besides using spatial autocorrelation measures to capture the clustering dimension of segregation (Massey and Denton, 1988), geographers also often equate positive spatial autocorrelation with the presence of spatial clusters. Strong positive spatial autocorrelation appears when similar values are closed to each other. But how close is sufficient to be 'close'? This is addressed in greater detail in the next section. Also, close proximity or spatial contiguity of similar values is a prerequisite for the formation of spatial clusters, but is not a sufficient condition. As shown in Wong (2011), a trend surface where no obvious clusters are present produces the highest level of positive spatial autocorrelation, but some apparently clustered arrangements do not produce high levels of spatial autocorrelation.

On the other hand, the spatial proximity index essentially compares the average intra-group distance with the overall average distance in the population (White, 1983). Measuring spatial separation within and between groups using distance is conceptually appealing and straightforward (Newby, 1982). However, the spatial proximity index is a deterministic index that compares to the absolute benchmark of one. The difference between the index and one cannot reflect the likelihood that the observed pattern is a result by chance or not. In addition, if the two population groups are relatively uneven, the averaged distance for the minority group tends to be larger. The effects of imbalance in population sizes between the two groups can be significant. A weighted distance was adopted for the measure in a recently proposed framework to evaluate spatial patterns (Wong, 2011). A specific form of the weights allows the measure to evaluate spatial proximity. This framework and associated measures is reviewed below. In this chapter, the averaged distance between population groups is used as a measure of segregation.

General measure of spatial patterns as a segregation measure

Spatial autocorrelation (SA) statistics evaluate the strength and direction of relationships of attribute values given the defined spatial relationships between areal units. In general, SA measures involve two components: a G matrix, reflecting the correlation of the attribute values, and a W matrix, capturing the spatial relationships between areal units (Hubert et al, 1981). The W matrix is often referred to as the spatial weights matrix with various specifications (Wong and Lee, 2005), but W is essentially a function of distances between units. However, in the formulations of most SA measures, the W matrix often acts as a filter. In the case of using the adjacency criterion, the W matrix is used to determine which pairs of units should be compared. In the case of using the distance criterion, the W matrix often includes a set of inverse-distance weights to control the importance of each pair-wise comparison. In other words, SA can be expressed as $G = p(G, W(D))$ where D is the distance matrix. The resultant measure is essentially a measure of similarity in attribute space.

Wong (2011) suggested that instead of using only distance as a control through the W matrix, an additional weights matrix M imposed on G, the attribute correlation, can filter or moderate pair-wise comparisons. Then, the general statistic for describing spatial patterns is $MW = q(M(G) \ W(D))$. If the objective is to evaluate the degree of spatial proximity between units with a certain level of similarity, as captured by G, then the measure MW is reduced to $q(M(G), D)$, where M is an attribute weights matrix imposing on G, determining how pair-wise comparisons can be made based on their similarities. The distances between areal units reflected by D are not modified, and q is a function of M and D in deriving a specific version of MW, which is a spatial proximity (SP) measure. It reflects the spatial extent of a set of similar values or a cluster. The observed SP value can be compared with an expected SP value and its standard deviation that can be derived from a spatial randomisation process to render a z-score for hypothesis testing.

Analogous to W in measuring spatial autocorrelation, M can carry many forms, partly based on the measurement scale depicting the attribute differences between units. If the attributes are in interval-ratio scale, the attribute weights may be specified as $m_{ij} = g_{ij}$ where g_{ij} is a function of the attribute difference between units i and j. If a non-linear relationship is possible, the specification may be modified to $m_{ij} = g_{ij}^{\alpha}$ where α is a power parameter. An alternative formulation of the attribute weighting scheme may adopt a threshold approach where an attribute similarity threshold u can be chosen such that $m_{ij} = 1$ if $g_{ij} =< u$, and 0 otherwise. In this case, the two units i and j will be compared if the difference between the two units falls within a threshold distance u. Attribute weights can also be constructed to evaluate attribute values in ordinary or nominal scale where differences are reflected by orders. For instance, if two attribute values are identical (that is, the two observations are in the same group – zero-order difference), then $m_{ij} = 1$, and 0 otherwise. This mechanism selects observations in the same group to determine how close they are in D. This weighting scheme is similar to the adjacency criterion in defining the spatial weights matrix, but is applied to the attribute values.

The spatial proximity measure can evaluate the closeness of population groups classified by different types of attribute variables. Conceptually, it can evaluate the proximity among different income groups. Depending how income information is reported, the income attribute may be measured at the interval-ratio scale or even at the ordinal scale if income levels are aggregated into income groups. Selecting observations with zero-order differences to evaluate their spatial proximity is unlikely to be meaningful for interval-ratio variables, as observations with identical values are not very common. However, for population defined by categorical variables such as income groups, occupation types or racial-ethnic groups, zero-order evaluations can reflect the spatial distributions of population in the same categories. Higher-order comparisons evaluate the cross-group spatial proximity levels.

Illustrative examples

To illustrate how the spatial proximity measure can reflect segregation levels, I analyse 13 hypothetical landscapes, each with 100 units. Then I use the population data of Washington, DC from the 2000 and 2010 Censuses in the second example.

Hypothetical hexagonal landscape

Figure 3.1 shows 13 hypothetical landscapes with configurations of 100 hexagonal units. Each hexagon represents an areal unit completely dominated by one group, or as the location of an individual. For the sake of simplifying the discussion, I assume each unit has one person. Having multiple individuals at one location will not alter the concept. Two groups of individuals, A and B, are in the region with 12 A and 88 B. This binary variable may represent two population groups or political parties, each dominating an areal unit. The 13 configurations range from an extreme clustered configuration in 1 to extreme dispersed configurations in 12 and 13, according to the

Figure 3.1: Thirteen two-group hypothetical landscapes ranging from extremely clustered (1) to extremely dispersed (13) patterns

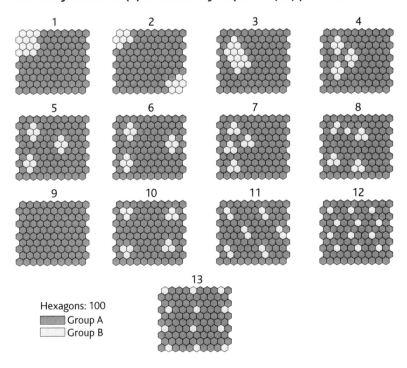

traditional conceptualisation of SA. Configurations 12 and 13 are slightly different in terms of the boundary effects levied onto group A hexagons along the edges of the region. Configurations in between the two extreme types have clustering levels gradually declining toward dispersion, or shifting from positive SA to negative SA, using traditional terminologies.

Table 3.1 reports the join count statistics with both free and non-free sampling assumptions. Both the numbers of AA and BB joins decrease from configuration 1 to 13, indicating a decline in positive spatial autocorrelation, while the numbers of AB joins increase, indicating an increase in negative spatial autocorrelation. Clearly, the boundary effect for configuration 13 is significant enough to produce the exceptional and somewhat counter-intuitive results. However, these levels and directions of spatial autocorrelation are only significant for the first few configurations, depending on the sampling assumption adopted. The non-free sampling assumption seems to provide more conservative results for the BB statistic (positive SA), but the free sampling assumption provides more conservative results for the AB statistic (negative SA). Using non-free sampling assumption, the negative SA for configuration 12 is highly significant, but the AA statistics are not significant under either sampling assumption.

Table 3.1: Join count statistics and their standardised scores under the two sampling assumptions for the 13 configurations (as shown in Figure 3.1)

Configura- tions	Join counts			Z-scores (free sampling)			Z-score (non-free sampling)		
	AA	BB	AB	Z(AA)	Z(BB)	Z(AB)	Z(AA)	Z(BB)	Z(AB)
1	226	23	12	1.5525	*7.143*	*−2.5563*	0.0707	*2.6774*	*−9.9936*
2	225	18	18	1.4875	*5.2868*	*−2.2007*	0.0677	*1.9916*	*−8.6209*
3	212	23	26	0.6424	*7.143*	−1.7264	0.0297	*2.6774*	*−6.7905*
4	204	15	42	0.1223	*4.1732*	−0.7779	0.0063	1.5801	*−3.1299*
5	204	15	42	0.1223	*4.1732*	−0.7779	0.0063	1.5801	*−3.1299*
6	204	15	42	0.1223	*4.1732*	−0.7779	0.0063	1.5801	*−3.1299*
7	201	12	48	−0.0727	*3.0595*	−0.4223	−0.0025	1.1686	−1.7571
8	201	12	48	−0.0727	*3.0595*	−0.4223	−0.0025	1.1686	−1.7571
9	201	12	48	−0.0727	*3.0595*	−0.4223	−0.0025	1.1686	−1.7571
10	201	12	48	−0.0727	*3.0595*	−0.4223	−0.0025	1.1686	−1.7571
11	196	6	59	−0.3978	0.8321	0.2298	−0.0171	0.3457	0.7596
12	189	0	72	−0.8528	−1.3952	1.0005	−0.0375	−0.4773	*3.7339*
13	205	0	56	0.1873	−1.3952	0.052	0.0092	−0.4773	0.0732

Note: Z-scores significant at 95% are in bold italics

For each configuration, I computed the spatial proximity version of the MW statistic, with the attribute weights matrix M taking a zero-order specification. Thus, the MW statistics report the averaged distance between pairs of observations in the same group (AA and BB). In other words, MW reflects the SP of observations within each group. The attribute weight M also took a first-order specification such that I could evaluate the SP between the two groups (AB). To test the significance of these MW statistics, I generated 9,999 randomisations to derive their expected values and standard deviations in order to determine the corresponding z-scores for the three MW statistics. I tested using 999 randomisations previously, and concluded that even 999 randomisations were sufficiently robust (Wong, 2011). Table 3.2 reports the z-scores of the calculated MW statistics for each configuration.

Overall, results from the join count statistics and the MW statistics are consistent, but significant differences are also apparent. For join count statistics, positive z-scores for AA and BB indicate that the numbers of neighbours in the same groups are more than those expected for a random pattern (that is, positive SA or sometimes interpreted as clustering). Their negative z-scores are interpreted in the opposite manner. For positive z-scores of AB, the numbers of neighbours in different groups are more than those expected of a random pattern (that is, the presence of negative SA). For those configurations with one big cluster (1 and 3) and regional clusters (2),

Table 3.2: Z-scores for the MW statistics for intra-group proximity (AA and BB) and inter-group proximity (AB)

Configurations	zMW(AA)	zMW(BB)	zMW(AB)
1	*−3.4504*	*−6.2594*	*4.9210*
2	*−4.5352*	*2.3620*	*4.7703*
3	1.9563	*−5.9191*	−1.2719
4	*2.4556*	*−4.6239*	*−2.0465*
5	1.7036	*−2.3093*	−1.5637
6	0.7455	−0.7698	−0.7230
7	1.4158	*−3.6048*	−1.0294
8	1.5653	−1.6943	−1.5055
9	0.2977	−0.4150	−0.2714
10	−1.2042	1.5487	1.1188
11	0.9324	−0.2386	−1.0202
12	1.7675	−1.1808	−1.8173
13	−1.8250	*2.4060*	1.6861

Note: Significant scores at 95% are in bold italics

they exhibit significant positive SA for the minority group (B), and negative SA between the two groups. But using the MW statistics, the clusters of the minority group are distinguishable between single clusters versus two-region clusters. The z-scores of MW for BB are negative (and significant) for configurations 1 and 3 with a single cluster, indicating that the group is closer than a random pattern, but is positive (and significant) for configuration 2 with two regional clusters, showing that the two clusters at the extreme corners separate the minority population apart.

Another major difference between results from the join count statistic and the MW statistic is their abilities to distinguish clustering at different geographical scales. Table 3.1 shows that the join count statistic cannot reflect the different degrees of dispersion of local clusters found in configurations 4, 5 and 6. Similarly, configurations 7, 8, 9 and 10 have different degrees of dispersion among local clusters, but join count statistic provides the same results. This weakness of join count statistics in these particular cases is due to the fact that this version of join count statistic considers only immediate neighbours, but not higher order neighbours. On the other hand, MW statistics capture spatial relationships using distance, not adjacency. Therefore, as shown in Table 3.2, MW statistics can distinguish very effectively the different levels of dispersion of local clusters among configurations 4, 5 and 6, and among the other set of configurations 7, 8, 9 and 10.

Washington, DC, 2000 and 2010 population data

In the above hypothetical landscape, the notion that each unit is occupied by an individual is not very realistic, even though at a very local scale such a framework is reasonable. But in most situations, population data are aggregated to geographical units to depict the spatial distribution of population over a region. Therefore, in the second illustrative example, 2000 and 2010 population data at the census tract level for Washington, DC were used. Three population groups, Whites, Blacks and Asians, were compared in terms of their spatial proximity levels. The maps in Figure 3.2 show the proportions of the three groups based on the three-group totals. Different from the hypothetical landscapes, each areal unit (census tract) has more than one person and was occupied by multiple population groups. Therefore, in computing the MW statistics, each individual in the unit is counted in the evaluation of the statistics. Because three groups are involved, MW statistics for intra-groups and all possible pairs were computed.

The plot in Figure 3.2 shows the MW statistics for all comparisons, including intra-groups. In addition, the lower and upper bounds of the 95 per cent confidence level of the statistics derived from randomisation were also plotted. The idea of this plot is similar to the clustergram concept proposed in Wong (2011). Analogous to the variogram that shows the (dis)similarity of observations over different spatial lags, the clustergram shows the spatial proximity/separation of observations over different levels of attribute differences or lags. In this specific example, because the variable is population group, which is in nominal scale, all possible pairs of comparison, including intra-groups (zero lag), are included. The statistics essentially show the averaged proximities or separation levels (in kilometres) between the corresponding groups.

Figure 3.2: Maps of proportions of Whites, Blacks and Asians as the three-group totals for census tracts in Washington, DC, 2000 Census (upper); MW statistics with their corresponding 95% confidence bounds for all group comparisons using 2000 U.S. Census at the tract level for Washington, DC (lower)

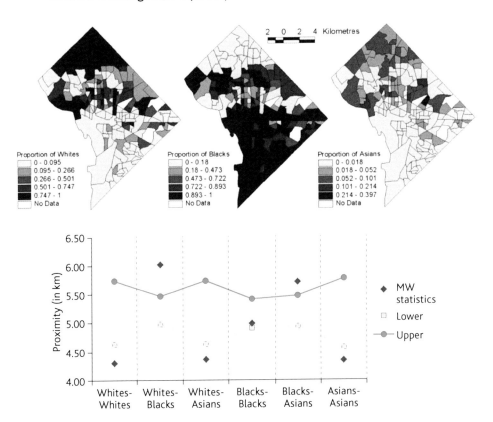

While all intra-group proximities are closer than expected, only the intra-group proximities of Whites and Asians are significant, but intra-group proximity for Blacks is not. For inter-group proximities involving Blacks (Whites-Blacks and Blacks-Asians), they are all above the expected values (and significant), meaning that Blacks are moderately separated from the other groups. The remaining inter-group proximity, Whites-Asians, shows below-average proximity and is significant. The z-values of the MW statistics for all comparisons are also reported in Table 3.3 showing that Blacks-Blacks proximity, which is below the expected value, is the only insignificant comparison.

I used the 2010 Census data for Washington, DC at the census tract level to perform the same analysis, and Table 3.3 reports the results. Similar to the situation in 2000, intra-group proximities for Whites and Asians were smaller than expected (and significant), but the intra-group proximity for Blacks was larger than expected, but insignificant. The overall inter-group comparisons for 2010 are similar to those in 2000. Proximities between Blacks and the other two groups were larger than expected (and more significant than in 2000), and the proximity between Whites and Asians was closer than expected (and significant).

While the overall patterns between the two decades have not changed dramatically, some interesting changes are recognisable. For intra-group proximities, both Whites and Asians had declined over the decade, implying that each of these groups has been increasingly closer. While the Black population had been spreading out slightly (a slight increase in MW statistics over time), such dispersions may be just the noise as their MW statistics were not statistically significant. For inter-group comparisons, the changes in the MW statistics between Blacks and the other two groups over the decade had been relatively small. Between Whites and Asians, these two groups tended to get closer

Table 3.3: MW statistics and their corresponding z-values for all three-group comparisons, 2000 and 2010 US Censuses at the census tract level of Washington, DC

Groups	2000		2010	
	MW statistics	zMW	MW statistics	zMW
Whites-Whites	4.2909	−3.1257	3.5451	−6.9213
Whites-Blacks	6.0131	6.3886	6.0034	9.5892
Whites-Asians	4.3547	−2.9428	3.4986	−7.3002
Blacks-Blacks	4.9787	−1.3864	5.2494	0.4975
Blacks-Asians	5.7035	3.5187	5.8742	6.8532
Asians-Asians	4.3363	−2.7073	3.4256	−7.2379

over the decade as the corresponding MW statistics have declined from 4.3547 to 3.4986.

In summary, Whites and Asians in Washington, DC exhibited some degree of spatial clustering in both 2000 and 2010, and each of the two groups has become more clustered over time. On the other hand, this study does not substantiate the claim that Blacks were more of a cluster than a random pattern, as Blacks have not exhibited statistically significant closer proximities than expected in both years. While Blacks have been relatively separated from the other two groups, the situations have not changed much between Blacks and Whites, but the separation between Blacks and Asians has increased over time. On the other hand, clustering between Whites and Asians has been increasing over time.

Discussion and conclusion

Spatial proximity as a measure of segregation

In this chapter, I demonstrated that a recently proposed general measure of spatial patterns could be used to measure segregation. The general measure becomes a SA measure if it compares the attribute similarities between observations when using the spatial weights matrix to control the comparisons. The general measure becomes a proximity measure when it selects observations based on their attribute similarity to evaluate their closeness. Population characteristics, including racial-ethnic identities or occupation groups (nominal scale), or income levels (interval–ratio scale) can be the attributes to divide population into groups. The general measure can evaluate the spatial proximities within and between population groups. Population groups are often nominal scale variables. If population groups exhibit an order, such as income classes, then some modified versions of spatial segregation measures may be more suitable than the one proposed here (Meng et al, 2006). In some recent approaches to measuring segregation and for neighbourhood studies using the activity space or social network concepts (see, for example, Maimon and Browning, 2010; Wong and Shaw, 2011), Euclidean or geographical distance were used to reflect the SP or spatial separation between groups. However, other distance metrics may also be used.

While using the concept of SP to evaluate segregation is not new (White, 1983), this concept is probably closest to the notion of spatial separation, a fundamental attribute of segregation. An advantage of the proposed measure is the feasibility of testing the significance of proximity levels. In this chapter, I analysed a hypothetical landscape with different population arrangements to illustrate the implementation of the measure. In addition, I used the population data of Washington, DC for 2000 and 2010 at the census tract level to show how the measure can be applied to aggregated data, and compare population compositions and distributions over time to show changes in dispersion or clustering within and between population groups.

A concern of the proposed measure in evaluating segregation is the robustness of the randomisation test. Specific situations determine the needs of different spatial randomisation tests. In the case of the hypothetical landscape, generating random configurations was easy to facilitate the testing, but for the cases in Washington, DC, only conditional randomisation was feasible. For instance, one may randomise the proportions of a specific group and derive the population counts based on the unit totals. While the total population in each unit is conditioned (and preserved), the total populations by groups derived from the randomised proportions may not match the original group totals. On the other hand, one may randomise the population counts in each population group across units. While the total counts by groups are preserved, the total population counts by units are not constrained by the original areal unit totals. Therefore, statistical testing results using these randomisation methods may be biased. Using latter approach in the Washington, DC cases, the standard deviations of the statistics are likely inflated, thus increasing the chance of committing a Type I error.

Is spatial autocorrelation the same as clustering?

The literature seems to support the idea that SA measures can measure clustering, and therefore they are segregation measures. If this logic is valid, then the proposed measure is redundant. As mentioned above, Massey and Denton (1988) include clustering as a dimension of segregation, and they grouped global SA measures under the clustering dimension. The literature is filled with studies using local SA measures in cluster detection, including hot-spot and cold-spot analyses (see, for example, Brown and Chung, 2006; Johnston et al, 2010). Theoretical formulations of these measures also support the use of these measures for cluster analysis (Getis and Ord, 1992; Anselin, 1995). However, as argued in Wong (2011), SA evaluates the similarity of the attribute, given the a priori definitions of a neighbourhood, and using different neighbourhood specifications captured by the spatial weights matrix will produce different results (see, for example, Getis and Aldstadt, 2004).

In addition, most SA measures deal with a single variable at interval-ratio scale. A few exceptions are for bivariate and multivariate attributes (Wartenberg, 1985; Lee, 2001). A high degree of clustering in one population group does not necessarily mean a high segregation level in the population, as other population groups may exhibit similar levels of clustering. Therefore, SA measures in general are not too useful in measuring segregation. A possible use of SA as a measure of segregation is to first derive a percentage variable, such as percentage of a minority population group, and the SA measure evaluates the level of similarity in minority percentages spatially. A more direct approach to evaluate the SA of population distributions is to use the actual population counts of multiple population groups. The recently proposed Q-statistic, a spatial association measure for qualitative variables, can use population counts to evaluate segregation levels (Ruiz et al, 2010). In Chapter Five (this volume), Páez and his collaborators demonstrate the use of Q-statistics in such a context for historical population data.

The concept of SP is related to SA, but focuses on the distance separating the populations within and between groups. The proximity measure is a distance metric indicating how far people are separated. This concept is intuitive, easy to understand and interpret. It is less 'restrictive' than clustering, which implies the presence of a spatially continuous distribution of similar values. The spatial continuity condition is not a 'prerequisite' condition for measuring SP, but spatial clusters assume spatial continuity of the phenomenon. In segregation studies, whether similar units are neighbours is not critically important; their distances separating them are more important. The implementations presented here evaluate the levels of separation for the entire study area and, therefore, these measures are global measures. As segregation varies spatially within the study area, local versions of the proposed measures can depict the local situations and variations across local units.

What do we measure in segregation?

Going back to the comment raised by Johnston et al in Chapter Two (this volume) about the importance of being able to measure segregation, we are by no means short of measures of segregation. The numerous measures reviewed by Massey and Denton (1988), and many more after their review, indicate that we have different types of measures lumped under the umbrella of 'segregation measures'. At one point, we were excited that the review exercise conducted by Massey and Denton (1988) was able to dissect the concept of segregation into five measurable dimensions, but later studies found that some of these dimensions were either not distinctive or not very useful (Reardon and O'Sullivan, 2004; Brown and Chung, 2006). Meanwhile, we can continue to develop new measures of segregation based on specific conceptualisations of segregation, just like the one proposed here (note that the notion of spatial separation is not new). As recent advances in segregation research have helped us understand what we have been measuring using various indices, the literature with almost a century-old history has not been clear about what we should measure in segregation, despite all the legal opinions and decisions rendered in the court of law and in legislation.

On the other hand, measuring segregation level is often not the end, but a means – a means to relate the segregation phenomenon to some tangible social ills, such as disparities in health outcomes (see Chapter Fourteen, this volume), access to resources, facilities or services, including education (see Chapter Ten, this volume). Apparently, segregation has multiple dimensions (spatial clustering-proximity-separation is one, and exposure seems to be another) and facets (residential, occupation, education, cultural, etc). Are all dimensions and facets equally relevant to a specific segregation outcome? Probably not! In other words, when we believe that segregation is undesirable, we have to lay out the causal pathway(s) of how a 'segregated' population will lead to a specific undesirable outcome. So far, the literature has been quite fuzzy in specifying these types of relationships, or has been overly abstract and general in depicting the relationships. Some of the fundamental and conceptual questions raised by Reardon (2006) should provide some potential directions for future segregation research, but being able to relate the study to specific social outcomes will likely provide more meaningful segregation research in the future.

References

Anselin, L. (1995) 'Local indicators of spatial association – LISA', *Geographical Analysis*, vol 27, no 2, pp 93-115.

Brown, L.A. and Chung, S.-Y. (2006) 'Spatial segregation, segregation indices and the geographical perspective', *Population, Space and Place*, vol 12, no 2, pp 125-43.

Cummins, S., Curtis, S., Diez-Roux, A.V. and MacIntyre, S. (2007) 'Understanding and representing "place" in health research: A relational approach', *Social Science & Medicine*, vol 65, pp 1825-38.

Getis, A. and Aldstadt, J. (2004) 'Constructing the spatial weights matrix using a local statistic', *Geographical Analysis*, vol 36, pp 90-104.

Getis, A. and Ord, J.K. (1992) 'The analysis of spatial association by use of distance statistics', *Geographical Analysis*, vol 24, no 3, pp 189-206.

Hewko, J., Smoyer-Tomic, K.E. and Hodgson, M.J. (2002) 'Measuring neighbourhood spatial accessibility to urban amenities: does aggregation error matter?', *Environment and Planning A*, vol 34, no 7, pp 1185-206.

Hubert, L.J., Golledge, R.G. and Costanzo, C.M. (1981) 'Generalized procedures for evaluating spatial autocorrelation', *Geographical Analysis*, vol 13, no 3, pp 224-33.

Kwan, M.P. (2009) 'From place-based to people-based exposure measures', *Social Science & Medicine*, vol 69, pp 1311-13.

Johnston, R., Poulsen, M. and Forrest, J. (2010) 'Evaluating changing residential segregation in Auckland, New Zealand, using spatial statistics', *Tijdschrift voor Economische en Sociale Geografie*, vol 102, no 1, pp 1-23.

Lee, S.-I. (2001) 'Developing a bivariate spatial association measure: an integration of Pearson's *r* and Moran's *I*', *Journal of Geographical Systems*, vol 3, no 3, pp 369-85.

Logan, J.R., Spielman, S., Xu, H. and Klein, P.N. (2011) 'Identifying and bounding ethnic neighborhoods', *Urban Geography*, vol 32, no 3, pp 334-59.

Maimon, D. and Browning, C.R. (2010) 'Unstructured socializing, collective efficacy, and violent behavior among urban youth', *Criminology*, vol 48, no 2, pp 443-74.

Massey, D.S. and Denton, N.A. (1988) 'The dimensions of residential segregation', *Social Forces*, vol 67, pp 281-315.

Meng, G., Hall, G.B. and Roberts, S. (2006) 'Multi-group segregation indices for measuring ordinal classes', *Computers, Environment and Urban Systems*, vol 30, pp 275-99.

Morrill, R.L. (1991) 'On the measure of geographical segregation', *Geographical Research Forum*, vol 11, pp 25-36.

Newby, R.G. (1982) 'Segregation, desegregation, and racial balance: status implications of these concepts', *The Urban Review*, vol 14, pp 17-24.

Peach, C. (1996) 'The meaning of segregation', *Planning Practice & Research*, vol 11, no 2, pp 137-50.

Páez, A., Ruiz, M., López, F. and Logan, J. R. (2012) 'Measuring ethnic clustering and exposure with the Q statistic: an exploratory analysis of Irish, Germans, and Yankees in 1880 Newark', *Annals of the Association of American Geographers*, vol 102, no 1, pp 84-102.

Reardon, S.F. (2006) 'A conceptual framework for measuring segregation and its association with population outcomes', in J.M. Oakes and J.S. Kaufman (eds) *Methods in social epidemiology*, Chichester: John Wiley & Sons, pp 169-92.

Reardon, S.F. and Firebaugh, G. (2002) 'Measures of multigroup segregation', *Sociological Methodology*, vol 32, no 1, pp 33-67.

Reardon, S.F. and O'Sullivan, D. (2004) 'Measures of spatial segregation', *Sociological Methodology*, vol 34, pp 121-62.

Ruiz, M., López, F. and Páez, A. (2010) 'Testing for spatial association of qualitative data using symbolic dynamics', *Journal of Geographical Systems*, vol 12, no 3, pp 281-309.

Schnell, I. and Yoav, B. (2001) 'The sociospatial isolation of agents in everyday life: space as an aspect of segregation', *Annals of the Association American Geographers*, vol 91, no 4, pp 622-36.

Schönfelder, S. and Axhausen, K.W. (2003) 'Activity spaces: measures of social exclusion?', *Transportation Policy*, vol 10, no 4, pp 273-86.

Taylor, C., Gorard, S. and Fitz, J. (2003) 'The modifiable areal unit problem: segregation between schools and levels of analysis', *International Journal of Social Research Methodology*, vol 6, no 1, pp 41-60.

Wartenberg, D. (1985) 'Multivariate spatial correlation: A method for exploratory geographical analysis', *Geographical Analysis*, vol 17, no 4, pp 263-83.

White, M.J. (1983) 'The measurement of spatial segregation', *American Journal of Sociology*, vol 88, no 5, pp 1008-18.

White, M.J. (1986) 'Segregation and diversity measures in population distribution', *Population Index*, vol 52, pp 198-221.

Wieczorek, W.F., Delmerico, A.M., Rogerson, P.A. and Wong, D.W.S. (2012) 'Clusters in irregular areas and lattices', *Wiley Interdisciplinary Reviews (WIREs): Computational Statistics*, vol 4, no 1, pp 67-74.

Wong, D. (2009) 'The modifiable areal unit problem (MAUP)', in A.S. Fotheringham and P.A. Rogerson (eds) *The SAGE handbook of spatial analysis*, London: Sage Publications, pp 105-23.

Wong, D.W.S. (1993) 'Spatial indices of segregation', *Urban Studies*, vol 30, pp 559-72.

Wong, D.W.S. (1998) 'Measuring multi-ethnic spatial segregation', *Urban Geography*, vol 19, no 1, pp 77-87.

Wong, D.W.S. (2011) 'Exploring spatial patterns using an expanded spatial autocorrelation framework', *Geographical Analysis*, vol 43, no 3, pp 327-38.

Wong, D.W.S. and Shaw, S.-L. (2011) 'Measuring segregation: an activity-space approach', *Journal of Geographical Systems*, vol 13, no 2, pp 127–45.

FOUR

Measuring neighbourhood segregation using spatial interaction data

Christopher D. Lloyd, Gemma Catney
and Ian G. Shuttleworth

Introduction

The term 'segregation' implies a lack of mixing between members of
different groups, and measures of segregation are often taken to indicate
the degree of possible interactions between members of these groups
(see Chapters Three and Five, this volume). Measures of segregation
reflect spatial patterning in group distributions. The development
of spatial measures, which make use of information on the relative
spatial locations of zones, has been a particular focus in the academic
literature concerned with improving methodologies for understanding
segregation (see, for example, Morgan, 1983; Morrill, 1991; Wong,
1993, 2003; Reardon and O'Sullivan, 2004). Such measures overcome
the spatial location independence of traditional measures (often
expressed as the 'checkerboard problem'). With traditional measures, if
we have a set of zones containing members of two (or more) population
subgroups, the spatial configuration of these zones will not alter the
results and could be misleading. For example, if half of the zones are
exclusively populated by members of group x and all other zones
contain members only of group y, then the segregation index values
will be the same irrespective of how much clustering or dispersion there
is in the zones. That is, the index values will be identical, whether the
x zones tend to cluster together in a group which is spatially distinct
from the y zones, or if the x and y zones are intermixed. More recently,
a variety of measures that enable the exploration of local variations
in residential segregation have been presented (Wong, 2002; Feitosa
et al, 2007; Lloyd and Shuttleworth, 2012), and local measures of
spatial autocorrelation have been applied in the analysis of population
clustering (Lloyd, 2010; Poulsen et al, 2010).

   Conventional segregation measures, such as the index of dissimilarity (*D*), are aspatial and are intended to measure how the population is distributed *across* a set of zones, but they disregard the spatial relationships *between* zones. Thus, the use of such measures could be taken to imply that there is no interaction between zones. In other words, the model suggests that nobody interacts with anyone who lives outside of their zone. Spatial and local measures offer a conceptual improvement on standard aspatial measures in that they account for possible interactions between zones (see Chapter Three, this volume). Most spatial and local measures are based either on contiguity weighting (immediate neighbours of a given zone are included in calculations) or distance decay functions. The latter are usually isotropic (the same in all directions) and based on Euclidean (straight line) distances. Definitions of neighbourhoods based on adjacency or simple functions of distance are used primarily for convenience, and it is difficult to assess how far such definitions reflect reality, especially given that what constitutes a neighbourhood is likely to differ between individuals, and between places. 'Neighbourhood' is a contested and problematic concept and, because of this, there are a variety of possible definitions and meanings; Kearns and Parkinson (2001) review alternative ideas while van Ham et al (2013) provide a set of studies that deal with ideas of neighbourhoods and neighbourhood effects. In their study, Östh et al (Chapter Seven, this volume) constructed progressively larger neighbourhoods according to the numbers of people around a location in order to evaluate the relationship between size of neighbourhoods and segregation levels. Similarly, Páez et al (Chapter Five, this volume) defined neighbourhoods as a few people at the scale of micro-geography.

   This chapter takes as its focus Northern Ireland, with the specific objective of exploring different ways of defining neighbourhoods for the measurement of residential segregation by community background ('religion or religion brought up in') using data from the 2001 Census of Population; context on segregation in Northern Ireland is provided later in the chapter, along with Catney (Chapter Fourteen), Shuttleworth et al (Chapter Nine), and Shuttleworth and Lloyd (2009). This chapter discusses some ways in which distance decay weighting schemes can be adapted to better reflect interactions between people in different areas. The use of data on migration as a proxy for daily interactions between Catholics and Protestants in Northern Ireland is explored. Proximity is a poor guide to interaction in some areas – a key example in Northern Ireland is the interface areas where Catholic areas border Protestant areas but there is likely to be negligible interaction between the two groups. Using migration data to model interactions will correctly suggest minimal movement between the two areas, while simple Euclidean distance-based measures would not. Of course, one-year migration might be argued to be a poor proxy for daily interaction by some since address changes are not daily events, but it is argued that they reflect perceptual awareness, or some form of familiarity, and thus possible interactions. Comparison of results using standard geographically weighted distance decay schemes suggests that the modified approach may offer benefits for assessing the degree of mixing between members of different population groups – this is most notably the case in interface areas, as suggested above.

Defining neighbourhoods

As noted above, in most quantitative analyses of residential segregation (and indeed analyses of population structures more generally) neighbourhoods are defined using adjacency or distance decay schemes (see Chapters Three and Nine, this volume). In the latter case, it is assumed that interactions between members of different areas are likely to decline with some function of distance. In other words, interactions between occupants of zones are less likely the greater the distance separating the two zones. A wide variety of distance decay (geographical weighting) schemes have been used in the study of population structures, and some of these are considered below.

Modelling of neighbourhoods can be based on simple spatial or attribute criteria, for example:

1. Defining individual zones (for example, census wards) as neighbourhoods
2. Distances or connections between places (for example, with straight lines or a transportation network)
3. Differences in zone population characteristics (that is, zones are not treated as neighbours if they are too different according to specific criteria; see Martin, 2002, for a discussion about the design of internally homogeneous census zones).

Cases 1 and 2 represent population mixing potentials that would occur if we assumed that there were no barriers between places with different population attributes (for example, there may be little mixing between areas with very different socioeconomic profiles), while case 3 assumes that different characteristics restrict interaction.

The first case corresponds to the case for a standard 'aspatial' segregation index, whereby values are computed for each zone (for example, proportional share of each group is computed per zone) and no account is taken of other zones relative to the central zone. The second case includes measures that take into account adjacent zones; distance decay measures are quite commonly encountered in the analysis of population structures (for example, geographically weighted regression, or GWR; Fotheringham et al, 2002 is based on a distance decay function). The third case is less well developed and possible approaches are reviewed later in this section.

In terms of distance decay functions (case 2 above), several general frameworks can be identified in terms of directional variation (anisotropy) and definition of the degree of decay with distance. A distance decay function may be:

- isotropic
- regular anisotropic (that is, using a simple anisotropy ratio)
- irregular anisotropic (for example, accounting for friction; see, for example, Lloyd, 2014).

With the first type of function, the distance decay function is the same in all directions at all locations. With the second function, some global trend in data values is accounted for by effectively 'stretching' the kernel (that is, the weighting function) in one direction so that observations in particular directions with respect to the central zone receive different weights than observations in other directions. The third function corresponds to modifying the directional effects locally. For example, there may be localised directional effects corresponding to physical barriers such as rivers or major roads.

The distance decay kernel is associated with a bandwidth that indicates its size. For some functions, the bandwidth corresponds to the distance at which zero weights are assigned, whereas in other cases the bandwidth might be analogous to the standard deviation of the normal distribution. Figure 4.1 provides a schematic example of the Gaussian weighting scheme (see Fotheringham et al, 2002; this function is defined in equation 1 below) for two different bandwidths. In either case, the bandwidth determines the degree of smoothing – in relative terms, for a small bandwidth fine scale features are emphasised, whereas with a large bandwidth coarser scale features are emphasised. The bandwidth can be fixed at all locations or varied as a function of, for example, zone/population density. In this chapter, two forms of distance decay kernel are used – one with a fixed bandwidth and the other with an adaptive bandwidth – and these are outlined below. For a fixed bandwidth, the weights are the same with respect to all locations

Figure 4.1: Gaussian weighting function for two bandwidths

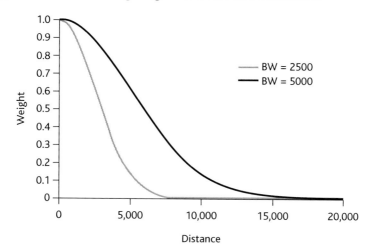

i and an observation distance *d* away. In the following case study, the geographical weights employed are determined by the Gaussian weighting function (Fotheringham et al, 2002):

$$w_{ij} = \exp[-0.5(d_{ij}/\tau)^2] \qquad (1)$$

Where d_{ij} is the distance between locations *i* and *j*, and τ is the bandwidth that determines the size of the kernel.

With a variable (adaptive) bandwidth based on observation density or population number, the kernel is small in areas with large numbers of zones and large in areas with small numbers of zones. As an example, the kernel may be adapted to include the nearest 10 observations to each location. In the case study presented below, the bi-square weighting function (see Fotheringham et al, 2002) is used:

$$w_{ij} = [1-(d_{ij}/\tau)^2]^2 \text{ if } d_{ij} < \tau$$
$$= 0 \text{ otherwise} \qquad (2)$$

The standard approach with distance decay functions such as those defined above is to use straight-line distances. This approach can be improved conceptually by using road distances (for example, Lloyd and Shuttleworth, 2005, who use road distances as inputs to GWR). A standard geographical weighting scheme, whether fixed or adaptive, may be a useful approximation, but one purpose of this chapter is to assess more sophisticated approaches.

With respect to the measurement of segregation, a geographical weighting scheme may be taken to represent interactions between people who live in different zones. Gatrell (1983) considers a variety of alternative concepts of distance (that is, temporal, economic, cognitive and social). The choice of areas to (and through) which people travel depends on necessity, convenience and the degree to which an individual feels comfortable in an area (Osborne, 2003). There is both a space (distance) and a time element – for example, some areas which may be considered 'safe' in the daytime will not be considered so at night or, indeed, vice versa. Interactions may vary in purpose and frequency. An individual may simply travel through an area to get to work, or there may be substantive day-to-day connections (particularly in terms of family and friends) between individuals in different areas. The focus of this chapter is residential segregation, and the particular concern is to attempt to determine how far there are likely to be regular interactions between people living in one area and another. In this respect, the concept of neighbourhood is an important one, and the definition of neighbourhood is considered later in the chapter.

A key problem addressed by this chapter is illustrated well by an example. Suppose that in an area of Belfast there are two neighbouring zones – one has 0 per cent Catholics while the other is 100 per cent Catholic. This area (or the boundary between the two zones) may be considered an interface area, and the two separate 'zones' may even be divided by a physical barrier such as a peace wall. In such cases, meaningful day-to-day interaction between people who live in each of the two zones is likely to be minimal or non-existent. A local measure of spatial autocorrelation would indicate negative autocorrelation and thus suggest that there is a high degree of mixing in this area. Thus, at least in terms of the clustering dimension of segregation (see Massey and Denton, 1988), the wrong impression would be formed in such a case. Integrating information on physical barriers such as peace walls (in the Northern Ireland context), or a river or major road, would provide a partial solution, and Lloyd (2014) uses a friction surface that incorporates information on peace wall locations to derive weights for local autocorrelation measures.

The notion of friction seems intuitively sensible in the context of residential segregation and interactions between social (and economic) spaces. Entry into 'unsafe' territory may entail greater (perceived) risk (in terms, perhaps, of physical threat or merely a lack of familiarity) the further an individual travels into that territory (Smith and Chambers, 1991). Put another way, the distance from 'safety' and 'escape' increases out of proportion to the actual distance travelled. Conceptually, in a threat-free environment, friction is a function of 'normal' factors such as distance and the necessity of the trip. Comparatively, in a segregated environment, the degree of friction is greater for a given distance. Thus, the notion of friction means that movement between different areas may not be prevented, but it is less likely than movement between similar areas.

In terms of physical processes, friction is often related to the degree of effort or cost associated with travelling over a particular area. The most obvious form of friction is the slope of the terrain in a given place. Given a friction value at each location (typically represented by a square cell), least-cost path algorithms can be used to ascertain the least-cost route between one place and another. Taking a short route over a mountain may take considerably more effort than a much longer route around the mountain, because the effort (and friction) of travelling a fixed distance over a mountain is considerably greater than for the effort of travelling the same distance over relatively flat terrain. The analogy can be extended to social spaces, whereby the relative 'cost' of passing through an unfamiliar area or an area perceived to be threatening is greater than the cost of passing through a familiar and 'safe' area. In a related context, Noonan (2005) considers barriers that create discontinuities in movement over space and the distance equivalence of these barriers is estimated. As such, the friction effect of barriers is evident. Greenberg et al (2011) explore the use of cost surfaces as an alternative to Euclidean distances in the context of spatial interpolation.

As well as sources of quantitative data such as the census, focused survey data provide indications of the perceptions of the safety of travelling into particular areas. Shirlow and Murtagh (2006), for example, report results from two surveys of, in total, over 9,000 individuals who lived in interface areas in Belfast in 2004. While focused specifically on interface areas only, the results provide an interesting example of how (non-)interactions between places may play out. In response to the question 'How safe do you feel when walking through an area dominated by the opposite religion during the day?', 49 per cent of males and 52 per cent of females said they would not venture into such areas. Only 15 per cent of males felt 'safe or quite safe', with an equivalent figure of 10 per cent for females. While walking through an area does not necessarily equate to meaningful interaction, these figures demonstrate the problem with assuming that individuals living in neighbouring zones with different communal backgrounds will interact. Given that this is exactly what standard spatial segregation indicators do, there is clearly scope for improvement in conceptual terms.

Another way of assessing perceptions of familiarity or safety is through the construction of mental maps. There is an extensive literature that deals with the concept of neighbourhood as a mental image (see, for example, Gould and White, 1986). In a Northern Ireland context, Green et al (2005) assessed free hand maps drawn by young people in Belfast which were intended to depict their knowledge of labour market opportunities and the areas in which they were, in principle, willing to work. For many individuals in Green et al's accompanying survey, areas dominated by the 'Other' group were considered unsuitable as locations within which to seek employment. Using data from The Hague (the Netherlands), Reynald et al (2008) present a study that explores the connections between residential locations of criminals and the locations where their crimes have been committed. The authors find that the 'flow' of crime between areas is a function of physical distance, and ethnic and economic differences between neighbourhoods, which the authors term 'social barriers'. The friction effect of (social) difference (in addition to physical distance) seems likely to affect interactions of many forms.

Most analyses of segregation are concerned with the residential context, while segregation in other 'activity spaces' (Wong and Shaw, 2011), such as work or leisure, is often ignored. Wong and Shaw (2011) make use of travel diary data to explore segregation in spaces other than the purely residential. Given that a concern with the measurement of segregation is on quantifying interactions, as discussed above, data that record movements of individuals would be of potential use. The UK censuses collect information on two forms of moves – one-year migration (the zone an individual resided in one year prior to census enumeration) and workplace (the zone of workplace). Quantitative data on interactions in a housing market context are thus available given that the present residence is recorded along with the residence (if in the UK) one year before the census. In addition, connections between place of residence and place of work can be explored. Catney (2008) examines one-year migration patterns in Northern Ireland using a spatial interaction modelling (SIM) framework, while Lloyd et al (2007, 2008) explore travel-to-work patterns using SIM. Information on the size of flows between places could be used to weight spatial segregation measures, and such an approach is detailed later in this chapter. As an alternative perspective, typical segregation measures represent a temporal cross-section; using one-year migration data, as applied in this study, two points in time (origin and destination) are considered.

Case study context: Northern Ireland

In Northern Ireland, residential segregation and perceptions of inequalities between groups are core concerns in political and public debate. Broadly, the population is often divided into two main (religious) groups, Catholics, and Protestants. In the 2001 Census, two questions were asked relating to religious identity – respondents were asked to state their religion as well as their community background ('religion or religion brought up in'). In 2001, approximately 40 per cent of the population were Catholic by religion and 46 per cent Protestant (including 'Other Christian'), while some 44 per cent were Catholic by community background and 53 per cent Protestant and 'Other Christian'. The link between religion and politics means that the changes in the percentage shares are of widespread interest in the region. In Figure 4.2, the percentage of Catholics by community background in 2001 is given by census ward (Catney, in Chapter Fourteen, this volume, gives an equivalent map for super output areas, SOAs). There are marked spatial patterns of Catholic/Protestant distributions, with large percentages of Catholics in the predominantly rural west and south and a predominantly Protestant east. Belfast is

Figure 4.2: Percentage of Catholics by community background in 2001

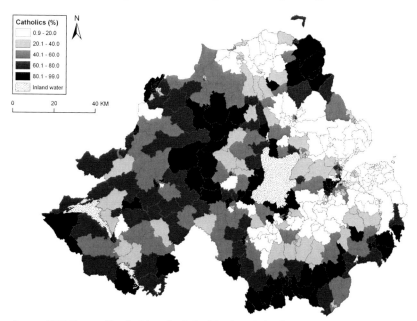

Source: 2001 Census: Standard Area Statistics (Northern Ireland). Output Area Boundaries, Crown copyright 2003. Data source: Census Key Statistics Table KS07b.

itself divided into a predominantly Catholic west and a predominantly Protestant east. Shuttleworth and Lloyd (2009) present a recent study of residential segregation in Northern Ireland, exploring changes in segregation between 1971 and 2001. Figure 4.3 shows the counties of Northern Ireland with the Belfast Urban Area (BUA) superimposed, for reference.

The analysis is based on data from the 2001 NI Census. The zones used are wards, of which there were 582, and with a mean population of approximately 2,400. The counts are of (1) Catholics, and (2) Protestant and 'Other Christians' (including Christian-related) (Census Table KS07b). For the purposes of this analysis, those in the categories of 'Other religions and philosophies' and 'None' were excluded. Counts of people who moved in the year before the census are used to obtain weights for the segregation measures, as detailed above.

Measuring segregation

Massey and Denton (1988) provide a useful, and much-cited, assessment of alternative dimensions of segregation that can be captured using different indices. In this chapter, the concern is with

Figure 4.3: Counties of Northern Ireland with Belfast Urban Area superimposed

two dimensions in particular – evenness and exposure (or, alternatively, isolation). (Un)evenness is most commonly measured using the index of dissimilarity (D). The isolation index ($_mP_m^*$, where m indicates a particular group) is widely used to measure isolation. Table 4.1 defines the measures used in this chapter. The primary focus is on geographically weighted global and local versions of D and $_mP_m^*$ (with m referring to Catholics and $_nP_n^*$ being the corresponding measure for Protestants). The geographical weighting schemes used were specified in equations 1 and 2 above. As defined in Table 4.1, global

Table 4.1: Definitions of segregation measures

	Dissimilarity (D)	Isolation (P)
Global aspatial measure (two group case)	$D = 0.5 \times \sum\limits_{i=1}^{N_i} \left\| \dfrac{N_{im}}{N_m} - \dfrac{N_{in}}{N_n} \right\|$	$_mP_m^* = \sum\limits_{i=1}^{N_i} \left(\dfrac{N_{im}}{N_m} \times \dfrac{N_{im}}{N_i} \right)$
Spatially weighted population	$\tilde{N}_{im} = \sum\limits_{i=1}^{N_i} d(N_{im})$	
Weighted proportion of group m	$\tilde{p}_{im} = \dfrac{\tilde{N}_{im}}{N_i}$	
Global spatial measure	$\tilde{D}(m) = \sum\limits_{i=1}^{I} \sum\limits_{m=1}^{M} \dfrac{N_i}{2NI} \|\tilde{p}_{im} - p_m\|$ with $I = \sum\limits_{m=1}^{M} (p_m)(1 - p_m)$	$_m\tilde{P}_m^* = \sum\limits_{i=1}^{I} \dfrac{N_{im}}{N_m} \tilde{p}_{im}$ with $I = \sum\limits_{m=1}^{M} (p_m)(1 - p_m)$
Local measure	$\tilde{D}_j(m) = \sum\limits_{m=1}^{M} \dfrac{N_j}{2NI} \|\tilde{p}_m - p_m\|$ with $I = \sum\limits_{m=1}^{M} (p_m)(1 - p_m)$	$_m\tilde{P}_{mj}^* = \dfrac{N_{jm}}{N_m} \tilde{p}_{jm}$

Description of terms:
   m = population group; m (Catholics in this study)
   M = number of population groups
   n = population group; n (Protestants in this study)
   i = index for zones
   N_i = number of zones
   N_{im} = number of people in group m in zone i
   N_i = number of people in zone i
   N_m = number of people in group m

spatial measures are computed as well as local measures, which allow assessment of unevenness and isolation in the neighbourhood (however defined) of each zone. Such approaches, as argued by Lloyd and Shuttleworth (2012), allow a far richer assessment of the characteristics of segregation than single global summaries.

As well as standard geographical weighting schemes, two alternative schemes were used, namely:

1. Weights based on physical distance *and* differences between zones in terms of the percentage of Catholics.
2. Weights based on flows of people between zones, as represented by one-year migration data.

With respect to (1), it is argued that by altering the weights to reflect differences (for example, social or economic) in addition to (functions of) distance, the resulting indices reflect the experiences of the population of the central zone. That is, if weights are made smaller for more distant zones, then similarly they can be made smaller for zones that are more dissimilar in terms of their population characteristics. A simple schema is as follows:

1. Weight distance using the Gaussian function (equation 1).
2. Measure the difference between zones (in terms of percentage Catholic) and compute weight, again using the Gaussian function.
3. Add weights from (1) and (2).

So, the bandwidth for (1) is in distance units, while that for (2) is in percentage differences. Therefore, if zone *j* is close to zone *i* and they have a very similar percentage of members of a given group (their difference in that respect is small), then the weight assigned will be large. As the bandwidth for attribute differences increases, differences between areas have a smaller impact on results.

An alternative approach would be to use thresholds for attribute similarity. For example, in a Northern Ireland context, if the difference between zone *i* and any of its neighbours *j* is greater than some fixed amount, then the boundary between these zones may be treated as an interface area.

Earlier in this section it was noted that migration flows are used to weight segregation indices. Such an approach is simple to implement and can be outlined as follows: for zone *i*, record the number of people who moved to zone *j* and this count becomes the weight with respect to zone *j*. Similarly, take all other counts of flows from zone *i* to all of the j zones and use these as weights. So, for zones j that have large flows from zone i, the weights will be large. The measures obtained using this approach can be conceived of in two ways:

1. Migration is used as proxy for (regular and 'meaningful') interaction between zones.
2. The measures represent segregation with respect to the housing market.

These possibilities are considered further in the Discussion at the end of this chapter. To put the migration data in context, a useful step is to assess the relationship between the sizes of flows, the distance between zones and the difference between zones in terms of the percentages of Catholics. Given that the dependent variables are counts, and that many of the counts are zeros, a Poisson regression model was applied, with flows as the response variables, and distance and difference (abs[Catholic % in zone i – Catholic % in zone j]) as the explanatory variables. The model coefficients were: β_1 (distance) = −0.088, β_2 (difference) = −0.026; the signs of the coefficients are as expected – that is, there is a negative effect of both distance and difference.

Analysis

As the first stage of the analysis, global segregation indices were computed using no weights and then geographical weights with both fixed and adaptive bandwidths. Table 4.2 reports values of D, $_mP_m^*$ and $_nP_n^*$ for different weighting schemes and a range of bandwidths. Clearly, for smaller bandwidths (whether in terms of fixed bandwidths or bandwidths determined given a specific number of neighbours), the index values are larger than those for larger bandwidths; thus there is a scale effect. This is as expected given that for larger areas the population is likely to be more heterogeneous and thus measured segregation will generally be less (Wong, 1997). As noted by Lloyd and Shuttleworth (2012) in a similar context, decreases in values of D with an increase in bandwidth size are proportionately larger than the decreases for $_mP_m^*$ and $_nP_n^*$. The minimum possible values of $_mP_m^*$ and $_nP_n^*$ are the proportions, respectively, of groups m and n, and Noden (2000) derives an alternative measure by extracting the relevant proportion from the isolation index. With this modified index, the proportional decreases with increases in bandwidth values are, as expected, larger.

The next stage of the analysis moves on to the assessment of segregation locally. This element of the analysis focuses only on

Table 4.2: Spatial segregation indices for 2001 population counts by community background for wards

Weights	Distance	BW	D	$_mP_m^*$	$_nP_n^*$
Equal	None	NA	0.601	0.701	0.753
Geographical	Euclidean	0.1km	0.601	0.701	0.753
Geographical	Euclidean	0.5km	0.575	0.689	0.742
Geographical	Euclidean	1km	0.526	0.664	0.718
Geographical	Euclidean	2.5km	0.460	0.629	0.681
Geographical	Euclidean	5km	0.363	0.589	0.642
Geographical	Euclidean	10km	0.288	0.539	0.616
Geographical	Euclidean	20km	0.228	0.492	0.599
Geographical	Euclidean	5NN	0.510	0.654	0.702
Geographical	Euclidean	10NN	0.459	0.616	0.679
Geographical	Euclidean	15NN	0.442	0.597	0.673
Geographical	Euclidean	20NN	0.419	0.583	0.665
Migration data	NA	NA	0.416	0.629	0.676

Note: m is Catholics, *n* is Protestants. NN = Number of nearest neighbours.

(un)evenness (D), rather than the isolation indices, for reasons of space. Figure 4.4 shows D ($\times100,000$ to avoid exponentiation) for a 5km bandwidth. Note that the local index values sum to the global values and they are not therefore proportions of 1, like the global measures. Figure 4.5 shows local D (again, $\times100,000$) for an adaptive bandwidth determined by 20 nearest neighbours. Figures 4.4 and 4.5 show some of the same general trends, but it is clear that a 5km fixed bandwidth effectively smoothes out variation and, most notably in Belfast, areas that are known to be highly segregated locally (in terms of unevenness and isolation, among other dimensions) appear mixed. Given the objectives of this study, it is clear that an adaptive bandwidth is more appropriate.

The interest here is in more subtle definitions of neighbourhood than simply functions of distance, and the focus of the analysis now moves on to alternatives to geographical weighting. The Poisson regression model coefficients given above suggested that distance and attribute difference are, as expected, negatively associated with migration flows between wards. Figure 4.6 presents an alternative summary – a plot of percentiles of absolute differences between wards (in terms of the proportional Catholic composition of sending and receiving wards) against the log of percentage total flows. The fitted linear model explains most of the variation, with the most obvious exceptions being at the ends of the x-axis. In short, difference in proportions of Catholics between zones is a key factor in migration

Figure 4.4: *D* × 100,000 for a 5km bandwidth

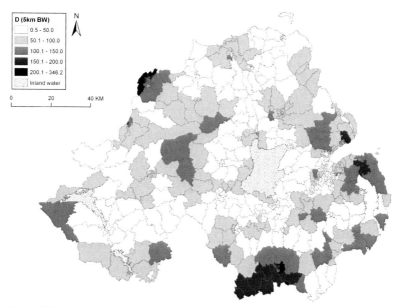

Source: 2001 Census: Standard Area Statistics (Northern Ireland). Output Area Boundaries, Crown copyright 2003.

Figure 4.5: *D* × 100,000 for an adaptive bandwidth determined by 20 nearest neighbours

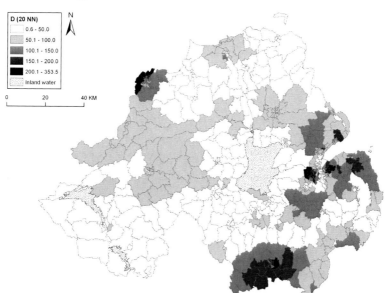

Source: 2001 Census: Standard Area Statistics (Northern Ireland). Output Area Boundaries, Crown copyright 2003.

Figure 4.6: Absolute difference (Catholic % for sending and receiving wards) against log(% flows) for percentiles

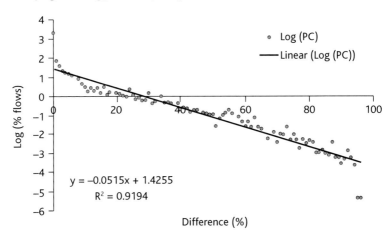

$y = -0.0515x + 1.4255$
$R^2 = 0.9194$

in Northern Ireland (Catney, 2008). This plot provides context for the next part of the analysis.

Figure 4.7 shows D (×100,000) using migration data for geographical weighting following the procedure summarised above. The map shares many similarities with Figure 4.5 in that many of the same regions

Figure 4.7: D × 100,000 using migration data for geographical weighting

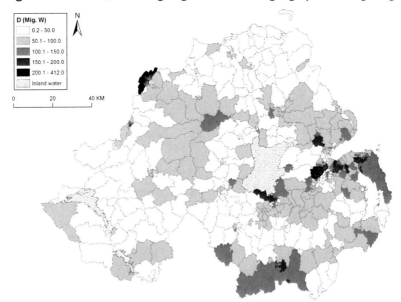

Source: 2001 Census: Standard Area Statistics (Northern Ireland). Output Area Boundaries, Crown copyright 2003.

with large values of D are apparent in both maps. For example, in both maps, Belfast and Derry/Londonderry have the most notable large values. The issue of what this map shows – in terms of segregation by housing markets or segregation more generally (with migration as a proxy for daily interaction) – is left for the following section.

The analysis so far has focused on Northern Ireland as a whole. The geographical focus now moves to the Belfast Urban Area (BUA), and this enables a more detailed perspective on the largest urban area of Northern Ireland. Figure 4.8 shows the percentage of Catholics by community background in 2001 in the BUA. Figure 4.9 is a map of local D ($\times$100,000) for an adaptive bandwidth determined by 20 nearest neighbours. Areas with large values in Figure 4.9 are, as expected, among those which Figure 4.8 shows to have very large or very small percentages of Catholics. But some areas with 'extreme' values in Figure 4.8 do not have large values in Figure 4.9. We would not expect an exact match between the two maps in this respect; indeed, there would be little point in computing local segregation indices if all of the variation was explained by per zone percentages. However, in parts of west and east Belfast, for example, Figure 4.9 appears to show smaller degrees of unevenness in some areas than we would expect. Figure 4.10 shows local D ($\times$100,000) using migration data for geographical weighting for BUA. In this map, the largest values of local D are larger than the largest values in Figure 4.9. In other words, the migration weighting scheme indicates greater degrees of unevenness at some localities than the scheme based on adaptive bandwidths (for 20 nearest neighbours). The larger values of local D in parts of west Belfast in Figure 4.10 than in Figure 4.9 are due to the migration-based weights emphasising east–west differentials in propensity to migrate. That is, the local D values suggest that those living in zones (that is, wards) in the predominantly Protestant east are more likely to interact with those in zones with more different community background profiles than those who live in zones in the predominantly Catholic west. Of course, strictly speaking, 'interaction' in this respect refers specifically to housing market choices, although it may be interpreted more widely if migration flows are considered representative of likely daily interactions.

Discussion

How far it is possible to represent neighbourhoods in a quantitative analysis framework is questionable. Definitions based on proximity or distance are simple to conceptualise and implement. However, a

Figure 4.8: Belfast Urban Area: percentage of Catholics by community background in 2001

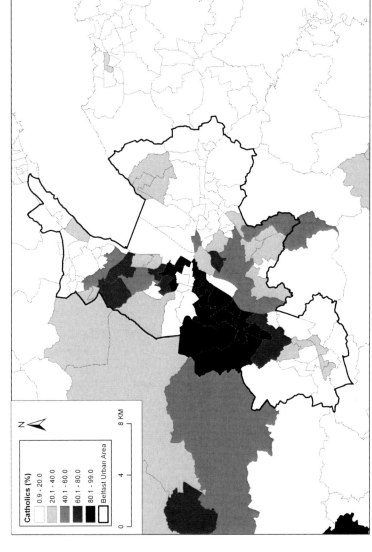

Catholics (%)
- 0.9 - 20.0
- 20.1 - 40.0
- 40.1 - 60.0
- 60.1 - 80.0
- 80.1 - 99.0
- Belfast Urban Area

0   4   8 KM

Source: 2001 Census: Standard Area Statistics (Northern Ireland), Output Area Boundaries, Crown copyright 2003.

Figure 4.9: Belfast Urban Area: D × 100,000 for an adaptive bandwidth determined by 20 nearest neighbours

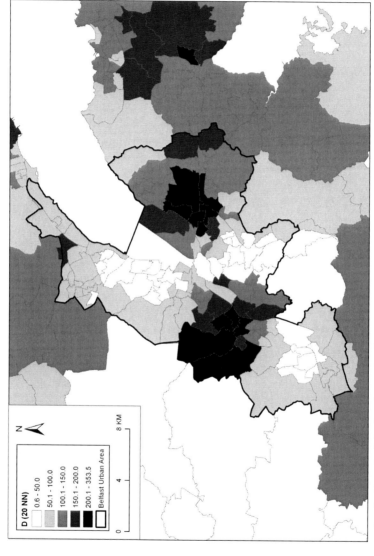

D (20 NN)
- 0.6 - 50.0
- 50.1 - 100.0
- 100.1 - 150.0
- 150.1 - 200.0
- 200.1 - 353.5
- Belfast Urban Area

Source: 2001 Census: Standard Area Statistics (Northern Ireland). Output Area Boundaries, Crown copyright 2003.

Figure 4.10: Belfast Urban Area: $D \times 100{,}000$ using migration data for geographical weighting

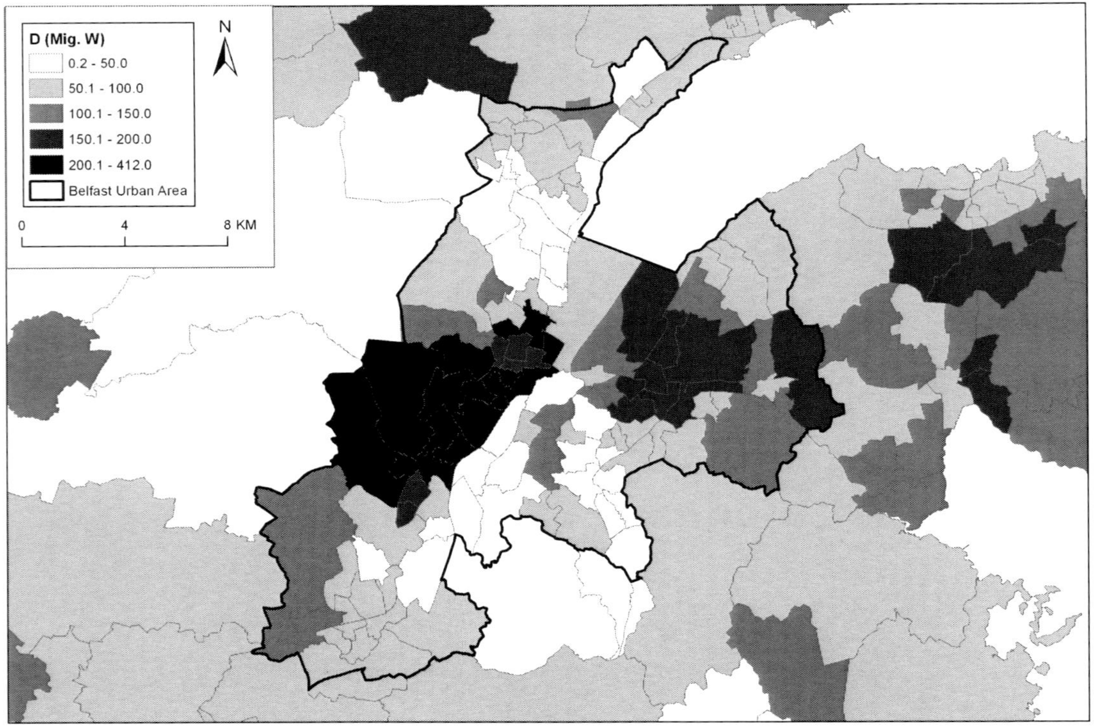
D (Mig. W)
0.2 - 50.0
50.1 - 100.0
100.1 - 150.0
150.1 - 200.0
200.1 - 412.0
Belfast Urban Area
N
0
4
8 KM

Source: 2001 Census: Standard Area Statistics (Northern Ireland). Output Area Boundaries, Crown copyright 2003.

critical assessment of segregation measures should consider how far individuals in different areas may interact meaningfully and how far these interactions can be represented. The present analysis offers some possible approaches that, it is argued, make better use of knowledge about interactions than simple distance-weighted measures, to construct more meaningful neighbourhoods as spatial units. However, further research, which marshals different data sources, is needed to more fully understand the nature of interactions.

Segregation indices with weights based on migration flows may be considered as representative only of segregation using housing markets as spatial units, rather than of residential segregation more generally (see Chapter Thirteen, this volume). Even so, the measurement of housing market segregation is, it is argued, useful and informative. The previous section concluded with a comparison of maps of local *D* generated using (i) adaptive bandwidths for geographical weights and (ii) migration-based weights. Irrespective of the specific meaning of indices with weights based on migration flows, these results suggested that weights based on adaptive bandwidths were appropriate but that, in some localities, degrees of unevenness appeared to be smaller than expected since we know that there are discrete concentrations of individual groups in these areas. In short, with an adaptive bandwidth, excessive smoothing is less marked than is the case for a fixed bandwidth scheme (with the caveat that the comparison is based on selection of particular fixed and adaptive bandwidths). There was still a suggestion that an adaptive bandwidth based on 20 nearest neighbours obscured local variation in some areas.

Zone-to-zone migration data are not available for a full range of census output zones and for areas smaller than wards (namely, output areas) – problems of small cell adjustments (see Duke-Williams and Stillwell, 2007) restrict their value. In some countries, migration data of this kind may not be available at all. These problems restrict the generalisability of an approach to the measurement of segregation based on migration flows.

The issue of how far migration patterns equate to meaningful interactions remains open. As noted above, such measures can simply be interpreted as summaries of housing market segregation, or we can go further and consider migration as a proxy for day-to-day interaction. One-year migration data provide evidence of a willingness to move between zones and, given connections between familiarity with places and residential choice, it can be argued that migration patterns mirror daily interactions. Moreover, most people in Northern Ireland migrate short distances (Shuttleworth et al, 2013), and this further supports the notion that these data provide a useful indicator of regular interactions. Of course, using migration data to determine the propensity for regular interaction between residents of different zones is likely to markedly exaggerate separation. Just because a person who lives in a given area does not want to (or is not able to) move to a different zone does not mean that they cannot have regular meaningful interactions with members of that zone. However, despite such weaknesses, it is argued that use of migration data as a proxy for daily (or at least regular) interactions between residential areas is an improvement conceptually on use of contiguity or distance decay measures. Most moves are short distance (see Chapter Nine, this volume), and thus they can be argued to be within one's daily activity space.

Spatial interaction models suggest that there is not a simple linear relationship between the communal composition of the areas of origin and destination (Catney 2008). This is not surprising – those movers who lived in a mixed area in 2000 are likely to have moved to a mixed area in 2001. In such cases, the definition of 'mixed' may vary to quite a large degree. For those movers who, in 2000, lived in a communally segregated area – say, an area with one group comprising more than 80 per cent of the population – a move to a similarly segregated area in 2001 will be more likely. In short, the nature of moves between segregated and mixed areas is (in most cases) likely to be distinct and, therefore, a linear relationship between the communal composition of sending and receiving areas would not be expected. Nonetheless, community background plays a major role in determining the places to which people move. Part of the explanation behind this relates to the spatial structure of the population by religion – some large contiguous areas are dominated by one group or the other, and a short-distance move is likely to take place from and to areas that are similar in terms of their religious profile (see Lloyd, 2012, for an analysis of the spatial scale of population concentrations by religion).

Conclusions and future work

This chapter provides a review of ideas about residential segregation and its connections to notions of neighbourhoods and (social) interactions. It is argued that more can be done to quantify interactions and, therefore, to produce more meaningful measures of segregation. Through a case study making use of census data on community background in Northern Ireland in 2001, it is demonstrated that alternative weighting schemes capture different aspects of segregation (specifically in terms of the dimensions of (un)evenness and isolation).

Furthermore, it is argued that measures based on neighbourhoods determined using combined geographical and attribute difference weights may better capture local characteristics of segregation than measures based on geographical weights alone.

Approaches like those presented in this chapter are much more difficult to implement than standard global aspatial segregation indices because of the number of choices that must be made concerning weighting schemes and bandwidths. But, in order to move beyond simple measures of the distribution of values within a set of predetermined zones, new and more flexible frameworks are required. Lessons could be learned from developments in local statistics generally (see Lloyd, 2011). A specific approach that would be worthy of further exploration includes local variograms (Lloyd, 2012), whereby dominant scales of variation in the variable of interest are captured directly. The clustergram approach of Wong (2011; and Chapter Three, this volume) allows direct assessment of the degree of clustering as a function of attribute similarity. An additional approach that could be used to collapse information given multiple bandwidths is to compute ratios of index values for particular bandwidths, which allows assessment of the spatial scale of segregation (Reardon et al, 2008). Different domains of segregation (for example, in the workplace) could also be explored – for example, commuting data could be used to weight segregation indices in the same way that migration data were used in this study. More generally, consideration of the role of urban environments in shaping neighbourhoods (Noonan, 2005) is an important objective that could enhance existing quantitative conceptualisations of neighbourhoods.

Acknowledgements

The Census Office, part of the Northern Ireland Statistics and Research Agency (NISRA), are thanked for provision of data from the Northern Ireland 2001 Census (NISRA, 2001 Census: digitised boundary data (Northern Ireland) [computer file]). Census output is Crown Copyright and is reproduced with the permission of the Controller of Her Majesty's Stationery Office and the Queen's Printer for Scotland.

References

Catney, G. (2008) 'Internal migration, community background and residential segregation in Northern Ireland', Unpublished PhD thesis, Belfast: School of Geography, Archaeology and Palaeoecology, Queen's University Belfast.

Duke-Williams, O. and Stillwell, J. (2007) 'Investigating the potential effects of small cell adjustment on interaction data from the 2001 Census', *Environment and Planning A*, vol 39, pp 1079-100.

Feitosa, F.F., Câmara, G., Monteiro, A.M.V., Koschitzki, T. and Silva, M.P.S. (2007) 'Global and local spatial indices of urban segregation', *International Journal of Geographical Information Science*, vol 21, pp 299-323.

Fotheringham, A.S., Brunsdon, C. and Charlton, M. (2002) *Geographically weighted regression: the analysis of spatially varying relationships*, Chichester: John Wiley & Sons.

Gatrell, A.C. (1983) *Distance and space*, Oxford: Clarendon Press.

Gould, P. and White, R. (1986) *Mental maps* (2nd edn), Boston, MA: Allen & Unwin.

Green, A., Shuttleworth, I.G. and Lavery, S. (2005) 'Young people, job search and local labour markets: the example of Belfast', *Urban Studies*, vol 42, pp 301-24.

Greenberg, J.A., Rueda, C., Hestir, E.L., Santos, M.J. and Ustin, S.L. (2011) 'Least cost distance analysis for spatial interpolation', *Computers & Geosciences*, vol 37, pp 272-6.

Kearns, A. and Parkinson, M. (2001) 'The significance of neighbourhood', *Urban Studies*, vol 38, pp 2103-10.

Lloyd, C.D. (2010) 'Exploring population spatial concentrations in Northern Ireland by community background and other characteristics: an application of geographically weighted spatial statistics', *International Journal of Geographical Information Science*, vol 24, pp 1193-221.

Lloyd, C.D. (2011) *Local models for spatial analysis* (2nd edn), Boca Raton, FL: CRC Press.

Lloyd, C.D. (2012) 'Analysing the spatial scale of population concentrations by religion in Northern Ireland using global and local variograms', *International Journal of Geographical Information Science*, vol 26, pp 57-73.

Lloyd, C.D. (2014) 'Local cost surface models of distance decay for the analysis of gridded population data', *Journal of the Royal Statistical Society: Series A*, DOI: 10.1111/rssa.12047 [online, pre-print version].

Lloyd, C.D. and Shuttleworth, I.G. (2005) 'Analysing commuting using local regression techniques: scale, sensitivity and geographical patterning', *Environment and Planning A*, vol 37, pp 81-103.

Lloyd, C.D. and Shuttleworth, I.G. (2012) 'Residential segregation in Northern Ireland in 2001: assessing the value of exploring spatial variations', *Environment and Planning A*, vol 44, pp 52-67.

Lloyd, C.D., Shuttleworth, I.G. and Catney, G. (2007) 'Commuting in Northern Ireland: exploring spatial variations through spatial interaction modelling', in A.C. Winstanley (ed) *GISRUK 2007. Proceedings of the Geographical Information Science UK Conference*, 11-13 April, Maynooth: National Centre for GeoComputation, National University of Ireland Maynooth, pp 258-63.

Lloyd, C.D., Shuttleworth, I.G. and Catney, G. (2008) 'Origin-specific models for analysing commuting flows in Northern Ireland: scale effects and other problems', in D. Lambrick (ed) *GISRUK 2008. Proceedings of the GIS Research UK 16th Annual Conference*, 2-4 April, Manchester: Manchester Metropolitan University, pp 145-9.

Martin, D. (2002) 'Output areas for 2001', in P. Rees, D. Martin and P. Williamson (eds) *The census data system*, Chichester: Wiley, pp 37-46.

Massey, D.S. and Denton, N.A. (1988) 'The dimensions of residential segregation', *Social Forces, vol* 67, pp 281-315.

Morgan, B.S. (1983) 'A distance-decay interaction index to measure residential segregation', *Area*, vol 15, pp 211-16.

Morrill, R.L. (1991) 'On the measure of geographical segregation', *Geography Research Forum*, vol 11, pp 25-36.

Noden, P. (2000) 'Rediscovering the impact of marketisation: dimensions of social segregation in England's secondary schools, 1994-99', *British Journal of Sociology of Education*, vol 21, pp 372-90.

Noonan, D.S. (2005) 'Neighbours, barriers and urban environments: are things "different on the other side of the tracks"?', *Urban Studies*, vol 42, pp 1817-35.

Osborne, R. (2003) 'Progressing the equality agenda in Northern Ireland', *Journal of Social Policy*, vol 32, pp 339-60.

Poulsen, M., Johnston, R. and Forrest, J. (2010) 'The intensity of ethnic residential clustering: exploring scale effects using local indicators of spatial association', *Environment and Planning A*, vol 42, pp 874-94.

Reardon, S.F. and O'Sullivan, D. (2004) 'Measures of spatial segregation', *Sociological Methodology*, vol 34, pp 121-62.

Reardon, S.F., Matthews, S.A., O'Sullivan, D., Lee, B.A., Firebaugh, G., Farrell, C.R. and Bischoff, K. (2008) 'The geographic scale of metropolitan racial segregation', *Demography*, vol 45, pp 489-514.

Reynald, D., Averdijk, M., Elffers, H. and Bernasco, W. (2008) 'Do social barriers affect urban crime trips? The effects of ethnic and economic neighbourhood compositions on the flow of crime in the Hague, the Netherlands', *Built Environment*, vol 34, pp 21-31.

Shirlow, P. and Murtagh, B. (2006) *Belfast: segregation, violence and the city*, London: Pluto Press.

Shuttleworth, I.G. and Lloyd, C.D. (2009) 'Are Northern Ireland's communities dividing? Evidence from geographically consistent Census of Population data, 1971-2001', *Environment and Planning A*, vol 41, pp 213-29.

Shuttleworth, I.G., Barr, P.J. and Gould, M. (2013) 'Does internal migration in Northern Ireland increase religious and social segregation? Perspectives from the Northern Ireland Longitudinal Study (NILS) 2001-2007', *Population, Space and Place*, vol 19, pp 72-86.

Smith, D.J. and Chambers, G. (1991) *Inequality in Northern Ireland*, Oxford: Clarendon Press.

van Ham, M., Manley, D., Bailey, N., Simpson, L. and Maclennan, D. (eds) (2013) *Understanding neighbourhood dynamics: new insights for neighbourhood effects research*, Dordrecht: Springer.

Wong, D.W.S. (1993) 'Spatial indices of segregation', *Urban Studies*, vol 30, pp 559-72.

Wong, D.W.S. (1997) 'Spatial dependency of segregation indices', *The Canadian Geographer*, vol 41, pp 128-36.

Wong, D.W.S. (2002) 'Modeling local segregation: a spatial interaction approach', *Geographical and Environmental Modelling*, vol 6, pp 81-97.

Wong, D.W.S. (2003) 'Implementing spatial segregation measures in GIS', *Computers, Environment and Urban Systems*, vol 27, pp 53-70.

Wong, D.W.S. (2011) 'Exploring spatial patterns using an expanded spatial autocorrelation framework', *Geographical Analysis*, vol 43, pp 327-38.

Wong, D.W.S. and Shaw, S.-L. (2011) 'Measuring segregation: an activity space approach', *Journal of Geographical Systems*, vol 13, pp 127-45.

FIVE

Micro-geography of segregation: evidence from historical US census data

Antonio Páez, Fernando A. López Hernández,
Manuel Ruiz and John Logan

Introduction

Segregation, the preferred or imposed separation of individuals in space and/or time, is a phenomenon observed for several traits of self-identity and labelling, including ethnicity, language, religion and economic status. Urban segregation is as old as the history of cities, with evidence indicating that it was practised in such disparate places as Hellenistic Babylon, *circa* 300 BC (van der Spek, 2009) and pre-Columbian Mesoamerica, *circa* 100 BC (Cowgill, 1997). Systematic study of segregation is a much more recent endeavour that is conventionally traced back to the Chicago School of Sociology in the first half of the 20th century (Dawkins et al, 2007). In contemporary academic and policy debates, the social phenomenon of segregation is considered an important factor to understand mobility (South and Crowder, 1998), opportunity (Musterd and Andersson, 2005), inequality (Chapter Fifteen, this volume; see also Massey and Fischer, 2000), social coherence (Baum et al, 2010), wellbeing (Chapter Sixteen, this volume; see also Ochieng, 2011), and individual health (Chapter Fourteen, this volume; see also Williams and Collins, 2001). Accordingly, numerous studies have been conducted in order to illuminate the possible existence of population segregation in the context of age (Smith, 1998), income (Chapter Thirteen, this volume; see also Fong and Shibuya, 2000; Feitosa et al, 2007), religion (Lloyd, 2010), and ethnicity (Alba et al, 1997; Wong, 1998), among other characteristics.

Segregation research can broadly be thought of as having two complementary branches, namely, the study of measurement and the study of process. The study of measurement is valuable to identify situations of interest, in particular, evidence of segregation, and to generate hypotheses about the processes that affect segregation (see, for example, Chapter Ten, this volume). The study of process is essential to understand the ways in which segregation originates, and how it is perpetuated, or abated. Research on segregation measurement has in recent years undergone a profound transformation. As chronicled by Gorard and Taylor (2002), segregation was conventionally measured by means of the index of dissimilarity, after the work of Duncan and Duncan (1955a, 1955b). The research of Massey and Denton (1988) on the dimensions of segregation, on the other hand, was hugely influential in clarifying the multidimensional nature of the concept, and the difficulties associated with trying to find an all-encompassing measure of segregation. It is now broadly accepted that segregation can be conceptualised as having two dimensions: in the evenness-concentration and clustering-exposure continua, according to Brown and Chung (2006), or exposure-evenness/clustering, according to Reardon and O'Sullivan (2004). Much research has been motivated by a more complex perspective of the components of segregation, and the measurement of patterns (see the discussion in Wong, 2008, p 458).

A particular area of research that has seen elevated levels of activity in the past two decades is concerned with the geography of segregation, and more specifically, with the ability of various indices to sufficiently capture spatial pattern, sufficiency being a key statistical criterion in the analysis of geographical data (see Griffith, 1988, pp 9-11). Following the early work of Jakubs (1981), Morgan (1983), White (1983) and Morrill (1991), a number of authors have raised awareness concerning the importance of measures that sufficiently summarise the locational information contained in population data. The use of alternative measures that do so has been promoted by, among others, Wong (1993, 2005), Reardon and O'Sullivan (2004), Brown and Chung (2006), Feitosa et al (2007) and Lloyd (2010). Johnston et al (2009) capped two decades of research on spatial measures of segregation with an exhortation to put more geography in. Several measures now exist that are better able to capture spatial relationships between units of analysis, and that are useful to discriminate, for instance, between a situation with a single ghetto and another with dispersed pockets of ethnic groups (that is, the checkerboard problem described by White, 1983). As a consequence, it is now technically feasible to put geography back in the way segregation is measured.

The subject matter of this chapter is the micro-geography of segregation. As observed from the literature, many of the difficulties ascribed to the analysis of segregation using aspatial indices have been much reduced through the use of measures that incorporate geographical relationships such as proximity and contiguity. This includes the use of kernel density estimation (see, for example, Reardon and O'Sullivan, 2004; O'Sullivan and Wong, 2007), and global and local spatial autocorrelation measures (see, for example, Feitosa et al, 2007; Poulsen et al, 2010; see also Chapter Three, this volume). Application of local and global autocorrelation measures depends on the availability of data aggregated for administrative areas, such as census tracts or dissemination areas. Although these measures generally consider only one population group, recent work has extended local statistics for two groups (see Farber et al, 2012). Nevertheless, contingent on scale and zoning schemes, the results may fail to illuminate spatial relationships of interest.

Consider the situation depicted in Figure 5.1. In each of the two zones shown, one of the two groups is in the minority. Measures based on zonal totals or proportions would be incapable of perceiving micro-arrangements that likely influence how the distribution of population is experienced by different individuals. For example, individual (a), who resides in a zone where his/her group is in the minority, is in fact clustered with other individuals of the same group – or conversely, has low exposure to individuals of the other group. Individual (b) is in a zone where his/her group is in the minority. However, barring the

Figure 5.1: Example of population in zones

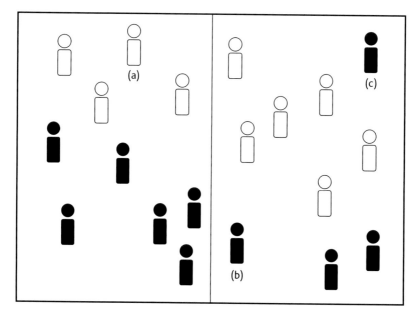

artificial and essentially invisible boundary of the zone, this individual is in fact part of a cluster of others who belong to the same group and, contrary to expectation, has comparatively low exposure to members of the other group. Individual (c), in contrast, does not form part of a cluster of others like him/her, and has high exposure to members of the other group, assuming that no population is on the other side of the zone (for example, an ocean).

Patterns such as illustrated above, while essentially impossible to retrieve using zone-based measures, can be captured by methods that shift the frame of reference from the zone to the individual. At least two such approaches have been discussed in the literature.

First, kernel-based approaches provide a way to analyse segregation, in principle unencumbered by arbitrary frames of reference (although in some discussions there is still a presumption that data is reported at the level of zones; see Reardon and O'Sullivan, 2004, p 128). Nevertheless, there are at least two limitations inherent in the use of kernel-based approaches. A kernel is essentially a smoothing device that is defined as a function of distance and a bandwidth. The degree of smoothing is controlled by the bandwidth, which defines the size of the window. A large bandwidth (in the limit, all units of analysis are inside the window) leads to over-smoothing, and local patterns could easily be obscured. On the other hand, a small bandwidth (in the limit, only one unit of analysis is encompassed) would tend to replicate the observed pattern exactly or almost exactly, and would thus be comparatively uninformative (that is, information is not summarised). In order to avoid under-smoothing, relatively large bandwidths are required (in previous analyses, in the range of several hundred metres to several kilometres; see Reardon and O'Sullivan, 2004; Feitosa et al, 2007; O'Sullivan and Wong, 2007; Reardon et al, 2008). Recent research adopts an activity-based perspective, whereby the areas scanned for potential patterns of contact or exposure is based on revealed spatial behaviour (Wong and Shaw, 2011; Farber et al, 2012). A limitation of these approaches is that kernels can be defined with respect to a population at risk, but are less apt for exploring patterns involving multiple groups.

The second approach discussed in the literature is the use of a statistic of spatial co-location for categorical data, as advocated by Páez et al (2012). Based on relatively small neighbourhoods around individual observations, the $Q(m)$ statistic of Ruiz et al (2010) affords an opportunity to investigate the micro-geography of segregation, specifically patterns of clustering and exposure at very high levels of resolution. Although individual-level data have traditionally not been available for segregation research, there are emerging opportunities for exploring segregation at this level of detail. Such is the case of historical data sources that are increasingly available in geographical format (see, for example, Lloyd et al, 2012; So and Wong, 2012), and, in some cases, at secure facilities sponsored by national or regional statistical agencies, such as the Research Data Centres Program in Canada,[1] or university-based data centres supported by Statistics Sweden (Chapter Seven, this volume). In this chapter, we use data from the Urban Transition Historical Geographic Information System (GIS) Project (Logan et al, 2011a) to investigate the micro-geography of segregation in three North American cities in 1880. Evidence that segregation exists at the meso- and macro-scales is plentiful. The research reported here provides evidence that segregation patterns may be present (and measured) at much smaller (that is, micro-) scales than previously reported.

The structure of this chapter is as follows. Next, the technical details regarding $Q(m)$ and its implementation are discussed. Subsequently, the data used in the analysis are described. This is followed by a presentation of the results of the analysis and discussion. Some concluding remarks and directions for future research are provided in the final section.

Methods

Using Q(m) for clustering and exposure analysis

Clustering and exposure are two aspects of the same dimension of segregation (Brown and Chung, 2006). Clustering can be defined in terms of geographical proximity between individuals who belong to the same group. Exposure can be defined in terms of geographical proximity between individuals who belong to different groups.

Shifting the perspective from zonal aggregations to the individual, the micro-geography of clustering and exposure can be investigated by making reference to the immediate neighbourhood in which a person is located (similar to the individualised neighbourhoods of Östh et al, in Chapter Seven, this volume). In order to do this, spatial data for all N individuals to be analysed, say, the coordinates of their place of residence s_i, are required ($i=1,...,N$). Furthermore, all individuals must be characterised by means of a variable, say Y, which describes their membership status with respect to one of k groups (for example, ethnicity, linguistic group, income class). Membership in a group is exclusive, that is, an individual cannot belong to two or more groups simultaneously. For instance, in the example in Figure 5.1, there are

k=2 groups, and so individuals are attributed with values of Y=1 (Black) or Y=2 (White).

Since the coordinates (that is, locational information) are available for the individuals under analysis, it is possible to identify for each individual his or her m-1 nearest neighbours, to generate a neighbourhood of size m, which includes the individual in question. This neighbourhood is called an m-surrounding. As an example, consider m-surroundings with m=4 (the size of m is determined by the analyst subject to some considerations discussed below). The m-surroundings of individuals (a), (b) and (c) in the example are shown in Figure 5.2.

Individual (a), who is attributed with Y=2, is at the centre of an m-surrounding that consists exclusively of individuals of the same group, or in other words, is part of a small neighbourhood with others like him/her. In a compact way, the configuration of (a)'s m-surrounding can be expressed as {0,4}, since there are no individuals who belong to Y=1, and all four individuals in this m-surrounding belong to Y=2 (that is, this is a cluster of Whites). Individual (b) is at the centre of an m-surrounding where all individuals are attributed with Y=1, and so the m-surrounding can be expressed as {4,0} (that is, the individual is in a cluster of Blacks). Individual (c) is part of a group where most members belong to a different group: the corresponding m-surrounding is {1,3}. While (c) has high exposure to members of a different group, the same is not necessarily true for other members in the m-surrounding.

It is straightforward to see that m-surroundings can be identified for every single individual under analysis. Furthermore, it should be clear that there are only a limited number of ways in which members of k different groups can combine to create distinct configurations of surroundings of size m. In the example, with k=2 (and disregarding the ordering of members within the group) there are exactly five unique combinations of neighbours in groups of four, as shown in Table 5.1. Each unique m-surrounding can be represented in a compact form by a means of a symbol, denoted by $\sigma*$ (an equivalent symbol, in the terminology of Páez et al, 2012). More generally, there are λ=k $(k+1)...(k+m-1)/m!$ symbols, that is, the number of combinations

Figure 5.2: Examples of m-surroundings with m=4

(a) (b) (c)

Table 5.1: List of unique *m*-surrounding configurations when *k*=2 and *m*=4, and corresponding symbols

Configuration of *m*-surrounding	Symbol
●●●● ▮▮▮▮	$\sigma_1^* = \{4,0\}$
●●●○ ▮▮▮▯	$\sigma_2^* = \{3,1\}$
●●○○ ▮▮▯▯	$\sigma_3^* = \{2,2\}$
●○○○ ▮▯▯▯	$\sigma_4^* = \{1,3\}$
○○○○ ▯▯▯▯	$\sigma_5^* = \{0,4\}$

with replacement of k different object types in groups of size m. Collectively, the symbols denote all forms of co-location in small neighbourhoods, of individuals belonging to different groups.

The process of identifying the m-surrounding corresponding to individual i at location s_i, and assigning it a symbol, is called *symbolisation*. Returning to the example, it is possible to see that the symbol corresponding to individual (a) is σ_5^*, or in other words, individual (a) is of type σ_5^*. Likewise, individual (b) is of type σ_1^*, and individual (c) is of type σ_4^*. Once all individuals have been symbolised (or an appropriate number of them – more on this below), the empirical relative frequency of each symbol can be calculated as the number of individuals whose symbol is of type j ($n_{\sigma_j^*}$), divided by the number of individuals who have been symbolised (S):

$$p_{\sigma_j^*} = \frac{n_{\sigma_j^*}}{S} \tag{1}$$

Intuitively, one would expect that if the members of the populations under analysis were located in a random fashion with respect to each other, the chances of being geographically proximate to individuals belonging to each of these groups would be approximately the same, contingent on the number of members in each group. Clustering would be evinced by a high frequency of symbols where members of one group are co-located (such as σ_1^* and σ_5^* in the example). Evidence of exposure would result if a high frequency of symbols where individuals tend to be co-located with members of a different group were observed (that is, symbols σ_2^* and σ_4^*).

To illustrate these ideas, consider again Figure 5.1, where group 1 has $n_1=10$ members and group 2 has $n_2=10$ members ($n_1+n_2=N=20$). Under the null hypothesis of a random sequence, the probability of observing an individual at the centre of an m-surrounding of type σ_1^* (which includes four Black individuals) is P($\blacksquare\blacksquare\blacksquare\blacksquare$)=$(n_1/N)^4=(10/20)^4$ $=1/16=0.0625$. Since there are 20 individuals, the expectation under the null hypothesis would be to observe approximately $20*0.0625=1.2$ m-surroundings of type σ_1^*. Clearly, this symbol type is observed in the empirical distribution with much higher frequency than 1.2, as a consequence of the clustering of members of group 1.

In an empirical situation, a certain inherent variability makes it extremely unlikely that the frequency of symbols will match the expectation for a random distribution of members of the population relative to each other, even if there are no underlying patterns of clustering and/or exposure. A key question, then, is to determine the probability that an empirical pattern of co-location of members of different groups is *not* random. One way to approach this question is to summarise the information available in the empirical pattern of co-location of members of different groups by means of a symbolic entropy function. The function is based on Shanon's formula, as follows (see Ruiz et al, 2010):

$$h(m) = -\sum_j p_{\sigma_j^*} \ln(p_{\sigma_j^*}) \qquad (2)$$

The value of $h(m)$ tends to zero when the pattern of co-location is highly organised, that is, when only one symbol, or a relatively small number of symbols, appears repeatedly. An upper bound, call it η, can be found for the converse situation, whereby the distribution is random. The expression for this is given by Ruiz et al (2010) as:

$$\eta = -\sum_i \frac{n_{\sigma_j^*}}{S} \sum_j \alpha_{ij} \ln(q_j) \qquad (3)$$

where a_{ij} is the number of times that members of class j ($j=1,...,k$) appear in symbol i, and q_j is the probability that $Y=j$, and again S is the number of locations that were symbolised.

The $Q(m)$ statistic is simply a likelihood ratio test that compares the value of the empirical entropy function to the value of the function under the null hypothesis of a random spatial sequence:

$$Q(m) = 2S(\eta - h(m)) \qquad (4)$$

The statistic in (4) is asymptotically χ^2-distributed, with degrees of freedom equal to the number of symbols minus one.[2] The value of the statistic can be associated with a probability (a p-value) that can be used by the analyst to decide whether to reject the null hypothesis of a random spatial sequence in favour of a systematic pattern of co-location of the members of the groups under analysis.

$Q(m)$ is a global statistic of spatial co-location of a qualitative variable. As such, it can be used to reject the hypothesis that the spatial distribution is globally random. A second way to assess the probability that a pattern of co-location is not random is to compare the empirical relative frequency of the symbols to the corresponding expected frequency under the null hypothesis. The empirical frequency of the symbols can be visualised by means of a histogram. As discussed by Páez et al (2012), the interval of confidence for the empirical frequency of a symbol can be calculated as follows:

$$\left(p_{\sigma_j^*} - z_{\alpha/2} \sqrt{\frac{p_{\sigma_j^*}\left(1 - p_{\sigma_j^*}\right)}{S}}, \; p_{\sigma_j^*} + z_{\alpha/2} \sqrt{\frac{p_{\sigma_j^*}\left(1 - p_{\sigma_j^*}\right)}{S}} \right) \tag{5}$$

where $z_{\alpha/2}$ is the cut-off value of the standard normal distribution corresponding to a level of significance of α.

The interval of confidence allows the analyst to assess whether a specific symbol is observed more or less frequently than expected under the null hypothesis. In other words, it becomes possible to assess, by examining symbols of interest, whether specific patterns of clustering and/or exposure are significant.

Before proceeding to the case study, discussion concerning some practical issues in the implementation $Q(m)$ is in order.

Practical issues for implementation

The statistic $Q(m)$ allows an analyst interested in segregation issues to investigate, in a descriptive and inferential framework, the question of clustering and exposure among members of different population groups. The statistic can be deployed at a micro-geographical scale, by using individual-level data, and considering small neighbourhoods of size m. The analyst selects the value of m (the size of the neighbourhood). There is some flexibility in terms of the selection of m, subject to some considerations, as discussed next.

First, a small value of m, say $m=1$, limits the analysis to the first nearest neighbour, and is thus limited in geographical extent. Larger values of m would therefore seem desirable, in order to employ more spatial information and to increase the geographical extent of the analysis. Larger values of m, however, can also face constraints. First, as discussed by Ruiz et al (2010, p 291), the number of symbolised locations must be at least five times the number of symbols used in the analysis (alternatively $S/\lambda \geq 5$), in order to provide reasonable asymptotic convergence conditions to the χ^2 distribution. Since the number of symbols depends on k (a value over which the analyst may have only limited control) and m, selection of m may be conditioned by the number of observations. For instance, as seen above, when $k=2$ and $m=4$, there are only five symbols. The number of symbols, however, rapidly increases as k and m grow. For instance, when $k=3$ and $m=5$, there are 28 symbols. When $k=4$ and $m=7$, there are 120 symbols. The latter situation would require at least 600 symbolised observations.

Second, the process of symbolisation naturally leads to some degree of overlap. In other words, some individuals will be part of multiple m-surroundings. This overlap, and lack of independence between m-surroundings, can have a deleterious impact on the power (ability to correctly reject the null hypothesis) and size (ability to correctly identify the null hypothesis) of the statistic, in other words, the ability of the statistic to correctly reject the null hypothesis when the pattern is not random, or the failure to reject the null hypothesis when the pattern is random, respectively. As a way to reduce the overlap between m-surroundings, and to sharpen the inferential capabilities of the statistic, Ruiz et al (2010) propose a procedure to symbolise a sub-set of observations S, with $S \leq N$, given a desired degree of overlap r. A value of $r=1$ implies that proximate m-surroundings have an overlap of at most one observation, $r=2$ implies an overlap of at most 2 observations, and so on. Reducing the degree of overlap (that is, selecting small values of r) leads to more stringent conditions for selecting observations for symbolisation. Consequently, the number of symbolised observations will tend to decrease, which can further limit the size of m that can be implemented. Simulations performed by Ruiz et al (2010) indicate that higher values of r increase the risk of false positives, but also the ability of $Q(m)$ to correctly reject the null hypothesis when the distribution is not random.

Finally, a greater number of symbols can also pose a challenge for interpretation, as the increasing level of detail creates minute differences between many symbols.

Data

The analysis reported below is based on data from the 1880 US Census. Retrieving historical data in a format amenable for modern spatial analysis can be an onerous task – albeit one with potentially large rewards. Information contained in the census was painstakingly collected and organised by a number of parties to generate an all-digital database suitable for contemporary computer-assisted research. Volunteers coordinated by the Church of Jesus Christ of Latter-Day Saints (LDS) undertook electronic transcription of archived census records over a period of 18 years by. Data cleaning and processing services of the electronic records were provided by Minnesota Population Center (MPC) at the University of Minnesota, as part of an agreement with LDS that would allow MPC to make the data freely available for academic use. Building on the efforts of LDS and MPC, the Urban Transition Historical GIS Project at Brown University (Logan et al, 2011a) has endeavoured to provide additional resources for use of the digital 1880 Census.

Resources generated by the Urban Transition Historical GIS Project include linking the records to accurate 1880 maps, and creating a web-based mapping application that allows users to easily access the information for enumeration districts in 39 cities, with minimal demands on GIS training (www.s4.brown.edu/utp). For more advanced users who want to implement their own mapping applications, the data is available for download. Comprehensive as these tasks are, perhaps the most ambitious aspect of the project has been to geocode, based on street addresses, the records corresponding to the 39 cities being mapped – approximately 5 million residents. As noted by Logan et al (2011a, p 49), this effort will make it possible to use large parts of the 1880 Census for analysis of 'urban spatial patterns at any scale, with no need to use administrative boundaries imposed by the census.' As the data become available, so do the opportunities for innovative research into urban structure (for example, the identification of ethnic neighbourhoods in 1880 Newark; see Logan et al, 2011b) and population geography (for example, the analysis of ethnic clustering and exposure in 1880 Newark; see Páez et al, 2012).

The current application complements the analysis of Newark reported by Páez et al (2012). Available data currently allows the analysis of three cities, namely, Albany and Buffalo in New York, and Cincinnati in Ohio. Household heads are extracted corresponding to three different ethnic groups: German, Irish and Yankee. Under this classification, an individual is considered to be ethnically German or

Irish if he or she was born in one of these countries, or at least one parent was. An individual is recorded as a Yankee if he or she is White, and born in the US with US-born parents. Members of these three ethnic groups comprise over 85 per cent of all household heads in Albany, approximately 75 per cent of household heads in Buffalo, and 83 per cent of all household heads in Cincinnati. The number and frequency of cases in each of these cities appears in Table 5.2.

As seen in Table 5.2, the three groups are well represented in the cities considered. In Albany, one group (Irish) is in the plurality, whereas in Buffalo and Cincinnati, one group (German) is in the majority.

Table 5.2: Descriptive statistics

| City | Sample size (*N*) | Total (and %) of household heads by ethnic group | | |
		German	Irish	Yankee
Albany, NY	15,938	3,667 (23.01%)	6,868 (43.09%)	5,403 (33.90%)
Buffalo, NY	22,944	13,252 (57.75%)	4,974 (21.68%)	4,718 (20.56%)
Cincinnati, OH	42,916	26,967 (62.84%)	7,575 (17.65%)	8,374 (19.51%)

Analysis and discussion

The results of the analysis are discussed next. The first step is to calculate the statistic $Q(m)$ for the three cities under study. As discussed above, there are several parameters that must be selected for the analysis. A surrounding of size $m=5$ is selected as this gives a manageable number of symbols for interpretation. Furthermore, various values of the degree of overlap r are tested. Table 5.3 reports the results for $r=1$ and $r=4$, as these are at the boundary of possible overlap values for $m=5$ (that is, the overlap cannot exceed the size of the selected m-surrounding). A lower value of r is used to verify that the analysis is not at risk of detecting a false positive. It can be seen in Table 5.3 that reducing the degree of overlap can substantially reduce the number of symbolised observations, and therefore the power of the statistic. For this reason, the larger value of r is also tested. In the present analysis, the results are very robust, and the null hypothesis is rejected in every case, at a very high level of significance, regardless of the value of r used. It is worthwhile noting that the ratio of number of symbols to number of symbolised cases handily exceeds the recommended value of 5, even for $r=1$.

Table 5.3: Results with *k*=3 (Yankee, Irish, German) and *m*=5

City	N	λ	r	S	S/λ	Q(m)	p-value[a]
Albany	15,938	21	1	3,984	189.71	6,049.04	<0.0001
			4	15,934	758.76	23,412.48	<0.0001
Buffalo	22,944	21	1	5,735	273.10	13,367.43	<0.0001
			4	22,940	1,092.38	53,195.13	<0.0001
Cincinnati	42,916	21	1	10,728	510.86	12,244.62	<0.0001
			4	42,912	2,043.43	49,214.23	<0.0001

Note: [a]D.F.= $n_{\sigma_j^*} - 1 = 20$

The results clearly indicate that the null hypothesis of a random spatial sequence can be rejected with a high level of confidence for the three cities. This implies that there is a non-random pattern of co-location among members of the three groups. Since $Q(m)$ is a global statistic, it does not provide further insight into the characteristics of the non-random pattern. The analysis can be expanded by exploring the empirical distribution of the frequency of symbols, and comparing this distribution to the expected frequency under the null hypothesis, as per equation (5).

Focusing the analysis, it is possible to generate Figures 5.3, 5.4 and 5.5, for Albany, Buffalo and Cincinnati, respectively. The figures (generated with *r*=4) show the frequency of the symbols on the vertical axis, and the symbols on the horizontal axis. The bars represent the empirical frequency of the symbol, and the whiskers are the 95 per cent confidence intervals. Bars are white when the empirical frequency is within the 95 per cent interval of the expected frequency under the null hypothesis. Dark grey bars correspond to symbol types that appear with significantly lower frequency than expected. Light grey bars correspond to symbol types that appear with significantly higher frequency than expected. The symbols in the horizontal axis are coded as #Y#I#G, where # indicates the number of individuals of that ethnic group in that type of surrounding (the number is omitted when there is only one member of the corresponding ethnic group). In this way, the number of members of each ethnic group in the symbol type can be readily identified. For instance, and recalling that *m*=5 (there are exactly five members in each surrounding), Y2I2G means that there is one Yankee, two Irish, and two Germans in this type of surrounding; 2Y3G indicates that there are two Yankees and three Germans in this type of surrounding, and so on.

Figure 5.3, for Albany, offers information about the characteristics of the co-location pattern of ethnic groups in this city. In particular, it

Figure 5.3: Frequency of symbol types and confidence intervals for Albany

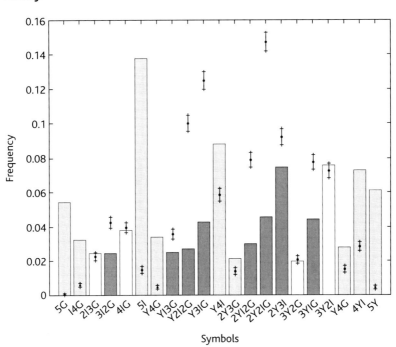

can be seen that there is significant clustering among members of the three ethnic groups. Symbols 5G, 5I and 5Y indicate a strong tendency of members of the same group to be found in close proximity of each other, when exploring small neighbourhoods of at most five neighbours. There is also evidence of a relatively high degree of exposure of isolated Irish, Yankees and Germans to members of one other group (see I4G, Y4G, Y4I, 4YG and 4YI). On the other hand, genuinely mixed neighbourhoods composed of members of all three ethnic groups appear to have been very rare, and are observed with significantly lower frequency than expected under the null hypothesis. Considering that the mix of ethnic groups in the city is relatively balanced at approximately 40, 30 and 20 per cent for German, Irish and Yankee residents, respectively, this suggests a high degree of segregation at this micro-geographical scale.

Buffalo and Cincinnati are similar in terms of the contribution of the three resident ethnic groups to the overall population, with ethnic Germans representing the majority group. It is interesting to note then that the results of the analysis regarding the composition of small neighbourhoods are also remarkably similar. There is evidence

Figure 5.4: Frequency of symbol types and confidence intervals for Buffalo

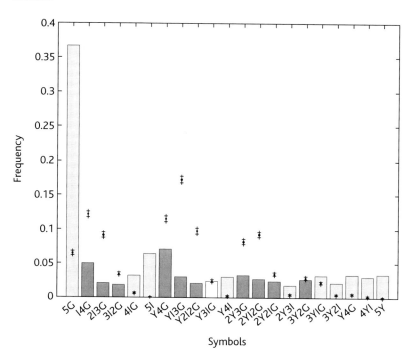

again of significant clustering (5G, 5I and 5Y). Unlike the case of Albany, in these two cities there was little exposure of isolated Irish and Yankees to Germans (I4G and Y4G). However, isolated Germans residing in proximity of four members of one other ethnic group were more common (4IG and 4YG). Mixed neighbourhoods tended to be of Yankees and Irish (2Y3I and 3Y2I), whereas those containing Germans were rare, and observed with significantly lower frequency than expected, even when Germans were in the majority (that is, YI3G, Y2I2G and 2YI2G, in both cities, and 2Y2IG in Cincinnati).

Conclusion

There is plentiful evidence that patterns of segregation exist at the meso- and macro-scale. Investigations of the micro-geography of segregation have been rare, largely due to the delicate sensitivities of working with contemporary individual-level data, caused by the imperative to maintain privacy and confidentiality. There are, however, emerging opportunities to conduct research into the geography of population without the impediment imposed by administrative

Figure 5.5: Frequency of symbol types and confidence intervals for Cincinnati

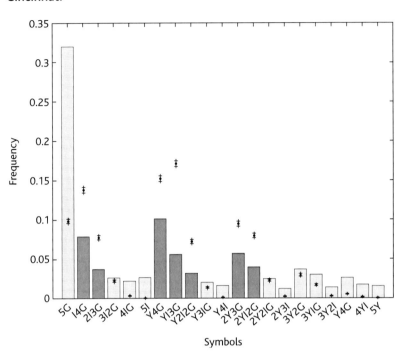

boundaries. Such is the case of dedicated and secure research facilities, or the use of historical information for which confidentiality issues are largely immaterial. One such opportunity is afforded by the Urban Transition Historical GIS Project (Logan et al, 2011a).

Analysis of the micro-geography of segregation was conducted for three cities for which newly geocoded data is available through the Urban Transition Historical GIS Project. More specifically, the focus was on the related issues of clustering and exposure among Yankees, Irish and Germans in the cities of Albany, Buffalo and Cincinnati in 1880. The results of the analysis applying the $Q(m)$ statistic provide significant evidence that patterns of clustering and exposure at the micro-geographical scale were common in these three cities. Together with the analysis reported in Páez et al for Newark (2012), this suggests that the processes that generated patterns of segregation in these historical cities may have operated at the micro-scale. The results of the analysis are limited to the scale at which $Q(m)$ was implemented, covering neighbourhoods of five spatially proximate residents. According to Ruiz et al (2010, pp 290-1), this means that the process also exists at more local scales. The geographical extents of these micro-scale neighbourhoods defined according to the numbers of neighbouring individuals could be smaller than the smallest neighbourhoods used in Östh et al (Chapter Seven, this volume). An outstanding question is whether the patterns observed at such micro-geographical scale translate into similar patterns at other scales, say, $m>5$. This is a matter for future research.

Notes

[1] See www.statcan.gc.ca/rdc-cdr/index-eng.htm

[2] The code to calculate the $Q(m)$ statistic is available on request from the authors.

References

Alba, R.D., Logan, J.R. and Crowder, K. (1997) 'White ethnic neighborhoods and assimilation: The Greater New York region, 1980-1990', *Social Forces*, vol 75, pp 883-912.

Baum, S., Arthurson, K. and Rickson, K. (2010) 'Happy people in mixed-up places: the association between the degree and type of local socioeconomic mix and expressions of neighbourhood satisfaction', *Urban Studies*, vol 47, pp 467-85.

Brown, L.A. and Chung, S.Y. (2006) 'Spatial segregation, segregation indices and the geographical perspective', *Population Space and Place*, vol 12, pp 125-43.

Cowgill, G.L. (1997) 'State and society at Teotihuacan, Mexico', *Annual Review of Anthropology*, vol 26, pp 129-61.

Dawkins, C.J., Reibel, M. and Wong, D.W. (2007) 'Introduction – further innovations in segregation and neighborhood change research', *Urban Geography*, vol 28, pp 513-15.

Duncan, O. and Duncan, B. (1955a) 'A methodological analysis of segregation indexes', *American Sociological Review*, vol 20, pp 210-17.

Duncan, O. and Duncan, B. (1955b) 'Residential distribution and occupational stratification', *American Journal of Sociology*, vol 60, pp 493-503.

Farber, S., Páez, A. and Morency, C. (2012) 'Activity spaces and the measurement of clustering and exposure: a case study of linguistic groups in Montreal', *Environment and Planning A*, vol 44, pp 315-32.

Feitosa, F.F., Camara, G., Monteiro, A.M.V., Koschitzki, T. and Silva, M.P.S. (2007) 'Global and local spatial indices of urban segregation', *International Journal of Geographical Information Science*, vol 21, pp 299-323.

Fong, E. and Shibuya, K. (2000) 'The spatial separation of the poor in Canadian cities', *Demography*, vol 37, pp 449-59.

Gorard, S. and Taylor, C. (2002) 'What is segregation? A comparison of measures in terms of "strong" and "weak" compositional invariance', *Sociology—Journal of the British Sociological Association*, vol 36, pp 875-95.

Griffith, D.A. (1988) *Advanced spatial statistics*, Special Topics in the Exploration of Quantitative Spatial Data Series, Dordrecht: Kluwer.

Jakubs, J.F. (1981) 'A distance-based segregation index', *Socio-Economic Planning Sciences*, vol 15, pp 129-36.

Johnston, R., Poulsen, M. and Forrest, J. (2009) 'Measuring ethnic residential segregation: putting some more geography in', *Urban Geography*, vol 30, pp 91-109.

Lloyd, C.D. (2010) 'Exploring population spatial concentrations in Northern Ireland by community background and other characteristics: an application of geographically weighted spatial statistics', *International Journal of Geographical Information Science*, vol 24, pp 1193-221.

Lloyd, C.D., Gregory, I.N., Shuttleworth, I.G. and Lilley, K.D. (2012) 'Exploring change in urban areas using GIS: data sources, linkages and problems', *Annals of GIS*, vol 18, pp 71-80.

Logan, J.R., Jindrich, J., Shin, H. and Zhang, W. (2011a) 'Mapping America in 1880: the Urban Transition Historical GIS Project', *Historical Methods: A Journal of Quantitative and Interdisciplinary History*, vol 44, pp 49-60.

Logan, J.R., Spielman, S., Xu, H.W. and Klein, P.N. (2011b) 'Identifying and bounding ethnic neighborhoods', *Urban Geography*, vol 32, pp 334-59.

Massey, D.S. and Denton, N.A. (1988) 'The dimensions of residential segregation', *Social Forces*, vol 67, pp 281-315.

Massey, D.S. and Fischer, M.J. (2000) 'How segregation concentrates poverty', *Ethnic and Racial Studies*, vol 23, pp 670-91.

Morgan, B.S. (1983) 'An alternate approach to the development of a distance-based measure of racial segregation', *American Journal of Sociology*, vol 88, 1237-49.

Morrill, R.L. (1991) 'On the measure of geographical segregation', *Geography Research Forum*, vol 11, pp 25-36.

Musterd, S. and Andersson, R. (2005) 'Housing mix, social mix, and social opportunities', *Urban Affairs Review*, vol 40, pp 761-90.

O'Sullivan, D. and Wong, D.W.S. (2007) 'A surface-based approach to measuring spatial segregation', *Geographical Analysis*, vol 39, pp 147-68.

Ochieng, B.M.N. (2011) 'The effect of kin, social network and neighbourhood support on individual well-being', *Health & Social Care in the Community*, vol 19, pp 429-37.

Páez, A., Ruiz, M., López, F. and Logan, J. (2012) 'Measuring ethnic clustering and exposure with the Q statistic: an exploratory analysis of Irish, Germans, and Yankees in 1880 Newark', *Annals of the Association of American Geographers*, vol 102, pp 84-102.

Poulsen, M., Johnston, R. and Forrest, J. (2010) 'The intensity of ethnic residential clustering: exploring scale effects using local indicators of spatial association', *Environment and Planning A*, vol 42, pp 874-94.

Reardon, S.F. and O'Sullivan, D. (2004) 'Measures of spatial segregation', *Sociological Methodology*, vol 34, pp 121-62.

Reardon, S.F., Matthews, S.A., O'Sullivan, D., Lee, B.A., Firebaugh, G., Farrell, C.R. and Bischoff, K. (2008) 'The geographic scale of metropolitan racial segregation', *Demography*, vol 45, pp 489-514.

Ruiz, M., López, F. and Páez, A. (2010) 'Testing for spatial association of qualitative data using symbolic dynamics', *Journal of Geographical Systems*, vol 12, pp 281-309.

Smith, G.C. (1998) 'Change in elderly residential segregation in Canadian metropolitan areas, 1981-91', *Canadian Journal on Aging–Revue Canadienne du Vieillissement*, vol 17, pp 59-82.

So, B.K.L. and Wong, D.W. (2012) 'Foreword', *Annals of GIS*, vol 18, pp 1-2.

South, S.J. and Crowder, K.D. (1998) 'Leaving the 'hood: residential mobility between black, white, and integrated neighborhoods', *American Sociological Review*, vol 63, pp 17-26.

van der Spek, R.J. (2009) 'Multi-ethnicity and ethnic segregation in Hellenistic Babylon', in T. Derks and N. Roymans (eds) *Ethnic constructs in antiquity: the role of power and tradition*, Amsterdam: Amsterdam University Press, pp 101-15.

White, M.J. (1983) 'The measurement of spatial segregation', *American Journal of Sociology*, vol 88, pp 1008-18.

Williams, D.R. and Collins, C. (2001) 'Racial residential segregation: a fundamental cause of racial disparities in health', *Public Health Reports*, vol 116, pp 404-16.

Wong, D.W.S. (1993) 'Spatial indices of segregation', *Urban Studies*, vol 30, pp 559-72.

Wong, D.W.S. (1998) 'Spatial patterns of ethnic integration in the United States', *The Professional Geographer*, vol 50, pp 13-30.

Wong, D.W.S. (2005) 'Formulating a general spatial segregation measure', *The Professional Geographer*, vol 57, pp 285-94.

Wong, D.W.S. (2008) 'A local multidimensional approach to evaluate changes in segregation', *Urban Geography*, vol 29, pp 455-72.

Wong, D.W.S. and Shaw, S.L. (2011) 'Measuring segregation: an activity space approach', *Journal of Geographical Systems*, vol 13, pp 1-19.

SIX

Neighbourhood racial diversity and White residential segregation in the United States[1]

Richard Wright, Mark Ellis and Steven R. Holloway

Introduction

The current interest in multiethnic metros (see, for example, Frey and Farley, 1996), global neighbourhoods (see, for example, Logan and Zhang, 2010), and urban intermixing (see, for example, Brown and Sharma, 2010) signal the emergence of urban environments characterised by growing and sizable non-White immigrant populations and their offspring. The emphasis on multiethnicity and mixing also draws attention away from Black–White isolation, the social division that motivated much of the original research on residential racial segregation in the US (see also Chapter Two, this volume). This chapter connects these newer diversities and older segregations by taking stock of recent changes in the neighbourhood geographies of people who identify as White. Using 1990, 2000 and 2010 US Census data to analyse all metropolitan areas exceeding one million people, we showcase the increasing racial diversity in these places and their census tracts. We focus on the neighbourhoods in which Whites constitute a large majority. The number and share of these tracts is diminishing everywhere, but the pace and form of this transition to greater diversity in neighbourhood space is uneven across and within metropolitan areas. We explore these transitions and their correlates and argue that 'White flight', a term redolent of the demarcation of the Black–White colour line and White suburbanisation in the late 20th century, has not slipped away in the multiethnic, global 21st century; it has found new spatial expression.

The racial and ethnic profile of the US has changed considerably in the last few decades. Immigration from Central and South America and parts of Asia drives these new demographic diversities and they play out on the ground in complicated ways. Newcomers and their offspring continue to settle, for the most part, in large metropolitan areas of the country. Additionally, new immigrants tend to concentrate within particular neighbourhoods, increasing Asian-White and Latino-White segregation in a number of places (Frey, 2011). At the same time, many urban neighbourhoods that were predominantly White are diversifying as non-Whites take up residence. These changes, of course, layer on top of the historic subordination of Blacks by Whites and the continued residential 'hyper-segregation' of African Americans from Whites (Massey and Denton, 1993; Wilkes and Iceland, 2004).

This chapter takes stock of these changes using decennial census data from 1990, 2000 and 2010 in three main ways. We first explain a new way of thinking about racial residential segregation and diversity. Conventional approaches to racial segregation tend to view neighbourhoods as either segregated or blended; pure segregation and complete diversity come to demark two extremes of a continuum of neighbourhood racial mix, with neighbourhoods being to some extent *either* racially segregated *or* racially diverse. The approach that racial segregation and diversity are 'mirror images of one another' (Holloway et al, 2012, p 2) fails to capture, however, the fact that segregated spaces are appearing in cities at the same time other parts of town are diversifying. Accordingly, we move away from this 'either/ or' viewpoint and instead take up an approach that understands large US urban areas – metropolitan statistical areas (MSAs) and their neighbourhoods – are best characterised as *both* segregated *and* diverse. This 'both/and' lens is not only ontological but also methodological and helps resolve the paradox that racial segregation and diversity occur at the same time, sometimes in very close proximity. We are, of course, not the only scholars to notice the coincident development of neighbourhood segregation and diversity. According to Reibel and Regelson, '... within cities, trends toward greater and potentially stable diversity in some neighbourhoods co-exist with continuing White flight and re-segregation in other local areas' (2011, Abstract). They call this 'fragmented diversity'.

Operationally, we characterise the census tracts of every MSA by placing them in three basic classes of tract diversity. We then note the numerically dominant racial group in each to arrive at neighbourhood taxonomy that we use to map and assess metropolitan neighbourhood change over time and across space. In terms of measurement, these new complexities stretch single-index assessments of racial residential patterns past their limits. The argument of this chapter moves beyond such measurements, and deploys a neighbourhood classification scheme that can better pinpoint patterns of change in a demographic environment that racially and ethnically is far more nuanced today than a generation ago. We locate change in two main ways: using neighbourhood transition matrices and cartographically. Building on these foundations, we then focus particular attention on people who identify as White.

While quite a bit of ink has been spilled about 'minority majority' populations and racial demographic change, Whites, of course, constitute the majority of the country. All population projections of which we are aware have them as the plurality for the foreseeable future. And even though most immigration is directed toward large MSAs, Whites represented the majority in the preponderance of these MSAs in 2010 and in the bulk of metropolitan neighbourhoods. As a second focus, the chapter is especially concerned with neighbourhoods that are predominantly White in the context of rising levels of neighbourhood racial diversity. Much of the growing diversity we find in MSAs stems from neighbourhoods that were heavily White (that is, over 80 per cent) becoming more diverse so that Whites in these places constitute less of a plurality. We pay attention to these transitions, as well as to predominantly White places that remained so between 1990 and 2010.

Third, we link these neighbourhood transitions to assessments of neighbourhood wealth measured by median household income at the census-tract scale. The analysis of racial and class divides in US metropolitan space is a grand theme in urban ecological analysis. Contemporary evaluations of the association between race and class tend to examine the socioeconomic status (SES) of racial and ethnic groups at the household scale and find that, for example, relatively wealthy non-White households are less segregated from non-Hispanic Whites than corresponding relatively less wealthy racialised groups (Iceland and Wilkes, 2006; Spivak et al, 2011). In contrast, we keep the analysis centred on census tracts and augment our neighbourhood classification system by analysing the median household income of tracts that remain predominantly White over the two decades and with those that have transitioned to another category.

White segregation amid increasing racial and ethnic diversity

Decades of research on residential racial segregation foregrounds the deleterious effects of neighbourhood isolation on racialised minority groups (see Charles, 2003, pp 167-9). Residents of unsafe, poorly resourced neighbourhoods, lacking educational and recreational opportunities and access to employment and basic services such as food stores and banks, are hugely disadvantaged relative to those who live elsewhere. Non-White minority urban populations, especially Blacks, reside disproportionately in such areas of deprivation (see also Chapters Thirteen, Fifteen and Sixteen, this volume).

Du Bois famously predicted the colour line would be the problem of the 20th century, and social science research from Du Bois' analysis of segregation 100 years ago to Myrdal (1944) to the *Black metropolis* (Drake and Cayton, 1945) to Clark (1965) to tipping-point studies (Schelling, 1971) to hyper-segregation and *American apartheid* (Massey and Denton, 1993) to present-day assessments (for example, Kennedy, 2011) confirm Du Bois' prescience (Du Bois, 1989). Other groups also live in segregated neighbourhoods and residential segregation analysis, of course, includes not only studies of Black–White neighbourhood segregation and concentration, but also that associated with immigrants. This scholarship on immigrant segregation also reaches back a century, to Park (1998 [1928]) and the analysis of the assimilation of immigrants. In both types of study, spatial distribution becomes a barometer of social distribution and the geography of White populations is often used as a benchmark for both (Wright et al, 2005).

It follows that one concern we have with research on 'the colour line' is that attention tends to fall on only one side of that boundary. It has been entirely appropriate to point out the social failures that have led to apartheid conditions in the US. It is vitally important that we expose and counter the forces that produce racialised inequality and subordination. When we devote exclusive attention to the spatial isolation of racialised non-White minorities, however, we often implicitly dis-acknowledge that Whites are segregated too. Segregation research tends to draw attention to places where Whites are relatively absent rather than where they are numerically dominant.

Only a handful of studies report on *White* segregation per se (for example, Iceland, 2004, 2011). More often, Whites are used as the referent in studies of segregation and spatial assimilation. Using Whites as a referent acknowledges them as socioeconomically politically dominant. But such research tendencies also veer toward using proximity to Whites and their spaces as a standard of social membership. Put bluntly, segregation studies have failed for the most part to engage with Whiteness studies. That scholarship aims to shift research away from the place where race is 'always an issue of Otherness that is not white' (hooks, 1990, p 54). Whiteness studies have additional goals, one of which alluded to by hooks – to bring attention to bear on the racialisation of Whites and to deconstruct the White category. In this chapter, we do not deconstruct the 'White' category in any way. Iceland (2011), for example, examines three different definitions of 'White' in calculating White segregation and isolation in large MSAs. We do, however, examine White neighbourhood segregation from several standpoints.

Segregation has different consequences for Whites than non-Whites. In that sense, this chapter (see also Chapter Thirteen, this volume) joins the conversation on what segregation means for different groups (Peach, 1996; Borjas, 1998; Marcuse, 1997; Wacquant, 1997). Following in the footsteps of those scholars, Beaulieu and Continelli (2011) develop a simple model wherein segregation is more likely to facilitate economic, political and cultural advantage for Whites while reinforcing disadvantages for Blacks. As others have shown, Black segregation is part of a vicious cycle wherein spatial isolation increases the odds of being poor, and this in turn leads to deteriorating neighbourhood resources, such as schools, which hamper the ability of future generations to escape adverse economic circumstances (see Chapter Ten, this volume). White segregation produces the opposite; it enhances social stability and fosters social and economic investment in communities. White segregation is thus a mechanism to ensure the future benefits of being White, or what Lipsitz (1998) calls, in the very title of his book, the 'possessive investment in whiteness.'

As US urban areas become more diverse at the metropolitan scale, and as White segregation from other groups slowly declines, the question arises about how Whites, and, crucially, which class of Whites, will maintain this 'possessive investment' through residential segregation. We approach this issue by situating White segregation relative to *both* (1) the residential segregation of racialised groups, including Whites, *and* (2) the increasing rates of overall demographic diversity and increasing neighbourhood diversity. We are particularly interested in the socioeconomic characteristics of White neighbourhood spaces that diversified between 1990 and 2010 compared to those that did not.

We expect to find that White neighbourhoods have higher median incomes than other neighbourhoods. We also expect that White-dominated tracts with lower median incomes are less likely to remain in this state than those with higher median incomes. Our reasoning is that higher-income White neighbourhoods are better able to retain their racial composition – their investment in Whiteness – because of the income barriers to entry. As the population of less well-off minority populations swells, selected members of these groups will find it easier to buy into moderate- than high-income White neighbourhoods. Thus the White spaces that remain in US MSAs in the face of increasing diversification are increasingly the preserve of higher-income groups.

In the last 20 years or so, the US has become more unequal economically, with the upper echelon of the income distribution garnering an increased share of the national wealth. Those in the top fraction are disproportionately White, and this group is best able to maintain a degree of separation from others. Whites, whose incomes are below these relatively well-off ranks, do not have the resources to buy into upscale neighbourhoods. We expect, therefore, that neighbourhoods with concentrations of Whites that also are home to medium- and low-income subpopulations are the places most likely to transition to higher diversity. White neighbourhood space under this process becomes increasingly associated with higher income and socioeconomic privilege.

Finally we estimate a simple model that predicts the gap between median income in what we come to call low-diversity White-dominated (LDW) tracts and those that transitioned from LDW status as a function of change in metropolitan racial and ethnic composition. We anticipate that where LDW tracts decline the most, the gap in median income between LDW tracts and others should be the largest. The idea here is that, again, the growing diversity in neighbourhood space – specifically the pace of that change – transforms remaining White-dominated spaces into wealthier enclaves of Whites. Racial and ethnic composition may mediate this process: where Asians and Latinos are numerous, we may find this relationship attenuated if well-off Whites can find spaces with suitable housing and other amenities where there are significant numbers of these other groups.

Methods

Reibel (2011) provides a useful recent review of the main approaches to neighbourhood taxonomy. He points out that, for many years, social scientists tended not to perform neighbourhood analysis based on racial or ethnic classification schemes. This stems back to the origins of research on residential segregation. Blacks and Whites in the US have been so starkly divided socially and geographically for much of the last 100 years, the notion of neighbourhood classification along the lines of race was redundant. What was important, and remains so, are means by which to assess the levels of segregation between and Whites and Blacks (and not just in neighbourhoods). So segregation measures came of age, as it were, aimed at calibrating the degree to which Blacks and Whites were segregated from one another.

The changes in the racial and ethnic composition of US society in the last few decades require, however, that we adjust the assessment of the relative residential geographies of racialised groups. First we must set aside segregation for a moment. Given the increases in overall racial and ethnic diversity of the US population and its constituent urban areas, our approach begins by measuring the extent to which groups live together using an effective and widely used method of evaluating compositional diversity – scaled entropy. Our classification system grew out of a set of explorations of the impact on scaled entropy of many configurations of ethnic/racial composition spread across six racialised groups (Whites, Blacks, Asians, Latinos, Native Americans and others). Tract diversity measured by entropy is:

$$E_j = s\left(-\sum_{i=1}^{k} \left(p_i \times \ln(p_i) \right) \right) \tag{1}$$

where E_j references the entropy of census tract j and p_i refers to group i's proportion of a particular area's population. The maximum value of E_j is the natural log of the number of groups ($k=6$ in our case), and occurs only when a tract's population is evenly divided among the six racial groups. Because this maximum value for E_j is a function of the number of groups in the analysis, we include a scaling constant s (1/ $\ln(k)$) so that E_j ranges from 0 to 1. Entropy is a widely used measure of neighbourhood diversity (White, 1986; Brown and Sharma, 2010; Farrell and Lee, 2011; Sandoval, 2011; Wilson, 2011).

Our scheme produced three basic classes of tracts, the rationale for which[2] appear in Holloway et al (2012):

- 'Low diversity' tracts have scaled entropy values less than or equal to 0.3707, with one group constituting at least 80 per cent of the population.
- 'High diversity' tracts are those with scaled entropy greater than or equal to 0.7414. This insures that (a) no group constitutes more than 45 per cent of the tract's population; (b) a tract's largest two groups have a combined percentage of no more than 80 per cent of the total population; and (c) the third and fourth ranking groups have meaningful representation because the value of E_j is sensitive to the population shares of the third and fourth largest groups. (E_j takes on larger values, that is, more diversity, when the numerically smaller groups in a tract have relatively equal shares of the remaining population. When the remaining population is concentrated in only one of the groups, entropy takes on a lower value.)

- 'Moderately diverse' tracts are those not captured by the other two categories.

We take the additional step of identifying the numerically dominant racial group in the low-diversity and moderate-diversity tracts.

We end up with a taxonomy wherein we talk about places that are 'low diversity, White dominant' (LDW), 'moderately diverse, Asian dominant' (MDA), and so on. We explicitly avoid terms such as 'enclave', 'ghetto' or even 'ethnoburb'. This discursive choice is important. Our system identifies different types of segregation and diversity without attaching a value-laden label, and avoids falling into the territorial trap, so to speak, of drawing attention to places where the density of non-White people is relatively high and thus away from locales where Whites retain a considerable plurality (cf Wright and Ellis, 2006; see also Holloway et al, 2012; Chipman et al, 2012, for details).

In our sample of MSAs, only a few tracts were Native American Indian-dominated, and people claiming 'some other race' numerically dominated only one metropolitan tract (in 1990). Although such tracts do not play a significant role in the narrative we develop about racial segregation and diversity, Native Americans and 'others' do factor in calculations of neighbourhood diversity. Note also that, following convention, we defined as 'Latino' all census respondents who reported having Hispanic origin, regardless of their reported race. We are fully aware of the limitations of this classification, and the other single race categories, to capture the rich and varied histories and contemporary realities of racial identity.

Being interested not only in patterns of both segregation and diversity but also in how they have changed over the last couple of decades, we also had to develop a consistent racial/ethnic taxonomy across a time period. The fact that the US census tinkers with racial and ethnic categorisation in almost every census complicated matters and forced us to adopt the census classification schema from 1990 for all three time periods. This had implications for two groups: Asians and census respondents who claimed a multiracial identity. Our 'Asian and Pacific Islander' category is a combination of two categories on the 2000 Census that mirrors the 1990 classification of Asian and Pacific Islander. Similarly, we aggregated Asian Indians, Chinese, Filipinos, Other Asians, Japanese, Koreans, Vietnamese, Native Hawaiians, Guamanians or Chamorros, Samoans and Other Pacific Islanders from 2010 into 'Asian and Pacific Islander'.

In line with other researchers who have compared 1990 with 2000, and noting that only 2.4 per cent of the population claims 2+ races in

2000 and 2.9 per cent in 2010, we collapsed mixed-race individuals into the set of single-race categories using a method of proportional assignment to non-White categories (cf Logan and Zhang, 2010). Individuals reporting multiple racial categories in 2000 and 2010 were allocated into single, non-White, racial categories using a minority preference proportional weighting algorithm. Specifically, we used the whole-race assignment method – largest group other than White – recommended by the Office of Management and Budget. This technique most closely resembles the choice multiracials would have faced on the 1990 Census form, before the option to 'check more than one (race) box' was available. This crosswalk must occur 'backwards' (we cannot change 1990 racial and ethnic groupings to approximate those in 2000 or 2010; we can match 2000/2010 to match 1990). These decisions produced six race/ethnicity classes: White, Black, Latino, Asian, Native American and 'Some other race' (or 'Other').

Just as racial categories change slightly with each census, so too do some census tract boundaries. As population densities change, the census must rearrange the boundaries of a proportion of tracts. To produce consistent census tracts in 1990, 2000 and 2010, we boundary-matched the 1990 and 2010 boundaries to 2000 tracts, using Census Bureau tables of changed tracts. We dropped from subsequent analysis any tract that had a population of less than 50. This yields a consistent set of tracts and groups for all locations.

This taxonomy applies the same 'grid' to any location within the US; it translates easily across contexts within the country. Unlike some related schemes, our measures of diversity or racial dominance are not relative to the MSA under investigation. Maly (2005) and Logan and Zhang (2010), for example, both adopt variants of such an approach. A relative system has the advantage of tailoring a local context relative to the larger metropolitan region of which it is a part, but in our view the disadvantages outweigh any advantages. The main problem for us is this. Consider two tracts that have precisely the same population and proportions of racial groups, but one is in, say, Los Angeles, and one in Cincinnati. The tracts could be classed differently – a relative system stymies inter-metropolitan comparison.

While our classification system applies generally to places in the US and facilitates straightforward comparisons across time and space (we focus on census tracts in this analysis, but the scheme works at various scales from the nation as whole to states, to MSAs to tract to blocks; see Wright et al, 2014), it is not 'universal' in the sense that it does not easily translate across international contexts. Johnston, Poulsen and Forrest's (see, for example, Johnston et al, 2006; Chapter Two, this volume) neighbourhood classification translates across national context. Like all such classification schemes, theirs, too, has some weaknesses (see Wright et al, 2011, for a critique and appreciation). One of the main strengths of their taxonomy is that it allows researchers to compare patterns of segregation in different metropolitan areas in different countries. This opens up a set of important research questions concerning public policy, comparative rates of spatial assimilation and differential levels of housing market discrimination in an international context.

We sought to produce a set of classes that made sense and, importantly, that could be mapped. So while a classification scheme with, say, 15 groups might have some strengths, that number of groups would pose a huge, probably insurmountable, cartographic challenge. This is a distinguishing feature of our work and sets it apart from related recent research (see, for example, Logan and Zhang, 2010; Farrell and Lee, 2011; cf Sandoval, 2011; Chipman et al, 2012). By restricting the analysis to six groups, this opens up the possibility to map and visually differentiate between low, moderate and high diversity tracts using proportional shading techniques. This move is only possible using different colours to represent different racial and ethnic groups. It is also an explicit response to the recent call by Johnston et al (2006) to the effect that although geographers have done a lot to infuse studies of segregation with a spatial perspective (notably the work of Wong – see Chapter Three, this volume) there remains plenty of room, as it were, to put even more geography into such research.

The exercise of actually mapping segregation leads research toward thinking about neighbourhood numerical dominance and away from approaches to segregation that summarises the relative (un)evenness of different racialised groups. We have published maps for each of the 53 MSAs and 50 US states in an interactive web-based atlas, www.mixedmetro.com. Some of those maps are reproduced in this chapter as part of our analysis. The cartographic symbology of these maps highlights both the diversity of each tract and the locally dominant racial group. For each state or metropolitan area, the reader can compare maps from the 1990, 2000 and 2010 Census years.

Analysis

We begin by examining the aggregate trends by aggregating counts in all the large MSAs in the US and comparing the distribution of tracts by classification in 1990 with 2010.

Starting with all low diversity neighbourhoods, between 1990 and 2010 these tracts declined from 24,712 to 14,792, driven largely by massive decline in LDW tracts. This type of tract dropped from 21,332 in 1990 to 11,112 in 2010: a reduction of 48 per cent. The majority of this decline occurred in the first 10 years. Between 1990 and 2000, the number dipped from 21,332 to 15,371, a decline of 5,961. Between 2000 and 2010, the count of LDW tracts shrank by 4,259 (15,371 to 11,112). Put differently, LDW tracts constituted 58.5 per cent of all tracts in these 53 MSAs in 1990; in 2010, they made up 30.5 per cent. The number of LDB tracts (low-diversity, Black-dominated) also declined but not as steeply as LDWs. The number of LDBs dropped from 2,685 in 1990 to 2,472 in 2010, an 8 per cent decrease. Their share of all tracts therefore contracted from 7.4 per cent to 6.8 per cent. In contrast, the number of LDL (low-diversity, Latino-dominated) tracts grew from 672 to 1,164, a 73 per cent increase. The handful of LDA (low-diversity, Asian-dominated) tracts in 1990 more than tripled to a total of 31 by 2010. That 2010 count, however, represents about 0.04 per cent of the total number of tracts in these MSAs.

The decline in the overall number of low-diversity tracts was, of course, taken up by increases in other types of neighbourhood. Between 1990 and 2010, such neighbourhoods grew 80 per cent, from 11,551 to 20,754. Half of that expansion was accounted for by growth in MDWs (moderate-diversity, White-dominated) (7,795 to 13,167, a 70 per cent increase). MDW tracts supplanted LDW tracts as the modal category in 2010. There was an explosive growth in MDLs (moderate-diversity, Latino-dominated) from 1,795 to 4,162, an increase of 132 per cent. MDLs now make up almost 11.5 per cent of the total number of tracts in these large MSAs. The highest rate of growth was recorded among MDAs (moderate-diversity, Asian-dominated): 214 per cent, with 745 such tracts representing about 2 per cent of the total. MDB tracts also increased significantly, from 4.7 per cent to over 7 per cent of the total. Tracts classified as 'high diversity' grew by 738 per cent between 1990 and 2010, from 188 to 905. Most of this growth was in the first half of this period (not shown). From 2000 to 2010, the number of highly diverse tracts increased from 811 to 905.[3]

The aggregate data in Table 6.1 conceal variation by region. To illustrate this, Table 6.2 shows the changing geography of LDW and MDW tracts grouped census region. The West and South were home to the MSAs that had sharpest rates of decline in LDWs. The Northeast and Mid West still had regional rates of decline, 37 and 34 per cent respectively.

Many LDWs transitioned into MDWs over this 20-year period, but certainly not all. In western MSAs, many transitioned into Latino-dominated tracts and in certain MSAs in that region (especially San

Table 6.1: US aggregate transition matrix for the 53 largest metropolitan areas: 1990-2010

| | 2010 | | | | | | | | | | | | | | |
All MSAs (1990)	White, low diversity	Black, low diversity	Asian, low diversity	Latino, low diversity	American Indian, low diversity	White, moderate diversity	Black, moderate diversity	Asian, moderate diversity	Latino, moderate diversity	American Indian, moderate diversity	Other, moderate diversity	High diversity	Total	% 1990	% 2010
White, low diversity	11,009	54		16		9,259	423	32	392			147	21,332	58.52	30.48
Black, low diversity	1	2,052		1		37	556		35			3	2,685	7.37	6.78
Asian, low diversity			6					3					9	0.02	0.09
Latino, low diversity	1			568		9	2	1	91				672	1.84	3.19
American Indian, low diversity					12				1	1			14	0.04	0.04
White, moderate diversity	95	107	5	93		3,559	802	431	2,123			580	7,795	21.38	36.12
Black, moderate diversity	3	259		13		166	862	14	328			75	1,720	4.72	7.35
Asian, moderate diversity			18			5	3	178	21			12	237	0.65	2.04
Latino, moderate diversity	3			472	1	129	23	53	1,090			24	1,795	4.92	11.42
American Indian, moderate diversity						1				1		1	3	0.01	0.01
Other, moderate diversity											0	1	1	0.00	0.01
High diversity	2		2	1		2	7	33	81	2		62	188	0.52	2.48
Total	11,112	2,472	31	1,164	13	13,167	2,678	745	4,162	2	0	905	36,451		

Table 6.2: Changes in the diversity of white dominated tracts by census region: 1990 to 2010

	Low diversity, White			Moderate diversity, White		
	1990	2010	% change	1990	2010	% change
North East	6,290	3,935	−37.44	1,473	2,938	99.46
Mid West	5,718	3,729	−34.78	886	2,171	145.03
South	5,072	1,943	−61.69	2,263	3,910	72.78
West	4,252	1,505	−64.60	3,173	4,148	30.73
Total	21,332	11,112	−47.91	7,795	13,167	68.92

Francisco and Los Angeles), a considerable proportion became Asian-dominated.

To provide a different view of how the 'both/and-' ness of segregation and diversity transitions played out in different places, we highlight patterns gleaned from several selected MSAs. Baltimore, Charlotte and San Diego represent three different MSAs. Baltimore – older, highly segregated along a Black–White divide. Charlotte is in the New South; it is smaller than the other two, but fast growing, like San Diego. San Diego is western, and relatively young; unlike Baltimore, but like Charlotte, it experienced rapid growth in last 20 years.

Table 6.3 shows the distribution of tracts by neighbourhood classification for 1990 and 2010. In 1990, over 80 per cent of tracts in each MSA were white-dominant. (Note that the proportion in all 53 MSAs was 79.9 per cent.) Between 1990 and 2010, the proportion of LDWs dropped considerably, and in each the percentage of MDWs also grew. San Diego experienced rapid growth in the number of Latino-dominated neighbourhoods, from about 12 per cent of the total to about 30 per cent. Growth occurred in both MDL and LDL

Table 6.3: Changes in tract diversity in three metropolitan areas: 1990 to 2010

	San Diego		Charlotte		Baltimore	
	1990	2010	1990	2010	1990	2010
White, low diversity (%)	41.11	11.24	74.00	32.33	62.86	35.21
White, moderate diversity (%)	40.60	52.18	11.00	44.33	16.08	33.44
Black, low diversity (%)	–	–	9.00	6.33	15.43	19.61
Black, moderate diversity (%)	1.34	0.00	6.00	14.00	5.63	11.25
Asian, low diversity (%)	–	–	–	–	–	–
Asian, moderate diversity (%)	1.34	4.53	–	–	–	0.16
Latino, low diversity (%)	1.85	4.53	–	–	–	–
Latino, moderate diversity (%)	10.07	25.34	–	2.33	–	0.32
High diversity (%)	3.69	2.18	–	0.67	–	–
Number of tracts	596	300	622			

classes. Seven tracts in Charlotte became MDL, two in Baltimore. San Diego had few Black-dominated neighbourhoods in 1990 and none in 2010. In Charlotte the number of LDB tracts declined while MDBs grew, gaining from transitions from both LDB and white-dominated tracts. The count of both LDB and MDB types of tracts in Baltimore increased in 1990 and 2010.

One of the advantages of our method of neighbourhood classification over some others is that we can map a metropolitan area at different points in time. Viewing patterns of neighbourhood racial dominance and diversity cartographically provides additional insight into the structures of urban morphology and change. To illustrate the geographies of neighbourhood transitions in the contemporary US, we provide maps of San Diego and Baltimore in 1990 and 2010.

Both Figures 6.1 and 6.2 depict the geography in the decline in LDW tracts in two very different metropolitan contexts. In San Diego, that decline in LDW tracts (from 245 in 1990 to 67 in 2010) leaves a

Figure 6.1: Changes in both racial segregation and diversity in Baltimore: 1990–2010

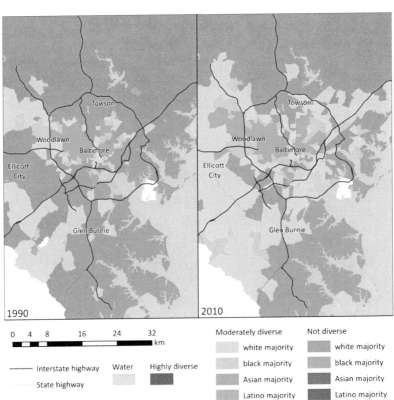

Figure 6.2: Changes in both racial segregation and diversity in San Diego: 1990–2010

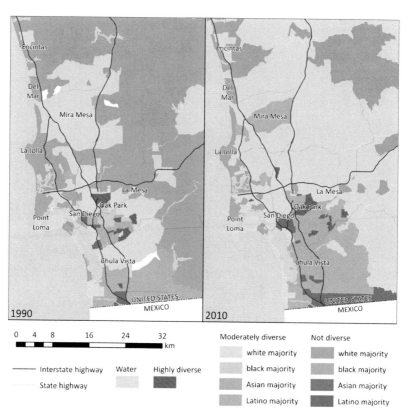

string of LDW neighbourhoods hugging the coast with a few sparsely settled tracts in the rural centre. In Baltimore, the count of LDWs drops from 391 to 219, occurring in the metropolitan area's outer suburbs. Both MSAs also experience growth in minority-dominated low-diversity neighbourhoods. In San Diego's case, the cluster of LDL and MDL tracts projecting north from the Mexican border more than doubles (71 to 177). In Baltimore, the count of Black-dominated tracts also increases, from 125 to 192. Both metropolitan areas have very different histories and different demographic trajectories, yet both exhibit in their own ways what we are calling the 'both/and-' ness of segregation and diversity.

The narrative about neighbourhood transition becomes more nuanced when we consider not just the racial make-up of neighbourhoods, but also the concentration of Whites in White-dominated tracts. In other words, we can build on our basic classification scheme to peel back another layer of the racial dynamics in MSAs. We simply connect our classification scheme with data on population counts by tracts to observe the changing concentration of Whites in tracts we designate as LDW.

Between 1990 and 2010, the percentage share of LDWs decreased in all MSAs, and not a single MSA bucked this trend. Of course, some MSAs recorded a faster decline than others. In Las Vegas, for example, the share of all tracts that were LDW in 1990 was 68.5 per cent; in 2010, it was 9.7. Other fast-growing MSAs also recorded considerable declines in shares of LDWs (notably Atlanta, Seattle, Orlando, Oklahoma City and West Palm Beach). MSAs that had low rates of decline partitioned into two main groups: (a) those with relatively few LDW tracts to start with (for example, Los Angeles; 22.7 per cent in 1990 and 4.4 per cent in 2010) and (b) older MSAs in the Northeast and Midwest, with relatively large shares of LDW-type neighbourhoods in 1990 (Pittsburgh; 90 per cent in 1990 and 76.7 per cent in 2010). The percentage of Whites in LDW tracts in most of these MSAs did not decline as fast. We show this for each metropolitan area by calculating the percentage of Whites in LDW tracts for 1990, 2000 and 2010 expressed as a ratio relative to the percentage of tracts that are LDW. This is a type of location quotient (LQ). If this value is 1, then the percentage of Whites in LDW equals the percentage of LDWs in a metropolitan area. If it is greater than one, then Whites tend to be concentrated in LDWs.

In 48 out of the 53 MSAs in the analysis,[4] the quotient for 2010 is larger than 2000 or 1990, meaning that the percentage share of Whites in LDW tracts is increasing. In other words, while the share of White-dominated tracts decreased between 1990 and 2010, the rate of decline in the number of tracts was not accompanied by a similar rate of decline in the proportion of Whites in those tracts. This resulted in an increase in the concentration of Whites in LDW neighbourhoods. This is another example of what we are calling the 'both/and-' ness of segregation and diversity; while many White-dominated tracts became MDW or other types, almost every MSA recorded a greater proportional concentration of Whites in those tracts that remained LDW. Some of the most racially diverse or 'immigrant gateway' MSAs (for example, Houston, New York, Los Angeles and Miami) registered some of the highest of these LQs in 2010. Similarly San Antonio is now majority Latino and has the highest LDW LQ for any of the 53 MSAs in the study. Again, segregation and diversity can occur at the time in the same places.

For perspective, we performed a parallel analysis of LDB tracts. Some MSAs have few such tracts; some have none. LDB tracts offer no consistent pattern of shrinkage. Atlanta, for example, had 112 LDB tracts in 1990, 123 in 2000 and 115 in 2010. Pittsburgh, one of the more segregated MSAs in the US based on Black–White dissimilarity, had 31 LDB tracts in 1990, 29 in 2000 and 24 in 2010. The number of such tracts increased in St Louis in the 20-year period; they stayed the same in West Palm Beach. Using the same LQ formula, however, we can also observe changing patterns of *Black* concentration in LDB tracts. While the degree of Black concentration in Black-dominated tracts is far higher than White concentration is in heavily White-dominated tracts, unlike the patterns we see in Whites, Black concentrations are lower in 2010 than 2000, and lower in 2000 than 1990 – *across the board*. So while Whites are increasingly concentrating in predominantly White tracts, Blacks are becoming less concentrated in predominantly Black tracts.

The final phase of the analysis exploits the temporality of the dataset in another way. We connect patterns of change or lack thereof (1990 to 2000 to 2010) in White-dominated tracts to average tract median household income at the midpoint (2000). As context, we note that the median household income for Blacks has been between 55 and 60 per cent that of Whites over the last few decades. Latinos have median household incomes roughly 70 per cent that of Whites. Asian median household income is higher by about 15 per cent (DeNavas-Walt et al, 2011, p 8).

Table 6.4, Panel A, contains all the transition 'paths' for LDW tracts in 1990[5] and can be read in the following way. Between 1990 and 2000, 15,273 tracts 'transitioned' from LDW to LDW. The chance of that occurring was 0.716. Of those tracts, 10,925 were recorded as LDW in 2010 and, of those, another 4,325 transitioned to MDW in 2010. The chance of a tract remaining LDW throughout was 0.512; the probability of following an LDW-LDW-MDW path was 0.203. The right-hand column records the weighted average median household income in 2000 for each set of transition possibilities.

Tracts that remained LDW from 1990 to 2010 were almost always the wealthiest. Others that started as LDW but transitioned to another category almost always had lower average median household incomes (Dallas, Las Vegas, Miami, Orlando, San Antonio, Seattle, Tampa and DC are the exceptions [not shown]; in these places, LDW-LDW-MDW tracts had higher average median household incomes than LDW-LDW-LDW tracts). Generally speaking, the higher the density of Whites in a path, the higher the median neighbourhood income. The path that stands apart from that comment is the one with 31 tracts that transitioned from LDW to MDW to MDA. The weighted

Table 6.4: Transition paths for low and moderately diverse white-dominated tracts: 1990-2010

All MSAs	1990	2000	2010	Tract count	Transition probability	Weighted median HH income
Panel A						
	LDW	LDW	–	15,273	0.716	61,666
	LDW	LDW	LDW	10,925	0.512	62,695
	LDW	LDW	MDW	4,325	0.203	59,212
	LDW	LDW	MDB	17	0.001	49,870
	LDW	MDW	–	5,830	0.273	52,942
	LDW	MDW	LDW	84	0.004	54,059
	LDW	MDW	MDW	4,931	0.231	54,183
	LDW	MDW	MDB	306	0.014	45,046
	LDW	MDW	MDA	31	0.001	73,468
	LDW	MDW	MDL	335	0.016	42,207
	LDW	MDW	HD	137	0.006	47,939
	LDW	MDB	–	145	0.007	41,870
	LDW	MDB	LDB	47	0.002	43,968
	LDW	MDB	MDB	96	0.005	41,078
	LDW	MDL	–	63	0.003	40,438
	LDW	MDL	LDL	14	0.001	43,197
	LDW	MDL	MDL	46	0.002	39,597
	LDW	HD	–	18	0.001	45,481
	LDW total			21,332	1.000	59,001
Panel B						
	MDW	LDW	–	96	0.012	65,802
	MDW	LDW	LDW	40	0.005	64,566
	MDW	LDW	MDW	54	0.007	66,857
	MDW	LDB	–	30	0.004	45,708
	MDW	LDB	LDB	29	0.004	45,911
	MDW	LDL	–	20	0.003	34,705
	MDW	LDL	LDL	19	0.002	34,789
	MDW	MDW	–	4,898	0.628	49,958
	MDW	MDW	LDW	51	0.007	49,132
	MDW	MDW	MDW	3,368	0.432	50,539
	MDW	MDW	MDB	256	0.033	42,210
	MDW	MDW	MDA	182	0.023	69,286
	MDW	MDW	MDL	807	0.104	44,381
	MDW	MDW	HD	233	0.030	54,579
	MDW	MDB	–	696	0.089	38,967
	MDW	MDB	LDB	77	0.010	46,773
	MDW	MDB	MDW	46	0.006	34,212
	MDW	MDB	MDB	508	0.065	38,362

(continued)

Table 6.4: Transition paths for low and moderately diverse white-dominated tracts: 1990-2010 (continued)

All MSAs	1990	2000	2010	Tract count	Transition probability	Weighted median HH income
Panel B (continued)						
	MDW	MDB	MDL	53	0.007	35,574
	MDW	MDA	–	226	0.029	61,945
	MDW	MDA	MDA	208	0.027	61,677
	MDW	MDL	–	1,232	0.158	38,604
	MDW	MDL	LDL	74	0.009	36,738
	MDW	MDL	MDW	33	0.004	34,272
	MDW	MDL	MDL	1,106	0.142	38,919
	MDW	HD	–	597	0.077	43,313
	MDW	HD	MDW	53	0.007	37,706
	MDW	HD	MDB	29	0.004	36,722
	MDW	HD	MDA	37	0.005	52,041
	MDW	HD	MDL	151	0.019	41,585
	MDW	HD	HD	327	0.042	44,516
MDW total				7,795	1.000	46,880

average median household income for these tracts is over US$73,000 and echoes the aggregate patterns of household income we find in the country as a whole. This particular finding is affected by six high-income neighbourhoods that followed this path in San Francisco. We also note that in every MSA but one, Las Vegas, the average median household income is higher in LDWs than in other tracts. In over half, it exceeds US$10,000; in Los Angeles, this difference is over US$40,000.[6]

By way of contrast, we repeat the same analysis for MDW tracts (Panel B). It is an obvious thing to say, even removing the transition sequences that had 10 or fewer tracts, Panel B shows that range possibilities for tracts that started out in 1990 is far greater than for those that started as LDW. The most common sequence of transition is MDW-MDW-MDW (MDW*3), but this probability is 0.432, meaning that 57 per cent of the tracts that started in 1990 as MDW ended up as some other status. Individual MSAs that had a relatively limited set of transition types tended to be in the Northeast or Mid West. Columbus, for example, had three (MDW*3; MDW-MDW-MDB; MDW-MDB-MDB). Dallas, on the other hand, had 18. MSA size, more than anything else, shaped the variety of transition path types, reminding us that urban racial diversity (usually immigrant-driven) remains a large MSA phenomenon. As before, adding a consideration of household income reveals a pattern wherein those tracts that become Whiter or more Asian are associated with higher neighbourhood median household incomes. Tracts that became Black or Latino-dominated were poorer. MDW neighbourhoods in 1990 that became highly diverse (HD) in 2010 tended to have median incomes in between those of Whites and non-Whites.

We can look at this relationship between racial diversity and White relative wealth from a different angle, by changing the scale of analysis. We ask how these transition sequences, these pathways, relate to overall metropolitan racial and ethnic change. Again, we focus on heavily White tracts that did not transition – the LDW*3s. Hypothesising a positive relationship between median household income in LDW*3 tracts averaged across the MSA and *metropolitan*-level diversity (that is, where *Ej* now references the entropy of metropolitan area *j*), we find the correlation between median household income in LDW*3 in 2000 by MSA entropy in 2000 to be +0.56 (significant at α=0.01). In other words, metropolitan areas that have the higher median incomes in White-dominant neighbourhoods that remained so from 1990 to 2010 also tend to be the more racially diverse.

Conclusion

The inauguration of Barack Obama did not erase the colour lines in US society (Kennedy, 2011); in some subtle ways, it actually redrew them. Using several different perspectives on the changing racial demarcations in large US urbanised areas, this chapter shows the complexity of these patterns and how they vary by geographical context. In most instances, however, we also demonstrate that Whites leverage considerable advantage from their segregation, and those Whites able to retain this spatialised form of their possessive investment in Whiteness are increasingly the most well-off.

This chapter is not so much concerned with 'White flight' per se in the classic Schelling sense, that is, seeking tipping points and so on. Rather, we used a new neighbourhood racial taxonomy to isolate new forms of White concentration and the persistence of *White* segregation. Our chapter contributes to the literature on Whiteness studies. Such scholarship challenges the idea that Whites are unmarked, ordinary and taken-for-granted. Accordingly, research on such White segregation moves Whites from being a point of reference and off to the side to centre-stage.

Our chapter also asks other questions relating Whites and Whiteness to racial diversity. What do increases in such diversity hold for US metropolitan areas? How does that actually translate into everyday life? There is a tendency in recent work on residential diversity to be celebratory. The focus on residential mixing and multiethnic metros sometimes comes very close to an anodyne understanding of our contemporary social condition. It's as if the subprime crisis, with its devastating effects particularly concentrated in non-White neighbourhoods, hardly happened. Moreover, the disconnection between the work on super-diversity, hyper-hybridity, diaspora space, new cosmopolitanisms and so on and the segregation/inequality literature is vast. Even when blending in new forms of social theory and offering new critiques of old approaches, much of this research is simply reinvented liberal multiculturalism or hybridity (dressed up in new terms – 'super-diversity', or some compound noun involving cosmopolitanism) divorced from class politics and global political economy dynamics.

Notes

[1] Sandy Wong, Akikazu Onda and Jonathan Chipman, Director of the Laboratory for Geographic Information Science and Applied Spatial Analysis at Dartmouth College, provided valuable research support. Grants from the National Science Foundation and the Russell Sage Foundation as well as a CompX Faculty grant from the Neukom Institute for Computational Science at Dartmouth College helped make this research possible.

[2] The thresholds used are specific to analyses using six racial groups. They could be modified for other studies using a different number of groups in the analysis.

[3] Tracts with significant numbers of Native Americans are few in number but regionally important. The number of metropolitan area tracts that were low diversity Native American stayed about the same.

[4] Dallas, Portland, Raleigh, Richmond and San Diego were the exceptions.

[5] Transition types involving less than 10 tracts (for example, LDW-LDW-LDB where $n=1$) are not included.

[6] This finding needs more analysis (space limits preclude it here), but we observe for now that between 1990 and 2010, Las Vegas was the fastest growing MSA in this sample. LDWs in Las Vegas were likely relatively poorer neighbourhoods in the building boom. And this place attracted lots of Latino and Asian migrants from southern California who were, by Las Vegas standards, relatively prosperous.

References

Beaulieu, M. and Continelli, T. (2011) 'Benefits of segregation for White communities: a review of the literature and directions for future research', *Journal of African American Studies*, vol 15, pp 487-507.

Borjas, G.J. (1998) 'To ghetto or not to ghetto: Ethnicity and residential segregation', *Journal of Urban Economics*, vol 44, no 2, pp 228-53.

Brown, L.A. and Sharma M. (2010) 'Metropolitan context and racial/ethnic intermixing in residential space: US metropolitan statistical areas, 1990-2000', *Urban Geography*, vol 31, no 1, pp 1-28.

Charles, C. (2003) 'The dynamics of racial residential segregation', *Annual Review of Sociology*, vol 29, pp 167-207.

Chipman, J., Wright, R., Ellis, M. and Holloway, S. (2012) 'Mapping the evolution of racially mixed and segregated neighborhoods in Chicago', *Journal of Maps*, vol 8, no 4, pp 340-3.

Clark, K.B. (1965) *Dark ghetto*, New York: Harper.

DeNavas-Walt, C., Proctor, B.D. and Smith, J.C. (2011) *Income, poverty, and health insurance coverage in the United States: 2010. Current population reports, P60-239,* Washington, DC: US Government Printing Office.

Drake, St Clair and Cayton, H. (1945) *Black metropolis: a study of negro life in a northern city*, New York: Harcourt, Brace & Company.

Du Bois, W.E.B. (1899/2010) *The Philadelphia negro*, New York: Cosimo Classics.

Du Bois, W.E.B. (1989) *The souls of black folk*, New York: Penguin Books.

Farrell, C.R. and Lee, B.A. (2011) 'Racial diversity and change in metropolitan neighborhoods', *Social Science Research*, vol 40, no 4, pp 1108-23.

Frey, W.H. (2011) *Brookings Institution and University of Michigan Social Science Data Analysis Network's analysis of 1990, 2000, and 2010 Census Decennial Census tract data* (www.psc.isr.umich.edu/dis/census/segregation2010.html).

Frey, W.H. and Farley, R. (1996) 'Latino, Asian, and black segregation in US metropolitan areas: are multiethnic metros different?', *Demography*, vol 33, no 1, pp 35-50.

Holloway, S., Wright, R. and Ellis, M. (2012) 'The racially fragmented city? Neighborhood racial segregation and diversity jointly considered', *Professional Geographer*, vol 64, no 1, pp 63-82.

hooks, b. (1990) *Yearning: race, gender, and cultural politics*, Boston, MA: South End Press.

Iceland, J. (2004) 'Beyond black and white – metropolitan residential segregation in multi-ethnic America', *Social Science Research*, vol 33, pp 248-71.

Iceland, J. (2011) 'White residential segregation in US metropolitan areas: conceptual issues, patterns, and trends, 1970 to 2009', Eastern Sociological Society meetings, Philadelphia, PA, 24-27 February.

Johnston, R., Poulsen, M. and Forrest, J. (2006) 'Blacks and Hispanics in urban America: similar patterns of residential segregation?', *Population, Space and Place*, vol 12, pp 389-406.

Kennedy, R. (2011) *The persistence of the color line: racial politics and the Obama Presidency*, New York: Pantheon Books.

Lipsitz, G. (1998) *The possessive investment in whiteness*, Philadelphia, PA: Temple University Press.

Logan, J. and Zhang, C. (2010) 'Global neighborhoods: new pathways to diversity and separation', *American Journal of Sociology*, vol 115, pp 1069-109.

Maly, M.T. (2005) *Beyond segregation: multicultural and multiethnic neighborhoods in the United States*, Philadelphia, PA: Temple University Press.

Marcuse, P. (1997) 'The enclave, the citadel, and the ghetto – what has changed in the post-Fordist US city', *Urban Affairs Review*, vol 33, no 2, pp 228-64.

Massey, D. and Denton, N. (1993) *American apartheid*, Cambridge, MA: Harvard University Press.

Myrdal, G. (1944) *An American dilemma: the negro problem and modern democracy*, New York: Harper.

Park, R.E. (1998 [1928]) 'Foreword', in L. Wirth *The ghetto*, Chicago: University of Chicago Press, pp lxv–lxvii.

Peach, C. (1996) 'Good segregation, bad segregation', *Planning Perspectives*, vol 11, no 4, pp 379-98.

Reibel, M. (2011) 'Classification approaches in neighborhood research: introduction and review', *Urban Geography*, vol 32, no 3, pp 305-16.

Reibel, M., and Regelson, M. (2011) 'Neighborhood racial and ethnic change: the time dimension in segregation', *Urban Geography*, vol 32, no 3, pp 360-82.

Sandoval, J. (2011) 'Neighborhood diversity and segregation in the Chicago metropolitan region, 1980-2000', *Urban Geography*, vol 32, no 5, pp 609-40.

Schelling, T. (1971) 'Dynamic models of segregation', *Journal of Mathematical Sociology*, vol 1, pp 143-86.

Spivak, A.L., Bass, L.E. and St John, C. (2011) 'Reconsidering race, class, and residential segregation in American cities', *Urban Geography*, vol 32, no 4, pp 531-67.

Wacquant, L.J.D. (1997) 'Three pernicious premises in the study of the American ghetto', *International Journal of Urban and Regional Research*, vol 21, no 2, pp 341-53.

White, M. (1986) 'Segregation and diversity measures in population-distribution', *Population Index*, vol 52, no 2, pp 198-221.

Wilkes, R. and Iceland, J. (2004) 'Hypersegregation in the twenty-first century', *Demography*, vol 41, no 1, pp 23-36.

Wilson, R.E. (2011) 'Visualizing racial segregation differently: exploring changing patterns from the effect of underlying geographic distributions', *Cityscape: A Journal of Policy Development and Research*, vol 13, pp 163-74.

Wright, R. and Ellis, M. (2006) 'Mapping others', *Progress in Human Geography*, vol 30, no 3, pp 285-88.

Wright, R., Ellis, M. and Parks, V. (2005) 'Replacing whiteness in spatial assimilation research', *City and Community*, vol 4, no 2, pp 111-35.

Wright, R., Holloway, S. and Ellis, M. (2011) 'Reconsidering both diversity and segregation: a reply to Poulsen, Johnston, and Forrest; and Peach', *Journal of Ethnic and Migration Studies*, vol 37, pp 167-76.

Wright, R., Ellis, M., Holloway, S. and Wong, S. (2014) 'Patterns of racial diversity and segregation in the United States: 1990-2010', *The Professional Geographer*, vol 66, no 2, pp 173-82.

SEVEN

Analysing segregation using individualised neighbourhoods

John Östh,[1] *Bo Malmberg and Eva K. Andersson*

Introduction

Discussions concerning the strengths and weaknesses of different measures of segregation have a long tradition (Wirth, 1938; McKenzie et al, 1967; Wilson, 1987; Massey and Denton, 1993). In 1988, Massey and Denton suggested that it is perhaps not very important which measure is used, since different measures generally tend to capture the same thing (1988). However, even if different measures are indeed correlated, there is still a need for precisely defined measures in order to allow comparisons between different urban areas (see Chapters Two and Three, this volume). A claim that the level of segregation is higher in City A than in City B presupposes that the measures used truthfully represent a real difference in the residential patterns of the two cities. This is even more so if measurements of segregation are going to be used to analyse the determinants of segregation patterns, to study the consequences of different levels of segregation, or in urban and regional planning and policy.

Having a measure that truthfully reflects differences in residential patterns between cities is important if segregation measures are to be used as explanatory variables in statistical analysis. Statistical theory teaches us that measurement errors in explanatory variables will lead to biased parameter estimates. This implies that there is a strong need for accurate measures in research focused on testing hypotheses about the effect of segregation on social outcomes as well.

It could be argued that there are two major shortcomings in existing measures of segregation, and that both are linked to the use of pre-defined statistical areas. The first shortcoming is that existing methods do not measure segregation as a phenomenon that affects individuals. Instead, available measures are derived from aggregate numbers in statistically defined areas. This implies that they do not focus on the residential context of individuals but rather provide information about an abstract spatial structure. This characteristic of current measures is most evident with respect to the index of dissimilarity (Duncan and Duncan, 1975). It is well known that this index gives a measure of the degree to which different groups would need to be redistributed to achieve a settlement pattern in which population shares in different neighbourhoods correspond to overall population shares – no segregation. Thus, in its formulation the index of dissimilarity is not clearly linked to the individual residential experience and the possible effects of segregation.

Another popular measure of segregation is the isolation index, which measures the probability that members of a certain minority group will meet other members of the same group if contacts between individuals in a certain neighbourhood are random. Clearly, this measure can be more directly linked to theories on the effect of residential segregation (Subramanian, 2004). There are, for example, different theories on how exposure to minority groups affects majority group views of the minority. Other theories claim that having few contacts outside the minority group can affect educational or employment outcomes for minority individuals (Brännström, 2004; Pinkster, 2009; Sykes and Kuyper, 2009). Segregation indices based on exposure and isolation can thus more easily be evaluated in terms of consequences than the index of dissimilarity. Still, the isolation index tends to be calculated on the basis of statistically defined areas, implying the somewhat arbitrary assumption that contact patterns follow the boundaries of these areas. Instead, the preferred approach would be to use individualised neighbourhoods, acknowledging the fact that individuals are always at the centre of their own life world (Husserl, 1978; see also Chapter Five, this volume).

A second problem that emanates from the use of pre-defined statistical areas is the well-known modifiable areal unit problem (MAUP) (Openshaw, 1984; Fotheringham and Wong, 1991). Clear evidence has shown that levels of segregation will change depending on the population size of statistical areas. This implies that redistricting can result in a shift in segregation indices even if the residential patterns of different groups are the same (Wong, 1997; Wong et al, 1999). MAUP also makes it more or less impossible to compare levels of segregation between urban areas. This is also an important reason why so few international comparative studies have been published (Johnston et al, 2007). It will always be difficult to determine the extent to which differences are due to a difference in residential patterns and the extent to which they are artefacts linked to the differences in the statistical subdivisions.

Given these two problems with current approaches to segregation measurement, the aim of this chapter is to present an approach that provides segregation measures based on the idea of individualised neighbourhoods and by which the difficulties associated with MAUP can be circumvented. A second aim is to compare the results obtained using individualised neighbourhoods with those obtained when predefined statistical areas are used. Finally, the chapter also addresses the question of whether residential segregation in Sweden limits the possibilities to have ethnically integrated neighbourhood schools.

The rest of the chapter is organised as follows. First, previous research on individualised neighbourhoods and segregation is presented. A software solution for obtaining segregation data using individualised neighbourhoods defined by population thresholds is presented. Next, some background is given on Swedish register data. The developed method is then used to analyse residential segregation among middle school-aged children in Sweden. The segregation measure used here is the isolation index. The analysis shows that when the pre-defined statistical areas provided by Statistics Sweden (SCB) are used, differences in segregation levels between municipalities primarily reflect differences in areal subdivisions, and this makes comparisons across municipalities close to meaningless. The second part of the case study discusses how the entropy index of segregation can be computed using INP (individualised neighbourhoods defined by population thresholds) data, and then applies this measure to a further analysis of segregation patterns in Swedish municipalities. The analysis shows that calculating entropy index values for different population thresholds allows for the production of a segregation profile that can distinguish between different spatial segregation patterns.

Individualised neighbourhood approach to segregation studies

One scholar who argued strongly that statistically or administratively defined areas are more of a hindrance than a help in geographical analysis was the late Torsten Hägerstrand (1955). Already in 1955, he proposed a coordinate method as the solution to this problem. Instead of being registered as living in a certain area, people's place of residence should be represented by its geographical coordinates. This would free researchers from the dependence on pre-defined statistical areas. The solution proposed in this chapter can be directly related to Hägerstrand's idea in that it makes use of a population register with geocoordinates to construct individualised neighbourhoods.

With access to geocoordinates representing where people live, *individualised neighbourhoods* can be constructed by extending a buffer around each dwelling and then counting the number of individuals from different groups living within this buffer. This would generate as many neighbourhoods as there are dwellings, with data on the distribution of different groups within each neighbourhood. This data can then be used to compute segregation indices such as the index of dissimilarity, the isolation or entropy index, or others. There will be some need to reformulate the indices to account for the fact that individualised neighbourhoods overlap but, as shown later in this chapter, this is relatively straightforward.

Still, the size of the buffer remains to be determined. Previously, neighbourhoods were constructed by including all individuals within a fixed radius (Reardon et al, 2008), or by including individuals from adjacent neighbourhoods (Wong, 2005). A drawback of these methods is that varying population density generates great differences in neighbourhood population size. An alternative approach, used earlier in epidemiology, is to allow a buffer radius to vary in response to shifts in density in a way that generates *individualised neighbourhoods of equal population size*. This is the approach adopted in this chapter.

Given that the individualised neighbourhoods should include the same number of people, the final question is what this number should be (Andersson and Musterd, 2010). How large, in terms of population size, is a neighbourhood? This is clearly not simply a question of definition. Instead, it involves substantive issues concerning the spatial scale of local interaction and local social networks (see Chapters Four and Five, this volume). It can also be argued that the definition of local can vary between different types of social interaction. Your immediate neighbours can be very small groups, while people you meet at the local shopping mall can make up a substantially larger group. The best solution, hence, is not to apply a fixed definition of neighbourhood population size. Instead, if possible, segregation indices for individualised neighbourhoods should be reported with an explicit population size subscript, k, denoting the population threshold that has been used to define neighbourhood size. Preferably, segregation levels should be reported for different values of k. The argument made in this chapter is that segregation measures based on INP can provide segregation studies with a measure equivalent to the total fertility rate used in fertility studies. While it is true that the computation of INP-based segregation measures is computationally more demanding than computing area-based measures, this is also true of the total fertility rate compared to the crude birth rate. The great gains are that segregation measures based on individualised neighbourhoods defined by population thresholds are theoretically sound, circumvent the MAUP problem by being explicit about the scale level used, and therefore make it possible to draw comparisons using measures that reflect differences in residential patterns, not differences in areal subdivisions.

Constructing individualised neighbourhoods using EquiPop

In order to analyse segregation in individualised neighbourhoods a new software package, EquiPop, has been developed. This section contains a brief introduction to the 'mechanics' behind EquiPop and to how the analyses are conducted.

The key parameter is k, a number representing the count of nearest neighbours. As k increases, more neighbours are included in the computation. Statistically, this leads to less variance in the estimate. But if k-nearest neighbour is used to analyse segregation, increasing k also implies that the concept of neighbourhood is redefined. A small k implies neighbourhoods that consist of relatively few people while a large k implies neighbourhoods that consist of many people. Strictly speaking, the k-nearest neighbour method presupposes that objects are located in a continuous space, but as shown below, it can be modified for use with gridded data.

In a standard geographic information system (GIS) analysis, counting individuals within a fixed radius is relatively straightforward. Finding the k-nearest neighbours, however, requires a much more computation-intensive approach. Tools for computation are available, but do not offer viable solutions for larger datasets. One way to find the k-nearest neighbours would be to compute distances between all locations. Then, for every location, its proximities to other locations are ranked. Individuals are counted according to the established proximity order until the k-nearest neighbours have been found for each location.

In most advanced GIS tools, users are able to create distance tables between any pair of locations. However, these tables grow very large as the number of locations increases. Rankings of distances are typically performed in a non-GIS environment, by searching through the entire distance vector for every location. As a consequence, computation of k-nearest neighbours is limited in this way to analyses involving hundreds or a few thousand populated locations. An alternative approach is therefore necessary to compute k-nearest neighbours in datasets involving hundreds of thousands or even millions of unique locations. The EquiPop software is specifically designed to handle *k*-nearest neighbour calculations involving vast amounts of data distributed over large areas.

To fully understand the *k*-nearest neighbour computations using EquiPop, an introduction to the 'mechanics' is necessary. The EquiPop program organises input data in the following way:

1. All locations (pairs of coordinates) are converted from point features in a matrix to a raster (gridded data). This procedure means that the raster resolution determines the geographical precision. In the examples presented in this chapter, all point features are converted to raster with a resolution of 100 × 100 metres. Feature specifications finer than specified in the raster resolution are truncated. In the examples published in this chapter, the entire Swedish surface is converted to a raster containing roughly 97.5 million 100 × 100 metre units (15,000 north–south × 6,500 east–west), of which 765,972 units were habituated in the year of study.

2. In the second step of EquiPop, a stepwise floating catchment procedure is used in order to accumulate neighbours. The principle is illustrated in Figure 7.1, below. Here, the zero represents the *origin grid cell*, the location for which the *k*-nearest neighbours are to be found. The number of neighbours in the origin grid cell, as well as the number of neighbours belonging to any specified subgroup, is saved in a coordinate-coded database.

   In the subsequent steps, the coordinate-coded database cumulatively adds neighbours from adjacent grid cells until the user-specified *k* value has been reached. The grid cell from which the next neighbour should be added is determined by an instruction vector in EquiPop. In short, the instruction works as follows: in relation to the origin grid cell, the four grid cells bordering the origin are all located at one unit's distance (see Figure 7.1a). First, all population values in the origin are saved, the finding of neighbours continues in the adjacent grid cell in quarter 1, followed by the adjacent grid cells in quarters 2, 3 and 4. The described scenario, having a user-specified *k*-nearest neighbour value of 10, is illustrated at the top left of Figure 7.1b, where a value of 10 is reached adding together the local value of 1 and adjacent values 3 (quarter 1), 5 (quarter 2) and 1 (quarter 3). The instruction vector is arranged so that the next grid cell to be counted always represents the closest grid cell not yet counted. However, since every grid cell, except the origin, will be located at the same distance as at least three

Figure 7.1: Illustration of stepwise floating catchment procedure

(a)   (b)

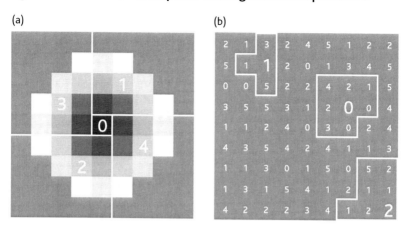

Part a. illustrates the principle behind counting the next k-nearest neighbour in quarter-sequences. Part b. illustrates three examples of space needed to reach a k-nearest neighbour value of 10.

other cells, the segmentation of the counts in quarters assures that the counting is balanced geographically. The instruction vector currently holds counting-order instructions for the 19,999,997 closest grid cells.

3. When the user-specified k-nearest neighbour value is reached for the current origin, the procedure sets a new origin grid cell and step 2 is repeated. This process continues until all populated grid cells in the datasets have reached the user-specified value of k-nearest neighbours.

EquiPop is currently programmed to count and report up to 40 user-specified k-nearest neighbour values (but also the count of subgroup population for each k value and/or the ratio of subgroup to population count value) and the distances needed to reach the specified k-nearest neighbour value. In addition, more distant individuals can be weighted less using the built-in support for distance decay functions.[2] The programme reads input data and exports results in tab-separated ASCII format.

The software package was originally designed for the analysis of Swedish coordinate-set register data, but has also been successfully used in the analysis of international data (Shuttleworth and Östh, 2012). Although the software was designed to work with point feature data, the transformation of block-level feature data to point data has also enabled the segregation analysis of population statistics from the US census (Clark et al, 2012).

The EquiPop software performs computations that are similar to those previously described in Chaix et al (2005), resulting in spatially adaptive areas. Adaptive kernel estimation (Davies and Hazelton, 2010) is a similar approach that has been used in epidemiological research, but the *k*-nearest neighbour approach has not been used to analyse urban segregation.

Swedish register data

In this section, two data-related issues are discussed. First, the organisation and use of Swedish population register data is briefly introduced, and second, the variables used in this study are presented.

According to the Swedish Official Statistics Act (2001), public authorities are required annually to compile and submit statistics to Statistics Sweden. Submitted datasets may be used in analysis by authorities and/or research institutions. The data play a key role in various fields of government, politics and administration. The extent to which the collected data can be used by organisations is determined by regulations in the Personal Data Act (1998, 2003), which forbids the disclosure of individual-level data unless the societal benefits clearly outweigh the risks connected to the intrusion on individual privacy. This formulation makes it possible for researchers to access and use individual-level data. Access to data is not self-evident, however. The right to access and use data is only available after an ethics review of the research project. Ethically approved research projects can use data in two ways: either through databases compiled by Statistics Sweden but located at the universities, or through a VPN-encrypted remote computer located at Statistics Sweden. In recent years, the latter access solution has been the only option for new research groups.

The Statistics Sweden databases comprise a wide range of variables assembled from the contributing public authorities. The data made accessible to research only comprise variables necessary for the research specified in the research projects. This means that researchers involved in several different projects may access different sets of variables depending on which project it concerns. These restrictions are set to meet the demands asserted in the Personal Data Act.

Statistics Sweden regularly publishes manuals and variable-content reports for users of their database. These reports explain variable classifications and summarise variable content changes. In these reports, the database containing the full set of variables is referred to as MONA (Micro data-ON-line-Access). Since the databases available to researchers contain fewer – but to some extent different – variables, Swedish research teams usually name their databases to distinguish between them. Among geographers, well-known research databases include GEOSWEDEN (see, for instance, Andersson and Subramanian, 2006; Andersson and Musterd, 2010) located at the Institute for Housing Research (IBF) in Gävle; the ASTRID database (see, for instance, Lundholm and Malmberg, 2009; Tammaru et al, 2010) located at the Department of Social and Economic Geography at Umeå University; and the PLACE database (see, for instance, Andersson et al, 2010; Åslund et al, 2010) located at the Department of Social and Economic Geography at Uppsala University.

The segregation analyses in this chapter focuses on the visible minority segregation of children aged 13-15 in Sweden for the year 2008. All variables used in the analyses come from the PLACE database. The variables used contain records of each individual's ethnic background, age and geographic location. In Table 7.1 the variables as well as their content and use are presented in detail.

The analysis of segregation in Sweden is typically conducted using planning areas (small area market statistics [SAMS]) as the smallest geographical units. However, using SAMS is problematic in studies of segregation. Besides the well-known MAUP-related risks of using administrative regions, size and number of planning areas vary significantly between municipalities. In Figure 7.2, the distribution

Table 7.1: Variables used in study of visible minority segregation among children aged 13-15, year 2008

Variables	Description	Use in study
Geography variables		
Coordinates (east/ west north/south)	Residential coordinates of all residents of Sweden are available on 100m × 100m units. In 2008, 181,471 units were populated with children aged 13-15.	Geographic unit of analysis in EquiPop.
SAMS (planning areas)	Small area market statistics. SAMS are the smallest area units used for the entire country. In 2008, 8,989 were populated. The geographies of SAMS are delimited by types of residence and economic use. Numbers and sizes of SAMS vary considerably between municipalities (see Figure 7.2).	Geographic de facto standard unit in Swedish segregation analysis. Used for comparison to EquiPop results (Figure 7.4).
Municipality	During 2008 a total of 290 municipalities existed in Sweden.	Geographic unit used for presentation of results.

(continued)

Table 7.1: Variables used in study of visible minority segregation among children aged 13-15, year 2008 (continued)

Variables	Description	Use in study
Demography variables		
Age	All Sweden-resident children born in 1995, 1996 and 1997 (13-15 years old in 2008) are included in the population used in this study. The population was chosen to represent pupils in the mandatory lower secondary school.	Used for population selection. Not used in analysis.
Visible minority	Children with at least one parent born in Africa, Asia or the Americas south of the US are defined as belonging to a visible minority. All others are categorized as non-visible minority children. Of the 348,026 children included in the studied population, 53,765 are categorized as visible minorities.	Share of visible minority children is used to compute isolation and entropy measures.

of planning areas in Sweden's three largest municipalities is illustrated. It reveals that the number of planning areas is considerably greater in Göteborg, especially compared to Stockholm. In this study, segregation analysis results using SAMS are compared to results using the k-nearest neighbour approach.

Case study: residential segregation among Swedish lower secondary school youth/children

In this section, individualised neighbourhoods are computed in order to analyse residential segregation in the 13-15 year age group using an isolation index. This age group makes up the majority of students in the Swedish mandatory lower secondary school. One important reason to focus on this age group is that high levels of residential segregation for this age group would make it difficult to attain balanced student composition with fixed school catchment areas. In fact, it has been argued that in the face of high levels of residential segregation, free school choice can be used as a means of reducing school-level segregation (Lindbom, 2010).

The minority definition used in this study is 'visible minority'. This is a term that has mainly been used in Canada, but it has also been employed in a number of Swedish studies (Andersson et al, 2010; Socialstyrelsen, 2010). In Sweden, race or ethnic identity is not registered. Therefore, parents' country/ies of birth are used as an indicator variable. Children with at least one parent born in countries in Africa, Asia or the Americas south of the US are defined

Figure 7.2: Between municipality differences in size and numbers of SAMS

Göteborg 1:300 000   Göteborg 1:100 000

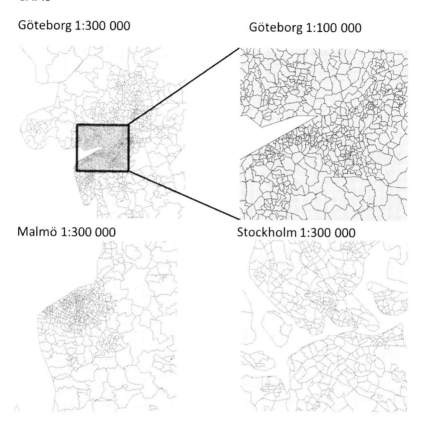

Malmö 1:300 000   Stockholm 1:300 000

Upper left, lower left and lower right maps illustrate SAMS in the three largest municipalities, scale 1:300 000. Upper right map illustrates city centre of Göteborg, scale 1:100 000.

as belonging to a visible minority. Using a dichotomous variable to represent belonging to a minority can, of course, be discussed, and additionally, what is seen as a *visible* minority is not constant over time or space. On the other hand, it has been argued that Swedes are not as race-blind as has been assumed. Therefore, analysing the extent to which this group is spatially sorted on the housing market can in itself be interesting.

Using the software described above and k-nearest neighbour values of 13, 25, 50, 100, 200, 400, 800 and 1,600, all Sweden-resident children in the age group 13-15 during 2008 have been analysed. Note that even the smallest of these k values is still much larger than the micro-geography scale used in Páez et al (see Chapter Five, this volume). The ratio of visible minority children at all locations for each k-nearest neighbour value forms the basis of the analyses below. The usage of differently sized k-values points to differences in contexts at various scales. The 13 nearest children ($k=13$) may represent the pool of friends available in the same block, whereas the 100–400 counts may represent children at the local school and finally the 800–1,600 ks represent the children the local child is likely to encounter in a small city, at a sports centre or at a church/mosque/temple. There are several advantages to combining the isolation index and a k-nearest neighbour approach for the study of residential segregation among Swedish school children. First, each visible minority child's isolation can be compared to other visible minority children's isolations. And second, the child's isolation can be compared at different neighbourhood scales.

Isolation index

A first look at the data for Sweden is provided on the left in Figure 7.3. The values of this graph show the probability that a visible minority student will meet another visible minority member if contacts are picked randomly from among 13, 25, ..., 800, or 1,600 students who live close to the student. The results illustrate that the chance that a random contact will be made with a visible minority declines as the number of k-nearest neighbours increases. In fact, the isolation index is 50 per cent higher when $k=13$ compared to a k of 1,600 (first and last points of the graph on the left in Figure 7.3). The intuition that the levels of segregation are scale-dependent is thus confirmed. It should be kept in mind that probabilities have been weighted by the number of visible minority students present in each location. This implies that locations with a concentration of visible minority students will have the strongest influence on the statistics shown. The right part of Figure 7.3 shows the same measure for the four most populous municipalities. With the exception of Uppsala, the isolation index values are higher in these municipalities compared to the isolation index values for all of Sweden, illustrated on the left in Figure 7.3. The same pattern of decline, with respect to increases in k, is evident, however. It can also be noted that there is a shift in the relative segregation level between the Malmö and Stockholm municipalities when k increases. For low values of k, segregation is higher in Stockholm, but for $k=800$ or larger, Malmö is the most segregated city. It should also be noted that Göteborg has the lowest level of isolation at all scale levels. This goes against the general view that Göteborg has the highest level of segregation, for example, in *Social rapport* (Socialstyrelsen, 2010). Uppsala displays levels of isolation that are considerably lower than in the other three municipalities.

Figure 7.3: (top) Isolation index for the entire student population in Sweden, n=348 026; (bottom) Isolation index for the four most populous municipalities: Stockholm, Göteborg, Malmö and Uppsala

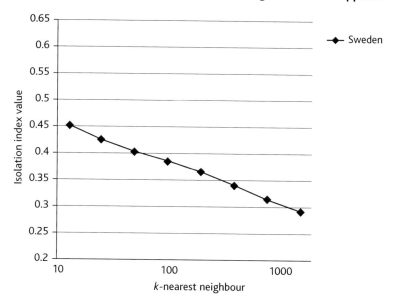

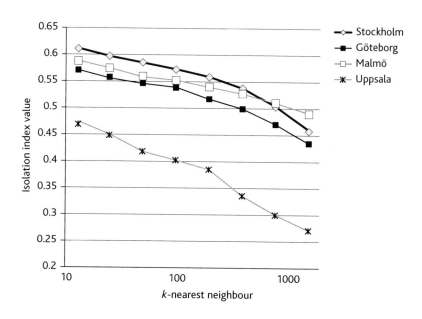

Interestingly, the reason why segregation measures have singled out Göteborg as more segregated than Stockholm is simply that the statistical aggregates used to compute these indices are not comparable in scale between Stockholm and Göteborg. These aggregates, called SAMS or planning areas, are generally small in Göteborg and large in Stockholm. There has been an awareness of the problem of comparison, but results have still been interpreted and accepted.

This problem is not restricted to Stockholm and Göteborg, however. Figure 7.4 shows index values for a selection of Swedish municipalities. The grey line shows the k-nearest neighbour-based values, the black line the isolation index based on the SAMS/planning areas. The point where these lines intersect, that is, the point where the k-nearest neighbour and the planning area are equal, gives an indication of the effective size of the planning areas in different municipalities.

The top row of the graphs in Figure 7.4 shows that if planning areas are used, Göteborg stands as the most segregated municipality, and Stockholm as less segregated. In Göteborg, the grey–black intersection occurs for a very low k value (near 25), but for Stockholm the corresponding k value is 400. This highlights an important difference between the sizes of the municipality's planning areas. The other graphs show a very large variation in the scale of planning areas across municipalities with no apparent patterns. There are big municipalities with large planning areas, big municipalities with small planning areas, small municipalities with large planning areas and small municipalities with small planning areas. This erratic pattern demonstrates that quantitative segregation studies based on Swedish planning areas are virtually meaningless. And certainly, the lack of methods for getting around this problem must have been an important obstacle to the analysis of segregation patterns in Sweden.

Entropy index

In 1971, the Dutch economist Henry Theil proposed a segregation measure based on the concept of entropy (Theil and Finizza, 1971). An advantage of this measure is that it can be both aggregated and disaggregated. Historically, the entropy index (also called the Theil index) has not been referred to as often in segregation studies as has the index of dissimilarity (according to the Web of Science database), and it has been used more frequently by sociologists and economists than by geographers (White, 1983; Hårsman, 2006). Recently, however, the popularity of the entropy index has increased.

Figure 7.4: Isolation index for different k values (grey line) and based on planning areas (black line) in a selection of Swedish municipalities. The four largest municipalities are in the top row, remaining municipalities have been randomly selected.

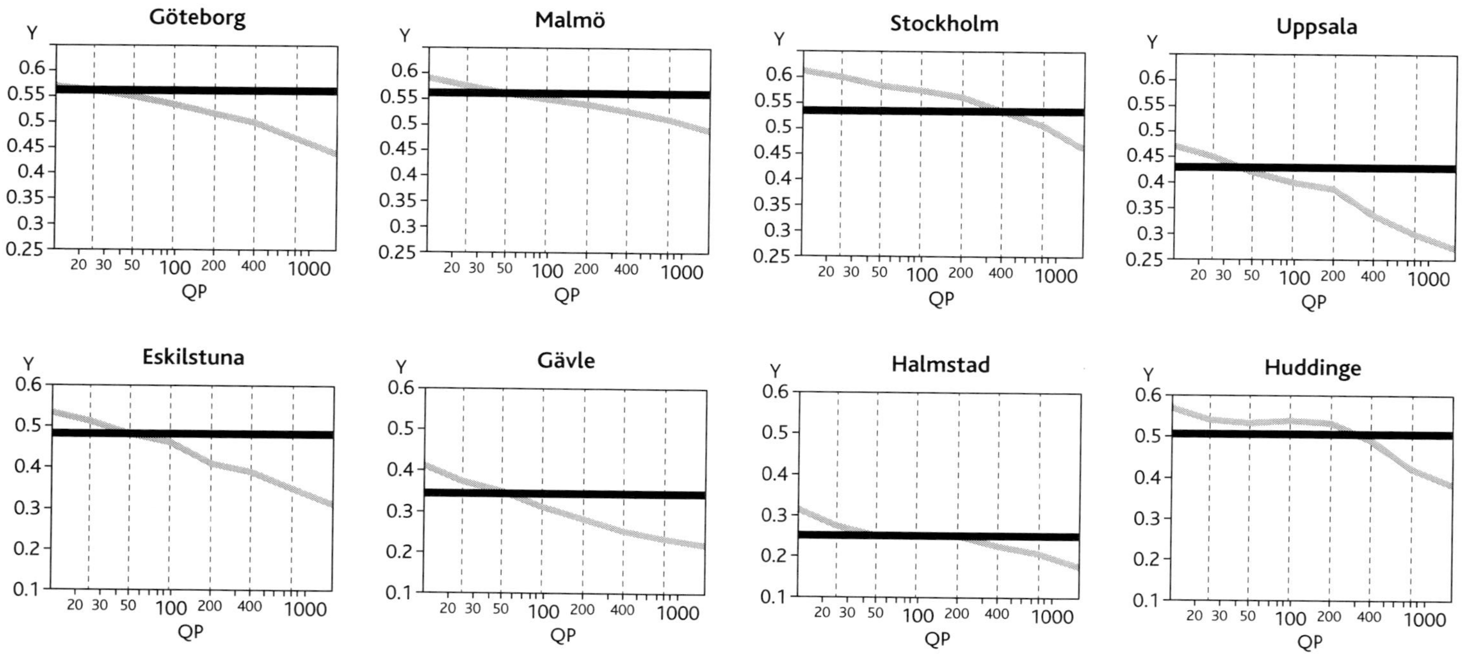

(continued)

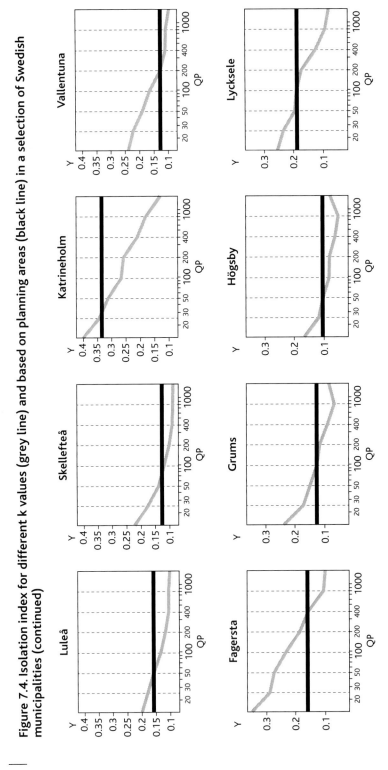

Figure 7.4. Isolation index for different k values (grey line) and based on planning areas (black line) in a selection of Swedish municipalities (continued)

The entropy index measures entropy normalised with benchmark entropy based on an equally distributed population. Suppose we have an urban area with N neighbourhoods. We define p^i_m and p^i_n as the minority and non-minority share in area I, and p_m and p_n as the city-wide minority and non-minority share. The entropy index e is then defined as:

$$e = \frac{N - N}{e} \tag{1}$$

with

$$H = -\sum_{i=1}^{N} p_{i,n} \log p_{i,n} + p_{i,m} \log p_{i,m} \tag{2}$$

and

$$\bar{H} = -N(p_n \log p_n + p_m \log p_m) \tag{3}$$

With some modifications, the entropy approach can also be used to compute a segregation index using k-nearest neighbour values simply by letting $p_{i,m}$ refer to the minority share among the k nearest neighbour of individual i.

Before equation 1 is used to compute the segregation index, however, it is necessary to modify the computation of $\bar{H}$. Normally $\bar{H}$ is computed using the urban level share of the minority, p_m, defined as the number of minority people divided by total population size. When individualised neighbourhoods are used, the relevant urban level minority share is instead the grid-cell population weighted mean of minority shares of the individualised neighbourhoods. This share need not be exactly the same as the share obtained by dividing the size of the minority population by the total population size.

The entropy index profiles for Sweden's four largest municipalities are shown in Figure 7.5. Again, the results indicate that Stockholm is the most segregated municipality in Sweden. According to the entropy index Göteborg is more segregated than Malmö, which is a reversed result compared to the pattern in Figure 7.3. This indicates that the high levels of isolation found in Malmö compared to Göteborg are linked to a high overall share of visible minorities, not to a stronger spatial concentration.

In Figure 7.5, the entropy profiles of larger municipalities are at higher levels than those of smaller municipalities. This link between municipality size and entropy profiles can, in fact, be found across the

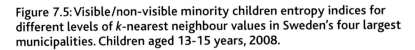

Figure 7.5: Visible/non-visible minority children entropy indices for different levels of *k*-nearest neighbour values in Sweden's four largest municipalities. Children aged 13-15 years, 2008.

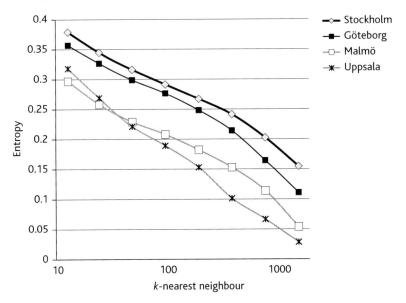

entire size distribution of the municipalities. This is shown in Figure 7.6. The municipalities have been divided into five different classes according to population size (rows). For *k*-nearest neighbour values from 13 to 1,600, the municipalities have been divided into those with an entropy index higher (dark grey) and lower (light grey) than 0.1 and 0.2. The graph shows that for *k*=13, all municipalities except a few in the smallest class have an entropy index above 0.2. In other words, individualised neighbourhoods defined by 13 visible minority children almost exclusively have pronounced segregation. In addition one could say that at this scale, visible minority segregation is a general phenomenon, not restricted to larger urban areas.

With an entropy value of 0.2, and with the value of *k*-nearest neighbour reaching 25 children, segregation is no longer a general phenomenon. Some of the smallest municipalities still have segregation at this scale, but it is only in municipalities with a population larger than 40,000 that a majority of the municipalities have an entropy index value higher than 0.2.

At *k*=50, municipalities with an entropy index higher than 0.2 become a minority in the 40,000 to 90,000 size class as well. With *k*≥100, only one of the municipalities with less than 40,000 inhabitants has an entropy index of 0.2 level of segregation. Similarly, at the *k*=100

Figure 7.6: Share of municipalities with an entropy index higher than 0.1 and 0.2 for different *k*-nearest neighbour values, by population size in municipality

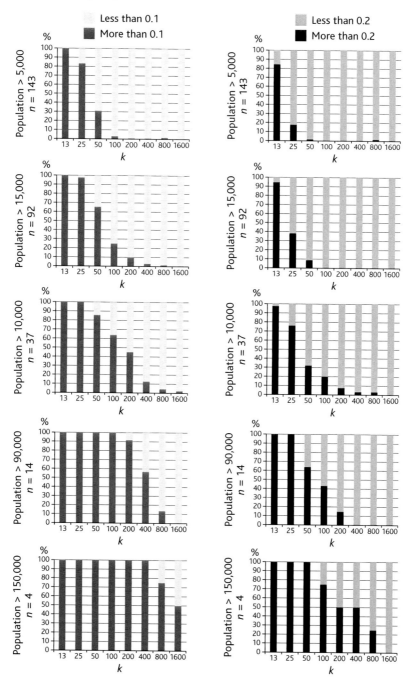

scale, only a minority of the municipalities with 40,000 to 150,000 inhabitants have a 0.2 entropy index level of segregation. Finally, at $k \geq 400$, entropy 0.2 segregation has become a phenomenon restricted to only two metropolitan municipalities (Stockholm and Göteborg). What conclusions can be drawn from this pattern?

First, it shows that in Sweden, visible minority residential segregation is a phenomenon that exists even at the very lowest levels of the urban hierarchy. Admittedly, this is a form of micro-scale segregation since it often disappears when the number of child neighbours is increased to 25 or 50. But still, visible minority children in these small municipalities will tend to live in neighbourhoods with an above-average share of visible minority children. This suggests that residential sorting of visible minorities also occurs in small municipalities. This result is supported by findings by Statistics Sweden (SCB, 2007).

A second conclusion is that in an overwhelming majority of Swedish municipalities, residential segregation does not hinder schools with fixed catchment areas based on a proximity principle from achieving a balanced ethnic composition. If a body of 400 students is not considered too large for a lower secondary school, then the entropy index for the 400 nearest neighbour children can be taken as an indicator of how unbalanced neighbourhood schools would become in different municipalities. Figure 7.6 then tells us that it is only in two metropolitan municipalities, Göteborg and Stockholm, that neighbourhood schools would be more imbalanced than is indicated by the 0.2 level of the entropy index.

Still, an entropy index of 0.2 corresponds to a high level of segregation. But even if the limit is lowered to an entropy index of 0.1, there are only 20 municipalities, most of them large, that fall into this category when $k=400$.

This is not to say that residential segregation is not a driving force behind school segregation in some municipalities. Instead, the main point is that the number of municipalities where residential segregation might hinder mixed schools due to catchment areas and concerning visible minorities is very low.

The third conclusion is that the close correlation between municipal population size and the neighbourhood scale of segregation deserves to be analysed further. Of course it can be argued that small municipalities cannot have large-scale (high k) segregation, but it is not self-evident that large municipalities must have large-scale segregation. Instead, a large municipality could in principle be composed of, as it were, several small municipalities joined together. Such a municipality would have a large population but only small-scale (low k) segregation. Why, then, is this not the pattern that has been found? The answer could be that the processes of segregation are influenced by city size. It could, for example, be the case that the stigmatisation of certain areas uses geographic labels that refer to larger areas in large cities than in smaller cities. This could reinforce a tendency towards 'White flight' in a broader area in large cities than in smaller cities (comparable to Andersson et al, 2010). A second reason could be the size of the units built, especially during the Swedish 'Million Programme' era (mainly during the 1960s). The residential areas built during this time, and later, are considerably larger than those in smaller cities, creating large homogeneous housing type and tenure type areas.

Notwithstanding the size–segregation scale correlation, there are also variations in segregation patterns that cannot be explained in this way. In Figure 7.7, the entropy index profiles for four of Sweden's largest non-metropolitan municipalities are shown. It shows that there are, in fact, great differences in the segregation patterns of these relatively similar-sized municipalities. In Örebro, levels of segregation are high, up to k=400, even higher than in Malmö. In Gävle and Västerås, on the other hand, levels of segregation are lower.

The results presented in Figure 7.7 reveal that segregation patterns can be very different even in relatively similar-sized municipalities.

Figure 7.7: Visible/non-visible minority children entropy indices for different levels of k-nearest neighbour values in four of Sweden's largest non-metropolitan municipalities. Children aged 13-15 years, 2008.

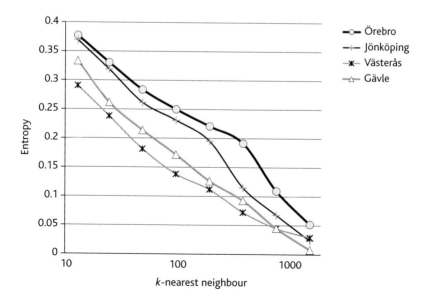

Through the illustration of entropy for different k-nearest neighbour at the urban level, the patterns of segregation on a local scale can be better understood.

Figure 7.8 shows the residential pattern of visible minority students in Örebro and Västerås, and how the share of visible minority changes as the number of the neighbours (k) increases. In Örebro (left column), visible minority children are strongly concentrated in housing areas in the north, and here the visible minority share does not decline rapidly as k increases. In Västerås (right column), visible minority children are represented more evenly across the city with some concentrations, but this is intermingled with areas with low visible minority shares (for small values of k). As the size of k increases, the red areas in Västerås turn blue (or grey), which indicates declining visible minority shares. It is this residential pattern that produces the different entropy profiles of Örebro and Västerås shown in Figure 7.8. The declining visible minority shares as k increases in Västerås imply rapid declines in the entropy index. Slow declines in visible minority shares as k increases in Örebro imply slow declines in the index.

This difference between Örebro and Västerås is intriguing. Both cities have a similar history of local politics having been dominated by the Social Democrats for many decades. Can the differences be explained by the adoption of contrasting planning ideals? Has the development in Västerås been influenced by the dominance of its one large manufacturing employer? Or can these different patterns emerge as a result of chance occurrences that send cities off, destined for different segregation paths. These are questions that cannot be addressed in depth here. The conclusion is instead that only access to a good, reliable and sensitive measure of urban structure allows these kinds of differences to be discovered, and hence, to be turned into objects of further research.

Conclusion

Researchers have long debated the usefulness of various types of segregation indices, but only limited attention has been given to the complications involved in using the administrative region as the statistical unit for computation. As a result, a key issue has been to compare levels of segregation between regions, or even within the same region, especially over time. In this chapter a new software tool (EquiPop) has been introduced, with which alternative statistical regions may be constructed. Using the residential coordinates of individuals, individualised regions are created around individuals.

Figure 7.8: Residential pattern of visible minority children in Örebro (right) and Västerås (left). Red colour indicates high share of visible minority in neighbourhood population, blue colour low shares. Size of circles shows size of visible minority population.

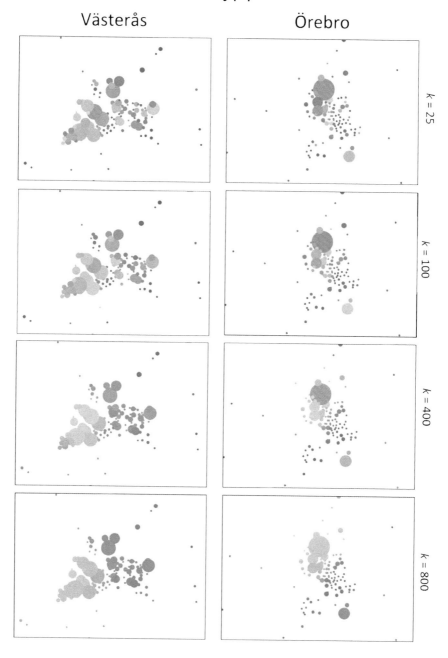

In addition, the created statistical regions are allowed to vary in population size (*k*-nearest neighbour), making it possible to construct several regions for each individual.

Our application of the *k*-nearest neighbour approach to the measurement of segregation, which shares some similarities with the micro-geography approach used in Páez et al (see Chapter Five, this volume), has demonstrated the following: first, that it is superior to the use of administrative areas especially when, as is the case for Sweden, areas are defined differently in different municipalities; second, that segregation also exists in small municipalities but that this segregation is small-scale in nature; third, that large urban areas are generally characterised by large-scale segregation, although this does not have to be the case; fourth, that *k*-nearest neighbour-based segregation profiles can capture differences in segregation patterns between urban areas that correspond to those that can be observed on distribution maps; fifth, that large non-metropolitan municipalities differ in the extent to which they suffer from large-scale segregation, the background of which should be further researched as it could potentially be of great interest from a policy/planning point of view; and finally, that it is only in a few Swedish municipalities that residential segregation restricts the ability of lower secondary schools to attain an ethnically balanced group of students based on fixed school assignment areas using a proximity principle. In our view, this range of important results demonstrates that the *k*-nearest neighbour approach can become a valuable tool for the analysis of urban segregation.

Notes

[1] Contact person for the EquiPop software program.

[2] Using this option means that neighbours located far away from the origin cell are weighted as less important compared to neighbours located nearby. Decay can, at this stage, be modelled using five different formulations: exponential, exponential-normal, exponential-square-root, log-normal and power.

Acknowledgement
Suggestions from Hannes Malmberg are gratefully acknowledged.

References

Andersson, R. and Musterd, S. (2010) 'What scale matters? Exploring the relationships between individuals' social position, neighbourhood context and the scale of neighbourhood', *Geografiska Annaler: Series B, Human Geography*, vol 92, no 1, pp 23-43.

Andersson, E., Östh, J. and Malmberg, B. (2010) 'Ethnic segregation and performance inequality in the Swedish school system: a regional perspective', *Environment and Planning A*, vol, 42, no 11, pp 2674-86.

Åslund, O., Östh, J. and Zenou, Y. (2010b) 'How important is access to jobs? Old question – improved answer', *Journal of Economic Geography*, vol 10, no 3, pp 389-422.

Brännström, L. (2004) 'Poor places, poor prospects? Counterfactual models of neighbourhood effects on social exclusion in Stockholm, Sweden', *Urban Studies*, vol 41, no 13, pp 2515-37.

Chaix, B., Merlo, J., Subramanian, S.V., Lynch, J. and Chauvin, P. (2005) 'Comparison of a spatial perspective with the multilevel analytical approach in neighborhood studies: the case of mental and behavioral disorders due to psychoactive substance use in Malmö, Sweden, 2001', *American Journal of Epidemiology*, vol 162, no 2, pp 171-82.

Clark, W., Malmberg, B. and Östh, J. (2012) 'Where does the mixed race population live? Evidence from Los Angeles', AAG Annual Meeting, Session: 'Changing Patterns of Segregation in Europe and the United States 2', 25 February, New York.

Davies, T.M. and Hazelton, M.L. (2010) 'Adaptive kernel estimation of spatial relative risk', *Statistics in Medicine*, vol 29, no 23, pp 2423-37.

Duncan, O.D. and Duncan, B. (1975) 'A methodological analysis of segregation indexes', in C. Peach, *Urban social segregation*, London: Longman Group Ltd, pp 35-51.

Fotheringham, A.S. and Wong, D.W.S. (1991) 'The modifiable areal unit problem in multivariate statistical analysis', *Environment and Planning A*, vol 23, no 7, pp 1025-44.

Husserl, E. (1978) *The crisis of European sciences and transcendental phenomenology: an introduction to phenomenological philosophy*, Evanston, IL: Northwestern University Press.

Hårsman, B. (2006) 'Ethnic diversity and spatial segregation in the Stockholm region', *Urban Studies*, vol 43, no 8, pp 1341-64.

Hägerstrand, T. (1955) 'Statistiska primäruppgifter, flygkartering och "data processing-maskiner. Ett kombineringsprojekt"', *Svensk geografisk årsbok*, vol 31, pp 233-55.

Johnston, R., Poulsen, M. and Forrest, J. (2007) 'The geography of ethnic residential segregation: a comparative study of five countries', *Annals of the Association of American Geographers*, vol 97, no 4, pp 713-38.

Lindbom, A. (2010) 'School choice in Sweden: effects on student performance, school costs, and segregation', *Scandinavian Journal of Educational Research*, vol 54, no 6, pp 615-30.

Lundholm, E. and Malmberg, G. (2009) 'Between elderly parents and grandchildren – geographic proximity and trends in four-generation families', *Journal of Population Ageing*, vol 2, no 3, pp 121-37.

McKenzie, R.D., Park, R.E. and Burgess, E.W. (1967) *The city*, Chicago, IL: University of Chicago Press.

Massey, D.S. and Denton, N.A. (1988) 'The dimensions of residential segregation', *Social Forces*, vol 67, no 2, pp 281-315.

Massey, S.D. and Denton, A.N. (1993) *American apartheid: segregation and the making of the underclass*, Cambridge, MA: Harvard University Press.

Openshaw, S. (1984) *The modifiable areal unit problem*, CATMOG (Concepts and Techniques in Modern Geography) 38, Norwich: Geobooks.

Pinkster, F. (2009) 'Neighborhood-based networks, social resources, and labor market participation in two Dutch neighborhoods', *Journal of Urban Affairs*, vol 31, no 2, pp 213-31.

Reardon, S.F., Matthews, S.A., O'Sullivan, D., Lee, B.A., Firebaugh, G., Farrell, C.R. and Bischoff, K. (2008) 'The geographic scale of metropolitan racial segregation', *Demography*, vol 45, no 3, pp 489-514.

SCB (2007) *Barn, boendesegregation och skolresultat* [*Children, segregated housing and school results*], Örebro: Statistics Sweden

Shuttleworth, I.G. and Östh, J. (2012) 'The geographical distribution of unemployment and economic inactivity in Northern Ireland and Sweden 1991 and 2001: concentration of dispersion?', AAG Annual Meeting, Session: 'Changing Patterns of Segregation in Europe and the United States 2', 25 February, New York.

Socialstyrelsen (The National Board of Health and Welfare) (2010) *Social rapport 2010*, Stockholm: Socialstyrelsen.

Subramanian, S.V. (2004) 'The relevance of multilevel statistical models for identifying causal neighborhood effects', *Social Science & Medicine*, vol 58, no 10, pp 1961-7.

Svensk författningssamling (1998) *Personuppgiftslag*, Stockholm: Regerings kansliet.

Svensk författningssamling (2003) *Lag om ändring i personuppgiftslagen 1998:204*, Stockholm: Regerings kansliet.

Sykes, B. and Kuyper, H. (2009) 'Neighbourhood effects on youth educational achievement in the Netherlands: can effects be identified and do they vary by student background characteristics?', *Environment and Planning A*, vol 41, no 10, pp 2417-36.

Tammaru, T., Strömgren, M., Stjernström, O. and Lindgren, U. (2010) 'Learning through contact? The effects on earnings of immigrant exposure to the native population', *Environment and Planning A*, vol 42, no 12, pp 2938-55.

Theil, H. and Finizza, A.J. (1971) 'A note on the measurement of racial integration of schools by means of informational concepts', *The Journal of Mathematical Sociology*, vol 1, no 2, pp 187-93.

White, M.J. (1983) 'The measurement of spatial segregation', *American Journal of Sociology*, vol 88, no 5, pp 1008-18.

Wilson, W.J. (1987) *The truly disadvantaged: the inner city, the underclass, and public policy*, Chicago, IL: University of Chicago Press.

Wirth, L. (1938) 'Urbanism as a way of life', *The American Journal of Sociology*, vol XLIV, no 1, pp 1-24.

Wong, D.W.S. (1997) 'Spatial dependency of segregation indices', *The Canadian Geographer*, vol 41, no 2, pp 128-36.

Wong, D.W.S. (2005) 'Formulating a general spatial segregation measure', *The Professional Geographer*, vol 57, no 2, pp 285-94.

Wong, D.W.S., Lasus, H. and Falk, R.F. (1999) 'Exploring the variability of segregation index D with scale and zonal systems: an analysis of thirty US cities', *Environment and Planning A*, vol 31, pp 507-22.

EIGHT

The international comparability of ethnicity and collective identity: implications for segregation studies

Pablo Mateos

Introduction

This book is devoted to the various factors that have recently brought urban segregation to the fore of contemporary public debates in most developed countries. However, despite a worldwide increase in interest in the study of ethnic, racial and migrant segregation, there is a clear lack of international comparative studies in this area. In other words, research that assesses the level of segregation between cities and consistent population groups across countries is almost non-existent. One of the consequences of this is a lack of agreed standards to conduct studies of socio-spatial differences as well as to benchmark results beyond entrenched national conceptions and meanings of 'otherness' and disadvantage. This situation, in turn, impedes the justification of segregation as a subject worth investigating, since many academic arguments at national level tend to be frequently shaped by the political and media representations and priorities of the moment, and as such, are often immune to robust long-term and international validation.

Such a state of affairs is largely a consequence of the serious methodological barriers faced by scholars in this area, as discussed by other authors in this book. These are derived from a strong dependence on the information provided by national Censuses of Population (Kertzer and Arel, 2002; Logan and Zhang, 2004; see also Chapter One, this volume). As such, different issues arise from the use of inconsistent units of analysis between countries, or even within countries when making comparisons over time (Mateos et al, 2009). The majority of the literature in this area focuses on the problems related to the comparison between incompatible geographical units of analysis, namely, issues of scale and extent of urban areas (Johnston et al, 2007; see also Chapter Two, this volume). The former refers to variations in the number and size of the basic spatial units of residence (that is, defining the meaningful scale of a 'neighbourhood'; see Krupka, 2007; see also Chapter Four, this volume), while the latter relates to the problem of delineating the external boundary of what we consider 'a self-contained city' or metropolitan area.

However, a key aspect that seems to be overlooked in segregation debates is the issue of varying definitions, measurements and meanings of the categorisation of human groups underpinning each investigation (Phillips, 2007). In other words, the problem of incompatible classifications of distinct human groupings, which has obvious consequences for (the lack of) comparability across studies. Such human groups are typically classified along one or several identity dimensions into migrant, racial, ethnic or religious groups, according to available data. These classifications are also heavily influenced by the aforementioned political priorities, collective memory and the contextual national perceptions and representations of minority groups. What surprises the outsider is how the apparently inert nature of ethno-racial categories in the census is commonly taken for granted in public and academic debates of segregation.

However, censuses typically utilise only a few self-assigned ethnic categories, the number, definition and reporting of which are highly inconsistent between countries, and even within countries through time (Kertzer and Arel, 2002). In this respect, it is interesting to note the persistence of the skin colour criterion when creating population classifications for the purpose of measuring segregation in neighbourhoods. In the majority of studies, the White/non-White divide seems to be a perennial axis of segregation, and is construed as 'a problem' (Iceland, 2004; see also Chapter Six, this volume), both in the early 20th century as well as in contemporary understandings of 'otherness'. It seems that the definition of the segregation/integration problem lies on a racial dichotomy, which seems to depict non-White concentrations as negative (Simpson, 2004), when the reality looks more like a complex spectrum of 'skin tones', migration histories, languages, beliefs and cultures (Vertovec, 2007).

Even when several ethnic groups are analysed, most research on segregation has been reduced to just a few of the largest ethno-religious minorities in a country. In the UK these have typically been South Asian (Indian, Pakistani and Bangladeshi) (Peach, 1998) and Black minorities (Phillips, 1998), or increasingly a Muslim minority (Peach, 2006a). In the US, most segregation studies just refer to the four 'pan-ethnic' groups: Whites, Asians, Blacks and Hispanics (Iceland et al, 2011). Little consideration is usually paid in segregation studies to what it means to be 'White' (Peach, 2000), who the 'Other' or 'Mixed' ethnic groups are (Connolly and Gardener, 2005; Mateos et al, 2009), or whether it is meaningful to use overarching groups such as 'Asians' (Aspinall, 2003b) or 'Hispanics' (Choi and Sakamoto, 2005).

Therefore, although the meaning of various aspects of segregation indices have been hotly debated in recent years (see Chapter Two, this volume), the meaning and ontology of ethnicity underlying such studies nevertheless seems to go unnoticed (Mateos, 2011). This is certainly the case at least in empirical social sciences, while in other disciplines, for example Public Health, it constitutes one of the most contentious issues in contemporary research (Bhopal, 2004).

On the contrary, the question that seems to be missing from segregation studies is: what are the key ethno-cultural differences or discrimination factors that justify the study of segregation as a vehicle for understanding the wider geography of ethnic inequalities? This chapter intends to make a contribution in this direction, addressing the key methodological issues of definition and measurement of ethnicity and human difference faced by international comparisons of segregation. It reveals that national identity classifications strongly shape the way we conceive ethnicity/race and broader identity dimensions, and thus prevent meaningful international comparisons in the study of segregation levels between cities and ethnic groups. However, some common lineages between categories can be made. The chapter concludes with recommendations for some analytical options that will allow the comparison of some ethnic groups when small area data for the 2010/11 Census round become available.

International comparisons of segregation

As stated in the previous section, international comparisons of segregation levels across ethnic/racial groups and cities are very scarce. Most of the few studies available in English tend to compare just two countries: the UK and the US (Peach, 1996, 1999; Johnston et al, 2002; Iceland et al, 2011). Several others focus on different sets of Anglo-Saxon countries: Australia, Canada, New Zealand, the UK and the US (Peach, 2005; Johnston et al, 2007; see also Chapter Two, this volume). The few examples available on Continental Europe are either comparative reviews of pre-existing national literature (Musterd, 2005; Arbaci, 2007) or edited collections with independent national chapters wrapped up in a comparative manner (Glebe and O'Loughlin, 1987; Musterd and Ostendorf, 1998). It is well known that the lack of such international comparisons is mostly caused by incompatible population statistics and research practices (Johnston et al, 2007). These not only refer to stark differences between the available units of analysis (issues of geographical scale and labels used for population groups), but more worryingly, between the ontologies underlying the definitions of neighbourhoods, cities and meaningful human groups underlying national conceptions of 'otherness'.

The following illustration will suffice to explain the nature of these important, yet often ignored, ontological and methodological problems. Sako Musterd (University of Amsterdam), one of the key scholars in European segregation studies, has been one of the few brave researchers who has attempted to empirically summarise the existing literature on segregation indices across European cities and 'ethnic' groups. A summary of one of his reviews (Musterd, 2005) is presented in Table 8.1. Although the geographic terms in the second column show the well-known *scale* and *extent* issues associated with various definitions of a neighbourhood and the limits of the city under investigation, we obviate its discussion in this chapter in order to avoid repetition (on this issue see, for example, Voas and Williamson, 2000; Simpson, 2007). However, this second column also shows the striking incompatibility between the definitions of 'population

Table 8.1: Segregation levels of a selection of population groups and cities in Europe, as represented by Musterd (2005)

Country	'Ethnic group' and city	Segregation rank
Austria	Vienna foreigners	46
Belgium	Antwerp North African, Bosnian, metro	7
Belgium	Brussels Moroccan	15
France	Lille non-French	49
France	Paris Algerians Dept 75	50
France	Paris Portuguese Dept 75	54
Germany	Düsseldorf Turks	45
Germany	Frankfurt Americans	51
Germany	Frankfurt Turks	53
Germany	Munich foreigners	55
Italy	Milan non-Italian	52
Netherlands	Amsterdam minorities	43
Netherlands	Amsterdam Moroccans	36
Netherlands	Amsterdam Surinamese	42
Netherlands	Amsterdam Turks 1,216 grids	27
Netherlands	Amsterdam Turks 369	32
Netherlands	Amsterdam Turks 93 neighbourhoods	31

(continued)

Table 8.1: Segregation levels of a selection of population groups and cities in Europe as represented by Musterd (2005) (continued)

Country	'Ethnic group' and city	Segregation rank
Netherlands	Amsterdam Turks metro area	33
Netherlands	Rotterdam minorities	35
Netherlands	Rotterdam Moroccans	28
Netherlands	Rotterdam Surinamese	48
Netherlands	Rotterdam Turks	22
Netherlands	The Hague minorities	30
Netherlands	The Hague Moroccan	23
Netherlands	The Hague Surinamese	40
Netherlands	The Hague Turks	19
Sweden	Oslo third world immigrants	47
Sweden	Stockholm Iranian 14 municipalities	16
UK	Birmingham Bangladeshi	8
UK	Birmingham Bangladeshi ED	1
UK	Birmingham Black African	41
UK	Birmingham Black Caribbean	29
UK	Birmingham Pakistani	9
UK	Bradford Bangladeshi	6
UK	Bradford Black Caribbean	38
UK	Bradford Pakistani	14
UK	Bristol Black Caribbean	17
UK	Bristol Pakistani	13
UK	Leicester Bangladeshi	5
UK	Leicester Black Caribbean	44
UK	Leicester Pakistani	25
UK	London Bangladeshi	12
UK	London Bangladeshi ED	4
UK	London Black African	37
UK	London Black Caribbean	26
UK	London Pakistani	24
UK	Manchester Bangladeshi	11
UK	Manchester Black Caribbean	21
UK	Manchester Pakistani	18
UK	Oldham Bangladeshi	2
UK	Oldham Black Caribbean	39
UK	Oldham Pakistani	3
US	US Asian metro areas	34
US	US Blacks metro areas	10
US	US Hispanics metro areas	20

Source: Adapted from Musterd (2005), reordering the table by country and replacing segregation level by the ranking of each group in the overall table from most (1) to least segregated (55)

groups' used across countries. In fact, the underlying conceptions of 'otherness' that arise from Table 8.1 refer to different dimensions of human identity, encompassing aspects of: 'citizenship' (*foreigners*, '*non-French*', etc), 'migration' and 'development' (*third world immigrants*), 'ethnicity' (*Pakistani, Bangladeshi, Black African* in the UK context, or 'minorities' in the Dutch case), 'geography' (*African, Caribbean*), 'race' (*Black, Asian*), 'culture/ancestry' (*Hispanics*), and a myriad of 'national groups' from developing as well as developed countries (*Moroccans, Turks, Portuguese, Americans, Algerians*) whose exact attribution to individuals is unclear (using 'nationality', 'country of birth' or other variables). These categories encompass whole continents, racial groups, citizenship binaries, individual nations, and even 'religions', as hidden in the example that amalgamates together *North African and Bosnians*, presumably because they are both assumed to be Muslim. Such disarray in the conceptions and measurements of population groups is derived from the geopolitical, cultural and temporal national contexts in which the original data were collected. Each individual study from which Musterd compiled this table adopted such categories not only because of restrictions in data availability, but also because of influences of collective perceptions of human difference deemed most relevant in each of the cities analysed. However, such conceptual disarray is also well exemplified by the definition of ethnic group offered by Musterd in the same paper:

> In Europe the use of the concept of ethnic group, or ethnic minority population, or foreigner usually relates to those who have roots in culturally relatively different countries, often in so-called non- or late-industrialized countries and/ or former colonies. (Musterd, 2005, p 332)

Again, this all-encompassing definition of minority ethnic groups tries to embrace different issues of ethnicity, migration, citizenship, cultural distance, colonialism and development into a single concept of 'otherness'. Together with the categories listed in Table 8.1, it reflects well the deeply routed underlying national conceptions of 'outsider identity' that are commonly assumed by governments, academics and the media across Europe without much reflection. The consequence of such a state of affairs is a clear lack of standardisation in data collection on minority groups in Europe. This situation has been repeatedly denounced by human rights organisations as well as the European Commission at least since 2010, since it impedes progress towards reducing discrimination (Simon, 2012).

Such conceptual and methodological disarray in minority group conception and measurement has profound and understudied consequences for segregation studies. Not only does this situation prevent monitoring the situation of comparable population groups across countries, but more worryingly, it precludes disentangling the different factors producing the segregation patterns found. That is, we cannot attribute higher levels of segregation in particular population groups or cities to differences in generation (migrants or the children of migrants), nativity, length of residence, legal status, physical appearance, religious beliefs, language ability, cultural upbringing and so on. We are not referring here to socioeconomic, geographical or demographic covariates that typically help to explain differences in segregation levels. Rather differently, the problem at stake lies on the side of delineating the actual population groups under study, before any explanatory variables are thrown into the analysis. For example, when comparing levels of segregation of, say, Blacks or South Asians across countries, we first need to make sure that the criteria for inclusion and exclusion into such groups are consistent across our datasets before we are able to say anything else about the meaning of segregation patterns using covariates. Elsewhere we have attempted to carefully choose comparable 'ethnic groups' between the US and Great Britain, by focusing exclusively on ethnicity and nativity (Iceland et al, 2011). This comparative exercise required extreme care in aligning population groups between both countries' censuses, being very explicit about any potential sources of bias. Given that these two countries share many common conceptions and practices in the census, attempting to repeat such an exercise across many other and much more different countries will undoubtedly be a daunting task. Johnston et al (2007) make a similar effort, leaving separate, partially overlapping, ethnic categories when the definitions substantially differed across the five countries compared. Apart from the most frequently used pan-ethnic groups – White, Black, Asian and Hispanic – these authors also use some nation-specific groups (New Zealand European, [Australian] European, Middle Eastern, South Asian, Māori, Pacific and [Canadian] Indigenous) that are obviously not directly comparable between countries.

The requirement of comparable population groups between countries may seem an obvious pre-requisite in any study in social science, yet this is more often than not the exception rather than the rule. Furthermore, most studies just assume that the reader will know, for example, what the categories 'non-Hispanic White', 'Black American' or 'Asian' mean in the US context, and how they differ from 'White British', 'Black Caribbean', 'Black African' or 'Asian' (South Asian) in the UK. In Europe, the examples shown in Table 8.1 seem to assume that 'we all know what we mean' when referring to minority ethnic groups in Europe. This widely accepted attitude seems to neglect the need for more clear-cut and comparable statistics on segregation, as we have proposed elsewhere (Mateos et al, 2009). This reinforces the stereotype of the White/non-White dichotomy as the prevalent axis of analysis in segregation studies, rather than bothering to disentangle the nuanced reality of an increasingly diverse population. This problem has key implications not only for the classification of minority groups, but equally importantly for the definition of the 'majority' from which the minority groups are perceived to be segregated.

To conclude, the argument developed in this section does not imply that the majority of the ethno-racial, religious or other classifications of population minorities in the study of segregation are at all incorrect, or have led to wrong results. Indeed, residential segregation levels might be high for some of these groups in whichever way they are defined. However, some of the segregation patterns repeatedly found may vary substantially if slight alterations on the definition of groups are introduced, such as, for example, including or excluding the native-born citizens by birth, language ability, skin colour, legal status and so on. In other words, the fact that Black Americans in the US and Bangladeshis in the UK always appear at the top in segregation rankings might be a consequence of their strong homogeneity along the identity dimensions discussed in this chapter, while many other groups present a much more heterogeneous character and hence show an apparent sparse distribution across the city. Making them more 'homogeneous' might result in other groups topping the segregation ranks (Mateos, 2011).

The aim of this chapter is to propose much more imaginative classifications of human difference (Wright and Ellis, 2006) in segregation studies, that not only go beyond such White/non-White, *us/others* dichotomies, but that actually disentangle identity into several of its many constituting dimensions, as measured by separate variables.

Widening conceptions of collective identity

Despite the picture presented so far in this chapter, delineating consistent human groups across countries for international comparisons is becoming easier over time. This is thanks to a general trend in official population statistics witnessed over the last two decades, which parallels a renewed political interest in equality and diversity (Aspinall, 2009). Such a trend is the independent measurement of several dimensions of a person's collective identity through separate questions in censuses and surveys. We now analyse how the traditional concept of ethnicity and race is being unbundled into such separate dimensions.

The concept of ethnicity is not common in many countries' vocabulary, public debates and hence its statistical systems. Max Weber defined ethnic groups as 'those human groups that entertain a subjective belief in their common descent because of similarities of physical type or of customs or both, or because of memories of colonization and migration (…) it does not matter whether or not an objective blood relationship exists' (Weber, 1922, cited in Guibernau and Rex, 1997, p 20). Therefore, at the core of the concept of ethnicity is a subjective belief of common origins without the necessary existence of genetic linkages or physical similarity. Over the last decades, the bio-medical world outside the US has tended to abandon the concept of race and adopt a broader conception of self-identity around ethnicity. Such a term includes certain shared characteristics in a 'population', including physical appearance, but most importantly, geographical and ancestral origins, cultural traditions, religion and language (Bhopal, 2004). Therefore, one of the most widely accepted notions of ethnicity today is a multidimensional concept that encompasses different aspects of a group's identity, in relation to kinship, religion, language, shared territory, nationality and physical appearance (Bulmer, 1996). Understood as such, ethnicity in social, as well as health, studies is considered to differ from race, nationality, religion and migrant status, sometimes in very subtle ways, although it is also considered to include traits of these other concepts (Bhopal, 2004).

Nonetheless, the characteristics that together define ethnicity are not fixed or easily measured, so ethnicity is considered in science as a subjective, contextual, transient and fluid concept (Senior and Bhopal, 1994), and probably the most controversial subject of study in social science (Nobles, 2000). The fluidity of the concept of ethnicity is at the root of the anti-essentialists' critiques, who challenge the whole idea of trying to classify people into discrete and immutable categories, such as social classes, but especially ethnic groups (Brubaker, 2004). These authors favour the concept of 'identities' that are subjective, fluid and always evolving, where people can assign themselves to several categories which, taken together, may better reflect the complexity of their lives (Pfeffer, 1998). Even the American Sociological Association describes race (in the US research context) as 'a social invention that changes as political, economic, and historical contexts change' (2006, p 7).

However, the increase in political interest on migration, minorities, multiculturalism and integration in the 21st century has brought a renewed demand for enhanced measures on population diversity. This trend has burst out of the original straitjacket of ethnicity, race and migration as a single axis of categorisation of populations (Aspinall, 2009), and led the way to introduce a range of variables that attempt to separately capture the increasing diversity of developed countries' societies (Vertovec, 2007). Even in countries with no tradition in collecting statistics on population diversity, there have been several initiatives to slowly and subtly introduce indirect questions in national censuses and surveys (Simon, 2012).

In order to assess the current state of the art in what we here loosely term 'collective identity measurement', the rest of this chapter is devoted to reviewing the way these are currently captured in 20 countries' national Censuses of Population.

Methods: a comparison of collective identity in national Censuses of Population

The objective of the rest of this chapter is to evaluate the way in which collective identity is currently conceptualised and measured by a selection of developed countries. Since the interest here is to study the categorisation of identity for residential segregation studies, the Census of Population (or its equivalent instrument in some countries) largely remains the only relevant spatially disaggregated source of data.

An attempt was made to collect the original forms used in the 2010/11 round of the Census of Population from a selection of immigration countries that conduct such a statistical exercise. The United Nations (UN) provides a useful resource with sample forms and English translations of some countries' national censuses, but this proved to be incomplete or outdated in some cases (UN, 2011). This resource was complemented with an internet search at the individual countries' national statistical agencies for such census forms or its equivalent complementary surveys. A total of 20 countries in America, Asia and Europe were finally included in the review. The selection of countries primarily focuses on key immigration countries where the census is conducted and forms are available. These include 11 European countries: Austria, the Czech Republic, Germany, France, Greece, Ireland, Italy, Russia, Spain, Switzerland and the UK; two in North America: Canada and the US; two in Oceania: Australia and New Zealand; and two in the Middle East: Israel and the United Arab Emirates (UAE). In addition to these 17 immigration countries, four others were also selected: in Asia – China, Korea and Japan – and in Latin America – Mexico. These all had relatively low levels of international immigration but represent regions of emigration and/ or recent industrialisation of interest for comparison purposes. In most cases the UN or the national statistical agencies provide English translations of such census forms, and when these were not directly available, they were translated by the author or acquaintances. Because of space limitations, a summary of data sources, references and method of translation into English is not included here, but is available from the author on request.

In those countries where the 'traditional' Census of Population is conducted in combination with large surveys, questions present in the survey are also included in the analysis (the US, France and Spain). It is acknowledged that some of the survey questions might not always be available at the detailed level of spatial disaggregation required for residential segregation studies. Nonetheless, it is judged that their consistent availability in a large national survey accompanying the census, as well as in other government statistics, merits their inclusion, since it allows a more even comparison across countries.

All questions present in each census form were evaluated, and those that could provide potential measures of collective identity were selected. Such selections were analysed in depth, interpreting their formulation as well as their contents and answer format. A list of all relevant questions across countries was compiled and summarised into 27 unique questions. Attempting to produce a common typology of census questions for 20 such different countries proved to be a difficult task. However, in the interest of conciseness, where questions were judged to present only slight differences of meaning between countries, they were amalgamated together under a common formulation. Finally, a matrix was then put together reporting for each country and census question, whether such a data variable is available, and coding the type of answer available according to the question format and the national context. A summary of such a matrix for the 20 countries analysed is provided in Table 8.2 (divided in subsections to fit the page space).

Results: six major themes that measure collective identity

The analysis of the 27 questions in the 20 countries presented in Table 8.2 yields clear clusters of countries according to the presence or absence of certain census questions and how these are formulated and codified. The questions were organised into six major *themes*:

Table 8.2: Matrix of census questions on collective identity available for each of the 20 countries compared

Theme and census question	No of countries No	No of countries %	AUS	NZ	CA	US	UK	IR
Census year			2011	2011[1]	2006 & 2011	2010 [2]	2011	2011
RESIDENCY AND MIGRATION								
Foreign country of residence 1, 5 or 10 years ago	12	60	1 & 5 (Y/N)	5		1	1	1
Year of arrival (1st/most recent/not specified)	13	65	1st, Yr	1st, Mth & Yr		Yr	Rec, Mth & Yr	Rec, Yr
Country of last residence abroad	4	20						CTY
Granted migrant settlement status	1	5			Y/N & Yr			
Current country of residence abroad (emigrant/visitor)	6	30						CTY
Second residence abroad	2	10					CTY	
CITIZENSHIP								
Person's charter citizenship and method of acquisition	17	85	Y/N		CB, CN	CB, CN, CP	Y/N	Y/N
Year of acquisition of charter citizenship	1	5						
Person's previous citizenship prior to naturalisation	2	10						
Person's foreign citizenship/s	15	75			OE		>2 MC, OE	>2 MC, OE
COUNTRY OF BIRTH								
Person's country of birth	13	65	CTY	CTY	CTY	CTY	CTY	CTY
Father's country of birth	5	25	A = Y/N					
Mother's country of birth	5	25	A = Y/N					
Mother's country of residence at person's birth	2	10						
ETHNICITY/RACE AND ANCESTRY								
Ethnic group	6	30	>2 MC		>2 MC	Hisp; MC	MC	MC
Race	1	5				>2 MC		
Indigenous group	4	20		Y/N + Group	1 MC, FSQ			
National identity	2	10					MC	
Person's ancestry	3	15	MC		>2 OE	OE		
Migrant parents	1	5						
LANGUAGE								
Childhood/mother language	3	15				1 MC; inc.		
Languages spoken	2	10			>2 MC; inc.	CE CLs		
Language/s most often spoken at home	7	35	FL; 1 MC		>2 MC; inc.	OE, exc.	1 OE, inc.	OE, exc.
Language/s most often spoken at work/ education	1	5						
National minority language spoken	2	10						Y/N, FSQ
Charter language proficiency	4	20	CE			CE	CE	CE
RELIGION								
Person's religion	10	50	MC	MC			MC	MC
Count of questions available (out of 27 possible questions)			12	6	10	9	11	12

FR	ES	DE	CH	AT	IT	CZ	GR	RU	IL	AE	KR	JP	MX
2008	2011 [3]	2011	2010	2001	2011	2011	2001	2010	2008	2005	2010	2010	2010
5	1 & 10				1 & 5	1	1 & 5					5 (Y/N)	5
Yr	Rec, Yr	Yr (>1955)	Yr						Yr	Len	Mth & Yr		Mth & Yr
	CTY	CTY											CTY
					CTY	CTY	CTY		Y/N				CTY
	CTY												
CB, OE	Y/N	Y/N	CB	Y/N	OE	Y/N	Y/N	Y/N		Y/N	Y/N	Y/N	
			Yr										
CTY			Lost? Y/N										
OE	OE	>2 CE	1 MC	2 MC	OE	OE	OE	OE		MC	MC	OE	
CTY	CTY			CTY	CTY			CTY	CTY				CTY
	CTY	A = Y/N			CTY				CTY				
	CTY	A = Y/N			CTY				CTY				
						CTY	CTY						
						2 OE							
									OE				OE
							OE						
		CTY, Yr [4]											
			MC			MC							
		>2 CE, inc. CE CLs	MC										
													OE
		CE	MC	MC		MC			MC				OE
6	9	6	11	5	7	8	5	4	7	3	3	3	8

Notes to Table 8.2:

Key elements in the type of question and answer

1st	First arrived to the country
A	Abroad
CB	Charter citizenship by birth
CL/CLs	Charter language/s
CN	Charter citizenship by naturalisation
CP	Charter citizenship through parents (jus sanginis)
CTY	Country name/code
FL	Foreign language
FSQ	Further specific questions asked on the topic
Hisp	Hispanic ethnicity only
inc./exc.	Including or excluding charter citizenship
Len	Length of stay (years)
Mth	Month
Rec	Most recent arrival to the country
Yr	Year

Formatting of answer

Y/N	Yes/no binary answer
MC	Multiple choice with pre-set questions plus open-ended options
OE	Open-ended question
CE	Close-ended question
1	One answer permitted
2	Two answers permitted
>2	More than two answers permitted

(1) Based on the 2011 Census form. This Census did not take place in 2011 due to the Wellington earthquake and has been postponed to 2013

(2) Combines the 2010 Census form with the American Community Survey 2010 questions

(3) The 2011 Census form is only collected in a 12% sample of the population. Therefore it might not be deemed useful for the study of segregation. The 2001 Census had similar questions enumerating the total population

(4) Question applies to father and/or mother who migrated after 1955 to current Germany's territory

Country codes: AE = United Arab Emirates; AT = Austria; AU = Australia; CA = Canada; CH = Switzerland; CZ = Czech Republic; DE = Germany; ES = Spain; FR = France; GR = Greece; IL = Israel; IR = Ireland; IT = Italy; JP = Japan; KR = Korea; MX = Mexico; NZ = New Zealand; RU = Russia; UK = United Kingdom; US = United States

(1) Residency and migration; (2) Citizenship; (3) Country of birth; (4) Ethnicity, race and ancestry; (5) Language; and (6) Religion. These six themes resemble well the different dimensions of ethnicity or collective identity previously identified in the literature (Bulmer, 1996), and are used here as the general framework with which to analyse these groups of countries.

Residency and migration

This theme includes six census questions, most of which have to do with different aspects of the act of international migration itself. That is, they deal with the change in a person's usual place of residence over national borders for a certain period of time. They therefore measure one aspect of migration commonly known as migration 'flows' (immigration or emigration). The most common question is the year of arrival into the country (present in 13 countries or 65 per cent out of 20 countries). Although formulated in different ways – first arrival to the country, most recent arrival to the country or not specified on the form – it provides a variable generally known as 'length of residence'. However, international comparisons must take into account that the 'universe', or total population, subject to answer this question, varies between countries, since it sometimes only applies to people born abroad or to non-nationals. The next most common question in this theme (60 per cent) was the person's 'previous place/country of residence' some time before the census (1, 5 or 10 years), measuring recent immigration flows, but again under different time spans. The other four questions in this theme are only present in a few countries: 'country of last residence abroad' (20 per cent), 'migrant granted settlement status' (5 per cent) and two questions on emigration. One of these two is 'current country of residence abroad' (30 per cent) present in countries with a long history of emigration (Ireland, Italy, the Czech Republic, Greece, Israel and Mexico) that attempt to capture part of their diaspora by asking members of the same household about an emigrant's whereabouts. Finally, the last question, 'second place of residence abroad' (10 per cent; UK and Spain) refers to owned or rented property abroad that is repeatedly used more than a number of days a year (15 and 30 days respectively). Both of these last two questions on emigration and transnational practices present a new and interesting avenue of research on emigration that has yet to be seized by segregation studies. It follows a trend that sees migration as part of circular and frequent movements across borders as opposed to unidirectional and definite migration flows that precede 'settlement'.

The implications of these trends and available measures is outlined in the Discussion section later.

Citizenship

The four questions under this theme refer to different aspects of the citizenship status or nationality/ies of the respondent. They include the two most common questions across the 20 countries and 27 questions evaluated here. These are the complementary questions of a 'person's charter citizenship' (85 per cent) and a 'person's foreign citizenship/s' (75 per cent) sometimes formulated as part of the same question. 'Charter citizenship' is the neutral term used in this chapter for the citizenship of the country in question, following the terminology proposed by Johnston et al (2007). The actual formulation of both questions present notable variations between countries, and the actual range of possible answers are coded in Table 8.2. The most important differences between countries relate to whether one or more citizenships can be declared, and whether complementary questions are asked (for example, specific country of citizenship/s or method of charter citizenship acquisition). The least informative of all countries is Germany that only permits a choice from four pre-set citizenship categories: 'German, EU; non-EU; or stateless'. There are only three countries that do not ask any question about citizenship: New Zealand, Mexico and Israel (although Israel asks for the national ID or passport number, which could be a proxy for citizenship). This means that citizenship is in fact the most commonly measured dimension of 'otherness' used in the 20 countries here analysed. This coincides with growing political interest in access to citizenship, around debates between proponents of facilitating the naturalisation of immigrants as a mechanism of integration (OECD, 2011) and those who prefer to restrict who is admitted into the polity. France and Switzerland include an additional census question on the person's foreign citizenship prior to naturalisation, assuming the respondent no longer holds such citizenship, and Switzerland on the year the person naturalised. The French case seems to reflect a rather anachronistic view of citizenship as unique and non-overlapping, while the Swiss case tries to further classify naturalised citizens into some sort of 'temporal gradations of national integration'. Overall, this theme provides a useful dimension to classify populations into citizens by birth, naturalised citizens, non-citizens and dual or multiple citizens mapping the geography of the passports present in a country's residents.

Country of birth

The classic proxy for measuring migration is the non-ambiguous question of a person's country of birth. It is asked in 65 per cent of the countries. Those where it is absent are Germany, Switzerland, the Czech Republic, Greece, UAE, Korea and Japan. Most of these countries tend to follow a *jus sanguinis* tradition in the transmission of citizenship and are perhaps less interested in the geography of birth of their residents and more on their passport. However, as it is well known, country of birth is not ideal to measure migration, since a person could have been born in a particular country during his/her parent's short visit or have subsequently emigrated in early childhood. Furthermore, this variable misses the second and subsequent generations of minority ethnic groups who are born in the country of interest and who might be citizens from birth. Because of these drawbacks, five countries ask further questions on the country of birth of both parents (Australia, Spain, Switzerland, Italy and Israel), following UN recommendations (UN, 2008) to 'establish a category of persons with a migration background' (Simon, 2012, p 14).

Finally, two of the countries that do not ask the respondent's country of birth, the Czech Republic and Greece, ask the very unusual question of 'the mother's country of residence at birth' (at the time of the respondent's birth). This question actually straddles between the three themes discussed so far: migration, citizenship and country of birth. This again relates to a blood transmission conception of citizenship and nationhood, common in many Central and Eastern Europe nations.

Ethnicity, race and ancestry

As discussed in the previous sections, ethnicity and race are the most contentious dimensions to measure in identity statistics, and the ones that have received most of the focus in the literature. We have grouped under this theme six rather different questions that attempt to build population categories through those identity traits that are somehow 'inherited from previous generations': ethnic group, race, indigenous group, national identity, ancestry, and migrant parents. These are all, however, 'rare' categories across national censuses. Only six countries (30 per cent) include ethnicity in their censuses. Anglo-Saxon countries clearly stand out in the ethnicity question (Australia, Canada, the UK and Ireland), with the only exception being the Czech Republic, and the US that asks about race and Hispanic ethnicity, both proxies for ethnicity. These questions tend to offer a few pre-set ethnic group categories or examples with additional open-ended options to write in other groups. The ontologies of ethnicity underpinning these census forms are clearly very different, placing different emphasis on the aforementioned dimensions of ethnicity (Bulmer, 1996).

The rest of the questions in this theme are quite rare in national censuses (≤20 per cent of countries). Specific questions on 'indigenous groups' are asked in countries with substantial indigenous minorities – New Zealand, Canada, Israel and Mexico – although in some other countries such groups are included within the ethnicity or race questions. 'National identity' is asked in the UK and Russia, generally intended to accommodate within-country regional identities (Scottish, Welsh, English, Chechen, Ossetian, etc), or ex-colonial nations (Commonwealth and ex-USSR nations respectively), but in theory open to allegiance to any type of 'nation' not reflected in citizenship status. A 'person's ancestry' is a concept only collected in three countries that have a tradition of 'White settler' societies: Australia, Canada and the US. This perhaps follows an objective of capturing 'within-White cultural variation' in a person's ancestors, mostly from Europe. Furthermore, ancestry today helps to trace more remote diversity in these traditional immigration countries (two/three generations ago and beyond) that might not be reflected in physical appearance (ethnicity/race), such as Irish, Greek, Arab, Lebanese, Armenian and so on. Finally, only Germany asks in a single question whether each of the respondent's parents migrated to Germany (after 1955), their country of origin and year of immigration. This question is related to the 'parent's country of birth' question previously discussed, but the fact that the emphasis is on a person's family migration history, regardless of the geography of birth, is perhaps closer to the idea of ancestry. This is a question most likely aimed at the *Aussiedler* or ethnic Germans who recovered German nationality and were spread all over Eastern Europe and Central Asia, more than two million of whom migrated to Germany after 1990 (Waldrauch, 2006).

Language

Several questions about a person's language/s have been recently introduced in many national censuses. This reflects two conflicting trends over the last decade-and-a-half. One is a move towards understanding population diversity and facilitating multicultural policies, while the other is a more recent *integrationist* set of policies that aim to promote proficiency in the 'mainstream language'. Six types of questions have been identified in this theme, all related to different ways of measuring the languages a person may speak, read or write at different stages in their lives. The most common formulation across countries is the 'language/s most frequently used at home' present in seven countries (35 per cent). There are four other questions that basically correspond to different formulations of a person's language/s, as listed in the language section of Table 8.2. For some multilingual countries, language diversity is clearly a major concern, with several of these questions simultaneously present in the census forms of Canada, Ireland and Switzerland. Finally, a question on 'proficiency in the charter language' (that is, the main official language of the country) is present in four Anglo-Saxon countries (20 per cent) – Australia, the US, the UK and Ireland – that all use the same four-level scale of proficiency. The introduction of these new language questions in the 2010 Census round also follows growing concern about the integration of minorities mentioned earlier.

Religion

The final theme is comprised by a single question, 'a person's religion'. Although formulated in many different ways, most national censuses seem to capture the same quality of a person's religious beliefs. They all only allow one choice of a 'person's current religion'. Subnational versions of census forms have not been analysed here, which, for example, in Northern Ireland ask the rather different question of a person's 'religious upbringing'. The religion question is present in 10 countries (50 per cent), demonstrating a renewed interest in religious diversity, most likely spurred on after September 11, 2001 and the subsequent world events and security concerns.

Results: clusters of countries

The analysis of the collective identity questions present in the 20 countries' census forms yields a set of interesting patterns and implications for the study of residential segregation. Just by analysing the presence or absence of the 27 questions across the six themes per country, a clear clustering of countries emerges.

A summary of such analysis is presented through the 'radar' graph in Figure 8.1. It shows, for each country, the percentage of questions available within each of the six major themes described in the previous section. Such a percentage is calculated out of the total number of questions identified for each theme and shown in Table 8.2 and

Figure 8.2, which are (number of questions in brackets): Residency and migration (6); Citizenship (4); Country of birth (4); Ethnicity, race and ancestry (6); Language (6); and Religion (1). To avoid cluttering, when no question is available for a theme (that is, 0 per cent), this is not shown on the graph (at the centre of radar). The graph is ordered clockwise following the same sequence of countries as shown in Table 8.2. These are ordered as follows: three pairs of Anglo-Saxon countries in Oceania, North America and the British Isles, followed by two similar EU countries (France and Spain), three German–

Figure 8.1: Percentage of questions per theme present in each country's Census

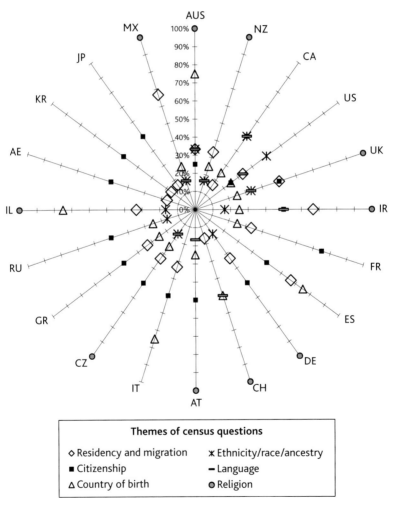

Note: see Table 8.2 to decipher country codes

speaking countries (Germany, Switzerland, Austria), four Southern and Eastern European countries (Italy, the Czech Republic, Greece, and Russia), two Middle Eastern countries (Israel and UAE), two East Asian countries (Korea and Japan), and finally, Mexico. This sequence and pairing of countries has a particular purpose. It attempts to group countries together according to the presence or absence of specific questions on collective identity as identified in their censuses. Figure 8.2 shows an alternative bar graph representation of the same data,

Figure 8.2: Number of Census questions and themes available per country

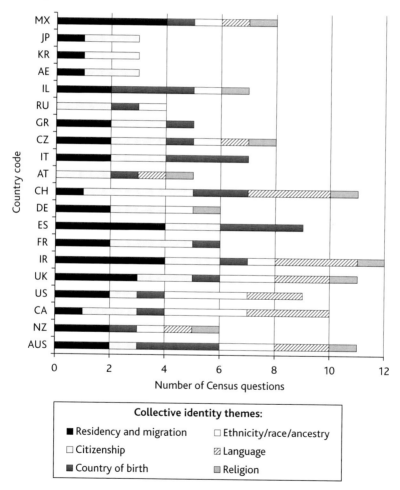

Note: Each horizontal bar represents a country (see Table 8.2 to decipher country codes). The number of Census questions available per country is broken down by each of the six themes of collective identity described in the text, and represented here by tinted/patterned codes.

displaying the absolute number of Census questions per theme and country. The rest of this section refers to both Figures 8.1 and 8.2.

The first group of six English-speaking countries of 'Anglo-Saxon stock' conform a clear cluster in the way they conceive and measure identity. They share a much higher presence of ethnicity, race and ancestry questions as well as the language questions, while featuring a small percentage of questions on citizenship. There is only a slight exception to the latter pattern in the UK and Ireland, which only adopted questions on citizenship in their 2011 Censuses. Within the Anglo-Saxon cluster, the differences are historical, with Australian, New Zealand and Canadian census forms being very similar in the formulation of most of these questions.

France and Spain form the second group. Although with very different types and number of questions, they both emphasise citizenship and avoid asking any questions on language, religion or ethnicity, race and ancestry. This resembles well the French tradition of avoiding collecting ethno-religious statistics (Simon, 2008), and distinguishing residents solely by citizenship and migration status.

The third group of countries is a large *jus sanguinis* cluster in Southern, Central and Eastern Europe. It is formed, by three subgroups: (a) German-speaking countries – Germany, Austria and Switzerland; (b) Italy, the Czech Republic and Greece; and (c) Russia and Israel. These eight countries seem to share a concern for immediate ancestry, probably deriving from a blood transmission conceptualisation of nationhood or a *jus sanguinis* tradition. All but Russia include a number of questions on the country of birth of the respondent's parents, or aspects of their migration history, and various questions on citizenship. However, they do not ask questions about ethnicity, race and ancestry, since these would be self-assigned, and they tend to avoid questions on immigration. Therefore, these are countries interested in distinguishing 'national stock' derived through one's parents and/or citizenship rights. Furthermore Italy, the Czech Republic, Greece and Israel share an interest in monitoring emigrants, with a question on current country of residence abroad, as does Ireland and Mexico. These are all traditional emigrant countries, except, perhaps, Israel, but which has a high rate of population churn.

The remaining four countries (UAE, Korea, Japan and Mexico) do not form a cluster but show how little information is typically available outside the main migration destination countries. Except for Mexico, they only ask some questions on residence/migration and citizenship, avoiding all the other themes.

Discussion

The evidence gathered from the international comparison presented in this chapter can be summarised in two types of general patterns. The 27 census questions on collective identity analysed here can be grouped into six broad themes or dimensions, that in turn somehow provide the key to group the 20 countries into four general clusters or 'traditions' on collective identity statistics. As stated above the themes are: (1) Residency and migration; (2) Citizenship; (3) Country of birth; (4) Ethnicity, race and ancestry; (5) Language; and (6) Religion, while the country clusters comprise: (a) Anglo-Saxon; (b) French–Spanish; (c) *jus sanguinis* Central, South and Eastern Europe; and (d) non–immigrant countries.

Such classification of these 20 countries into four clusters can be useful for the international comparability of residential segregation of minority groups. Comparisons *within* those clusters are likely to be much more meaningful than *between* clusters. This is not surprising since countries within a cluster share a series of common census questions and more importantly seem to present closer underlying conceptions of human difference. The scarce comparative segregation literature has tended to follow such clusterings, perhaps for convenience. As mentioned in the Review section, the few studies available (in English) all compare Anglo-Saxon countries.

However, more interesting is the empirical confirmation that collective identity can increasingly be measured in most countries using a much richer, multidimensional perspective on human difference and collective identity than is common in segregation studies. The fact that we can do so using the Censuses of Population means that such nuanced measurements are becoming available at the necessary finely grained geographical scale required for studies of residential segregation: the immediate neighbourhood. This proposition primarily consists in cross-tabulating, at such detailed scales, the different identity dimensions available in each country or cluster of countries, reflected in the census questions listed in Table 8.2. For example, in the Anglo-Saxon countries cluster one could be interested in creating cross-tabulations of respondents by ethnicity, world region of birth, length of stay, type of citizenship, religion and language spoken at home. In the *jus sanguinis* cluster of countries, one could perhaps cross-tabulate the respondent's world region of birth with that of each of their parents, the type and number of citizenships and if naturalised, as well as stated religion. Similar cross-tabulations could be created for the other clusters of countries.

For some specific countries, the multidimensionality in collective identity measurement offered by the 2010/11 round of censuses is perhaps the largest ever in history. Let's discuss in particular two sets of countries, the UK and Ireland (UK-IR), both sharing very similar census forms on identity questions, and Switzerland. In the UK-IR we can distinguish whether the respondent is a migrant and length of residence through the year of arrival question, and probable geographical origin through the country of birth and citizenship questions. We can also assess whether she was born in the UK-IR or in which other country, and if she has British/Irish citizenship together with any other passports. Furthermore, we also know her ethnic group, language spoken at home, English proficiency and religion. In the UK we are also told of her preferred 'national identity' allegiance, and whether she uses a second residence abroad for over 15 days, two more aspects that could be helpful in analysing 'transnational lives'. In Ireland we know whether she is a current emigrant and in which country, and whether she speaks Gaelic.

In Switzerland we are told whether a respondent is a migrant and for how long, but also whether his father and/or mother were born abroad. This ancestral data are very useful to build typologies of first and second-generation minorities. Moreover, the spectrum of information available on citizenship and language is outstanding. We know whether the person is a Swiss national by birth or naturalised, and if so, in which year he naturalised. We are also told of the respondent's mother language, important in a multilingual country, the language/s spoken at home, and those at work, and finally his religion. Again all of these variables are very useful to classify populations into alternative 'gradients of integration', rather than the common binary of 'us and them'.

All in all, each of these three countries offers 11-12 questions that have the potential to re-shape the way in which we conceive collective identity and 'otherness', of interest here when applied to segregation studies. Given that each question has a wide range of possible answers (that is, in those questions reporting a country there are around 220 answers, while for those allowing write-in free text answers there is a much larger number), the number of potential dimensions in which one can exploit these data is enormous. Such high dimensionality necessarily introduces more complexity in data analysis and interpretation, but the most plausible and useful cross-tabulations for each type of application are likely to prevail over time.

However, such cross-tabulations between these dimensions or variables are increasingly difficult to obtain for research purposes, because of risks of individual disclosure amidst a growing public distrust in government statistics. Nevertheless, some techniques do exist that would make such types of special cross-tabulations available for researchers. The most common of these is 'controlled access rooms', where approved researchers can submit queries cross-tabulating information at the individual level, but only retrieving aggregated outputs that are deemed 'safe' by appointed specialist staff (Chapters Nine and Fourteen, this volume, present analyses based on data accessed in such a way). This, for example, would allow a researcher to test different aggregations of the categories available within each question (for example, regional groupings of countries of birth), in order to increase the final people counts in the cross-tabulation cells. It is important that the researcher is allowed to create her or his own aggregations, rather than been given a set of pre-established groupings. However, the latter seems to be the rule, for example, in the UK sample of anonymised records (SARs) that only provides a reduced number of pre-set pan-ethnic groups for some cross-tabulations. This means that someone has decided for the researcher how to group the detailed ethnic groups into a construct of human difference that might not suit the aforementioned objective of challenging stereotypes in the study of segregation. The same goes, of course, for all the other variables identified in Table 8.2 when creating amalgamations of possible answers, such as ranges of years since immigration, world regions of birth or groupings of citizenship, languages, religions and so on.

Furthermore, the clearest obstacle for researchers studying residential segregation is accessing such cross-tabulations at a small area level. This proves impossible, however, in most cases, and hence most analyses using a bivariate conception of identity, such as religion and ethnicity, have to be performed at higher levels of geography, such as electoral wards in the UK (approximately 10,000 people) (Peach, 2006b). Nonetheless, this limitation could be substantially relaxed if the researcher is allowed to calculate segregation indices directly on the controlled access room, so that only those indices are released for the selected cross-tabulation of identity, but with no geographical detail below the city level, for example. This would require the possibility of running computer code in a common statistical package within the controlled room servers in order to calculate such indices with no access to small area data. This possibility has already been demonstrated by Shuttleworth et al (2011) at Queen's University Belfast for the Northern Ireland Census. This team developed code to compute segregation indices based on customised aggregations of individual level, which was subsequently run in-house by the census agency.

Finally, although the focus of this chapter has been on census data from the last 5/10 years, we acknowledge that the future of the traditional censuses is widely questioned worldwide. Over the next decades, current decennial practices of whole population, face-to-face and door-by-door, enumeration are very likely to be replaced in most countries by complex person-level longitudinal linkage of administrative data, continuous population registers and complementary surveys. Most of the issues discussed in this chapter will undoubtedly apply to such future datasets. In fact, these methods based on a myriad of individual-level micro-data offer new possibilities to be very creative in the way in which such human groupings are classified, as we have already seen in various Nordic and Northwestern European countries that use longitudinal population registers (Musterd and Deurloo, 1997; Edin et al, 2003; Guiraudon et al, 2005; Andersson, 2007). However, these practices of micro-data linking have already generated tensions with the government, on the one hand, with conservative proponents of small government and a hands-off approach to personal information, and on the other, with certain libertarians who see these statistical practices as reifying identities (Skerry, 2000; Kertzer and Arel, 2002).

Conclusion

The evidence presented here indicates that we can somehow start to grasp Vertovec's (2007) concept of super-diversity and apply it to cross-national segregation studies. The review of 20 countries' statistical practices accomplished here demonstrate that there are a large and growing number of dimensions of collective identity available in official statistics, which in fact provide a unique resource 'to re-imagine [...] how we map others' (Wright and Ellis, 2006, p 286) and to 'move beyond simplistic interpretations that set racially coded "others" apart' (Phillips, 2007) in the analysis of segregation. This chapter has analysed 27 questions on identity present in the censuses of 20 countries between 2000 and 2011. These have been grouped into six themes and proposed four clusters of countries that should benefit intra-cluster international comparisons of segregation. This comparative exercise has revealed interesting issues and discrepancies about the way in which 'otherness' is officially constructed in each country (Morning, 2008), and its relationship to power and identity (Anderson, 1991; Kertzer and Arel, 2002). Different statistical practices in different countries seem to be reflecting their particular socio-political and historical developments, sometimes making explicit each society's fears and concerns (Lesser, 1999; Christopher, 2002; Simpson, 2002; Aspinall, 2003a; Mezey, 2003). This is indeed a promising avenue for future multidisciplinary joint research in residential segregation from both empirical and theoretical social science perspectives, as we have justified elsewhere (Mateos et al, 2009; Mateos, 2011). National statistical agencies need to provide the necessary means for analysing flexible cross-tabulations between various identity dimensions, that is, through a 'controlled access room' type of setting in order to calculate segregation indices at small area level (Shuttleworth et al, 2011). Only in this way will researchers be able to construct innovative classifications of human groups out of a complex 'otherness continuum', with the ultimate aim to test entrenched stereotypes in residential segregation debates.

We hope to have made a contribution to this debate and sparked interest in overcoming traditional ethno-racial stereotypes by creating new, internationally comparable, alternative groupings of people for the study of residential segregation.

References

American Sociological Association (2006) *Statement of the American Sociological Association on the importance of collecting data and doing social scientific research on race*, Washington, DC: American Sociological Association.

Anderson, B. (1991) *Imagined communities: reflections on the origins and spread of nationalism*, London: Verso.

Andersson, R. (2007) *Residential segregation and the integration of immigrants: Britain, the Netherlands and Sweden*. Discussion Paper no SP IV 2007-602, Berlin: Social Science Research Center Berlin.

Arbaci, S. (2007) 'Ethnic segregation, housing systems and welfare regimes in Europe', *European Journal of Housing Policy*, vol 7, no 4, pp 401-33.

Aspinall, P.J. (2003a) 'The conceptualisation and categorisation of mixed race/ethnicity in Britain and North America: identity options and the role of the state', *International Journal of Intercultural Relations*, vol 27, no 3, pp 269-96.

Aspinall, P.J. (2003b) 'Who is Asian? A category that remains contested in population and health research', *Journal of Public Health Medicine*, vol 25, no 2, pp 91-7.

Aspinall, P.J. (2009) 'The future of ethnicity classifications', *Journal of Ethnic and Migration Studies*, vol 35, no 9, pp 1417-35.

Bhopal, R. (2004) 'Glossary of terms relating to ethnicity and race: for reflection and debate', *Journal of Epidemiology & Community Health*, vol 58, no 6, pp 441-5.

Brubaker, R. (2004) *Ethnicity without groups*, London: Harvard University Press.

Bulmer, M. (1996) 'The ethnic group question in the 1991 Census of Population', in D. Coleman and J. Salt (eds) *Ethnicity in the 1991 Census. Volume 1. Demographic characteristics of the ethnic minority populations*, London: Office for National Statistics, HMSO, pp xi-xxix.

Choi, K.H. and Sakamoto, A. (2005) *Who is Hispanic? Hispanic ethnic identity among African Americans, Asian Americans, and Whites*, Austin, TX: Population Research Centre, University of Texas at Austin.

Christopher, A.J. (2002) '"To define the indefinable": population classification and the census in South Africa', *Area*, vol 34, no 4, pp 401-8.

Connolly, H. and Gardener, D. (2005) *Who are the 'other' ethnic groups?*, Newport: Office for National Statistics.

Edin, P.-A., Fredriksson, P. and Aslund, O. (2003) 'Ethnic enclaves and the economic success of immigrants – evidence from a natural experiment', *The Quarterly Journal of Economics*, vol 118, no 1, pp 329-57.

Glebe, G. and O'Loughlin, J. (1987) *Foreign minorities in continental European cities*, Stuttgart: Steiner Verlag.

Guibernau, M. and Rex, J. (1997) *The ethnicity reader: nationalism, multiculturalism and migration*, Cambridge: Polity Press.

Guiraudon, V., Phalet, K. and Ter Wal, J. (2005) 'Monitoring ethnic minorities in the Netherlands', *International Social Science Journal*, vol 57, no 183, pp 75-87.

Iceland, J. (2004) 'Beyond black and white: metropolitan residential segregation in multi-ethnic America', *Social Science Research*, vol 33, no 2, pp 248-71.

Iceland, J., Mateos, P. and Sharp, G. (2011) 'Ethnic residential segregation by nativity in Great Britain and the United States', *Journal of Urban Affairs*, vol 33, no 4, pp 409-29.

Johnston, R.J., Forrest, J. and Poulsen, M. (2002) 'The ethnic geography of EthniCities: the "American model" and residential concentration in London', *Ethnicities*, vol 2, no 2, pp 209-35.

Johnston, R.J., Poulsen, M. and Forrest, J. (2007) 'The geography of ethnic residential segregation: a comparative study of five countries', *Annals of the Association of American Geographers*, vol 97, no 4, pp 713-38.

Kertzer, D.I. and Arel, D. (2002) *Census and identity: the politics of race, ethnicity, and language in national censuses*, Cambridge: Cambridge University Press.

Krupka, D. (2007) 'Are big cities more segregated? Neighbourhood scale and the measurement of segregation', *Urban Studies*, vol 44, no 1, pp 187-97.

Lesser, J. (1999) *Negotiating national identity: immigrants, minorities, and the struggle for ethnicity in Brazil*, Durham, NC: Duke University Press.

Logan, J.R. and Zhang, W. (2004) 'Identifying ethnic neighborhoods with census data', in M.F. Goodchild and D.G. Janelle (eds) *Spatially integrated social science: examples in best practice*, New York: Oxford University Press, pp 113-26.

Mateos, P. (2011) 'Uncertain segregation: the challenge of defining and measuring ethnicity in segregation studies', *Built Environment*, vol 37, no 2, pp 226-38.

Mateos, P., Singleton, A. and Longley, P.A. (2009) 'Uncertainty in the analysis of ethnicity classifications: issues of extent and aggregation of ethnic groups', *Journal of Ethnic and Migration Studies*, vol 35, no 9, pp 1437-60.

Mezey, N. (2003) 'Erasure and recognition: the census race and the national imagination', *Northwestern University Law Review*, vol 97, pp 1701-68.

Morning, A. (2008) 'Ethnic classification in global perspective: a cross-national survey of the 2000 Census round', *Population Research and Policy Review*, vol 27, no 2, pp 239-72.

Musterd, S. (2005) 'Social and ethnic segregation in Europe: levels, causes, and effects', *Journal of Urban Affairs*, vol 27, no 3, pp 331-48.

Musterd, S. and Deurloo, R. (1997) 'Ethnic segregation and the role of public housing in Amsterdam', *Tijdschrift voor economische en sociale geografie*, vol 88, no 2, pp 158-68.

Musterd, S. and Ostendorf, W. (1998) *Urban segregation and the welfare state: inequality and exclusion in western cities*, London: Routledge.

Nobles, M. (2000) *Shades of citizenship: race and the census in modern politics*, Stanford, CA: Stanford University Press.

OECD (Organisation for Economic Co-operation and Development) (2011) *Naturalisation: a passport for the better integration of immigrants?*, Geneva: OECD Publishing.

Peach, C. (1996) 'Does Britain have ghettos?', *Transactions of the Institute of British Geographers*, vol 21, pp 216-35.

Peach, C. (1998) 'South Asian and Caribbean ethnic minority housing choice in Britain', *Urban Studies*, vol 35, no 10, pp 1657-80.

Peach, C. (1999) 'London and New York: contrasts in British and American models of segregation', *International Journal of Population Geography*, vol 5, pp 319-47.

Peach, C. (2000) 'Discovering white ethnicity and parachuting plurality', *Progress in Human Geography*, vol 24, no 4, pp 620-6.

Peach, C. (2005) 'The mosaic versus the melting pot: Canada and the USA', *Scottish Geographical Journal*, vol 121, no 1, pp 3-27.

Peach, C. (2006a) 'Islam, ethnicity and South Asian religions in the London 2001 census', *Transactions of the Institute of British Geographers*, vol 31, no 3, pp 353-70.

Peach, C. (2006b) 'Muslims in the 2001 Census of England and Wales: gender and economic disadvantage', *Ethnic and Racial Studies*, vol 29, no 4, pp 629-55.

Pfeffer, N.D.A. (1998) 'Theories in health care and research: theories of race, ethnicity and culture', *British Medical Journal*, vol 317, pp 1381-4.

Phillips, D. (1998) 'Black minority ethnic concentration, segregation and dispersal in Britain', *Urban Studies*, vol 35, no 10, pp 1681-703.

Phillips, D. (2007) 'Ethnic and racial segregation: a critical perspective', *Geography Compass*, vol 1, no 5, pp 1138-59.

Senior, P.A. and Bhopal, R. (1994) 'Ethnicity as a variable in epidemiological research', *British Medical Journal*, vol 309, pp 327-30.

Shuttleworth, I.G., Lloyd, C.D. and Martin, D.J. (2011) 'Exploring the implications of changing census output geographies for the measurement of residential segregation: the example of Northern Ireland 1991-2001', *Journal of the Royal Statistical Society: Series A*, vol 174, no 1, pp 1-16.

Simon, P. (2008) 'The choice of ignorance: the debate on ethnic and racial statistics in France', *French Politics, Culture & Society*, vol 26, no 1, pp 7-31.

Simon, P. (2012) 'Collecting ethnic statistics in Europe: a review', *Ethnic and Racial Studies*, vol 35, no 8, 1366-91.

Simpson, L. (2002) '"Race" statistics: theirs and ours', *Radical Statistics*, vol 79, pp 1-19.

Simpson, L. (2004) 'Statistics of racial segregation: measures, evidence and policy', *Urban Studies*, vol 41, no 3, pp 661-81.

Simpson, L. (2007) 'Ghettos of the mind: the empirical behaviour of indices of segregation and diversity', *Journal of the Royal Statistical Society: Series A*, vol 170, no 2, pp 405-24.

Skerry, P. (2000) *Counting on the census? Race, group identity, and the evasion of politics*, Washington, DC: Brookings Institution Press.

UN (United Nations) (2008) *Principles and recommendations for population and housing censuses*, New York: Department of Economic and Social Affairs, Statistics Division, Series M, nr 67/Rev 2.

UN (2011) 2010 World Population and Housing Census Programme, United Nations Statistics Division, Demographic and Social Statistics (http://unstats.un.org/unsd/demographic/sources/census/censusdates.htm).

Vertovec, S. (2007) 'Super-diversity and its implications', *Ethnic and Racial Studies*, vol 30, no 6, pp 1024-54.

Voas, D. and Williamson, P. (2000) 'The scale of dissimilarity: concepts, measurement and an application to socio-economic variation across England and Wales', *Transactions of the Institute of British Geographers*, vol 25, no 4, pp 465-81.

Waldrauch, H. (2006) 'Statistics on acquisition and loss of nationality in EU15 member states', in R. Bauböck, E. Ersbøll, K. Groenendijk and H. Waldrauch (eds) *Acquisition and loss of nationality. Volume 1: Comparative analyses. Policies and trends in 15 European countries*, Amsterdam: Amsterdam University Press, pp 269-315.

Wright, R. and Ellis, M. (2006) 'Mapping others', *Progress in Human Geography*, vol 30, no 3, pp 285-8.

PROCESSES

Perspectives on social segregation and migration: spatial scale, mixing and place

Ian G. Shuttleworth, Myles Gould and Paul Barr

Introduction

Most studies of residential segregation in the UK and the US are based on census data. This means that they are cross-sectional as they capture geographical population patterns as they exist at one moment in time when the census is taken. Despite this, there is a long-standing awareness that segregation is shaped by changes in population distributions through time and the process is dynamic. One major early contribution that considered these dynamic aspects was Schelling (1969, 1971) who developed, with regard to Black/White segregation in US cities, a conceptual model that demonstrated how small differences in individual residential preferences with regard to the colour of neighbours could lead to large group/place differences. Schelling's approach was influential and was later elaborated on (for an example, see Clark, 1991) to show how these small differences should lead to complete segregation once a 'tipping point' had been passed – as a stable equilibrium with population mixing was unlikely. Yet, despite these expectations, in some situations segregation patterns/levels do not always move inexorably towards complete segregation as might be expected. Although high levels of residential segregation remain a persistent and intractable feature of US cities (South and Crowder, 1998), there is rarely complete segregation across an urban area, and in some cases segregation levels remain relatively stable through time. Clark (1992), using the example of the Los Angeles Metropolitan Area, argues that this stability can arise through a combination of short distance housing moves and residential preferences. He goes on to suggest that urban structure(s) and morphology also play a part in maintaining stable levels of segregation through time.

This chapter aims to explore and to elaborate on the points made by Clark (1992) with special reference to geographical population patterns and the distances moved when people change address. It uses, as an example, Northern Ireland (NI), albeit one with a very different political and historical context. This is another place where residential segregation has remained stable over a long period of time – since 1991 – despite many reports to the contrary. The chapter considers how this might be so despite differences in residential preferences between Catholics and Protestants that might be assumed to lead to complete segregation once a 'tipping point' is past. It explores the limits to the Schelling Model and offers some comments on its general applicability beyond the historical and geographical circumstances in which it was developed. In approaching this task, the chapter draws together a wide range of evidence of residential segregation in NI (derived using different statistical measures). It starts, in the next section, by pulling together previously published evidence based on a consideration of political discourses and aggregated data secondary sources. This is then followed by original analyses undertaken by the authors. Taken together this outlines and charts how residential segregation has changed through time. Special attention is given to the temporal discontinuities where processes of political unrest and other factors have driven relatively sudden increases in segregation (as, for example, the period of 'The Troubles' at their height between 1971 and 1991) and have then been followed by much longer periods of stability (as between 1991 and 2001). The succeeding section then focuses more closely on migration – as measured by changes in address – and its impact (or lack of it) on residential segregation patterns after 2001 using micro-data contained in the Northern Ireland Longitudinal Study (NILS; see also Chapter Fourteen, this volume). It is argued that 'normal' short-distance migration and mobility patterns are insufficient to radically change population patterns during a relatively stable and quiescent phase in NI's history, and that dramatic political events and policy responses, with associated exceptional population movements/changes, would be required for major increases/decreases in segregation. The chapter concludes by calling for evidence of underlying population geographies – that, as Clark (1992) suggested, reflect how population spatial structures can limit the possibilities for *either* greater (re)mixing *or* greater segregation in certain circumstances.

A review of residential segregation in Northern Ireland: 1921-2001

NI is characterised by residential segregation on the basis of ethnicity or nationality (Boal, 2002; see also Chapters Four and Fourteen, this volume). The existence of NI as a political entity has itself been questioned since its establishment by partition in the early 1920s on the basis of demography (with Catholic and Protestant population numbers being used as a marker of Irish Nationalist and British Nationalist [Unionist] strength respectively) (Anderson, 2008). The years after partition have seen continual political disagreements about whether NI should remain within the UK or (re)join the Irish state. Besides these external dimensions, there are also disputes about the internal political arrangements of NI. Sometimes, politics has been characterised by communal violence, most notably in The Troubles from 1969-98, but at other times political violence has been less overt and less apparent. This ethno-national background to residential segregation (the very terms used to describe the conflict are themselves contested) puts the situation in NI on a different footing to that seen in the US and the rest of the UK. Black/White or other racial dimensions to segregation in cities here are not characterised by, for example, national conflict about the existence of the state, and violence largely has a different rationale to NI where nationality (and its religious marker) is the key dimension. NI is different to 'normal' societies but it would, however, be unwise to stress its uniqueness as in its national dimensions the conflict in NI finds historical echoes in Eastern Europe, where legacies of colonial settlement and complex population patterns led to similar situations where the existence, shape and extent of nation states was contested.

It is not easy to create an authoritative first-hand quantitative account of segregation throughout NI since partition because of the lack of consistent small-area data before 1971. Therefore, to understand developments before this date it is necessary to piece together evidence from a variety of secondary sources. Many of these are concerned solely with the City of Belfast. Belfast is significant because it is the largest urban area in NI and within it is concentrated the large fraction of the NI population. Changes here thus play a large part in shaping the NI story, but it has to be acknowledged that, although important, it is not the full picture. Nevertheless, given these caveats, it is possible to identify two major features between 1921 and 1971 that can then be measured quantitatively for the period 1971-2001, as they continue to be present today. The first of these features is the segregation 'ratchet effect' identified by Smith and Chambers (1991). This describes upward leaps in segregation within a short time period followed by stability (or moderate decrease) in the intervening periods (Boal, 2002). Boal (2002, p 691) explains these 'upward jolts' in terms of 'ethno-national earthquakes'. The first of these occurred in the early 1920s when the island of Ireland was partitioned and there was rioting and political discord between Catholics (who were/are usually Irish nationalists) and Protestants (who were/are normally in favour of union with the UK). This period saw Catholics leaving areas where they had lived near Protestants – leading to increased segregation as a 'result of the bitter rioting that occurred in the city between 1920 and 1923' (Jones, 1960, p 195) – and also exiting workplaces (such as the shipyards) where they had worked with Protestants (Jones, 1960, p 195). Jones (1960) and Boal (2002) note that the easing of this segregation after 1926 was slight and, despite apparently positive attitudes towards cross-community relationships (Rose, 1971), a second 'ethno-national earthquake' in 1969 with the advent of The Troubles resulted in another sharp increase in residential segregation with forced housing moves as a consequence of rioting, violence and intimidation (Bardon, 1992). Such violent episodes that puncture periods of calm and equilibrium appear to be a long-term feature of Belfast's history. Jones (1960), for example, notes that violence associated with parades in the late 1850s and the various Irish Home Rule Crises of the late 19th century led to increased separation between Catholics and Protestants.

The second major theme, which is a consequence of the first, is that segregation has increased over a very long time scale. Jones (1960), for example, notes the increasing concentration and separation of Catholics and Protestants in Belfast in the 19th and early 20th centuries. Boal (1982) observes that at the street level some 60 per cent of the city's inhabitants were living in highly-segregated streets (90 per cent or more one community or the other) in 1901, with this rising to 67 per cent by the late 1960s, and by the end of the 20th century to 77 per cent. It is worth noting, however, that Gregory et al (2012), albeit using different spatial units, find little evidence of segregation increasing in NI as a whole over the 20th century. This means that it is necessary to be cautious in interpreting the various sources of information. Outside Belfast, Poole and Doherty (1996) report higher levels of segregation in 1991 compared to 1971. This evidence all taken together generally suggests increasing segregation through time. It also accords well with popular and media understandings of NI society which have tended to emphasise the growing separation of the two communities, a process that is seen as something that is inexorable and ongoing (Anderson and Shuttleworth, 1998). This discourse echoes some of the features of the British debate about ethnicity that some have argued has shaky empirical foundations (Finney and Simpson, 2009). Shuttleworth and Lloyd (2009) demonstrate using census data for 1km grid squares that residential segregation increased between 1971 and 2001, but they qualify statements about its ongoing and inexorable nature by pointing out that all the increase was restricted to the period between 1971 and 1991, and that the 1990s saw stability – or even slight declines – in segregation. This, of course, accords well with the picture of the long-term evolution of segregation sketched by Boal (2002) where large increases – in this case sometime between 1971 and 1991 – ratchet segregation up only for it to remain steady or slowly decline afterwards. There are other published insights, based on the analysis of NI grid square census data, into how the geographical structure of the population changed between 1971 and 2001. These reaffirm the 1971-2001 increase in segregation and its timing noted by others. Lloyd (2012) shows that the NI population became more geographically clustered by religion between 1971 and 2001, with the majority of this increase occurring in the two decades after 1971. This supports the finding of Shuttleworth and Lloyd (2009) that the Catholic population across NI became more concentrated in areas where it was already a majority over the same time periods. Furthermore, Lloyd (2010) shows that the degree of positive spatial autocorrelation by religion is greater than that observed for socioeconomic variables. In other words, the population geography of NI has become more structured through time by community background, with the growth of larger more homogeneous blocks, and it is structured far more strongly by religion than socioeconomic factors – religion remains the primary geographical divide. These are significant observations to which reference is made later.

It is probably useful at this stage to reflect more broadly on NI society so as to place it and its experience of segregation in context. A good place to start is the way in which religion was used to label the two communities in conflict during the NI Troubles. Although the division is not primarily about religion, it is used as the main marker and a shortcut to the wider and more important socio-political issues of national affiliation and identity (Macourt, 1995). Boal (2002) describes Belfast as a 'frontier city' that experienced 'ethno-national conflict'. This description is apt for NI society as a whole since it exists on the frontier between the failed state building projects of British and Irish nationalism in this part of the island of Ireland. This means that the issue at stake in NI is the existence and the nature and form of the state (Anderson, 2008). For much of the post-partition period the Protestant/Unionist population was politically, socially and demographically dominant (Patterson, 2006) and also in the 'majority' [sic] in this part of the island of Ireland. This period could be described by the term 'ethnocracy' (Yiftachel, 2006), where the state is not run for the benefit of the whole people – the *demos* – but for one ethnic group – the *ethnos*. This description is particularly suitable for NI during the period from partition until the suspension of Stormont Parliament in 1972 given the evidence for systematic bias against Catholic/Irish Nationalists (Smith and Chambers, 1991; Patterson, 2006). However, the introduction of Direct Rule from Westminster and the institutions established by the 1998 Good Friday Agreement weakened ethnocracy, and it is less plausible now to claim NI as an ethnocratic unit.

This discussion is important insofar as segregation occurs, and is interpreted, in a very different way in NI to that seen in Britain, the US and most parts of Europe. In these places, although there is segregation by race and ethnicity, it is not understood as part of a demographic trial of strength over the future of the state; although cities like Bradford in Britain and Detroit in the US are segregated, segregation is not associated with national divisions. NI has more in common with other societies that have grown along the fault lines at the edges of empire and should be placed along a continuum of politically and ethnically divided cities including the Balkans and most parts of the Middle East (Anderson, 2008). Residential segregation in NI can be about residential choice and preferences – 'normal' processes that happen in the Birminghams on both sides of the Atlantic for instance[1] – but in NI this normality is punctuated by extreme political events and these always remain in the background. However, as discussed later, while politics are important in understanding and interpreting segregation and its discontinuities, there is a tendency to over-emphasise this factor in NI, and the leap in segregation between 1971 and 1991 can also be partly attributed to *both* global socioeconomic forces that apply elsewhere, as well as NI-specific factors such as conflict and political violence.

Migration and segregation patterns after 2001

The redistribution of population through internal migration is implicit in popular interpretations of NI segregation with many accounts emphasising forced housing moves during times of political tension (see, for example, Boal, 2002). Furthermore, selective migration, and its impacts on segregation, has been an explicit subject for empirical investigation in a variety of other contexts outside NI (Crowder et al, 2006; Finney and Simpson, 2009; Bailey, 2012). It is also, via housing preferences, implicated in conceptual perspectives as the Schelling Model. Despite this, there have been no previous large-scale quantitative analyses in NI that have attempted to deal with the dynamics of segregation with special reference to migration. This section therefore summarises some recent work on migration and its relationship to segregation in NI. Before doing so, it is worthwhile briefly reflecting a little further on population dynamics and how they might relate to segregation. In this wider framework, of course, migration is only one of three elements that drive changes in the geography of population and thus segregation. The other two elements are births and deaths. Their net balance leads to differences between places in either natural increases or decreases and *in situ* population changes. Migration acts to modify local changes arising from these processes. A comprehensive understanding of population dynamics and migration would therefore, as Finney and Simpson (2009) argue, require information on natural increase as well as migration.

The data

In NI births and deaths are not registered by community background, so the analysis is forced to concentrate on migration but this, as can be seen above, is a theme of wider interest. The data that are used are from the NILS and are based on the Northern Ireland Health Care Registration (NIHCR) system, covering approximately 28 per cent of the NI population (Johnston et al, 2010). These data are matched to records from the 2001 NI Census of Population and to subsequent registration data such as births, deaths and address changes. This means that it is possible to examine residential location and address changes at an individual level after 2001 with the full range of 2001 Census information as explanatory variables and as context. The analysis focuses on migration – as measured by address change – of people aged over 25 but less than 75 in 2001. This group was selected because they have largely completed the moves associated with entry to and exit from higher education but have not yet fully entered the 'very old' age group where residential moves are associated with entrance to care homes. No information is available on residential preferences or perceptions – the tables and charts presented in this chapter show what people actually do rather than what they say. More sophisticated analyses will become possible when data from other censuses (for example, 2011) are linked to the NILS and by the expansion of the work to account for natural increase/decrease.

The community background variable is the focus for analysis. This was chosen as it gives fuller coverage than the voluntary religion question. In summary, the community background variable includes responses from the voluntary religion question (when this is given), information on religion individuals were brought up in (if the voluntary religion question is not answered), and imputed information when no response at all is given. The categories in the community background question are simply Catholic, Protestant, None and Other. Most attention is given to Catholics and Protestants as they form the majority of responses. Address data from the NIHCR were provided in regular six-monthly downloads from the Business Service Organisation (BSO) with 'migration' defined as a change of address. The analysis starts in April 2001, just after the census, and its end date was April 2007 with the first update of BSO information for that year. This is a significant point when it is remembered that a large and measurable increase in residential segregation took place over the 20 years between 1971 and 1991 (Shuttleworth and Lloyd, 2009) since the analytical period is about a third of this time, and so should yield measurable change either way. The finest NILS geography that is easily accessible by researchers is the super output area (SOA). SOAs are an aggregation of output areas (OAs) and are used as a census output geography in the UK. In NI, they have a mean population of 1,894 and range from a minimum population of 1,300 to a maximum of 2,956. They vary in spatial extent because population numbers are one of the main criteria in their design. In sparsely populated rural areas they therefore tend to cover greater areas than in densely populated urban locations. Spatial data on deprivation and community background were linked via SOA of residence to NILS members.

Does community background influence how people move in NI?

On average just over 30 per cent of people changed address at least once, and there appears to be little difference in the propensity to move between individual Catholics and Protestants. However, this masks important socio–spatial differences that Figures 9.1 and 9.2 help uncover. Figure 9.1 shows the proportion of NILS members who made at least one move (that is, an address change) between 2001 and 2007, and summarises the 'type of move' made *simultaneously* with respect to the community background of both individuals (that is, the

Figure 9.1: Proportions of NILS study members making at least one address change 2001-07 by individual community background and decile of community background of origin (1=least Catholic/most Protestant, 10=most Catholic/least Protestant)

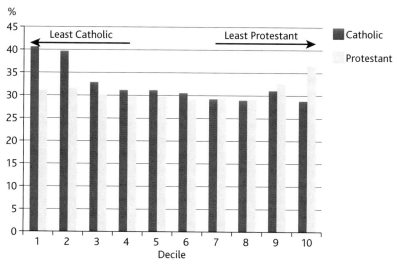

different bars representing Catholics and Protestants) and the nature of the SOA origins (that is, the different deciles summarising relative Catholic/Protestant population mix of areas – with the concentration of Catholics increasing from left to right). For example, looking at the first two bars for the first decile in Figure 9.1, approximately 40 per cent of Catholics compared to approximately 30 per cent of Protestants made at least one residential move during the study period for this first decile of SOA origin areas that contain the most Catholic/least Protestant populations.

Figure 9.2 shows the 'directionality' of first moves by individual community background in terms of the community background composition of 2001 SOA of origin. It is very clear from the chart that there are 'ceiling' and 'basement' effects that influence the interpretation of this chart – if someone lived in an SOA that was 95 per cent Catholic in 2001, for instance, then there is less chance for them to move to an SOA that is much more Catholic than if they started in an SOA that was only 20 per cent Catholic. Likewise, if the origin SOA is only 5 per cent Catholic, there is much less chance of moving to an even less Catholic SOA than if the starting point had been, say, 70 per cent Catholic. Each bar in the figure shows the mean difference in community background (percentage Catholic) between the origin SOA and the destination SOA for migrants with

Figure 9.2: Mean percentage difference between the community background of origin and of destination by individual community background and community background of decile of origin (1=least Catholic/most Protestant, 10=most Catholic/least Protestant)

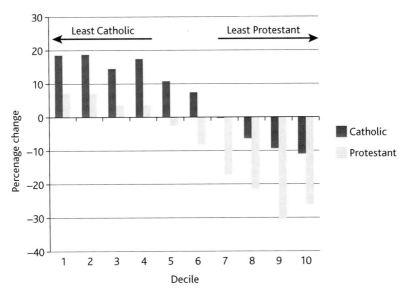

Note: Positive percentage changes are moves to more Catholic areas and negative to less Catholic areas

bars above the *x*-axis (for example, positive moves) being to more Catholic areas and negative bars (for example, below the *x*-axis) moves to less Catholic (or more Protestant) SOAs. What is noteworthy is that there are differences between Catholic and Protestants in their mean moves to more/less Catholic SOAs. For example, Catholics whose moves start in decile 1 move, on average, to SOAs that are 18 percentage points more Catholic than their starting SOA. Protestants starting in decile 1, on the other hand, move to SOAs, on average, that are 7 percentage points more Catholic. At the other end of the scale, for moves starting in decile 10, the mean move for Protestants is to SOAs that are 25 percentage points less Catholic as compared with 11 percentage points for Catholics.

Both Figures 9.1 and 9.2 show that in the most polarised kinds of SOA origins – those that are least Catholic/most Protestant (deciles 1 and 2 which are 20 per cent or less Catholic) and those that are at least 80 per cent Catholic (deciles 9 and 10 which are the most Catholic/ least Protestant) – there is a greater propensity to change address for minority populations and that there are more general differences in the propensity to move to more/less Catholic SOAs by individual community background. Other multivariate analysis that has been undertaken (but not presented here) shows that these differentials in the propensity to move, and in the direction of moves by individual community background, are robust and persist once other individual social and demographic factors such as age, occupation, gender, housing tenure and education are taken into account.

Do these findings matter?

These observations could be construed as being surprising. After all, much overt political violence has ceased in NI after the paramilitary ceasefires of the 1990s, and it might therefore be expected that sectarian factors would also cease to be important, or at least become less salient in all walks of life. There is evidence, for example, that NI did not become more segregated in the 1990s (Shuttleworth and Lloyd, 2009), and that the labour market has become less segregated through time as employment equality legislation and employment growth has taken effect (Osborne and Shuttleworth, 2004; McNair, 2006). However, despite survey evidence that the NI population is in favour of mixed housing, the actual directionality and types of move made by people when they changed address in the recent past would suggest that sectarian factors are still important in the housing market. The findings described here using NILS data are in tune with the comments of O'Dowd and Komarova (2009). However, O'Dowd and Komarova (2009) strike a note of caution, stating that sectarian divisions have existed for a long time, and their form of reproduction has proved to be remarkably durable despite large-scale political and economic changes. Taken at face value, the results presented so far in this chapter might indicate that residential segregation has persisted or continued to increase into the very recent past. The question therefore arises as to whether migration has recently acted to increase residential segregation through population redistribution. If so, a further question arises as to whether this contradicts other previously published evidence that segregation was approximately the same in 2001 as it was in 1991 (Shuttleworth and Lloyd, 2009), or whether it has even started to increase after 2001 after being stable during 1991–2001. The answer to these questions is that internal migration has had a very small impact on residential segregation and, if anything, has led to slightly less residential segregation between 2001 and 2007. Differential propensities to move, and the directionality of moves, by individual community background, as seen in Figures 9.1 and 9.2, have been outweighed by other factors.

Shuttleworth et al (2012) calculated a simple global value for the index of dissimilarity (D) in 2001 (the start of the study period) and also again in 2007 (the end of the study period). The index took account of the changed population distribution after migration – as measured by the first move/change of address. Findings showed very little change with differences only observable to two decimal places. It might be argued that if subsequent address changes had been included, there would be a larger impact, but this seems doubtful. Over this six-year study period most people did not change address, and of those who moved, the majority made only one move, and those who made two or moves were in the minority. Moreover, there is no reason to expect that second or other subsequent address changes would differ markedly from first moves. Naturally, a longer study period would give migration greater opportunity to take effect,[2] but it should be noted that six years is an appreciable fraction of the 20 years that saw a large increase in segregation between 1971 and 1991. The result that migration has only a weak effect on geographical segregation patterns should not, perhaps, be surprising. Catney (2008) came to the same conclusion for NI, while Bailey and Livingston (2008) and Bailey (2012) found the same thing with respect to social segregation in Scotland, and we have already noted above the persistence of racial segregation in US cities.

The empirical evidence therefore suggests that there can be group differences in migration destinations (and presumably the residential preferences that can be inferred from these differentials) but that, *contra* the Schelling Model, these do not lead inevitably to complete segregation as there seems to be the possibility of reaching a stable equilibrium with only very minor changes over a time period of more than half a decade despite these differentials. This, of course, raises other questions. How is this possible? And how and why did residential segregation in NI increase comparatively rapidly in the past? The next section offers possible answers to these questions, framing them in terms of a 'segregation ratchet' in NI and its 'periodisation' in terms of rapid step-changes followed by relative stability (as suggested by Boal, 2002).

Interpreting the relationship between internal migration and residential segregation in NI

The suggested answers to the questions outlined above draw on evidence about the geographical structure of population in NI and its associated nature of internal migration. They provide some insights into the NI experience and give some indications as to why internal migration has a weak impact on segregation, not only in NI, but also elsewhere. The key to this, as noted by Bailey (2012), is that most migratory flows are 'sideways moves' – in the Scottish case to and from areas with roughly the same social characteristics. In NI they are mainly sideways with regard to community background, as shown in Figure 9.3. This shows the percentage distribution of internal migratory moves (as measured by change of address) according to the decile of origin ranked by community background or multiple deprivation measure (MDM). The *x*-axis is scaled so moves from the least Catholic (and least deprived) decile – decile 1 – to the most deprived (or most Catholic decile) – decile 10 – are given a score of +9 and the reverse move a score of –9. There are very few large moves between deciles either upwards or downwards, and the most striking feature of Figure 9.3 is that most moves start and end in the same decile – there is almost zero change. The great majority of moves start and end in similar places – the change in decile lies between –2 and +2. Not unsurprisingly, there are very few moves from the least

Figure 9.3: Percentage distribution of moves through community and deprivation space (changes in decile)

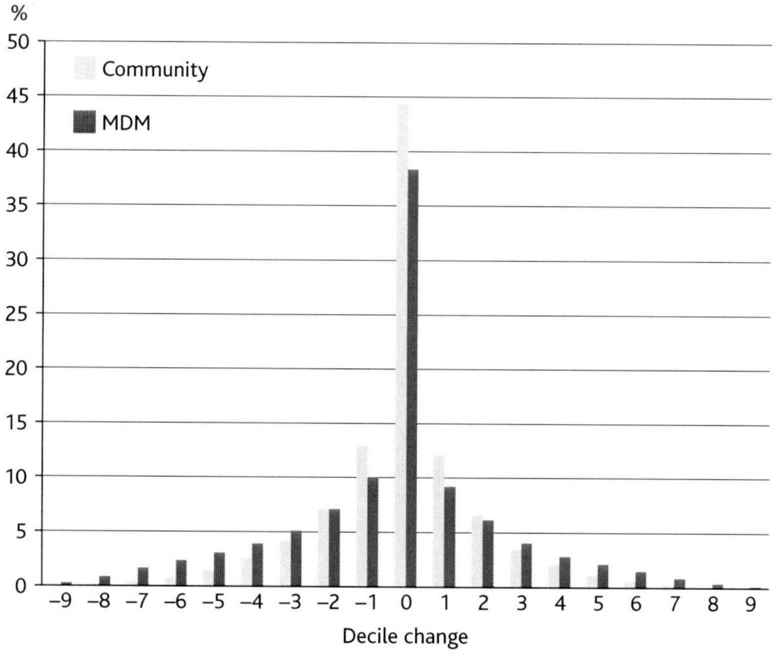

Source: Shuttleworth et al, submitted

Catholic SOAs to the most Catholic SOAs (a change of +9), and a similarly small number move from the most Catholic SOAs to the least Catholic (a change of −9).

One major reason for this is that most internal moves in NI, as elsewhere, are only over very short distances. As Table 9.1 shows, the majority of internal moves in the UK occur over distances of 9km or less. NI does not have the lowest mobility in the UK – in the North East and the North West English regions, the majority of moves happen over distances of 2km or less. However, on average, the NI population moves over much shorter distances than those in the South of England. Much internal migration therefore 'churns' populations between areas of similar type/composition in all regions, but especially so in NI. Migrants who move to areas that are very different from where they originated are, in fact, few and far between. Everything else being equal, then, internal migration would not be expected to sort the population radically, and this partly explains why six years of migration did not markedly change segregation levels in NI.

However, short distance moves are not sufficient on their own to explain why migration has only a small impact on segregation levels. Here, the comments made by Clark (1992) about population structure and the starting conditions in which residential preferences operate are elaborated on in Maps 9.1 and 9.2 that deal, respectively, with community background and social deprivation. They show SOA

Table 9.1: Distance moved by people changing address within the UK in the year prior to the 2001 Census: by UK country and Government Office Region of usual residence in 2001

Region	0-2km	3-9km	10-49km	50-199km	>200km	Total
North East	53.80	20.80	11.30	6.50	7.50	100
North West	50.40	22.80	12.20	8.00	6.60	100
Northern Ireland	47.20	21.10	17.10	6.70	8.00	100
Yorkshire & the Humber	46.80	22.60	13.40	10.20	7.00	100
Scotland	46.70	19.80	15.70	8.70	9.10	100
Wales	46.20	20.20	14.80	11.10	7.70	100
West Midlands	45.00	24.70	14.30	12.60	3.40	100
United Kingdom	*43.00*	*22.70*	*15.80*	*11.80*	*6.70*	*100*
East Midland	42.90	21.20	15.40	16.20	4.20	100
South West	38.90	20.50	14.40	15.60	10.60	100
London	38.00	30.20	16.90	9.00	6.00	100
South East	37.50	21.30	18.80	16.10	6.40	100
East	37.30	21.00	21.90	14.30	5.40	100

Source: Champion (2005)

Map 9.1: Community background for SOAs – Moran's I clusters

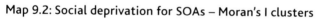

Map 9.2: Social deprivation for SOAs – Moran's I clusters

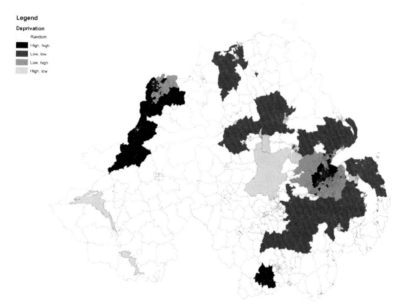

clusters derived from spatial autocorrelation patterns (Anselin, 1995; see Chapter Two, this volume, for a discussion about such measures) – high, high clusters occur where an SOA which has a high percentage of Catholics (or a high level of social deprivation) is surrounded by SOAs with similar high values. Low, low clusters are where SOAs with low values are surrounded by similar SOAs with low scores; high, low where high-value SOAs are surrounded by others with lower scores; low, high where low-scoring SOAs have neighbours with higher values. Comparing the two maps, it is apparent that NI is more strongly patterned by community background than multiple social deprivation, there are fewer random areas where clusters are not statistically significant and far more SOAs that belong to the high, high and low, low clusters (that is to say, SOAs with either high Catholic percentages surrounded by SOAs with a similar community background composition or else low Catholic percentages with neighbouring SOAs with the same background). This observation is corroborated in work by Lloyd (2010, 2012) who also notes that community background is more strongly positively spatially autocorrelated than other social or economic variables, and that it became more structured by religion between 1971 and 2001. Exploring the geography of the NI population over the same time period using variograms, Lloyd observed that the magnitude of variability between places grew by religion, meaning that polarisation increased, especially at local scales. An important point that emerged was that the dominant spatial scale (or support) over which community background varied on average across NI as a whole was around 5km. This means that on average the NI population falls into blocks that are 'clumps' of around 5km by community background. This average, of course, conceals some variation between places – urban areas such as Belfast, for instance, are more spatially fragmented, whereas other more rural areas are more homogeneous over greater distances. However, the 5km figure is used for clarity, although the argument will be stronger in some places than others.

Since the median distance moved by internal migrants in NI is 3.58km, many moves will start and end by default in the same type of SOA in which they started in terms of the community background composition of that area. When there is no change in decile by community background, the median distance moved is only 1.70km, presumably because many moves start and end in the same or immediately neighbouring SOA. So, for many internal migrants, the circumstances in which they find themselves (that is, the underlying neighbourhood population geography) mean that 'typical' moves of the same distance seen elsewhere in the UK will not usually cross boundaries with respect to community background in NI. This clearly limits the potential (re)sorting effects of migration on the population in terms of community background, and also downplays the role of individual residential preferences and choice in some places since it would take a deliberate decision to move a greater distance to make a transition to another SOA with a considerably different community background composition. Naturally, in some places, particularly those with a more fragmented population structure by community background, individual preferences would be more relevant, but even in Belfast, a move of 1.70km would be enough to remain in a homogeneous population 'clump' in some parts of the city, most notably the Catholic West and the Protestant East. Looking back at Figure 9.3 and comparing social mobility (measured by MDM) and community background, there is some evidence that people in NI are slightly more mobile through social deprivation space than community background space (for example, more likely to move from the most deprived decile to the least deprived than from the most Catholic to the least Catholic). This might be attributed to greater residential fears (and preferences) associated with community background, but part of the explanation may also be that NI is more geographically structured by community background than socioeconomic variables. If the underlying population geography of NI is less structured (for example, more fragmented and falls into smaller 'clumps') by social deprivation than community background, then everything else being equal, internal migratory moves of the same distance should cross social deprivation space more easily.

This is illustrated by Figure 9.4 taking the hypothetical case of Jedis (a 'religious' [sic] category that some respondents chose to identify with in the 2001 UK Census) and Wookiees and their social class. Short distance moves such as (b) and (c) can easily cross from high to low social class areas while remaining within larger community clumps of Jedi or Wookiee simply because they are larger. It takes a much longer distance move – such as (a) – to move from a Jedi to a Wookiee neighbourhood, but these moves are uncommon since most moves are

Figure 9.4: Geographical population structures and types of internal migratory move

High class Jedi	High class Jedi	Low class Jedi	High class Jedi	Low class Jedi	High class Jedi	Low class Wookiee	Low class Wookiee	High class Wookiee	Low class Wookiee

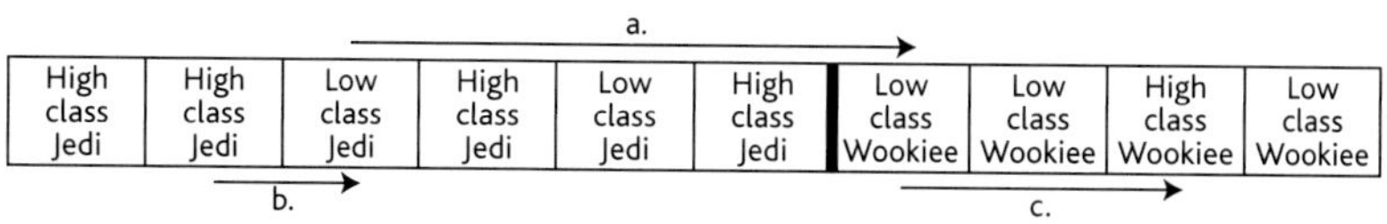

of short distances like (b) and (c). Of course, this is an oversimplification, but the principle is clear – population agglomerations that are larger than the average internal migratory distance mean that migration is unlikely to have a large (re)sorting impact and lead either to greater residential segregation or to its lessening. In the NI case, the past ratcheting up of residential segregation, and the average large spatial scale of population agglomerations by community background, mean that everyday migration processes – in which NI is similar to other UK regions with respect to distances moved – are unlikely to restructure the population. Quite simply, it will take considerably more people to move far greater distances than was evident in the 2001–07 period before segregation levels change, and this can also be demonstrated empirically. Other multilevel modelling undertaken by the authors (not presented here) of the directionality of moves through community background space (either to more Catholic SOAs or to less Catholic SOAs) has shown that individual-level community background was a major predictor of the SOA to which the move was made. However, the explanatory variables that measured population structure – the clusters shown in Map 9.1 – were also important with those, for example, resident in the low, high cluster (a Protestant SOA with more Catholic neighbours) more likely to move to a more Catholic place than those in the random reference group. Likewise, those in the high, low category were significantly more likely to make a move that made a transition to a more Protestant (that is, less Catholic) SOA. Besides residential choice and individual preferences, the spatial structure of population therefore also matters.

The underlying population structure of NI is a partial explanation of why migration has not changed residential segregation levels. There are, however, other factors that are also significant. First, only around a third of the population changed address at least once during the six-year study period. The comparative immobility of the NI population where the majority of people remain *in situ* is likely to be important. Second, gross migration flows partly cancel themselves out – although Catholics are more likely to move to more Catholic SOAs, some Protestants also make similar moves – and there are return flows where Catholics move to less Catholic SOAs. Third, the moves of minority groups originating from areas where the 'Other' group is a large majority (for example, Protestants in highly Catholic SOAs), while appearing striking, are numerically unimportant given the existing segregated starting point where these minorities are very small. They are insufficient to shift population patterns enough to cause either greater segregation or to reduce it substantially. The question therefore arises as to how segregation increased so markedly in the past in NI between 1971 and 1991.

It is impossible to give a clear and certain answer to this question given the lack of data on the components of small area population change by community background. It is obvious, however, that the NI population system was faster-changing and more dynamic in the 1970s and 1980s than it was from 1991 onwards. Many popular and academic discourses, as seen above, have emphasised fear and political violence in the early 1970s as the primary drivers of changing segregation – largely through forced housing moves. However, *in situ* natural increase and decrease cannot be discounted (Finney and Simpson, 2009), along with migration, but the size of their effect relative to migration remains uncertain. Despite these caveats, internal migration was undoubtedly important at some level. Given this, it is tempting to speculate about its causes, although again, there can be no certainty in this.

It would be rash to dismiss the significance of forced moves and political violence as a causative factor leading to a more dynamic population system in NI during the 1970s and 1980s as there is a lot of documentation on the large-scale population shifts caused by the onset of The Troubles in NI in 1969. However, these are unlikely to be sufficient enough on their own to move enough people long enough distances to lead to greater segregation between 1971 and 1991, as observed by Shuttleworth and Lloyd (2009). Another factor that might lead to population changes of a sufficient magnitude is counter-urbanisation. Industrial cities such as Belfast in Europe and in North America, for instance, lost population in the absence of political violence during the 1970s and the 1980s, and during this same time period, Belfast saw the loss of population from its urban core from 1971 onwards to the suburban fringe and beyond (Power and Shuttleworth, 1997). The population of Greater Belfast fell by almost 200,000 – a large number relative to the NI total – between 1971 and 1991. This can be attributed to political violence experienced in central Belfast and also the shared experiences that Belfast had with other industrial cities over the same period. These include the loss of manufacturing jobs through de-industrialisation (Martin, 1988) as well as urban clearance in the inner city with the building of public and private housing estates at the edge of the city (Hall, 2002). It may well be, therefore, that the latest upward leap of the segregation ratchet in NI between 1971 and 1991 can be attributed to political violence, and also the large-scale population changes associated with the decline of Belfast as an industrial city. What is more certain is segregation between 1991 and 2001 was stable in NI as a whole and also Belfast, and post-2001 there is no sign of migration leading to population changes of a sufficient magnitude to alter segregation levels.

Conclusion

In showing the effects of migration on population patterns during this latest quiescent stage of the 'segregation ratchet', this chapter echoes the findings of Bailey (2012), that internal migration has only a weak redistributive effect. The implications of this are, that in the absence of dramatic policy interventions in the housing market to increase residential mobility and the distance over which people move when they change address, greater residential mixing is highly unlikely given 'normal' migration distances, as seen in other UK regions. This suggests that policies encouraging a shared and integrated society would be better directed at the labour market where people commute longer distances and in which there is already evidence of less segregation (Osborne and Shuttleworth, 2004). More imaginatively, the domains of education, particularly at school level, and leisure may be more effective routes to more social integration than housing. This chapter also suggests that the periods when segregation moves sharply upwards in NI, such as between 1971 and 1991, are very different to when the population system remains in equilibrium. *In situ* population increase/decrease may be significant, but a large part might be played in these dynamic periods by large-scale migration, although this could occur for a variety of reasons.

More broadly, the chapter also shows the circumstances in which segregation remains stable despite differing residential preferences and the expectations of the Schelling Model. Building on the hints of Clark (1992), segregation levels can remain relatively stable when most internal migratory moves are less than the agglomerations (or 'clumps') into which the population falls according to the variable of concern. In this case, the tendency of the NI population to fall into 'clumps' of 5km and the median migration distance of 3.58km mean that many internal migratory changes of address start and end in the same type of place. Residential preferences can be important where the population is more finely spatially grained and also when people change address over longer distances. But in this latter case, there are comparatively few long-distance internal migrants, and numerically they can do little to alter population distributions to lead to larger changes in segregation. The Schelling Model is therefore a useful conceptual device which forefronts individual residential choices. These factors cannot be discounted, but in communally divided societies like NI, 'dramatic' political and economic events are probably more significant in the long run. In the short term, as we have seen, limitations on the potential for internal migration to redistribute the population are imposed by underlying geographical population structures that are themselves the product of history. In this case, the starting point for analysis is everything, and in the historical and geographical context of NI as it was in 2001, there are clear limitations on the redistributive potential of internal migration.

Notes

[1] Alabama, US and West Midlands, UK.

[2] It will be possible to extend the analysis in the future with subsequent linking of the 2011 Census with the NILS and also perhaps with the addition of 1991 Census data to evaluate population change over a much longer duration.

References

Anderson, J. (2008) *From empires to ethno-national conflicts: a framework for studying 'divided cities' in 'contested states' – Part I*, Divided Cities/Contested States Working Paper 1. Belfast: Queen's University Belfast.

Anderson, J. and Shuttleworth, I. (1998) 'Sectarian demography, territoriality and policy in Northern Ireland', *Political Geography*, vol 17, pp 187-208.

Anselin, L. (1995) 'Local indicators of spatial association – LISA', *Geographical Analysis*, vol 27, pp 93-115.

Bailey, N. (2012) 'How spatial segregation changes over time: sorting out the sorting processes', *Environment and Planning A*, vol 44, pp 705-22.

Bailey, N. and Livingstone, M. (2008) 'Selective migration and neighbourhood deprivation: evidence from 2001 Census migration data for England and Scotland', *Urban Studies*, vol 45, pp 943-61.

Bardon, J. (1992) *A history of Ulster*, Belfast: Blackstaff.

Boal, F.W. (1982) 'Segregating and mixing: space and residence in Belfast. Integration and division, in F.W.J. Boal, N.H. Douglas and J.A.E. Orr (eds) *Integration & division: Geographical perspectives on the Northern Ireland problem*. London: Academic Press, pp 249-80.

Boal, F. (2002) 'Belfast: walls within', *Political Geography*, vol 21, pp 687-94.

Catney, G. (2008) 'Internal migration, community background and residential segregation in Northern Ireland', Belfast: Unpublished PhD thesis, Belfast: School of Geography, Archaeology and Palaeoecology, Queen's University Belfast.

Champion, A. (2005) *Focus on people and migration: population movement within the UK*, London: Office for National Statistics.

Clark, W. (1991) 'Residential preferences and neighborhood racial segregation: a test of the Schelling Model', *Demography*, vol 28, pp 1-19.

Clark, W. (1992) 'Residential preferences and residential choices in a multiethnic context', *Demography*, vol 29, pp 451-66.

Crowder, K., South, S. and Chavez, E. (2006) 'Wealth, race and inter-neighborhood migration', *American Sociological Review*, vol 71, pp 72-94.

Finney, N. and Simpson, L. (2009) *'Sleepwalking to segregation'? Challenging myths about race and migration*, Bristol: Policy Press.

Gregory, I., Cunningham, N., Lloyd, C. and Shuttleworth, I. (with Paul Ell) (2013) *Troubled geographies: a spatial history of religion and society in Ireland*, Bloomington, IN: Indiana University Press.

Hall, P. (2002) *Urban and regional planning* (4th edn), London: Routledge.

Johnston, F., Rosato, M. and Catney, G. (2010) *The Northern Ireland Longitudinal Study: an introduction*, NILS Working Paper 01, Belfast: NILS Research Support Unit.

Jones, E. (1960) *A social geography of Belfast*, Oxford: Oxford University Press.

Lloyd, C.D. (2010) 'Exploring population spatial concentrations in Northern Ireland by community background and other characteristics: an application of geographically weighted spatial statistics', *International Journal of Geographical Information Science*, vol 24, pp 1193-221.

Lloyd, C.D. (2012) 'Analysing the spatial scale of population concentrations by religion in Northern Ireland using global and local variograms', *International Journal of Geographical Information Science*, vol 26, pp 57-73.

McNair, D. (2006) 'Social and spatial segregation: ethno-national separation and mixing in Belfast', Unpublished PhD thesis, Belfast: School of Geography, Archaeology and Palaeoecology, Queen's University Belfast.

Macourt, M. (1995) 'Using census data: religion as a key variable in studies of Northern Ireland', *Environment and Planning A*, vol 27, pp 593-614.

Martin, R. (1988) 'The political economy of Britain's north–south divide', *Transactions of the Institute of British Geographers*, vol 13, pp 389-418.

O'Dowd, L. and Komarova, M. (2009) *Regeneration in a contested city: a Belfast case study*, Divided Cities/Contested States Working Paper 10. Belfast: Queen's University Belfast.

Osborne, R. and Shuttleworth, I.G. (eds) (2004) *Employment equality: a generation on*, Belfast: Blackstaff.

Patterson, H. (2006) 'In the land of King Canute: the influence of border unionism on Ulster Unionist politics, 1945-63', *Contemporary British History*, vol 20, pp 511-32.

Poole, M. and Doherty P. (1996) *Ethnic residential segregation in Northern Ireland*, Coleraine: University of Ulster.

Power, J. and Shuttleworth, I.G. (1997) 'Population, segregation and socio-economic change in the Belfast Urban Area (BUA) 1971-1991', *International Journal of Population Geography*, vol 3, pp 91-108.

Rose, R. (1971) *Governing without consensus: an Irish perspective*, London: Faber.

Schelling, T. (1969) 'Models of segregation', *The American Economic Review*, vol 59, pp 488-93.

Schelling, T. (1971) 'Dynamic models of segregation', *Journal of Mathematical Sociology*, vol 1, pp 143-86.

South, S.J., and Crowder, K. (1998) 'Leaving the 'hood: residential mobility between black, white and integrated neighbourhoods', *American Sociological Review*, vol 63, no 1, pp 17-26.

Shuttleworth, I.G. and Lloyd, C.D. (2009) 'Are Northern Ireland's communities dividing? Evidence from geographically consistent Census of Population data 1971-2001', *Environment and Planning A*, vol 41, pp 213-29.

Smith, D. and Chambers, G. (1991) *Inequality in Northern Ireland*, Oxford: Clarendon Press.

Yiftachel, O. (2006) *Ethnocracy: land and identity politics in Israel/Palestine*, Philadelphia, PA: University of Pennsylvania Press.

TEN

'Sleepwalking towards Johannesburg'? Local measures of ethnic segregation between London's secondary schools, 2003–08/09

Richard Harris

Introduction

Because segregation is the spatial outcome of spatial processes it makes sense to measure it in spatially intelligent ways. To that end, this chapter applies innovative methods of geocomputation (see also Chapters Three and Four, this volume), with particular emphasis on local indices of ethnic segregation to examine the claim that London's schools are 'sleepwalking towards Johannesburg'. It does so by looking at the flows of pupils from primary to secondary schools, using those flows to analyse the spatial patterns that form in the distribution of ethnic groups between schools, and to determine the geographies of competition between schools. Those geographies are codified in the form of a spatial weights matrix to compare any school with locally competing schools, giving a local index of segregation. The chapter finds that although there is 'segregation' in the sense that the distribution of the ethnic groups differs from randomness, from a nearest school assignment and with some substantial differences between geographically proximate schools, the evidence, focusing on the Black African and Bangladeshi groups, is not that ethnic segregation is increasing but that it is fluctuating with demographic changes over the period 2003 to 2008/09. The core argument advanced by the chapter is that segregation should be measured within its local context.

Context

> [Headline:] Headteacher expresses alarm over racial
> segregation in London schools: "It can't be a good thing
> for London to be sleepwalking towards Johannesburg,"
> conference warned […] with classrooms in some parts of
> the capital teaching almost exclusively black or Asian pupils.
> (Shepherd, 2011)

The headline and text above appeared in the guardian.co.uk with
another version featuring the following day in the print edition of it
and other British newspapers. The report is of a presentation given
by the vice-chair of the Headmasters' and Headmistresses' Conference
(HMC, an association of 250 fee-charging schools) in which he voiced
alarm at the way the capital was alleged to be dividing into ghettos
and "becoming a silo society".

The language mimics that used by Trevor Philips in a speech given
in September 2005 as chair of the Commission for Racial Equality in
which he stated that the country was "sleepwalking into New Orleans-
style racial segregation". Although Philips' speech was as much about
residential communities as schools *per se*, it was linked to the debate
about schools dividing on ethnocultural lines following the civil
disturbances in three English cities in 2001 (Cantle, 2001; Ouseley,
2001). Indeed, Philips is himself quoted as saying on a national radio
news programme in 2008 that "we all know schools are becoming
more segregated than the areas they are in" (quoted in Finney and
Simpson, 2009, p 106).

Analysis by Johnston et al (2006) revealed some of the divisions
within England. Although about 75 per cent of the Black population
were living in census neighbourhoods with a majority White
population (in 2001), only 42 per cent of Black primary school pupils
and 51 per cent of Black secondary pupils attended a school where
the same was true. Similarly, although about 60 per cent of the South
Asian population lived in White majority neighbourhoods, only
35 per cent of South Asian pupils were in White majority primary
schools, and 46 per cent in White majority secondary schools. Overall
the results of the study showed greater ethnic segregation in schools
than in neighbourhoods, more so for primary schools than secondary
schools, more so for Black and South Asian pupils, especially Pakistani
pupils, and generally more so in London than in other places.

Johnston et al's comparison of neighbourhoods with schools is
not exact, however. It is possible that the apparent post-residential

sorting of different ethnic groups into different schools is explained by demographic trends, leaving the 2001 Census population with a different composition to the school-age population. A study by Harris and Johnston (2008) offered a more direct analysis, contrasting the ethnic profile of primary school intakes with the ethnic profile of pupils living in areas from which the schools could plausibly recruit students but do not necessarily do so. It also compared the profile of each school with those of other schools recruiting locally from the same areas. In both London and Birmingham, the study found clear examples of where the intake of a school had an ethnic profile very different from the places from which the pupils were drawn, and from other nearby schools. For example, it found a community school in Birmingham where the percentage of Pakistani pupils was expected to be 38.1 per cent was actually 12.5 per cent, and where its most immediate 'competitor' was recruiting no Pakistani pupils at all. This and other examples gave evidence of what might be regarded as ethnic polarisation occurring locally between schools.

However, to find particular examples of apparent segregation (or polarisation) is not to show it is the norm or that it is increasing in the way the dynamic of 'sleepwalking' implies. In a cohort analysis of pupils entering English primary and secondary schools in each of the years 1997 to 2003, Johnston et al (2007, p 88) found, with one exception, that 'levels of segregation remain as they were – considerable but not growing', with any apparent increase in segregation explained by an increase in the non-White groups' share of the entry cohort in each local authority. The exception is relevant: Black Africans in London's secondary schools, one of the groups about which the headteacher quoted at the beginning of this chapter was concerned.

This chapter proceeds as follows. The next section provides a review of what is meant by segregation, taking as a starting point that it is 'the spatial separation of groups within a region' (Rey and Folch, 2011, p 432). Although a rather loose definition (as Rey and Folch acknowledge), it usefully emphasises that processes of segregation lead to spatial patterns of, say, ethnicity within a city. This leads to a number of measurement challenges, including how to apply segregation indices based on geographically meaningful comparisons of geographically meaningful places. In this, the modifiable areal unit problem (MAUP) will be recognised. However, the availability of suitable micro-data and a more geocomputational approach to analysis makes it less a problem, more an opportunity – the opportunity to dispense with measures of segregation over arbitrary regions and to move to an approach that better suits the context of the analysis.

Here that context is educational research, and whether ethnic segregation has grown in London's state-funded secondary schools from the academic year 2003/04 to the year 2008/09. The third section considers the geographies of ethnicity for those schools, giving focus to how the proportions of ethnic groups within schools differ from what would be expected under a nearest-school or random allocation of pupils. That there is a difference is due to a quasi-choice system operating in England without any requirement that a pupil must necessarily attend their nearest school, but with geographical constraints operating on the pupils'/parents' decision-making and on the final allocation of pupils to schools.

The fourth section considers how to form localised indices of segregation that incorporate local patterns of admissions into their measurement and also the local competition for pupils and places. Having applied those indices to educational micro-data for London, the chapter concludes by observing that there are some schools with an almost exclusively Black or Asian (or White) intake and also some stark local differences between schools. However, there is little evidence to suggest that these differences are growing over and above demographic changes.

Segregation, measurement and the modifiable area unit problem

Broadly defined, segregation is the separation of one or more groups of people that have, or are given, characteristics that they or others imbue with particular meaning (for instance, race, religion, gender, wealth, age, social class). The separations are place-bound, by residential neighbourhood or by institutions such as schools or workplaces. The implication is that people who might otherwise be coming together and interacting are not doing so, a situation that is generally assumed to create distrust, a lack of mutual empathy, misunderstanding and/or to hinder life chances and social mobility, therefore reinforcing factors that may have created segregation in the first instance.

This (presumed) lack of mixing could be directly enforced – most perniciously by apartheid – or indirectly due to complex and multiple processes of selection and exclusion, including the workings of the housing and employment markets, the geographies of public sector provision such as housing (see Chapter Eleven, this volume), the consequence of social attitudes and behaviours, the legacy of past or present immigration policies, and so forth.

Segregation can be voluntary, at least in part – an action that is, to some degree, self-determined, such as choosing a residential neighbourhood or school where one's own cultural group is more prevalent (Clark and Rivers, 2013) – or it could arise as a forced response to the lack of other options available. It is usually treated pejoratively, a stain on society that reveals prejudice or inequality of opportunity (Cantle, 2012), although living or being with one's peers or kin can also have positive supporting effects, strengthening a sense of identity, inspiring confidence (which might be important for learning; see Weekes–Bernard, 2007) and promoting civic engagement in one's locality (Merry, 2013).

Despite the complexity of what is actually meant by segregation and whether it is necessarily a bad thing (and if so, for whom, and why; see also Chapters Fourteen and Sixteen, this volume), what can be agreed is that segregation is a spatial and comparative phrase. The word means a person of a particular group is more likely to be found in one place more than other places. This spatial patterning can be described and conceived in various ways including as (un) evenness, exposure, concentration, centralisation and clustering (Massey and Denton, 1988); differing conceptions lead to different forms of measurement, different forms of segregation index (Johnston and Jones, 2010). However, in all cases there is an expectation that if places are compared, then differences in their composition will be found. To measure segregation is to measure the spatial separation of groups within (or between) regions (Rey and Folch, 2011).

As Rey and Folch note, all segregation measures are in principle spatial, although rarely in the spatial statistical sense that if the georeferences of the base units of measurement within some larger region were changed, then the index value would also change. Most indices ignore the specific locations of the schools or neighbourhoods being analysed (their particular spatial configuration), and simply consider them jointly within a wider region. As Duncan and Duncan (1955, p 215) observed more than a half-century ago: 'all of the segregation indexes have in common the assumption that segregation can be measured without regard to the spatial patterns of white and non-white residence in a city.'

For example, the index of dissimilarity, widely used in segregation research, is usually interpreted (but not entirely correctly; see Cortese et al, 1976) as the proportion of a minority group that would have to change their place of residence to make the distribution of the group even throughout the study region. What it does not consider is how far people would have to travel to achieve evenness. In response, modified distance-based indices (MDBIs) have been proposed that use linear programming and spatial optimisation procedures to determine the minimum total distance movement required (Jakubs, 1981; Morgan, 1983), or the minimum relocation effort (Waldorf, 1993).

However, applications of even an explicitly geographical index such as an MDBI have been limited to data tied to formal administrative geographies such as census tracts, the boundaries of which may or may not be congruous to those of segregation. As Wright observed 75 years ago: 'a simple area coefficient [...] depends in part upon the scale of the system of areal distributions employed and in part upon the manner in which the boundary lines between the several areal distributions happen to subdivide both the area (distributary) and the population (distribution)' (1937, p 196).

What Wright is describing is today referred to as the modifiable areal unit problem (MAUP). It has two components. The first is the zoning problem. Segregation is marked by a greater density/concentration/prevalence of a particular group in some places more than others, but any measure of it depends on where the boundaries of the places are drawn. Some have more obvious and fixed boundaries (school buildings, for example) but others have either indeterminate and subjective boundaries (communities) or somewhat arbitrary boundaries imposed for governmental or administrative purposes (for example, electoral wards and census tracts) (Martin, 1998).

The second is an issue of scale dependency. Any measure of density is, by definition, dependent on the area or population size of the place for which the measurement is made (either area or population will feature in the denominator for the density calculation). Using the index of dissimilarity referred to above, Wong (1997) shows how using large areal units will typically result in lower segregation scores than if smaller area units are adopted.

In the context of segregation indices, there is, in fact, a third problem. Having decided on the type and scale of the areal unit (for example, schools, census tracts or districts), a decision also needs to be made about which places should be compared with which others across or within a wider region. It is common for measures of segregation to sum across a region such as a local or regional authority area with the implicit assumption that these provide the units that best capture the spatial extent and boundaries of the segregation-forming processes and their resultant patterns. The assumption is often questionable precisely because the group of interest has an uneven geographical distribution, because it is segregated within the region.

Consider a minority group that is concentrated only in a small part of a local authority. Looking at differences across the entire region does not make a tremendous amount of sense: in most or many places there is little or no difference to detect, so those that do exist are averaged away or, at least, understated. But being too myopic doesn't help either.

A chess or checkers board provides an analogy. There is no segregation within a single square: the colour is uniformly distributed. It is only with the wider view when the boundary between two squares is considered that the separation of black from white is seen. If we pull back further and consider the whole board, we could conclude that the two colours are, in fact, very well mixed.

Rather than regarding the MAUP as a problem, it can also be conceived as an opportunity. The opportunity is not to fix the scale of the analysis in advance, but to calibrate it to the study and data at hand. This is important for educational research determining patterns and trends of social and ethnic segregation between schools. In the UK, such research has focused on a wave of education reforms from the Education Act 1988 onwards that have sought to promote school choice to parents, to provide attainment data and school inspection reports as information to guide that choice, to allow (within the limits of the national curriculum) greater subject or vocational specialisation, to encourage charitable, private sector and cross-school partnerships, and by linking funding to the number of pupils on the school roll, to introduce marketisation and competition within the sector.

To ask whether segregation is increasing or decreasing, perhaps as a result of the reforms (direct causation is exceptionally tricky to establish), empirical evidence is sought, most often at the local authority scale. The problem is that local authorities vary greatly in size: in area, population count and the number and types of school they contain. They are not standardised units designed for comparative studies. In addition, there is no particular reason to assume that their boundaries are congruous to the geographies over which schools 'compete' in the general sense of sharing admission spaces, the places from where they recruit pupils. To compare the composition of a school in one corner of an authority with another in an opposite corner some miles away makes little sense if they have little in common other than they happen to be within the same yet arbitrary boundaries of the local authority. An alternative comparison is of each school with its local competitors, including those across local authority borders, since parents are open to apply to those schools as well. Before considering this local perspective further, the scene is set by considering the spatial distribution of various ethnic groups across London's state-supported secondary schools.

Geographies of ethnicity for London's secondary schools

Figure 10.1 maps the prevalence of various ethnic groups in London's secondary schools according to their proportion of new entrants to the schools in September 2008 (the proportion of pupils entering Year 1 of those secondary schools in the academic year 2008/09).

The maps are cartograms where the size of the symbol is relative to the proportion of 'not White British' pupils per school, except in the map of White British pupils where it is relative to the proportion of that White British group. The re-projection of the original mapping units into a cartogram space combined with the use of random data swapping between nearby schools preserves the overall geography, but means the true values for specific schools should not be presumed from their locations on the maps. The class breaks are at the 50th, 75th, 90th and 95th percentiles of the distribution, a non-linear scale to highlight the schools where a group is most prevalent.

Looking at the geography of where the groups are distributed, Black African and Black Caribbean pupils constitute a higher proportion of the secondary schools' intakes in areas especially to the south/south east of the city centre (the centre being where the dotted lines intersect). Bangladeshi pupils are prevalent in schools towards the centre and east of the city. Indian and Pakistani pupils are found especially to the north east of the city and to the west/south west in areas close to Heathrow airport. White British pupils tend to be educated in outer London schools.

Table 10.1 gives the results of a Moran test comparing the proportion of the ethnic group in any one school with the average proportion in locally competing schools (defined below). The effect size (the Moran value, I) is sizable – greater than 0.5 – in all cases, and significant at a greater than 99.9 per cent confidence. It is greatest for the Bangladeshi

Table 10.1: Results of Moran tests comparing the proportion of the ethnic group in one school with the average proportion for locally competing schools

	I	p
Black African	0.541	<0.001
Black Caribbean	0.602	<0.001
Bangladeshi	0.803	<0.001
Indian	0.530	<0.001
Pakistani	0.649	<0.001
White	0.707	<0.001

Note: In each case there is significant positive spatial autocorrelation.

Figure 10.1: The proportion of the 2008 entry into London's state-supported secondary schools that are of each ethnic group

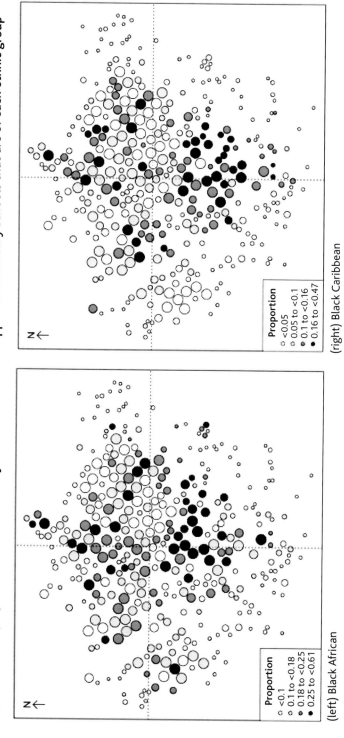

(left) Black African

(right) Black Caribbean

Note: The locations of the schools are indicative only

(continued)

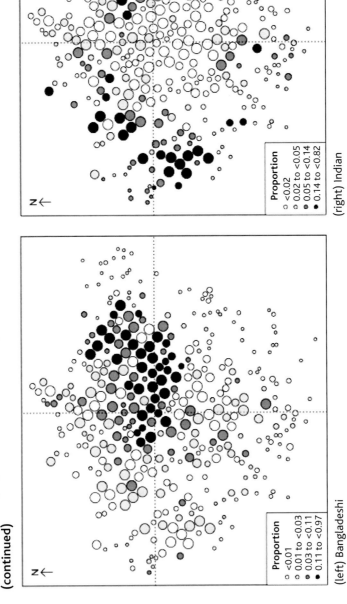

Figure 10.1: The proportion of the 2008 entry into London's state-supported secondary schools that are of each ethnic group (continued)

(left) Bangladeshi

Proportion
- <0.01
- 0.01 to <0.03
- 0.03 to <0.11
- 0.11 to <0.97

(right) Indian

Proportion
- <0.02
- 0.02 to <0.05
- 0.05 to <0.14
- 0.14 to <0.82

(continued)

Note: The locations of the schools are indicative only

Figure 10.1: The proportion of the 2008 entry into London's state-supported secondary schools that are of each ethnic group (continued)

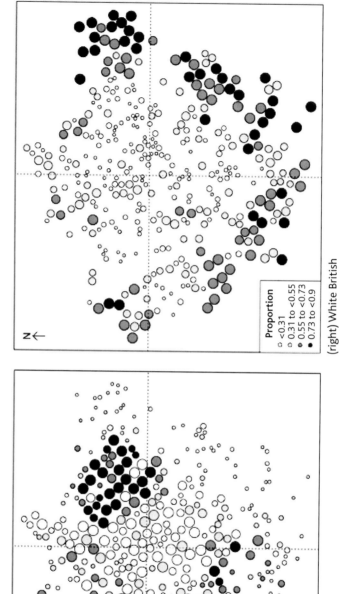

(left) Pakistani

(right) White British

Note: The locations of the schools are indicative only

group and least for the Indian group. This may hint at the Indian pupils being more likely to separate from pupils of other ethnicities when they make the transition to secondary schools, or it may simply mean they are in more mixed schools. In any case, the general trend is that schools recruiting a higher proportion of any one ethnic group tend to be competing with other schools that do likewise. The pattern is one of clustering with the meaning described by Massey and Denton (1988, p 293): 'the extent to which areal units inhabited by minority members adjoin one another, or cluster, in space.' It should be noted that neither this definition nor the Moran values of Table 10.1 mean that any one group is necessarily separated from the others. The clusters can and (in Figure 10.1) do overlap.

It is not surprising to find the patterns of spatial clustering; we may assume they reflect the residential geographies of where the various groups are located in London. However, they are not an inevitable outcome of those residential geographies because England does not operate a neighbourhood-based schooling system that would require pupils to attend a nearest or some other designated secondary school. Instead, the system is one of constrained choice. Schools are ranked by applicants in terms of preference, but in the event of there being more applications than places available, admissions criteria will be employed. Typically these give priority to children in public care and to those with siblings already in the school. The next consideration is usually geography, giving priority to those living closest, or at least close, to the school.

A study by Burgess et al (2006) estimated that only one-quarter of pupils in London attended their nearest school. Similarly, of the 2008 cohort of pupils in this study, a little more than one-quarter (27.7 per cent) attends the secondary school closest to their primary school. The average primary school is sending 90 per cent of its pupils to one of five secondary schools, with an interquartile range (IQR) from three to eight secondary schools. Reciprocally the average secondary school is receiving 90 per cent of its intake from approximately 27 primary schools, with an IQR from 17 to 36. The focus on the 90 per cent is to ignore the exceptional links between primary and secondary schools due to the one or very few pupils travelling long distances or appearing to because of a change of address. Even so, the statistics risk an exaggerated impression of the impact of choice on the transitions from primary to secondary school. There are three reasons for this.

First, the secondary school attended by a pupil is not necessarily a matter of their own or parental choice. In 2008, 36 per cent of pupils in London were not allocated to their first preference school, and 14 per cent did not receive any of their first three preferences. These values vary by local authority with the rate of unsuccessful first preference applications ranging from 9.9 per cent (Harrow, to the north west and edge of London) to 49.2 per cent (Wandsworth, near the centre, south of the River Thames). The percentage unsuccessful for any of their first three preferences ranges from 1.6 per cent (Harrow again) to 21.6 per cent (Hackney, to the north east of the centre). (The data are available from www.education.gov.uk/researchandstatistics)

Second, even if a pupil does not attend the most proximate school, it does not mean they are travelling far. There are supply-side and demand-side constraints limiting such travel. In regard to the former, the use of geographical-based admissions criteria will impose limits for over-subscribed schools. For the latter, there are practical and pragmatic reasons why a pupil is likely to prefer a reasonably close school, including transportation and wanting to stay with existing friendship groups. For the 2008 cohort of pupils, 56.1 per cent attend a secondary school that is within 2km (1.24 miles) of their primary school, and 82.5 per cent are within 4km. As Butler and Hamnett, (2010) and Hamnett and Butler (2011) observe, geography matters.

Third, the propensity to attend the nearest or a near secondary school varies by ethnic group, with 22.2 per cent of Black African and 18.3 per cent of Black Caribbean pupils attending the secondary school nearest to their primary, compared to 38.7, 32.7, 36.7 and 30.6 per cent of Bangladeshi, Indian, Pakistani and White British pupils, respectively. Whereas less than half (45.3 per cent) of Black Caribbean pupils attend a secondary school within 2km of their primary, over four-fifths (82.0 per cent) of Bangladeshi pupils do.

Table 10.2 summarises these differences by ethnic group in the transitions from primary to secondary school. It also shows the proportion of the group that are in voluntary-aided (VA) Church of England or Roman Catholic schools, and the proportion that are in academically selective schools. Such schools are of relevance because they are among the minority for which admissions criteria showing commitment to the faith group or testing academic ability are of greater importance than residential location, allowing them to recruit over greater distances. It is notable that 34.2 per cent of Black African pupils and 29.7 per cent of Black Caribbean pupils (the groups travelling furthest to school) attend a VA faith school, compared to 20.4 per cent of all pupils in the 2008 cohort. Almost double the proportion of Indian pupils attends an academically selective school compared to the proportion for all pupils in the cohort.

Table 10.2 also shows how unevenly each group is distributed among the schools relative to how uneven that distribution would be if:

(a) the pupils were randomly assigned to schools, respecting capacity constraints but not the logistical problems posed to the pupils were such a policy actually adopted; or

(b) all the pupils attended the nearest secondary school to their primary, ignoring any real-world capacity constraints.

Specifically, an unevenness ratio is calculated as,

$$U_k = \frac{n^{-1} \sum_{i=1}^{n} \left| p_{ik(\text{OBS})} - p_k \right|}{n_2^{-1} \sum_{i=1}^{n_2} \left| p_{ik(\text{EXP})} - p_k \right|} \quad n_2 \leq n \qquad (1)$$

where p_k is the proportion of all pupils that are of the ethnicity group (in the 2008 cohort), $p_{ik(\text{OBS})}$ is the observed proportion of the group in each of the n secondary schools and $p_{ik(\text{EXP})}$ is either (a) the expected

Table 10.2: Summary statistics describing the distances travelled by members of the various ethnic groups in the transition from primary to secondary schools in London, the proportion that attend VA or academically selective schools and whether the groups are more unevenly distributed than if all pupils (a) were randomly allocated to a secondary school, and (b) attended the nearest secondary school to their primary

	All	Black African	Black Caribbean	Bangladeshi	Indian	Pakistani	White	FSM
Proportion of all pupils	–	0.116	0.064	0.053	0.052	0.038	0.408	0.268
Proportion in nearest secondary school to primary	0.277	0.222	0.183	0.387	0.327	0.367	0.306	0.299
Proportion within 2km of primary school	0.561	0.503	0.453	0.820	0.698	0.754	0.568	0.628
Proportion within 4km of primary school	0.825	0.788	0.769	0.946	0.880	0.912	0.855	0.867
Proportion in a VA faith school	0.204	0.342	0.297	0.066	0.071	0.040	0.175	0.154
Proportion in a selective school	0.038	0.021	0.004	0.014	0.073	0.030	0.046	0.004
Unevenness ratio (a)	–	3.832	3.437	4.873	3.966	3.636	7.169	5.074
Unevenness ratio (b)	–	1.081	1.054	1.019	1.109	1.062	1.017	1.163

Note: FSM = free school meals.

proportion if the pupils are assigned randomly (without replacement), or (b) the expected proportion if every pupil attended the nearest primary. The random assignment uses a Monte Carlo approach averaging over 10,000 simulations. For scenario (a) n_2 could be written as n: it is simply the number of schools. For (b), however, n_2 is less than n because assigning pupils to the secondary school closest to their primary can leave some schools empty. In either case, a U_k value exceeding 1 indicates the unevenness is greater than under a random/nearest school assignment.

Table 10.2 shows that pupils are markedly more unevenly distributed by ethnicity group than if they were randomly distributed. This is not surprising given the clear patterns of positive spatial autocorrelation shown in Figure 10.1 and Table 10.1. Here the unevenness ratio can be interpreted as a measure of how concentrated any one group is in schools across the study region. Notably, it is White British pupils that are, in this sense, the most 'segregated'.

Using the second scenario, the Indian group are found to be the most unevenly distributed relative to if all pupils had attended the secondary school nearest to their primary. Care must be taken with the interpretation of this finding. It does not mean that the Indian group is the most self-segregating; it just means that if *all* pupils attended the nearest secondary, it would leave Indian pupils more evenly distributed across schools. In fact, we know that Indian pupils are more likely than many to be attending a near school so we should not conclude that the unevenness as it currently exists is a consequence of their decisions. It is a function of decisions made across the groups.

In any case, the increase in unevenness found for the Indian group is about 11 percentage points against the benchmark. The Black African group are found to be about 8 percentage points more unevenly distributed than if they attended the nearest secondary school. The Black Caribbean pupils are about 5 percentage points more unevenly distributed, the Bangladeshi pupils about 2, the Pakistani pupils 6, and the White British pupils 2. In short, the distributions of the groups across the schools do not differ that greatly from if the pupils were all choosing and allowed to attend the closest primary school to the secondary. This finding implies that the main cause of differences in the ethnic composition of secondary schools is 'simply a reflection of the clustered patterns of residence, which are largely a result of a sequence of labour shortages, immigration, natural growth and suburbanisation' (Finney and Simpson, 2009, p 105).

Moreover, and by way of comparison, Table 10.2 includes the same information for pupils eligible for free school meals (FSM, a crude but widely used measure of living in a low or lower-income household). None of the (non-White) groups is as unevenly distributed as the FSM-eligible group. A Department for Children, Schools and Family study (DCSF, 2008), cited by Finney and Simpson (2009), showed the same: that school sorting does occur over and above sorting by neighbourhoods but more so by income than by ethnicity, with the possibility that the two are confounded.

Measuring ethnic segregation within the local market for schools

The statistics presented in the previous section are global statistics, ones calculated for the entire study region. Earlier the case was made for measuring segregation in its local context. Here that means calculating localised measures of between-school segregation that compare locally competing secondary schools.

The idea links back to the Moran scores of Table 10.1. These were based on a comparison of each school with its average local competitor where locally competing secondary schools are defined as those that draw their intakes from one or more of the same primary schools (Harris, 2011). Specifically, competing schools are defined by a spatial weights matrix where the weight of competition between any two secondary schools (i and j) is based on the probability that a pupil selected at random from secondary school i also attended the same primary school as a pupil selected at random from secondary school j. This probability is calculated empirically. For example, if 40 of secondary school i's total intake of 120 pupils are from primary school A, and 20 of secondary school j's intake of 160 are also from primary A, the probability is $40/120 \times 20/160 = 0.042$. The probabilities are then scaled (row-standardised) so that the sum of the weights for any school equals one.

Having defined the weights in this way, a simple index of local difference (ID) is formulated as

$$ID_{ikt} = p_{ik} - \sum_{j=1}^{n-1} w_{ij} p_{jkt} \quad -1 \leq ID_{ikt} \leq 1, \quad j \neq i, 0 \leq w_{ij} \leq 1, \sum w_{ij} = 1 \tag{2}$$

The properties of this index are described in Harris (2012). The index ranges from −1 to 1, where a value above zero indicates that a school recruited a greater proportion of an ethnic group, k, at time t, than the (weighted) average proportion for locally competing schools. A value below zero indicates it recruited a smaller proportion.

The index is local in that a value is calculated for each secondary school in turn: the composition of each is compared to locally competing schools. Hence, a distribution of values is obtained. It is also spatial in the same sense that Wong (1993) means it: the index value depends on the location of the measurement unit vis-à-vis other units in the study region. (If the locations of the schools could be changed, the index values would also change because the flows between the schools would undoubtedly be altered, affecting the weights matrix and therefore the results.) However, whereas Wong is concerned with zoned data and with the shape and geometry of neighbouring zones, here the spatial weights matrix is configured by the flows of pupils from primary to secondary schools.

The left-side plots of Figure 10.2 show the distributions of the ID values as a sequence of box plots for each of six ethnic groups and for each of the cohorts entering the schools in London in the years from 2003 to 2008. To aid the comparison, the weights matrix is fixed to the year 2003 so, for example, the ID for 2008 is comparing schools that were competing in 2003, regardless of whether they still do. (If the weights matrix is not fixed, the comparison is complicated by changing patterns of admission which, although itself of interest, makes interpretation of the results harder.)

Taking Figure 10.2(a) as an example, we can see that in 2003 there is a school with an ID score of 0.3, meaning that its intake that year had 30 percentage points more Black African pupils than the weighted average percentage for other schools recruiting from the same primary schools. At the other extreme, there is a school with an intake that had 20 percentage points fewer Black African pupils than its average competitor (an ID score of −0.2).

Working down the left side of Figure 10.2, for any ethnic group it is possible to find schools that strongly differ from others locally: schools that have 70–80 percentage points more Indian pupils, for example. This is not trivial. Recall that the weights matrix defines locally competing schools as those that recruit from the same primary schools. The differences are therefore subsequent to any prior sorting by ethnicity between primary schools.

Clearly there are local differences between secondary schools. They are not all equally mixed and some contain a much greater proportion of an ethnic group than others that are nearby. There is also an asymmetry in the distribution of the ID values, with more schools with high positive than negative scores. As such, there is evidence of clustering. With the exception of the Pakistani group, in all years there are secondary schools that are predominantly or wholly filled

Figure 10.2: Showing (left) the distribution of the index values by year and by ethnic group and (right) standard deviation of the index values by year group

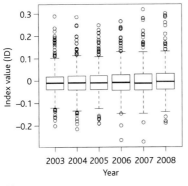
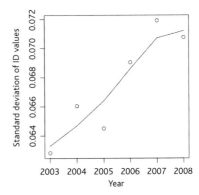

(a) Black African

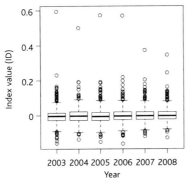
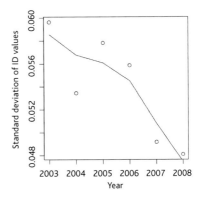

(b) Black Caribbean

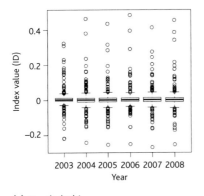
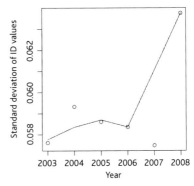

(c) Bangladeshi

(continued)

Figure 10.2: Showing (left) the distribution of the index values by year and by ethnic group and (right) standard deviation of the index values by year group (continued)

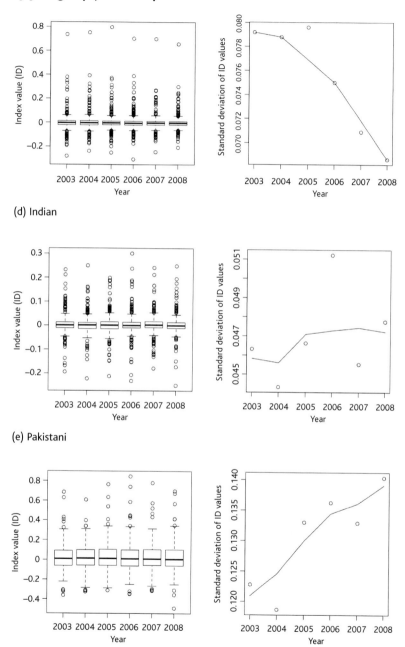

(d) Indian

(e) Pakistani

(f) White British

by pupils from a single ethnic group, especially so for the Bangladeshi and Indian groups.

As such, 'segregation' exists, but is it also increasing? If it is, then one way this could be revealed is by increasing differences in the ethnic composition of locally competing schools, and therefore an increase in the standard deviation of the ID scores for at least some ethnic groups over time. With the important caveat that six years is not a very long period over which to infer a trend, we may still observe an increasing standard deviation for the Black African and White British groups especially, and perhaps also for the Pakistani group. The apparent upward trend for the Bangladeshi group is solely dependent on one year. However, given the two groups the headteacher was reported to be concerned about were the Black Africans and Bangladeshis, both are now considered in more detail.

Taking the Black African group first, in addition to the trends in the index values, the proportion of Black Africans in the schools where the group are most prevalent also appears to be rising. However, the prevalence of the group among all school pupils is also rising. In 2003, 8.79 per cent of the school population (as recorded in the data) was Black African, 9.76 per cent in 2004, 10.1 per cent in 2005, 10.9 per cent in 2006, 11.6 per cent in 2007 and 11.6 per cent in 2008.

Comparing the cohorts for the years 2003 and 2008, a sizeable proportion of Black African pupils are found in an increasing number of London schools. In 2003, 4.45 per cent all of schools were 30 per cent or greater Black African but not majority Black African; by 2008 the corresponding value was 5.19 per cent. In 2003, 34.3 per cent of all schools were 10 per cent or greater but not majority Black African; by 2008 the value was 49.7 per cent. These changes suggest not a process of segregation but the opposite: of the group being more widely dispersed across schools.

The same is true of Bangladeshi pupils. Although the ID may again be increasing in the most extreme cases, as with Black African pupils the group forms a growing proportion of the school population (4.19 per cent in 2003, 4.23 per cent in 2004, 4.54 per cent in 2005, 4.80 per cent in 2006, 4.96 per cent in 2007 and 5.35 per cent in 2008), and has become more widely distributed across London's schools. In 2003, 6.81 per cent of all schools were 10 per cent or greater but less than 75 per cent Bangladeshi; by 2008 the value was 10.1 per cent.

The suspicion is that the apparent increases in the ID are driven by demographic changes. Asking if the rate of change is proportional to the group's increased prevalence among the local school population can test this. That is, if,

$$\frac{\text{ID}_{t2}}{\text{ID}_{t1}} = \frac{p^*_{t2}}{p^*_{t1}}$$

$$\Rightarrow \frac{\text{ID}_{t2}}{p^*_{t2}} = \frac{\text{ID}_{t1}}{p^*_{t1}}$$

(3)

where the local prevalence of the group, $p*$ can be estimated as proportional to its prevalence in a school and its average competitor. This logic gives rise to the index of clustering, which is

$$ICL_{ikt} = \frac{\text{ID}_{ikt}}{p_{ikt} + \sum_{j=1}^{n-1} w_{ij} p_{jkt}} - 1 \leq ICL_{ikt} \leq 1, j \neq i, 0 \leq w_{ij} \leq 1, \sum w_{ij} = 1$$

(4)

This index measures the local differences between schools relative to the local prevalence of the ethnic group. The index reaches its maximum when a school is completely filled by one ethnic group but none is found in that school's competitors (and its minimum when the opposite is true).

Figure 10.3 shows the distribution of the index values for the Black African and Bangladeshi groups. Once demographic effects are taken into account there really is no evidence to suggest that segregation has increased in the local markets for schools. To be sure, there are notable differences between the schools, but relative to the group's presence in the local population, these differences are not increasing. For the Black African group they may, in fact, be decreasing.

Conclusion

This chapter has used methods of geocomputational analysis to consider the extent to which segregation by ethnicity exists in London's secondary schools and, if it does, whether it is increasing. It presents a mixed picture. There are certainly differences between schools locally, and some of these differences are quite stark. However, we need to be wary of presenting the most extreme cases as the norm. More commonly the differences do not seem to veer too greatly from what would occur if all pupils simply attended the nearest secondary school to their primary. There is also little, if any, evidence to suggest those differences are growing, at least not when demographic changes are taken into consideration.

Figure 10.3: Showing the distribution of the index of clustering values and their standard deviation for (top) Black African and (bottom) Bangladeshi pupils

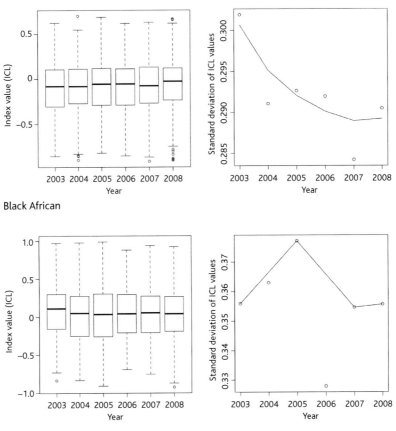

Black African

Bangladeshi

Of course, the debatable words are 'too greatly'. For anyone who would aspire for schools to either represent the ethnic mix of their surrounding neighbourhoods or, even better, to ameliorate residential differences by being more mixed than neighbourhoods, any increase in the concentration of particular ethnic groups in particular schools will be a disappointment, a sentiment that is laudable.

However, let us assume for a moment that the outcomes seen in this chapter are the consequence of the school choices that pupils or their parents make for those children's education. Even if that were entirely so – which it cannot be, because of the individual and system-wide constraints limiting that choice – there would still remain social justice arguments in favour of school choice and in not simply reproducing patterns of, for example, neighbourhood disadvantage by prescribing which school a pupil must necessarily attend. Choice, precisely because it is choice, can produce outcomes that some do not approve of but that are attractive, for whatever reasons, to those who make the choices. To deny them that choice, either directly or indirectly by overt criticism of them, raises issue of power as well as equality of opportunity.

The 'unspoken' presumption is that school choices are made such that pupils can be schooled with others of a similar ethnocultural kin. There are at least three arguments that weaken this presumption. First, school allocations are not necessarily a matter of choice but of the overall matching of supply and demand for school places. Second, sorting by ethnicity will be confounded with sorting by income. In 2008, the (non-parametric) Spearmen's rank correlation between the proportion of pupils in a London secondary school of any of the Black African, Black Caribbean, Bangladeshi, Indian and Pakistani groups, with the proportion eligible for FSM, was $r_s=0.568$ ($p<0.001$). Third, research by the Runnymede Trust has shown overall preferences among minority ethnic parents for their children to attend ethnically mixed schools (Finney and Simpson, 2009, citing Weekes-Bernard, 2007).

But even if the presumption were correct, it would still need to be demonstrated why the dominance of a particular ethnic group in particular schools is harmful to society and/or to those children's educational prospects. The fear is, of course, that if children of different ethnocultural backgrounds do not meet in school, then they will not meet at all, fostering fear or resentment of 'the other'. There may be validity to this argument in some circumstances, but it is not, presumably, without limit, or else we would pay more concern to the greater numbers of schools in England and Wales that are majority White British.

In summary, and taking the evidence in the round, while it is true that in 2008 there were 16 secondary schools in London with an entry cohort among whom more than half the pupils were of a single ethnic group other than White British, that is less than 5 per cent of schools. In contrast, 110 of schools (30 per cent) were majority White British in their intake. The dynamic implied by the phrase 'sleepwalking towards Johannesburg' is unhelpful, no matter how well intentioned (or possibly misreported) it may be.

More generally, the chapter has argued that the word 'segregation' is a spatial and comparative phrase, measured by looking at differences between places within a region. The importance of making geographically meaningful comparisons has been stressed, giving emphasis to measuring segregation within the local context and with consideration to the local processes in and by which the segregation is generated.

References

Burgess, S., Briggs, A., McConnell, B. and Slater, H. (2006) *School choice in England: background facts*, Bristol: Centre for Market and Public Organisation, University of Bristol Available (www.bris.ac.uk/cmpo).

Butler, T. and Hamnett, C. (2010) '"You take what you are given": the limits to parental choice in education in east London', *Environment and Planning A*, vol 42, no 10, pp 2431-50.

Cantle, T. (2001) *Community cohesion: a report of the Independent Review Team*, London: Home Office.

Cantle, T. (2012) *Interculturalism. The new era of cohesion and diversity*, Basingstoke: Palgrave Macmillan.

Clark, W.A.V. and Rivers, N. (2013) 'Community choice in large cities: selectivity and ethnic sorting across neighbourhoods', in M. van Ham, D. Manley, N. Bailey and D. Maclennan (eds) *Understanding neighbourhood dynamics*, London: Springer, pp 255-79.

Cortese, C.F., Falk, R.F. and Cohen, J.K. (1976) 'Further considerations on the methodological analysis of segregation indices', *American Sociological Review*, vol 41, no 4, pp 630-7.

DCSF (Department for Children, Schools and Families) (2008) *The composition of schools in England*, London: DCSF.

Duncan, O.D. and Duncan, B. (1955) 'A methodological analysis of segregation indexes', *American Sociological Review*, vol 20, no 2, pp 210-17.

Finney, N. and Simpson, L. (2009) *'Sleepwalking to segregation'? Challenging myths about race and migration*, Bristol: Policy Press.

Hamnett, C. and Butler, T. (2011) '"Geography matters": the role distance plays in reproducing educational inequality in East London', *Transactions of the Institute of British Geographers*, vol 36, no 4, 479-500.

Harris, R. (2011) 'Measuring segregation? A geographical tale', *Environment and Planning A*, vol 43, no 8, pp 1747-53.

Harris, R. (2012) 'Local indices of segregation with application to social segregation between London's secondary schools, 2003-2008/9', *Environment and Planning A*, vol 44, pp 669-87.

Harris, R. and Johnston, R. (2008) 'Primary schools, markets and choice: studying polarization and the core catchment areas of schools', *Applied Spatial Analysis and Policy*, vol 1, no 1, pp 59-84.

Jakubs, J.F. (1981) 'A distance based segregation index', *Journal of Socio-Economic Planning Sciences*, vol 15, pp 129-41.

Johnston, R. and Jones, K. (2010) 'Measuring segregation – a cautionary tale', *Environment and Planning A*, vol 42, no 6, pp 1264-70.

Johnston, R., Burgess, S., Harris, R. and Wilson, D. (2007) '"Sleepwalking towards segregation?" The changing ethnic composition of English schools, 1997-2003: an entry cohort analysis', *Transactions of the Institute of British Geographers*, vol 33, no 1, pp 73-90.

Johnston, R., Burgess, S., Wilson, D. and Harris, R. (2006) 'School and residential ethnic segregation: an analysis of variations across England's local education authorities', *Regional Studies*, vol 40, no 9, pp 973-90.

Martin, D. (1998) 'Automatic neighbourhood identification from population surfaces', *Computers, Environment and Urban Systems*, vol 22, no 2, pp 107-20.

Massey, D.S. and Denton, N.A. (1988) 'The dimensions of residential segregation', *Social Forces*, vol 67, no 2, pp 281-315.

Merry, M. (2013) *Equality, citizenship and segregation*, Basingstoke: Palgrave Macmillan.

Morgan, B.S. (1983) 'An alternative approach to the development of a distance-based measure of racial segregation', *American Journal of Sociology*, vol 88, no 6, 1237-49.

Ouseley, H. (2001) *Community pride not prejudice: making diversity work in Bradford*, Bradford: Bradford Vision.

Rey, S.J. and Folch, D.C. (2011) 'Impact of spatial effects on income segregation indices', *Computers, Environment and Urban Systems*, vol 35, no 6, pp 431-41.

Shepherd, J. (2011) 'Headteacher expresses alarm over racial segregation in London schools', *The Guardian*, 4 October (http://bit.ly/nsmyXy).

Waldorf, B.S. (1993) 'Segregation in urban space: a new measurement approach', *Urban Studies*, vol 30, no 7, pp 1151-64.

Weekes-Bernard, D. (2007) *School choice and ethnic segregation*, London: Runnymede Trust.

Wong, D.W.S. (1993) 'Spatial indices of segregation', *Urban Studies*, vol 30, no 3, pp 559-72.

Wong, D.W.S. (1997) 'Spatial dependency of segregation indices', *The Canadian Geographer*, vol 41, no 2, pp 128-36.

Wright, J.F. (1937) 'Some measures of distributions', *Annals of the Association of American Geographers*, vol 27, no 4, pp 177-93.

ELEVEN

Segregation, choice-based letting and social housing: how housing policy can affect the segregation process

Maarten van Ham and David Manley

Introduction

In this chapter we investigate the process of minority ethnic segregation in English social housing. Successive governments have expressed a commitment to the contradictory aims of providing greater choice – through the introduction of choice-based letting (CBL) – for households accessing an increasingly marginalised social housing sector, while also expressing a determination to create more mixed communities and neighbourhoods. We consider the concept of choice in the context of a heavily residualised social housing sector, arguing that, for social housing tenants at least, the concept of real choice is a misnomer. We draw on research that has utilised unique administrative data and analysed the moves of all entrants into and movers within the social renting sector over a 10-year period in England. The conclusion is that the introduction of CBL has influenced the residential outcomes of minority ethnic groups and resulted in highly structured neighbourhood sorting that has segregated minority populations into the least desirable neighbourhoods of English cities.

Many of the chapters in this volume report on the ways in which segregation can be measured (see, for example, Chapter Two, this volume), or the degree to which specific populations are segregated in the residential or even school context (see, for example, Chapter Ten). At the heart of these chapters is a discussion about segregation indices, either as a means through which the state of segregation can be measured and reported, or as a problematic indicator that requires careful consideration and deployment. This chapter takes a different approach by investigating neighbourhood sorting (see also Chapters

Nine, Ten and Thirteen). The study of segregation is, at one level, the study of variance in neighbourhood characteristics. That is to say, the amount by which the population in one place varies compared to the expected mean level of variation. While it is important to identify where high and low levels of variation occur, of more importance is the understanding of how the variation occurs in the first place. As a consequence, we explicitly explore the dynamic nature of the neighbourhood and the flows of households into neighbourhoods of different types. This chapter combines previous research by the authors of this chapter (van Ham and Manley, 2009; Manley and van Ham, 2011), which investigates the effect of CBL on how prospective social housing tenants sort into dwellings and neighbourhoods, and how household choice influences the composition of a neighbourhood. CBL was introduced in the early 2000s by the then labour government in England to enable social housing tenants to select their property, moving away from a landlord-led allocation system through which social housing had previously been let. CBL was also charged with promoting letting in neighbourhoods that were traditionally hard to allocate, either through reputation or perceived undesirability. A focus on these sorting processes within the social housing sector is largely missing in the current segregation literature.

This chapter draws on three literatures. The first is concerned with the issue of household residential choice and demonstrates that, when households are able to exercise choice over their residential location, they will, all other things being equal, choose to live in residential environments that are comprised of other households with similar characteristics (see Schelling, 1969; Clark, 1991, 1996; Peach, 1998). Of course, choice itself is a luxury good or activity, one that some households are better able to exercise than others. Real choice can be thought of as having the ability to choose a preferred outcome from a set of distinct options. However, even in the owner-occupier housing market, real choice rarely exists. A key determinant of choice in the residential housing market is finance – the ability to pay for access to better neighbourhoods and dwellings is crucial to being able to express one's own choice. Thus, households with limited access to financial resources will be less well placed to exercise choice.

The second literature on which this chapter draws is concerned with the changing role of the social housing sector in the UK. Successive governments in the UK have sought to reduce the size of the social housing sector. Through policies such as the Right to Buy, reduction of new social landlord building grants, and through the introduction of mixed tenure communities replacing large social housing estates, the proportion of the population living in the social housing sector has fallen from a peak of 32 per cent in 1971 to 17 per cent in 2011. Clearly, against a backdrop of a falling tenure mode, the notion of choice has a very specific meaning, and we enter into a discussion about this below.

The third literature on which this chapter is based is concerned with segregation in neighbourhoods. We briefly highlight the way in which segregation has been portrayed in the academic literature and the concern of the British government to the assumed negative effects of concentrations of minority ethnic groups in specific spaces within many of the towns and cities. We related this concern to the policy context as a means to understand the policy context within which CBL was launched. This chapter proceeds as follows. First, we identify key themes from the literature outlined above and set out how housing and neighbourhood choice can lead to segregated outcomes. Following on from this, we discuss the changing nature of social housing in the UK over the last 30 years. These discussions are then brought together when we outline the policy environment that led to the marketisation of social housing and the introduction of CBL. Second, we discuss two case studies originating from van Ham and Manley (2009) and Manley and van Ham (2011) on the effects of CBL on neighbourhood sorting and segregation. The third and final section presents some conclusions.

Background

Residential and tenure segregation in the UK[1]

The spatial concentration of minority ethnic groups in specific neighbourhoods is of great concern to the British government, and was highlighted as one of the causes of the 2001 riots in several towns and cities in Northern England (Independent Review Team, 2001; CRE, 1990, 2004). The severity of both ethnic and socioeconomic segregation in England has been strongly debated, and in these discussions terminology such as 'segregation' and 'ghettoisation' has become severely loaded. Champion (1996) used data from the 1991 UK Census to report that in England minority ethnic groups were spatially dispersed, and that ethnic concentration areas did not match images of US racialised 'ghettos' (see also Peach, 1996; Johnston et al, 2002). This national trend of dispersion of minority ethnic groups (with pockets of ethnic concentrations) was confirmed in more recent analysis using the 2001 Census (Johnston, 2006, p 988). Dorling and

Rees (2003) used both 1991 and 2001 Census data to suggest that there was evidence at the local authority level of increasing segregation between the White majority and minority ethnic groups. They used proxy measures for socioeconomic status – such as access to bathrooms and central heating – and reported growing segregation between housing tenures: '[t]o be growing up in a council house now marks a household out geographically far more than it did a decade ago' (Dorling and Rees, 2003, p 1301). The fact that minority ethnic groups concentrate in the social housing sector has led to concerns, as it suggests that minority ethnic groups are less able than others to satisfy their housing needs in the market (Home Office 2001; Cabinet Office, 2003). Of course, socioeconomic and ethnic segregation are strongly linked. About 14 per cent of the overall population in England could be classified as belonging to a minority ethnic group at the time of the 2011 Census, an increase of 5 per cent since the 2001 Census. These minority ethnic groups are generally concentrated in large urban areas, and are over-represented within the social housing sector. In line with the 2001 Census (see SEH, 2007), the 2011 Census showed that in England 9 per cent of the total population live in social housing, although the split is highly unequal between ethnic groups, with 17 per cent of the White population, while 25 per cent of the minority ethnic population lives in social housing.

Neighbourhood patterns of deprivation and segregation are partly created by selective residential mobility behaviour into and out of neighbourhoods (Bailey and Livingstone, 2008; van Ham and Feijten, 2008; Feijten and van Ham, 2009; van Ham and Clark, 2009; see also Chapter Nine, this volume). Preferences of moving households regarding the ethnic composition of their neighbourhood and their direct neighbours can lead to highly segregated neighbourhoods at the aggregate level (Schelling, 1969, 1971; see also Clark, 1992; Emerson et al, 2001; Ihlanfeldt and Scafidi, 2002; Ionnides and Zabel, 2003). An alternative explanation of segregation can be found in the 'racial proxy hypothesis', which argues that residents (mainly those who are members of the majority population) who leave ethnic concentration neighbourhoods do not do so because they do not want to live near minority group members, but because these ethnic concentration neighbourhoods are often also deprived (Taub et al, 1984; Clark, 1992; Harris, 1999; Crowder, 2000). Minority ethnic concentration neighbourhoods are often also deprived neighbourhoods because minority ethnic groups are more likely to be unemployed and have lower incomes than the majority population. On the other hand, minority ethnic groups often end up in low-income, deprived and unstable neighbourhoods as a result of limited choice in the housing market (Manley and van Ham, 2011).

Simpson (2004) has criticised the idea that ethnic neighbourhood segregation is largely caused by selective migration. He has used demographic data for Bradford to show that significant changes in the relative distribution of the South Asian community, relative to the rest of the population, were caused by the natural population growth of the population. This is an important conclusion in the context of Bradford that was one of the cities in the North of England that experienced riots during the summer of 2001. The official government report mainly focused on self-segregation of minority ethnic groups through their residential choices as the cause of segregation (Independent Review Team, 2001), which contributed to the social unrest. The same government report did not acknowledge that 'self-segregation' is often rooted in poverty and deprivation, and not necessarily the result of real choice (Robinson, 2005; Hickman and Robinson, 2006; van Ham and Manley, 2009; Manley and van Ham, 2011).

Social housing allocation in the UK

The current patterns of segregation in the UK have been linked to housing allocation practices that go back as far as the 1950s. Several studies have shown that the intentional and unintentional behaviour of housing officers, who were responsible for allocating social housing to applicants, resulted in segregation at the neighbourhood level (see also Manley and van Ham, 2011). They were shown to discriminate applicants based on their ethnicity and socioeconomic background, and as a result they allocated households dwellings partly based on whether they 'deserved' a dwelling or were 'suitable' for a neighbourhood (Simpson, 1981; Clapham and Kintrea, 1984; Henderson and Karn, 1984; Sarre et al, 1989; Malpass and Murie, 1994; Peach, 1996; Somerville, 2001). Prior to the 1970s, social housing in the UK was allocated by housing officers who were able to exercise a high degree of discretion in judging whether or not a family 'deserved' to live in a property. This process was not very transparent and has been acknowledged as a means through which minority ethnic segregation was reproduced overtime. From the 1970s onwards, social housing in England was allocated following a needs-based system. However, the needs-based system did not completely democratise the system. In many cases, front-line housing officers and local councillors still maintained some discretionary powers (Henderson and Karn, 1984). Needs-based systems were designed to introduce objectivity into the housing allocation process. Categories of reasonable preference were created and enabled a mechanism through which groups competing for the same properties could be prioritised. Even after needs-based systems were introduced, research still demonstrated that the allocation processes through which tenants gain access to social housing have tended to concentrate the most disadvantaged individuals in the least attractive areas (see, for example, Clapham and Kintrea, 1984; Henderson and Karn, 1984). This finding is important, as it is through the house and, therefore by extension the neighbourhood, that individuals locate their lives. In short, where you live has an effect on your ability to gain access to many public and private services, and also to employment and social opportunities. As Pawson and Kintrea (2002, p 646) noted, 'housing processes have the potential to be a force for social exclusion by creating and maintaining social and spatial divisions and thereby providing barriers to jobs, education and other services.' There are a number of competing issues to be considered here. First, the allocation systems through which prospective tenants must navigate are set up, in many cases, not to assist them to achieve the best housing outcome based on their own characteristics and desires, but to assist landlords to manage their housing stock and the demand for properties with varying levels of attractiveness. Research by Fitzpatrick and Pawson (2006) and Mullins and Pawson (2005) has shown that the traditional routes into social housing restrict prospective tenants in terms of the type of housing, including the location, available to them. Further restrictions on households exercising choice are apparent in the allocation system itself. Households who were offered a dwelling by a social landlord could reject this offer (often because they wanted to wait for a more suitable property), but such a rejection usually led to penalties. These included, for example, temporary suspension from the housing waiting list (Pawson and Watkins, 2007), or even exclusion from the waiting list through one-offer-only policies (Pawson and Kintrea, 2002). Of all the factors that can influence the outcome of a move into or within the social housing sector, waiting time is a key driver (Pawson and Kintrea, 2002; Mullins and Pawson, 2005). It was noted by Fitzpatrick and Pawson (2006, p 172) that 'the importance of the "ability to wait" in driving spatial polarisation is germane to the potential impact of the "choice" agenda.' In those cases where housing applicants with similar needs bid on the same property, waiting time is often used to allocate the dwelling to the applicant with the longest waiting time (Manley and van Ham, 2011). All other things being equal, turnover rates are greater in less popular housing and in less popular neighbourhoods. As a result, more popular properties and more popular neighbourhoods tend to become available less often. Households with more urgent housing needs, and with less time to wait, are less likely to be able to invest time in the search for a new property in a popular neighbourhood. This is particularly an issue for new entrants into the social housing sector, accessing housing because of eviction or repossession, or other groups requiring accommodation quickly such as those fleeing domestic violence.

CBL was introduced in the UK in 2001 as an instrument to empower people in social housing and to give them a say over how and where they live. The CBL model originated from the so-called 'advert' or 'supply' model, which was developed in the late 1980s in the Netherlands city of Delft (Kullberg, 1997, 2002). The idea behind the CBL system was to 'open up the letting of social housing' by enabling eligible households to bid on a range of vacant properties in the local housing market (Pawson et al, 2006, p 5). As more households bid on the same property, eligibility is often determined using 'currency' to rank bidders. These currencies include waiting time or housing need bands or points based on household characteristics, such as the presence of children (Marsh et al, 2004). Also within the CBL framework, social landlords still have the legal obligation to operate a needs-based allocation system. The main idea behind introducing a quasi-market system into social housing allocation was that it was hoped that housing demand would be stimulated in harder-to-let areas (Marsh et al, 2004), and that households would be encouraged to become stakeholders in their neighbourhoods of choice (Manley and van Ham, 2011).

Neighbourhood and housing 'choice'

The concept of 'choice' in relation to housing and neighbourhoods is often used in policy documents and academic literature and frequently has positive connotations. However, the concept of 'choice' is highly misleading in housing studies: it is unlikely that a household behaving rationally would choose to live in poor-quality housing or a dangerous neighbourhood (van Ham, 2012). Instead, housing and neighbourhood outcomes are the result of an interplay between preferences, opportunities and restrictions on the one hand, and housing stock availability and allocation mechanisms on the other. Real choice is assumed to exist when individuals are able to choose a preferred option from a set of distinct alternatives (Elster, 1999; Brown and King, 2005). Within the social housing sector it is hardly possible to speak of real choice as there are often no real distinct alternatives. Examining housing choice is complicated by the fact that housing is a composite good. It can be thought of in many terms, including size, number of bedrooms, style, quality and relative location. However, none of these aspects can be purchased individually, and dwellings come as a bundle of goods. This bundle also includes the neighbourhood and access to jobs as well as to private and public facilities (van Ham, 2012).

There are substantial differences in the degree to which choice can be exercised between tenures. For instance, those searching in the owner-occupied market are likely to be able to express a greater degree of choice than those households depending on the social housing sector. Brown and King (2005) describe social housing as a gift from the bureaucracy that controls it, as even under CBL the state sets the rules governing which households can bid on which properties.

Housing choice and segregation

There is a long history of work investigating the role of neighbourhood choice as a driver for neighbourhood segregation. The work of Schelling (1969, 1971) is often regarded as the starting point of this literature. He argued that many households have a preference for living in neighbourhoods with households of similar (ethnic) background, and that these preferences can lead to highly segregated neighbourhoods (see the related discussions in Chapter Nine, this volume). Using empirical data from the US, Clark (1991) demonstrated that the Schelling hypothesis was broadly correct, and that even small differences in preferences between ethnic groups with regard to the ethnic composition of neighbourhoods can lead to highly segregated communities (see also Fossett, 2006). Similarly, evidence from both Europe and the US indicates that ethnic segregation is primarily driven by own-group preferences held by the majority population. In addition, the majority population tends to have the greatest level of resources and, therefore, the ability to put these preferences into action. For example, Clark (1991) reports that while Whites preferred the ethnic mix in their neighbourhood to be at least 80 per cent White, Blacks seemed to prefer a 50/50 mix. Work from Sweden by Brämå (2006) demonstrated that the most immigrant-dense neighbourhoods are truly multicultural, making the notion of voluntary minority ethnic clustering unlikely. Ethnic mix preferences (or rather, preferences for relative homogeneity) by the majority population are apparent at the aggregate level through patterns of White avoidance of minority ethnic neighbourhoods. However, while Schelling and others have emphasised household preference as a means to understand residential sorting patterns, especially with respect to minority ethnic concentration in neighbourhoods, other authors have highlighted the importance of discrimination within housing markets, either through realtors not showing properties to families from minority ethnic backgrounds or finance companies making credit harder to obtain (see, for instance, Galster, 1976).

Studies from various countries have found that minority ethnic groups are more likely than natives to move to ethnic concentration neighbourhoods. It has been hypothesised that these moves to ethnic concentration neighbourhoods are (partly) motivated by the desire to live in areas with others who have common life experiences and by the availability of ethnic-specific services (see Bowes et al, 1997). Other studies have emphasised the impact of socioeconomic differences between ethnic and non-ethnic groups (see, for example, South and Crowder, 1997, 1998; Clark and Ledwith, 2006). In Sweden minority ethnic groups are over-represented among the lower-income groups, and as a result are concentrated in low-cost neighbourhoods. Similar evidence has been presented for the Netherlands (see Bolt et al, 2008). Bråmå and Andersson (2005, 2010) have shown that recent immigrants in Sweden initially move to areas with high densities of immigrants. When their income improves, they are more likely to leave these neighbourhoods and move to less ethnically concentrated neighbourhoods. Discrimination has also been shown to influence neighbourhood ethnic sorting (see, for example, Turner et al, 2002, for the US), although the extent to which this is valid for Sweden is unclear (Bråmå, 2007).

Choice-based lettings and segregation[2]

Giving people the opportunity to choose their own dwelling, as is the case in the CBL system, can lead to sustained or even increased levels of segregation as a side-effect of choice. As highlighted above, households that are empowered to express their preferences will on average choose dwellings in neighbourhoods that have a majority of other residents similar to themselves (as suggested by Schelling, 1971). We suggested in van Ham and Manley (2009) and Manley and van Ham (2011) that there is also an alternative explanation: a lack of real choice in CBL, and not self-segregation, might be a cause of social and ethnic segregation in neighbourhoods (see also Pawson and Watkins, 2007). Real choice means that people are able to select a preferred option from distinctive alternatives (Manley and van Ham,

2011). In the social housing sector, which functions as a safety net for those without options, such distinctive alternatives might not be available. Tenants who accessed social housing using CBL (Marsh et al, 2004) identified the lack of real choice as a real problem. It was stated by tenants that they frequently ended up bidding on properties and neighbourhoods which they thought were of poor quality. An essential prerequisite for having real choice is the availability of information about alternatives (see Elster, 1999, as in Brown and King, 2005). Such information is not equally available to everyone: some social housing applicants will have more and better information than others. This could be as a result of English language skills (Pawson et al, 2006), time to assess alternatives, skills in using the CBL system, or greater knowledge about the local housing market. An information advantage will bias the allocation system in favour of the information-rich (Brown and King, 2005). Research in the Netherlands has shown that this is indeed the case: applicants with low incomes and those from minority ethnic groups were likely to lack an understanding of the CBL system and were therefore less successful in securing a desirable dwelling and neighbourhood (Kullberg, 2002).

Those who have urgent housing needs, but no priority status, might use CBL to bid on the easiest-to-get dwellings. This is likely to lead to segregation because such dwellings are often located in less desirable areas (van Ham and Manley, 2009). As said earlier, the ability to wait is crucial in exercising real choice, and concerns have been expressed that CBL might be detrimental to the interests of already disadvantaged groups with urgent housing needs (Pawson and Watkins, 2007). As a result, minority ethnic groups may end up in ethnic concentration neighbourhoods, and especially deprived ethnic concentration neighbourhoods, not as a result of their own choice, but as a result of a lack of real choice (van Ham and Manley, 2009).

Prior to our own work (van Ham and Manley, 2009; Manley and van Ham, 2011), research assessing the impact of CBL on residential segregation has mainly focused on changes in the level of segregation in the neighbourhoods affected. Pawson and colleagues (2006; Pawson and Watkins, 2007) did some work for the Department for Communities and Local Government (CLG), in which they used a number of case studies from social housing estates and concluded that 'there is no evidence that [CBL] has resulted in more ethnically polarized patterns of letting than those arising from previous lettings systems where decisions on which properties to offer to which applications were largely in the hands or landlord staff' (Pawson et al,

2006, p 14; see also Pawson and Watkins, 2007). Regarding the ethnic mix in neighbourhoods, Pawson and colleagues found that '[m]any applicants preferred ethnically mixed areas, rather than areas where one ethnicity predominated, which suggests that diffusion is more likely than segregation under CBL' (2006, p 183). However, measuring a change in neighbourhood segregation requires information on the outflow of households from neighbourhoods as well as the inflows. If the outflow of a neighbourhood was comprised solely of one ethnic group (such as in extreme cases of 'White flight'), then the ultimate degree of segregation would be very different for a neighbourhood in which an equal share of ethnic and non-ethnic minority individuals were leaving. In their study, Pawson and colleagues (2006) only collected information about the households entering neighbourhoods (inflow) and not those households leaving the neighbourhoods. As such, they are not correct in concluding that under CBL, segregation is decreasing. The CBL process also requires that prospective tenants are willing and able to invest time in understanding the housing system that they are using, and that they will make rational, normative decisions in their housing and neighbourhood choices.

An English case study

The empirical evidence presented in this chapter originates from two papers by the authors of this chapter (van Ham and Manley, 2009; Manley and van Ham, 2011). Both of these use unique data from lettings made to tenants in social housing in England during the 2000s collected by the CLG. Each time a socially rented dwelling was let (either from a housing association or local authority), a record was created. This record was stored as part of the CORE database (COntinuousREcording), and contained information on both the property and household. Legislation in England meant that all social landlords with more than 250 units or bed spaces were legally required to complete the CORE logs fully. In practice, many landlords smaller than the regulation size also participated. Because of the comprehensive level of coverage, the CORE dataset can be treated as a census of all social housing lettings made in England during any given year, and can be regarded as flow data depicting the flows of households into social housing. It is also possible to include detailed information about local neighbourhoods because CORE data includes low-level geocoding for each letting. This information includes neighbourhood characteristics such as the level of neighbourhood deprivation, or the proportion of the neighbourhood belonging to minority ethnic groups.

In van Ham and Manley (2009) we investigated the probability that minority ethnic households are more likely to enter neighbourhoods with a high concentration of other members of minority ethnic groups. Neighbourhoods were defined using the administrative units super output areas (SOAs). SOAs contain on average 1,500 people and were designed to represent 'neighbourhoods' for the publication of low-level statistics in the UK. Using SOAs, neighbourhoods were classified using the proportion of minority ethnic residents, derived from the 2001 Census of Population for England. The groups were: '0 to 2.5%; 2.5 to 5%; 5 to 10%; 10 to 20%; 20 to 40%; and 40 to 100%' (van Ham and Manley, 2009, p 414). The models were used to predict if a minority ethnic household was more likely to enter a neighbourhood with a high concentration of minority ethnic groups than White households, and whether or not that likelihood was increased when properties were let under CBL. The results of the analysis show that for minority ethnic households, the most likely neighbourhood outcome is to enter into a neighbourhood with between 20-40 per cent of the population also belonging to a minority ethnic group. This outcome is more likely for minority ethnic residents using CBL than those using one of the other allocation systems. In all cases, minority ethnic households are more likely than White households to enter neighbourhoods with a high proportion of households also from minority ethnic groups, especially when using CBL. In comparison, the White population are most likely to enter neighbourhoods with 0-10 per cent and 10-20 per cent concentration of minority ethnic groups, even when they move from neighbourhoods with higher concentrations of minority ethnic groups. Unlike the minority ethnic group, there are no differences in the probabilities between White households who use CBL and those using the other access routes.

In Manley and van Ham (2011) we combined multiple years of CORE data to conduct two analyses. In the first analysis areas were matched where 100 per cent of the lettings were made using CBL in 2008/09 with the same areas in 1999/2000 (before CBL was introduced). This allowed the geography of the areas to be held constant and a direct pre-CBL to post-CBL comparison made. The second analysis used all the letting data from 2008/09 and analysed the flows of individuals using either CBL or non-CBL allocation routes in that year. The dependent variable of the models was also adjusted to combine measures of ethnic concentration and neighbourhood deprivation. The percentage of minority ethnic groups in neighbourhoods was measured using data from the 2001 Census and neighbourhood deprivation was measured using the Index of

Multiple Deprivation (IMD) for England (DCLG, 2007). The IMD data was not available for exactly the same years as the lettings data. We linked the IMD 2004 data to the 1999/2000 lettings data and the IMD 2007 to the 2008/09 lettings data. We argue that it is not a big problem to use deprivation information from different time periods, as deprivation at the neighbourhood level is largely static over time (see Meen et al, 2007). The neighbourhood characteristics allow us to rank neighbourhoods nationally, but given that most households search on local housing markets, and not on national housing markets, we decided to create variables reflecting the relative position of a neighbourhood in the local housing market (see Manley and van Ham, 2011, for more details). For this purpose we used travel to work areas (TTWAs) to represent local housing markets. A TTWA is defined so that 75 per cent of those living in the area also work in the area and vice versa. This means that TTWAs capture local housing search areas effectively (see Coombes and Raybould, 2004).

The outcome variable for the analysis was constructed using a combination of deprivation from the IMD and the proportion of the population identified as belonging to a minority ethnic group. We identified the 20 per cent most deprived SOAs in each TTWA, which gave a bespoke relative measure of neighbourhood deprivation and ethnicity for each housing market. We then classified the dependent variable into four groups: (1) non-deprived and White concentration neighbourhoods; (2) deprived but not ethnic concentration neighbourhoods; (3) non-deprived but ethnic concentration neighbourhoods; and (4) deprived and ethnic concentration neighbourhoods (Manley and van Ham, 2011). Using these four categories can be justified by research that shows that many see deprived neighbourhoods and ethnic concentration neighbourhoods as less desirable living environments (Harris, 1999; Bolt et al, 2008). In Manley and van Ham (2011) we argued that these four types of neighbourhoods can act as a proxy for neighbourhood desirability within local housing markets, where the first type of neighbourhood is more desirable than the other three types (although there is no particular order between types 2, 3 or 4). With a multinomial response variable (with four outcomes) and clear hierarchical structures within the data (local neighbourhoods as SOAs within TTWA housing markets), the most appropriate model was a multinomial, multilevel model.

The results of the analysis are presented in Table 11.1 (see Manley and Ham, 2011). For both the comparative 1999/2000 with 2008/09 approach and the cross-sectional 2008/09 approach, minority ethnic groups are found to be consistently more likely to end up in neighbourhoods with a high level of deprivation and high concentrations of other minority ethnic groups. In Table 11.1 the White population before the introduction of CBL is the control group. It can be seen that compared to this group (see the top half of the table) minority ethnic groups (also before the introduction of CBL) were 1.29 times more likely to end up in deprived neighbourhoods, 2.63 times more likely to end up in ethnic concentration neighbourhoods and 3.08 times more likely to end up in deprived ethnic concentration neighbourhoods (Manley and van Ham, 2011). After CBL, the sorting effects are stronger, with members of minority ethnic groups 4.6 times more likely to enter the same type of neighbourhood than the White population. It is also notable that the White households using CBL are actually less likely than White households renting prior to the introduction of CBL to enter deprived and minority ethnic concentration neighbourhoods. Thus, there were strong sorting mechanisms present in the allocation of social housing prior to the introduction of CBL. After CBL had been introduced, this sorting pattern became more pronounced, with minority ethnic groups 4.6 times more likely to enter deprived and ethnically concentrated neighbourhoods compared with White households prior to CBL. It is notable that White households are less likely (0.9 times) to enter these neighbourhoods after the introduction of CBL compared with the same households before CBL. The bottom half of the table reports the findings of the analysis post-CBL, and a similar trend can be seen.

Table 11.1: Total effects of ethnicity and choice-based letting (odds ratios)

Neighbourhood type	Deprived	Ethnic concentration	Deprived and ethnic concentration
Total effects using data from 1999/2000 and 2008/09 for housing association lettings in urban areas			
White before CBL	1.00	1.00	1.00
Ethnic before CBL	1.29	2.63	3.08
White after CBL	1.48	1.24	0.90
Ethnic after CBL	2.10	4.05	4.60
Total effects using data from 2008/09 for housing association and local authority lettings			
White, not using CBL	1.00	1.00	1.00
Ethnic minority, not using CBL	1.59	1.24	1.60
White, using CBL	1.19	1.07	1.13
Ethnic minority, using CBL	2.20	1.70	2.68

Source: Author's own calculations using CORE and LACORE lettings data 1999/2000 and 2008/09. Table adapted from Manley and van Ham (2011).

Minority ethnic households are more likely than White households to enter areas with higher concentrations of minority ethnic groups as well as areas with higher levels of deprivation. The minority ethnic groups are 1.5 times more likely than the White group to enter a deprived neighbourhood, 1.2 times more likely to enter an ethnic concentration neighbourhood and 1.6 times more likely to enter a neighbourhood with high levels of deprivation and ethnic concentration. Again, the results show an effect of CBL: minority ethnic groups using CBL are far more likely than others (including minority ethnic groups not using CBL) to rent a dwelling in deprived neighbourhoods, ethnic concentration neighbourhoods and especially deprived ethnic concentration neighbourhoods (Manley and van Ham, 2011). Compared to those renting without CBL, minority ethnic households are now 2.2 times more likely than the White group to enter a deprived neighbourhood, 1.7 times more likely to enter an ethnic concentration neighbourhood and 2.7 times more likely to enter a neighbourhood with high levels of deprivation and ethnic concentration than the White population. This demonstrates that there is a clear sorting of the population through social housing letting. These results suggest that ethnic segregation through CBL is not just the result of choice as minority ethnic groups are also more likely to end up in the more deprived neighbourhoods, even when these are not ethnic concentration neighbourhoods. We discuss this finding further in the final section of this chapter.

Discussion and conclusion

This chapter has suggested that in order to understand residential segregation, a number of literatures need to be brought together, and that segregation analysis should focus on flows of households into neighbourhoods rather than on static indices. This chapter combined background information and empirical results from two of our own studies (see van Ham and Manley, 2009; Manley and van Ham, 2011, for more details and information) on the flows of social housing tenants. These studies have demonstrated the implications that these flows have for the degree to which socioeconomic and more specifically ethnic segregation can occur. By combining literatures on housing choice and neighbourhood sorting, we highlighted the likely outcomes of government policies introducing choice into the social housing market. Given the spatial fixity of housing – once located in a neighbourhood a property cannot be moved, and changes to the characteristics of the neighbourhood tend to occur slowly over time – understanding how households are sorted into dwellings and neighbourhoods is crucial for understanding how residential segregation develops and is maintained over time. The vast majority of the residential segregation literature tends to assume that households are able to exercise choice and do not face substantial spatial constraints. When turning the discussion to the social housing sector, the third of our literatures, the debate must be refocused and the limited number of options recognised. When discussing the social housing sector choice is a much more restricted good, and the potential for prospective tenants to use choice to subvert the social housing allocation system and in a non-rational manner increases. No longer does choice become about exercising a preferred option among a range of distinct alternatives, but it becomes more about satisfying other, more immediate housing needs.

In contrast to the CLG-sponsored research (see CLG, 2006; Pawson and Watkins, 2007), which was based on a limited number of early CBL case studies, we argue that the process of CBL is contributing to, at best, a stabilising of segregation levels across social housing communities or, at worst, an increase in segregation. Based on the analyses from van Ham and Manley (2009) and Manley and van Ham (2011), as presented above, we draw a number of conclusions about the structure of social housing allocations and the potential of that sector to create segregated communities. The first conclusion is that among those who do not use CBL to acquire a dwelling, minority ethnic households are far more likely than White households to end up in deprived ethnic concentration neighbourhoods (Manley and van Ham, 2011). In other words, there are differences in households and letting structures that lead to differential outcomes for ethnic and White tenants even when choice is not exercised through CBL. The second conclusion is that those who use CBL (including non-minority and minority ethnic households) are more likely to rent a dwelling in a deprived neighbourhood than those who access their dwelling using the other allocation systems. Those who use CBL are also slightly more likely to end up in an ethnic concentration neighbourhood (Manley and van Ham, 2011).

These results emerged from the analyses presented in both van Ham and Manley (2009) and Manley and van Ham (2011) using multiple years' worth of data and multiple analytical methods. It is likely that the results are partly a function of the neighbourhoods in which CBL has been rolled out in the initial phases of the policy development. CBL was used primarily as a means to stimulate demand in areas that had traditionally been harder for landlords to let. As such it was less of a vehicle to promote real choice for prospective tenants by providing desirable residential alternatives for households looking for properties to choose from, and more a means to stimulate demand. The third conclusion is that for those minority ethnic groups who found their rented dwelling through CBL, the neighbourhood outcome is much more likely to be one of ethnic concentration compared to any other group (Manley and van Ham, 2011). This is clear evidence of a sorting process in social housing, and one that could lead to higher levels of segregation. This outcome is in stark contrast to Pawson and Watkins (2007), and fits with the theoretical and empirical literature of housing and neighbourhood choice (see Schelling, 1971; Clark, 1991).

We can conclude that allocation mechanisms for social housing will always lead to sorting simply because they act as bureaucratic gatekeepers to a restricted resource. However, that there are sorting differences among minority ethnic and White households, even when other socioeconomic factors are taken into account, is potentially worrying if the sorting mechanisms are leading to and reproducing spatial disadvantage. One aspect of segregation that this chapter has deliberately not commented on is how the level of segregation in neighbourhoods has changed after the introduction of CBL. Neither of the studies used in this chapter has investigated this, and to do so would require information about the outflow as well as the inflow of individuals. What we can conclude is that minority ethnic groups using CBL are not only the most likely to end up in ethnic concentration neighbourhoods, but also the most likely to end up in deprived neighbourhoods. This suggests that selective sorting into neighbourhoods is not only a result of choice and self-segregation of minority ethnic groups. The results can be interpreted as if this sorting is also partly the result of a lack of real choice within the social housing sector. This lack of real choice is a substantial structural characteristic of the social housing sector, as CBL seems to be mostly offered in the most deprived neighbourhoods and the most difficult-to-let stock. For CBL to make a real difference and to empower people to execute some level of choice, it needs to be implemented across the full range of social housing stock, including the most desirable houses. Of course, it is possible for the housing authorities to go further: the importance of waiting time as a key determinant could be removed for part of the stock if allocation was connected to a lottery system, which gives people the opportunity to get a desirable dwelling in a desirable neighbourhood without needing to play the waiting game.

Notes

[1] This section draws heavily on previous work by the authors, Manley and van Ham (2011).

[2] This section draws heavily on previous work by the authors, Manley and van Ham (2011).

References

Bailey, N. and Livingston, M. (2008) 'Selective migration and area deprivation: evidence from 2001 census migration data for England and Scotland', *Urban Studies*, vol 45, pp 943-61.

Bolt, G., van Kempen, R. and van Ham, M. (2008) 'Minority ethnic groups in the Dutch housing market: spatial segregation, relocation dynamics and housing policy', *Urban Studies*, vol 45, pp 1359-84.

Bowes, A., Dar, N. and Sim, D. (1997) 'Tenure preference and housing strategy: an exploration of Pakistani experiences', *Housing Studies*, vol 12, pp 63-84.

Bråmå, A. (2006) '"White flight"? The production and reproduction of immigrant concentration areas in Swedish cities, 1990-2000', *Urban Studies*, vol 43, pp 1127-46.

Bråmå, A. (2007) *Etnisk diskriminering po bostadsmarknaden. En forskningsoversikt*, IBF WP 54, Gavle: Institute for Housing and Urban Research.

Bråmå, A. and Andersson R. (2005) 'Who leaves Sweden's large housing estates?', in R. van Kempen, K. Dekker, S. Hall and I. Tosics (eds) *Restructuring large housing estates in Europe*, Bristol: Policy Press, pp 169-92.

Bråmå, A. and Andersson R. (2010) 'Who leaves rental housing? Examining possible explanations for ethnic housing segmentation in Uppsala', *Sweden Journal of Housing and the Built Environment*, vol 25, pp 331-52.

Brown, T. and King, P. (2005) 'The power to choose: effective choice and housing policy', *European Journal of Housing Policy*, vol 5, pp 59-75.

Cabinet Office (2003) *Ethnic minorities and the labour market: interim analytical report*, London: Cabinet Office.

Champion, T. (1996) 'Internal migration and ethnicity in Britain', in P. Ratcliffe (ed) *Social geography and ethnicity in Britain: geographical spread, spatial concentration and internal migration ethnicity in the 1991 Census*, vol 3, London: HMSO, pp 135-73.

Clapham, D. and Kintrea, K. (1984) 'Allocation systems and housing choice', *Urban Studies*, vol 21, pp 261-9.

Clark, W. (1991) 'Residential preferences and neighbourhood racial segregation: a test of the Schelling segregation model', *Demography*, vol 28, pp 1-19.

Clark, W. (1992) 'Residential preferences and residential choices in a multiethnic context', *Demography*, vol 29, pp 451-66.

Clark, W. and Ledwith V. (2006) 'Mobility, housing stress and neighbourhood contexts: evidence from Los Angeles', *Environment and Planning* A, vol 38, pp 1077-93.

CLG (Department for Communities and Local Government) (2006) *Monitoring the longer-term impact of choice-based lettings*, London: CLG.

CRE (Commission for Racial Equality) (1990) *Racial discrimination in an Oldham Estate Agency*, Report of formal investigation into Normal Lester & Co, London: CRE.

CRE (2004) *Race and council housing in Hackney: a general investigation*, London: CRE.

Coombes, M. and Raybould, S. (2004) 'Finding work in 2001: urban–rural contrasts across England in employment rates and local job availability', *Area*, vol 36, pp 202-22.

Crowder, K. (2000) 'The racial context of white mobility: an individual-level assessment the white flight hypothesis', *Social Science Research*, vol 29, pp 223-57.

DCLG (Department for Communities and Local Government) (2007) The English indices of deprivation (www.communities.gov.uk).

Dorling, D. and Rees, P. (2003) 'A nation still dividing: the British census and social polarization 1971-2001', *Environment and Planning A*, vol 35, pp 1287-313.

Elster, J. (1999) *Strong feelings: emotion, addiction and human behavior*, Cambridge, MA: Bradford Books, MIT Press.

Emerson, M., Chai, K. and Yancey, G. (2001) 'Does race matter in residential segregation? Exploring the preferences of white Americans', *American Sociological Review*, vol 66, pp 922-35.

Feijten, P. and van Ham, M. (2009) 'Neighbourhood change ... reason to leave?', *Urban Studies*, vol 46, pp 2103-22.

Fitzpatrick, S. and Pawson, H. (2006) 'Welfare safety net or tenure of choice? The dilemma facing social housing policy in England', *Housing Studies*, vol 22, pp 163-82.

Fossett M. (2006) 'Including preference and social distance dynamics in multi-factor theories of segregation', *Journal of Mathematical Sociology*, vol 30, pp 289-98.

Galster, G. (1976) 'Prejudice versus preference: what do we really know about housing market discrimination?', *Journal of Regional Analysis and Policy*, vol 6, pp 17-27.

Harris, D. (1999) 'Property values drop when blacks move in, because ...: racial and socioeconomic determinants of neighbourhood desirability', *American Sociological Review*, vol 64, pp 461-79.

Henderson, J. and Karn, V. (1984) 'Race, class and the allocation of public housing in Britain', *Urban Studies*, vol 21, pp 115-28.

Hickman, P. and Robinson, D. (2006) 'Transforming social housing: taking stock of new complexities', *Housing Studies*, vol 21, pp 157-70.

Home Office (2001) *Building cohesive communities: a report of the Ministerial Group on Public Order and Community Cohesion*, London: Home Office.

Iaonnides, Y. and Zabel, J. (2003) 'Neighbourhood effects and housing demand', *Journal of Applied Econometrics*, vol 18, pp 563-84.

Ihlanfeldt, K. and Scafidi, B. (2002) 'Black self-segregation as a cause of housing segregation: evidence from the multi-city study of urban inequality', *Journal of Urban Economics*, vol 51, pp 366-90.

Independent Review Team (2001) *Community cohesion. A report of the Independent Review Team*, London: Chaired by Ted Cantle, Home Office.

Johnston, R. (2006) 'School and residential ethnic segregation: an analysis of variations across England's local education authorities', *Regional Studies*, vol 40, pp 973-90.

Johnston, R., Forrest, J. and Poulsen, M. (2002) 'Are there ethnic enclaves/ghettos in English cities?', *Urban Studies*, vol 39, pp 591-618.

Kullberg, J. (1997) 'From waiting lists to adverts: the allocation of social rented dwellings in the Netherlands', *Housing Studies*, vol 12, pp 393-403.

Kullberg, J. (2002) 'Consumer's responses to choice based letting mechanisms', *Housing Studies*, vol 17, pp 549-79.

Malpass, P. and Murie, A. (1994) *Housing policy and practice* (4th edn), London: Macmillan Press.

Manley, D. and van Ham, M. (2011) 'Choice-based letting, ethnicity and segregation in England', *Urban Studies*, vol 48, pp 3125-43.

Marsh, A., Cowen, D., Cameron, A., Jones, M., Kiddle, C. and Whitehead, C. (2004) *Piloting choice-based lettings: an evaluation*, London: Office of the Deputy Prime Minister.

Mullins, D. and Pawson, H. (2005) '"The land that time forgot": reforming access to social housing in England', *Policy & Politics*, vol 33, pp 135-48.

Pawson, H. and Kintrea, K. (2002) 'Part of the problem or part of the solution? Social housing allocation policies and social exclusion in Britain', *Journal of Social Policy*, vol 31, pp 643-67.

Pawson, H. and Watkins, D. (2007) 'Quasi-marketising access to social housing in Britain: assessing the distributional impacts', *Journal of Housing and the Built Environment*, vol 22, pp 149-75.

Pawson, H., Donohoe, A., Jones, C., Watkins, D., Fancy, C., Netto, G., Clegg, S. and Thomas, A. (2006) *Monitoring the longer-term impact of choice-based lettings*, London: Department for Communities & Local Government.

Peach, C. (1996) Does Britain have ghettos?', *Transactions of the Institute of British Geographers*, vol 21, pp 216-35.

Peach, C. (1998) 'South Asian and Caribbean ethnic minority housing choice in Britain', *Urban Studies*, vol 35, pp 1657-80.

Robinson, D. (2007) 'Living parallel lives? Housing, residential segregation and community cohesion in England', in H. Beider (ed) *Neighbourhood renewal and housing matters*, Oxford: Blackwell, pp 163-85.

Sarre, P., Phillips, D. and Skellington, R. (1989) *Ethnic minority housing: explanations and policies*, Aldershot: Avebury.

Schelling, T. (1969) 'Models of segregation', *The American Economic Review*, vol 59, pp 488-93.

Schelling, T. (1971) 'Dynamic models of segregation', *Journal of Mathematical Sociology*, vol 1, pp 143-86.

SEH (Survey of English Housing) (2007) *Housing in England 2005/06: a report principally from the 2005/06 Survey of English Housing*, London: Department for Communities and Local Government.

Simpson, A. (1981) *Stacking the decks*, Nottingham: Nottingham Community Relations Council.

Simpson, L. (2004) 'Statistics of racial segregation: measures, evidence and policy', *Urban Studies*, vol 41, 661-81.

Somerville, P. (2001) 'Allocating housing or letting people choose?', in D. Cowan and A. Marsh (eds) *Two steps forward: housing policy into the new millennium*, Bristol: Policy Press, pp 113-32.

South, S. and Crowder, K. (1997) 'Escaping distressed neighbourhoods: individual, community and metropolitan influences', *American Journal of Sociology*, vol 102, pp 1040-84.

South, S. and Crowder, K. (1998) 'Avenues and barriers to residential mobility among single mothers', *Journal of Marriage and the Family*, vol 60, pp 866-77.

Taub, R., Taylor, G. and Dunham, J. (1984) *Paths of neighbourhood change*, Chicago, IL: University of Chicago Press.

Turner, M., Ross, S., Galster, G, and Yinger, J. (2002) *Discrimination in metropolitan housing markets: national results from Phase I HDS 2000*, Washington, DC: The Urban Institute.

van Ham, M. (2012) 'Housing behaviour', in D. Clapham, W. Clark and K. Gibb (eds) *Handbook of housing studies*, London: Sage, Chapter 3.

van Ham, M. and Clark, W. (2009) 'Neighbourhood mobility in context: household moves and changing neighbourhoods in the Netherlands', *Environment and Planning A*, vol 41, pp 1442-59.

van Ham, M. and Feijten, P. (2008) 'Who wants to leave the neighbourhood? The effect of being different from the neighbourhood population on wishes to move', *Environment and Planning A*, vol 40, pp 1151-70.

van Ham, M. and Manley, D. (2009) 'Social housing allocation, choice and neighbourhood ethnic mix in England', *Journal of Housing and the Built Environment*, vol 24, pp 407-22.

TWELVE

Demographic understandings of changes in ethnic residential segregation across the life course

Albert Sabater and Nissa Finney

Introduction

This chapter presents analyses of changes in the level of ethnic residential segregation in Britain taking a life course perspective. Changes are separately analysed for age cohorts, ethnic groups and subnational areas. The results show ethnic residential desegregation in the 1990s across age cohorts and ethnic groups, and this is particularly marked for young adults. The second part of the chapter examines how age differentiation in migration patterns might explain these changes in segregation. It shows that what has been described as 'White flight' and 'minority self-segregation' (see also Chapters Two and Six, this volume) can alternatively be seen as one of the dynamics of desegregation in which age-differentiated migration is common across ethnic groups: young adult urbanisation and family/older adult suburbanisation with immigration of a similar magnitude to the least and most diverse areas. The chapter concludes that it is necessary to take age into account to understand ethnic residential segregation and its dynamics. The chapter uses census-based population and components of population change estimates for small areas linking the 1991 and 2001 Censuses in England and Wales and also 2001 UK Census micro-data.

The fear of ethnic ghettos has been established over centuries (Wirth, 1928), although the modern idea that has dominated the topic both theoretically and methodologically was developed during the first decades of the 20th century by the ecological paradigm of the Chicago School of Sociology. Since the seminal work on the subject by Robert Park (1924) on *The concept of social distance* and Ernest Burgess (1928) on *Residential segregation in American cities*, the study of separation of groups has drawn on the political and intellectual idea of how elites have viewed the relationship between ethnicity and poverty in the city (Ward, 1989).

In his classic book *The ghetto*, Louis Wirth (1928, p 6) incorporates the 'Little Sicilies, Little Polands, Chinatowns, and Black Belts in our large cities' as the equivalent of Jewish ghettos of medieval Europe. In Duncan and Lieberson's (1959) classic paper, the authors demonstrate an inverse relationship between residential segregation and assimilation of immigrants. This landmark publication gave rise to the development of indices of dissimilarity as well as a quantitative framework based on the idea that high levels of segregation are problematic, because these imply that a subgroup of the population is isolated from opportunities, resources and amenities (Logan, 1978; Massey et al, 1987; Kaplan and Holloway, 1998). Such correlation between segregation and social and economic wellbeing has also become a public debate in Europe, generally associated with the African American model of inner-city segregation (Fortuijn et al, 1998). Although these ideas have influenced thinking about race relations in Europe, considerable literature has challenged the 'straight line' view of integration (Alba and Nee, 1997) and the notion that residential segregation represents both negative causes and negative consequences (Peach, 1996a, 1996b, 2009).

Residential integration may not have occurred as quickly or straightforwardly as early theories suggested, but decreasing residential segregation has been a characteristic of European cities (Musterd, 2005; Finney and Catney, 2012). The topic of residential ethnic segregation has also become highly political, becoming a priority on the agenda in both academic and policy circles over the last decade in Britain and elsewhere. The study of processes and patterns involved in residential segregation has become a matter of interest, and results suggest the overall importance of the assimilation model, 'with the clustering of some ethnic groups reflecting the first stages of its process of concentration followed by dispersal' (Johnston et al, 2002, p 609).

While initial reaction was quick to assume 'bad' segregation (see also Chapters Fourteen, Fifteen and Sixteen, this volume), more recent debate has turned to understandings of the processes of population change that underpin ethnic geographies. Demographic work has shown that the underlying processes of residential patterns of ethnic groups represent common experiences of migration and expected patterns of natural change (Stillwell and Hussain, 2008; Simpson et al, 2008b; Finney and Simpson, 2009a; Simon, 2009; Simpson and Finney, 2009; Finney and Catney, 2012). The result is increased ethnic diversity and ethnic mixing (Rees et al, 2011). There is little evidence that continued clustering represents retreat and ethnic division (Phillips, 2006).

Nevertheless, political concerns with residential segregation remain, and the community cohesion agenda represents a shift in political rhetoric from concern with multiculturalism and anti-discrimination (Cantle, 2001; Flint and Robinson, 2008; Kalra and Kapoor, 2009). The centuries-old myths about ethnic segregation have returned to shape political responses (Simpson, 2007; Finney and Simpson, 2009a). In turn there has been renewed interest in research on ethnic group population change which has tried to understand in greater depth the causes and meanings of residential clustering and dispersal.

One aspect of this literature on ethnic group population dynamics is its concern with demographic change through the life course. Natural population change (births and deaths) is inherently related to stage of life, and migration has long been recognised to be strongly associated with age. Although migration studies have been present in the development of life course research over the past two decades (Mulder, 1993; Mortimer and Shanahan, 2004), it is only relatively recently that substantial attention has been paid to the interaction between migration and life course (see, for example, Wingens et al, 2011 and special issues of *Population, Space and Place* [2008] and *Demographic Research* [2007]). This emerging arena of research has been propelled by findings that transitions to adulthood, migration's relation to family change and geographies of migration across the life course are more complex than previous understandings recognised (Bailey and Boyle, 2004; Clark and Withers, 2007; Kulu and Milewski, 2007; Geist and McMacus, 2008; Plane and Jurjevich, 2009).

There are reasons to theorise that both the ethnic mix of the neighbourhood of residence and patterns of migration in relation to ethnic mix vary for people of different ages, and through the course of an individual's life. It is well established that the geographies of migration vary across age groups with, for example, young adults favouring movement to urban centres while older adults suburbanise (Champion, 1989; Plane and Jurjevich, 2009). Thus, neighbourhoods can be classified according to their patterns of internal migration, and the resulting classifications have a strong age and life course dimension (Dennett and Stillwell, 2011).

Given these processes, we can expect young adults to be exposed to greater ethnic mix in their residential environments than families and older adults. We may also expect some variation across ethnic groups, not only because of uneven geographical distributions of ethnic groups across Britain, but also because of different traditions of living arrangements, home-leaving and associates of migration at key life stages (Dale et al, 2002; de Valk and Billari, 2007; Finney, 2011). Ethnic mix of a neighbourhood may also influence migration location decisions (van Ham and Feijten, 2008), although housing and migration aspirations have been found to be similar across ethnic groups (Phillips, 2006).

This chapter builds on the demographic body of work in this area by bringing the concepts of age and life course into debates about ethnic segregation and the processes of ethnic group population change (Sabater, 2010). It examines, first, changes in ethnic residential segregation by age cohorts nationally and locally, and second, migration patterns of young adults in relation to ethnic concentrations. The chapter addresses two specific questions:

1. Over the life course, how do people's experiences of ethnic residential segregation change, and how does this vary across ethnic groups and neighbourhoods?
2. Has migration resulted in decreased segregation for young adults, and if so, is this the case for White and minority ethnic groups?

The chapter shows that the dynamics of desegregation are age-differentiated migration common across ethnic groups – young adult urbanisation and family/older adult suburbanisation – and concludes that it is necessary to take age into account to understand ethnic residential segregation and its dynamics.

Data and methods

Three data sources are used in this chapter: full population estimates (1991-2001 by ethnic group and age), components of population change estimates (1991-2001 by ethnic group and age) and 2001 UK Census micro-data. The full population estimates are complete mid-1991 and mid-2001 population estimates for subnational areas in England and Wales. Even though many users of demographic statistics will find census data sufficient to compare the geographical patterns of settlement of ethnic groups over time, such comparisons are subject to four types of bias (Simpson et al, 1997; Sabater, 2008; Sabater and Simpson, 2009a): (1) the population definition, which defines who is a resident, has changed between the 1991 and 2001 Censuses; (2) the treatment of non-response in the 1991 and 2001 Censuses was different, and varied between ethnic groups, areas and ages; (3) key classifications changed between 1991 and 2001, including ethnic group and age in standard outputs; and (4) geographical boundaries used for standard census outputs changed after local government reviews between 1991 and 2001. The full population estimates take into account these four sets of bias (see Sabater and Simpson, 2009b). The data exclude counts of individuals in institutional establishments, such as prisons.

The components of population change estimates are a decomposition of the population change between 1991-2001 in the full population estimates into their demographic components of births, deaths and net migration. Components of change have been estimated for wards and districts of Britain, separately for ethnic groups by sex and single year of age. As vital statistics in Britain do not record ethnic group, demographic estimation procedures have been applied using the full population estimates (Sabater and Simpson, 2009a), which give net migration for subnational areas as a residual. Full technical details of the method can be found in Simpson, Finney and Lomax (2008a).

Additionally, the research has used the individual samples of anonymised records (SARs) and the controlled access micro-data sample (CAMS) from the 2001 UK Census. These datasets provide information on migration with an age and ethnic group breakdown, and with geographic detail in the CAMS. As a result this presents a higher risk of disclosure (that is, the identification of information about individuals) and, therefore, the use of the CAMS dataset has to be approved and in a secure setting.[1] Migration data in the 2001 UK Census are based on a question about place of usual residence one year prior to census day. If this is different from the address on census day, the individual is considered to have migrated in the year prior to the census.

For the calculation of residential segregation, two common measures have been used, the index of dissimilarity (D), the most common index in the segregation literature, and a corrected version of the isolation index ($P*$). These segregation measures are employed here to review the level and direction of change in two dimensions of spatial variation: *evenness* and *exposure* (Massey and Denton, 1988).

Residential evenness is measured with D, which indicates how evenly people of different ethnic groups are distributed across areal units in a city or metropolitan area. D is conceived to measure an unequal geographical spread of one group relative to another group, and is generally expressed as a percentage, with index values between 0 and 100. This value can be interpreted as the percentage of the ethnic group of interest that would have to move neighbourhood in order to have a distribution of the same evenness as the reference population.

Thus, the higher the index value, the greater the unevenness. One formula for the dissimilarity index is:

$$D = 0.5 * \sum_{i} \left| \frac{N_{gi}}{N_{g\bullet}} - \frac{N_{\bar{g}i}}{N_{\bar{g}\bullet}} \right| \tag{1}$$

Where N_{gi} refers to the population of the ethnic group g of interest in locality i; $\bar{g}$ means the population of the reference group (White British in this analysis); and the summation over an index is represented by the dot symbol.

Residential exposure is computed using $P*$, which is used to indicate the degree of potential contact between members of the same ethnic group. The interpretation of this index is also straightforward as a percentage. If the index is close to zero, it indicates that the probability of contact or interaction between two members of the same group is very low, whereas if the index values are close to 100, it highlights a high likelihood of sharing the same neighbourhood for two members of the same ethnic group. $P*$ is conceived as a measure of isolation (from people of a different ethnic group) to indicate the experience of segregation in daily lives (Massey and Denton, 1988). $P*$ can be expressed as follows:

$$P^* = \sum_{i} \left(\frac{N_{gi}}{N_{g\bullet}} \right) \left(\frac{N_{gi}}{N_{\bullet i}} \right) \tag{2}$$

In order to take into account of the relative size of the ethnic group, $P*$ has been adjusted using the following expression (see Noden, 2000):

$$PA^* = P^* - \left(\frac{N_{g\bullet}}{T} \right) \tag{3}$$

where T is the total population of the city or metropolitan area; and $PA*$ is the modified index of isolation.

Although D has become the preeminent summary statistic for the measurement of residential segregation, a much more complete description of spatial trends is possible in combination with $PA*$ (Robinson, 1980). Although residential evenness and exposure tend to be correlated empirically, they are two conceptually different measures. For example, while D is invariant to the size of the populations, $PA*$ depends on the relative size of the groups being compared. Therefore, if an ethnic group represents a small proportion of the total population of the area, they will experience a low level of isolation regardless of the evenness of their spatial distribution.

D has been computed across wards for England and Wales as a whole region. Overall, there are 8,800 wards in England and Wales, each containing an average population of around 6,000. Additionally, *D* and *P*A* have been calculated across census output areas (OAs) (with an average population size of about 300) for Bradford. When reviewing the analysis of *D* and *P*A*, it should be kept in mind that 'smaller areal units generally yield higher indices of segregation because they are more homogeneous' (Massey and Denton, 1988, p 299).

Since index values can be highly sensitive where the group size is small (Voas and Williamson, 2000), it is important to focus attention on those areas with large groups and where minority ethnic groups represent a substantial percentage of the total population (Peach, 1996b). For this purpose, in addition to the analysis for England and Wales, index values of evenness are reviewed in six ethnically diverse urban areas where non-White groups represented a significant percentage of the total population in 2001 at district level (Southwark −36.7 per cent, Leicester −36.1 per cent, Croydon −30.0 per cent, Birmingham −29.7 per cent, Bradford −21.8 per cent and Manchester −19.0 per cent), and with particular emphasis given to the following ethnic groups: Black Caribbean in Croydon (7.7 per cent), Black African in Southwark (15.9 per cent), Indian in Leicester (25.7 per cent), Pakistani in Bradford (14.6 per cent), Bangladeshi in Birmingham (2.1 per cent) and Chinese in Manchester (1.3 per cent).

For the purposes of comparison over time census ethnic group categories have been aggregated to eight compatible groups: White, Black Caribbean, Black African, Indian, Pakistani, Bangladeshi, Chinese and Other, with the 2001 Mixed groups being included in the residual Other category. The first seven of these groups are the most coherent and stable classification from 1991 to 2001 (ONS, 2006; Simpson and Akinwale, 2007). The residual eighth category is used for completeness, but is very diverse and of different composition in the two years.

Residential segregation across age cohorts

In this section residential segregation of ethnic groups between 1991 and 2001 across wards in England and Wales is analysed for different age cohorts. Despite the interest in recent years in the study of geographical mobility over the life course, with particular interest in its motivations and implications (Clark and Withers, 2007; Geist and

McMacus, 2008), as well as its specific relationships with, for example, women's economic activity (Dale et al, 2006) or family change and the need for domestic space (Bonney et al, 1999; Kulu and Milewski, 2007), only in some older studies, specifically in the US context, has residential segregation of Whites and Blacks been examined across the life course (Taeuber and Taeuber, 1965; Edwards, 1972). In Rossi's classic study of residential mobility (1955), residential mobility of Blacks to White neighbourhoods is seen as a spatial expression of vertical social mobility, the rate of which varies depending on age and stage in the life course. This relationship between spatial mobility and the life course is also well established through age migration schedules (Rogers et al, 1978; Rogers and Watkins, 1987), a framework based on constant migration that is affected by four peaks of migration over the life course (early childhood, early participation in the labour force, retirement and late old age).

This section first explores changes in residential segregation for various age cohorts through the index values of D across wards in England and Wales and for selected districts in 1991 and 2001. Within this context, the age cohort change analysis is used as a proxy to examine the relationship between residential segregation over the life course. It must be noted that the cohorts used are synthetic, based on age groups rather than groups of the same individuals at two time points. Thus, the populations of the age groups in 1991 and 2001 have been influenced by natural change and migration. So, the analysis compares index values of the resident population aged 0-6 in 1991 with index values for those aged 10-16 in 2001. Similarly, those aged 7-16 in 1991 are compared with the equivalent for those aged 17-26 ten years later. In other words, the analysis shows how residentially segregated in ethnic terms people are at two time points, a decade apart, thereby indicating the changing experience of ethnic segregation as people age. This is taken to illustrate changes in the level of segregation for different life stages. For example, people aged 0-6 in 1991 (and 10-16 in 2001) are a first age segment whose life stage can be considered to be primarily influenced by education. Similarly, other age segments can be related to life stages of family building and work, and retirement.

Figure 12.1 shows the index values of D by age cohorts across wards in England and Wales (top row) and for selected districts between 1991 and 2001 (bottom row). A separate line is presented for each ethnic group, and the three graphs in each row present D values in 1991, in 2001 and change in D over the decade.

Figure 12.1: *D* **values of ethnic groups by age cohorts across wards in England and Wales and for selected districts, 1991-2001**

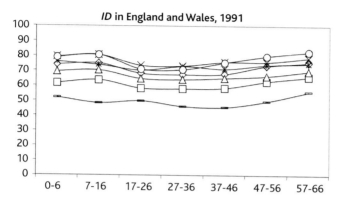

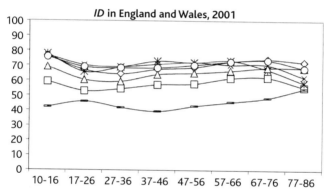

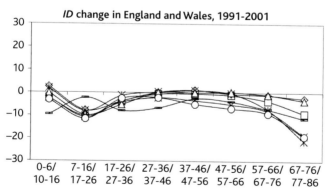

(continued)

Source: CCSR components of population change estimates and full population estimates (Sabater and Simpson, 2009)

Figure 12.1: *D* values of ethnic groups by age cohorts across wards in England and Wales and for selected districts, 1991-2001 (continued)

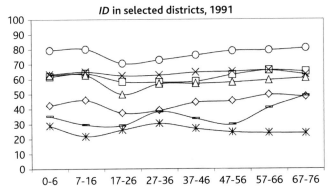

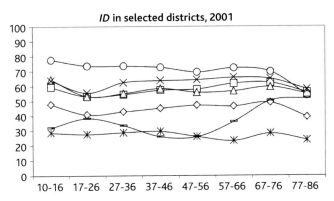

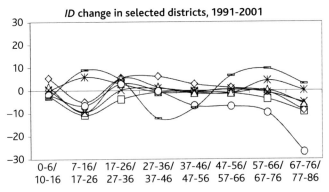

Source: CCSR components of population change estimates and full population estimates (Sabater and Simpson, 2009)

The analysis of the index values nationally clearly indicates a decrease in the level of residential segregation for each age cohort, a reduction that appears to be generally greater among minority ethnic groups (with an average decrease of 4.9 per cent) compared to the White British group (with an average decrease of 4 per cent). The analysis across age cohorts indicates a decrease in the level of unevenness during the decade for all ethnic groups in a similar fashion: the youngest group (which refers to children living with their parents) and adult ages show similar changes, while a clear decrease in segregation (D) is found among young adults. It is readily understood that the lower levels of residential segregation for young adults are a consequence of the difference in the residential distribution of school children and young adults (some of them university students).

In addition, international migration can affect residential segregation, particularly of young adults, given that most immigrants are in this age group. This is exemplified by the Chinese group, whose overseas migration to UK universities would explain the relative increase in the index values of D for Chinese young adults compared to other ethnic groups. Recent Chinese immigration, largely of higher education students (in their late teens and early twenties), has increased the proportion and clustering of the Chinese population in urban centres across the UK.

In the middle-aged phase – those age cohorts 17-26, 27-36 and 37-46 in 1991 – the patterns of desegregation suggest moves from big urban concentrations to less urban environments, following the suburbanisation process (Champion, 1989, 1996, 2005; Finney and Champion, 2008). Since older age cohorts of minority ethnic groups are affected by a significant number of neighbourhoods with small numbers of ethnic groups, it is difficult to provide a confident interpretation of the changes for these ages. Within this context, two aspects should be considered: on the one hand, the role of morbidity and mortality, which is more marked with increasing age among minority ethnic groups (Nazroo, 2003, 2006) and, on the other, the fact that minority ethnic groups are more likely to live in communal establishments than the White British group (over 25.5 per cent of people living in communal establishments were from minority ethnic groups in England and Wales, yet they only represented 8.8 per cent of the total population in 2001), thus adding further complexity to any meaningful comparison, particularly for the older age cohorts.

In the analysis of ethnic residential segregation by age cohorts for selected districts, results tend to replicate the reduction in index values of D obtained nationally for England and Wales. However, these also reveal situations of increased unevenness locally during the decade for some age cohorts, particularly during the early adulthood phase. For example, ethnic groups other than White generally experienced increased segregation, which is most likely a result of immigration between 1991 and 2001 of young adults, accentuating the clustering of these groups in these gateway districts. During the middle adulthood phase, an increase in unevenness is seen only for the Black Caribbean group in Croydon, which is likely to be caused by an over-representation of Black Caribbean in conjunction with White out-movement from Croydon, the latter being greater than the minority out-movement (Simpson and Finney, 2009).

The maps in Figure 12.2 show the index values of D for non-White groups (taken as a whole) across wards in districts of England and Wales in 2001 during the early adulthood phase, thus allowing comparisons of the index values for an area across the decade. They illustrate how the age cohorts 7-16 in 1991 and 17-26 in 2001 have become more evenly spread across districts, particularly from districts where non-White groups were most clustered. Although minority ethnic groups in the UK have very different residential geographies due to the timing and reasons for their immigration (Dale et al, 2006), those districts in traditional industrial areas in the North West, Yorkshire and Lancashire and the West Midlands appear to have the largest decreases in the index values of D for the early adulthood cohorts. This is in line with the idea that while the demographic consequences of immigration initially lead to greater isolation and segregation, the impact of growth and the unavailability of housing leads to dispersal from settlement areas to other parts of the country (Simpson et al, 2008b).

Figure 12.3 examines changes in segregation for one Yorkshire city, Bradford, over the 1990s. Although residential segregation by age group in Bradford has previously been examined for 2001 (McEvoy, 2009), showing variations with age in a consistent direction, there is still no evidence of changes over time. In this chapter, D and $PA*$ indices by age cohort are presented specifically for 1991 and 2001, with calculations based on OAs within the district of Bradford. The indices for the White and Pakistani populations are compared. In Britain the concern with concentrations of Asian (particularly Muslim) populations has been politically evident since disturbances in northern British cities, including Bradford, in 2001 (Cantle, 2001; Phillips, 2005). The historical concentration of South Asian groups in the inner areas of cities such as Bradford with the cheapest private housing originates from international migration to fill the unpopular night shifts of textile industries in response to competition after the Second World War.

Figure 12.2: Early adulthood phase D values of non-White groups across wards in 2001 districts. England and Wales, 1991-2001

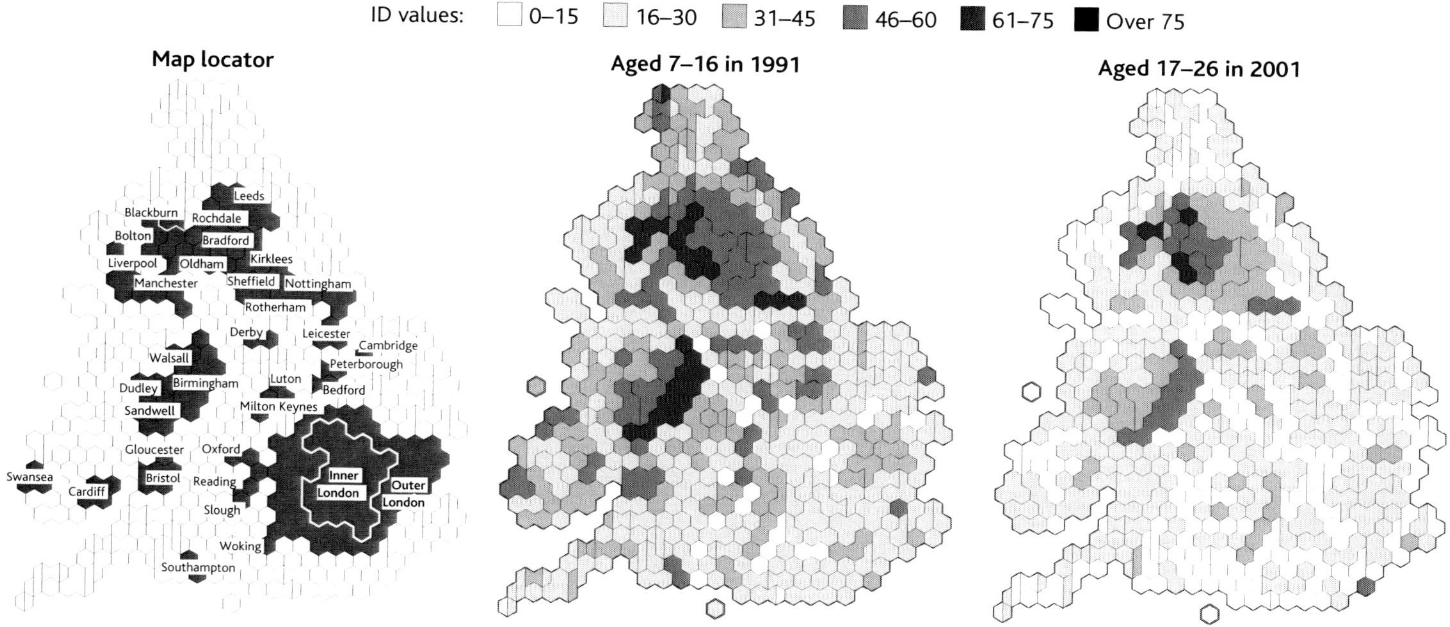

ID values: ☐ 0–15 ☐ 16–30 ▨ 31–45 ▨ 46–60 ■ 61–75 ■ Over 75

Aged 7–16 in 1991

Aged 17–26 in 2001

Map locator

Leeds, Rochdale, Bradford, Kirklees, Sheffield, Nottingham, Rotherham, Leicester, Cambridge, Peterborough, Bedford, Derby, Luton, Blackburn, Bolton, Oldham, Manchester, Liverpool, Walsall, Birmingham, Milton Keynes, Dudley, Sandwell, Gloucester, Oxford, Bristol, Reading, Slough, Woking, Southampton, Cardiff, Swansea, Inner London, Outer London

Source: CCSR Components of Population Change Estimates and Full Population Estimates (Sabater and Simpson, 2009).
Note: The areas in these cartograms are districts represented in proportion to the population size in 2001, maintaining the topology wherever possible. The shapefiles for the cartogram were created by Dorling and Thomas (2004).

Figure 12.3: *D* and *PA** values of White and Pakistani groups by age cohorts across Output Areas in Bradford, 1991-2001

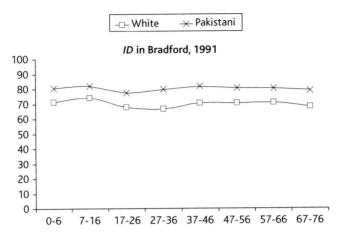

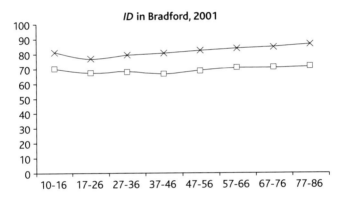

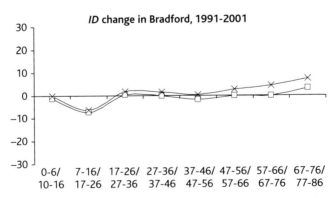

(continued)

Source: CCSR components of population change estimates and full population estimates (Sabater and Simpson, 2009)

Figure 12.3: *D* and *PA** values of White and Pakistani groups by age cohorts across Output Areas in Bradford, 1991-2001 (continued)

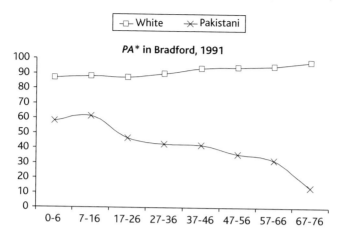

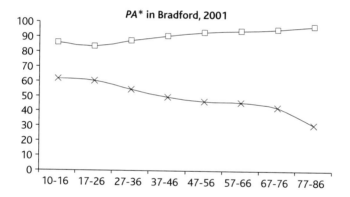

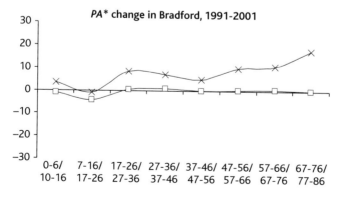

Source: CCSR components of population change estimates and full population estimates (Sabater and Simpson, 2009)

Considering the demography of immigration, D and $PA*$ are expected to change after significant streams of immigration. As expected, after the early years of immigration and the strong urban pattern of their natural growth in existing areas of Pakistani settlement, the index values of D of the Pakistani group for all age cohorts are greater (that is, show greater unevenness) than those of the White group. This tendency is characteristic where the influence of kinship ties is strong, thus reflecting the settlement pattern of international migration around the family, and cultural and religious support given by social networks (Peach, 1996a). Also, as expected, $PA*$ shows how all the age cohorts of the White group are more isolated from other ethnic groups than is the case for the Pakistani population of Bradford. Despite these differences in the values of D between the White and the Pakistani groups, it becomes evident that the most notable feature is how the D change depicts a similar pattern of age cohort segregation for both groups. The most remarkable change in $PA*$ over the decade is an increase for most age cohorts for the Pakistani population, and particularly for the youngest cohort (due to natural growth) as well as for older groups, thus reflecting increases in the population as a result of in-migration from elsewhere in Britain and overseas (Finney and Simpson, 2009b) as well as ageing in place for the oldest groups, although the latter needs caution as is clearly affected by small numbers. Finally, a significant feature of change in both D and $PA*$ for White and Pakistani populations of Bradford in the 1990s is the reduction in segregation of young adults. The role of age-differentiated migration patterns in explaining this change is the subject of the following section.

Role of migration in residential desegregation

Residential segregation, measured using two commonly used indices, has been shown to have decreased over the 1990s in England and Wales for young adults of all ethnic groups. Although changes in segregation may occur as a result of *in situ* population growth, particularly for minority populations with young age structures (see Finney and Simpson, 2009b), it is migration that redistributes the population. In the previous section it was suggested that migration patterns of young adults can explain this desegregation. This section looks explicitly at the migration patterns of young adults for evidence of processes of increased ethnic mixing (decreased residential segregation) through the 1990s.

Political concern has focused on movement of minorities towards areas in which they are most concentrated, a process that has become described as a combination of 'self-segregation' of minorities and 'White flight' of the majority population (see Chapter Six, this volume, which focuses on the US). However, analysis of internal migration patterns has revealed a process of dispersal from settlement areas to other types of area is occurring not only for the White group but also for non-White groups (Stillwell and Hussain, 2008; Simon, 2009; Simpson and Finney, 2009). In conjunction with this evidence, research based on surveys of households has found that many South Asians, particularly young adults, would like to move, with others, to areas outside the current settlements (Ratcliffe, 2000; Phillips, 2002):

> Contrary to the popular perception that South Asians, especially in places like Bradford, prefer to self-segregate, we found evidence of the desire for more mixing on the part of all ethnic/religious groups. Almost all respondents who talked about mixing characterised this as a process of Asian integration into ethnically mixed neighbourhoods rather than dispersal to white areas.... Movement to the outer areas of Leeds and Bradford was motivated by a better quality of physical environment, ... better housing, ... better schools, ... a safer environment, ... a more independent lifestyle, away from the sanctions and gossip of the ethnic cluster. (Phillips, 2002, p 10)

First, it is important to assess whether the migration of young adults is in any way distinct from migration at other ages and whether this holds for each ethnic group. Table 12.1 presents within-Britain migration rates by age and ethnic group, and shows a peak in migration rates for young adults (ages 16-29) for each ethnic group. More than for any other age group, therefore, migration has the potential to alter local ethnic group compositions of young adults. The question then arises of whether the migration is re-enforcing ethnic concentrations or dispersing them.

Table 12.2 presents the balance of migration (net migration) between districts grouped according to level of concentration of either White or minority ethnic (non-White) population. Districts are allocated into quintiles after being sorted according to the percentage of their population that is White/minority and then divided into five groups with roughly equal White/minority populations. Thus, the quintile groups contain similar numbers of White/minority people but in differing concentrations, meaning that there are different numbers of districts in each quintile. The migration is within Britain between 2000

Table 12.1: Within Britain migration rates (%), 2000-01, by ethnic group and age

	White British	White Irish	White Other	Mixed	Indian	Pakistani	Bangladeshi	Other Asian	Black Caribbean	Black African	Black Other	Chinese	Other	Total
0-15	10.9	9.6	15.0	11.9	8.6	8.5	8.2	11.4	8.9	13.5	9.4	10.7	15.0	10.9
16-19	15.8	24.0	24.4	15.9	12.3	8.6	9.8	15.2	14.3	17.7	12.7	20.5	24.0	15.8
20-24	32.6	45.4	48.1	33.7	23.7	17.9	15.6	29.4	22.0	33.2	19.6	42.8	37.0	32.4
25-29	24.0	32.6	36.2	28.1	19.5	15.9	15.4	23.7	17.0	28.6	16.2	25.2	32.3	24.3
30-44	11.4	13.5	17.7	14.8	10.3	10.2	9.2	16.7	10.7	16.4	11.4	13.5	18.9	11.7
45-59	5.0	4.7	6.4	7.9	3.7	5.6	5.6	6.4	6.7	9.6	9.2	5.1	7.8	5.0
60-64	3.8	3.1	4.4	4.1	2.9	3.5	5.8	5.0	3.7	6.0	2.0	5.3	6.6	3.8
65+	5.7	7.2	5.1	3.8	8.0	7.0	4.6	8.3	7.7	4.7	9.7	11.1	16.4	5.7
Total	10.5	10.2	18.0	15.0	10.1	10.0	9.7	14.3	9.9	17.0	11.3	16.1	18.7	10.8

Source: 2001 Census SAR, GB. Numerator is population who changed address in the year prior to the census; denominator is 2001 population in each age/ethnic group.

Table 12.2: Net migration between districts classified by ethnic concentration, 2000-01, by age and ethnic group

a) Migration of minority ethnic young adults

	Net gain to highest minority concentration districts from:	Net gain to high minority concentration districts from:	Net gain to medium minority concentration districts from:	Net gain to low minority concentration districts from:
Highest minority concentration districts				
High minority concentration districts	−16			
Medium minority concentration districts	7	28		
Low minority concentration districts	−31	11	12	
Lowest minority concentration districts	−18	−5	48	49

b) Migration of minority ethnic groups of other ages

	Net gain to highest minority concentration districts from:	Net gain to high minority concentration districts from:	Net gain to medium minority concentration districts from:	Net gain to low minority concentration districts from:
Highest minority concentration districts				
High minority concentration districts	−57			
Medium minority concentration districts	−42	−21		
Low minority concentration districts	−75	−31	−42	
Lowest minority concentration districts	−73	−37	−64	−23

(continued)

Table 12.2: Net migration between districts classified by ethnic concentration, 2000-2001, by age and ethnic group (continued)

c) Migration of White young adults

	Net gain to highest White concentration districts from:	Net gain to high White concentration districts from:	Net gain to medium White concentration districts from:	Net gain to low White concentration districts from:
Highest White concentration districts				
High White concentration districts	36			
Medium White concentration districts	−44	−17		
Low White concentration districts	−100	−65	−116	
Lowest White concentration districts	−298	−131	−597	−1,173

d) Migration of Whites of other ages

	Net gain to highest White concentration districts from:	Net gain to high White concentration districts from:	Net gain to medium White concentration districts from:	Net gain to low White concentration districts from:
Highest White concentration districts				
High White concentration districts	38			
Medium White concentration districts	0	390		
Low White concentration districts	117	152	255	
Lowest White concentration districts	300	452	608	943

Source: 2001 UK Census CAMS. Population: GB. Young adults are aged 18-29. Internal migration 2000-01.

Note: Districts have been grouped into five categories based on their percentage of non-White/White population. This division is such that each quintile of districts has the same non-White/White population but in differing concentrations.

and 2001 using data from the 2001 Census CAMS. The top two panels of the table (a and b) show movement of minority ethnic groups between districts classified by concentration of minority ethnic population; the lower two panels (c and d) show movement of Whites between districts classified by concentration of White population. For minorities and Whites, results are presented for young adults (aged 18-29) and for all other ages taken together. The net migration figures for the White group are expected to be higher than for the non-White group because of their larger population size and hence greater number of migrants. A negative value indicates dispersal from co-ethnic concentration, that is, migration from areas of more to less co-ethnic concentration.

Non-White young adults are on balance moving away from areas of highest non-White concentration to other areas (Table 12.2a). At the same time, areas of moderate and high concentration are gaining minority young adults from areas of low minority ethnic concentration. Thus, for non-White young adults there could be said to be a convergence to the 'middle ground' of areas of moderate to high ethnic diversity. The pattern for young adult Whites is clearer: they are dispersing from White concentrations and therefore moving into more ethnically diverse districts (Table 12.2c).

For both non-White and White populations aged under 19 and over 30, the direction of movement differs from that for young adults: families and older adults are moving to more White areas. This is illustrated in Table 12.2b by dispersal of non-White families/older adults from non-White concentrations and in Table 12.2d by movement of White families/older adults to more White areas. The different geographical patterns for young adults and others can be understood in terms of urbanisation of young adults and counter-urbanisation of families and older adults (Champion, 1989). Young adults, both White and non-White, are moving to diverse urban areas while families/older adults, White and non-White, are suburbanising away from urban centres. In terms of residential integration, Whites and non-Whites of young adult and other ages are moving to the same types of districts, thereby creating ethnic mixing.

Table 12.3 presents net migration for areas classified by concentration of minority ethnic population for Whites and minorities, for young adults and people of other ages taken together. Total net migration from the components of change estimates has been decomposed into internal migration and international migration in the final two columns of Table 12.3. This decomposition should be read as indicative because of discrepancies in the three measures of migration used in the table (see the table notes).

Table 12.3: Net migration for neighbourhoods grouped by minority ethnic concentration, by ethnic group and age

Quintile of minority concentration	Total migration		Migration within Britain		International migration (indicative estimate)	
	Whites	Minorities	Whites	Minorities	Whites	Minorities
Young adults						
Lowest	−65,914	5,883	−73,300	−2,467	7,400	8,400
Low	34,527	7,220	29,733	1,900	4,800	5,300
Medium	25,755	6,787	21,733	833	4,000	6,000
High	10,541	5,255	8,300	1,667	2,200	3,600
Highest	3,258	4,119	13,533	−1,933	−10,300	6,000
Non-young adult						
Lowest	121,298	12,735	76,767	6,567	44,500	6,200
Low	−36,942	2,168	−13,967	4,200	−23,000	−2,000
Medium	−31,162	−2,465	−15,767	−1,433	−15,400	−1,000
High	−21,728	219	−31,867	−1,100	10,100	1,300
Highest	−12,353	132	−15,167	−8,233	2,800	8,400

Sources: For total migration: components of change estimates, 1991-2001 divided by 10 to approximate a yearly figure. Based on wards of England and Wales.

Notes: White is all Census White groups; minorities are all others.

For migration within Britain: 2001 Census CAMS, 2000-01 scaled to 100% from figures for 3% sample. Based on districts of Britain.

White is White British; minorities are all non-White groups.

Young adults are aged 18-29; non-young adults are all other ages taken together.

International migration has been estimated by subtracting migration within Britain from total migration and is only indicative of patterns due to the discrepancies in the total and internal migration measures as described above. Figures have therefore been rounded to the nearest 100.

The table reveals two important findings. First, the pattern of dispersal/suburbanisation which has been seen for the White and minority populations as a whole is evident for children and older adults but not for young adults. Second, there is not a clear pattern of net immigration of minority populations being greater in areas in which they are concentrated compared to other areas. In fact, for young adults both White and minority, immigration is greatest to the areas of least minority ethnic concentration.

The dynamics of desegregation are summarised diagrammatically in Figure 12.4. The figure represents the net direction of internal and international migration for the most and least diverse areas, for Whites and minorities of young adult and other ages.

The least diverse areas, which can be alternatively seen as the most White areas and also the most rural areas, grow through net immigration of young adults and families/older adults, White and minority. They also gain families and older adults, White and minority, from elsewhere in Britain. They lose young adults, White and minority, to elsewhere in Britain. These dynamics result in the least diverse areas losing White young adults but gaining minority young adults, and also gaining Whites and minority families/older adults.

The most diverse areas in Britain, alternatively seen as central urban neighbourhoods, gained families/older adults, both White and minority, from overseas due to net immigration and simultaneously lost this population, on balance, to elsewhere in Britain. The same dynamic is seen for minority young adults: net gain from overseas and net loss to elsewhere in Britain. For White young adults, however, the migration dynamics are in the opposite direction: the most diverse areas gain White young adults from elsewhere in Britain and lose them, on balance, through emigration. Overall, these dynamics result in the most diverse areas gaining minorities (young adults and families/older adults) and White young adults but losing White families/older adults. Thus, the picture that has been described as 'White flight' and 'minority self-segregation' can alternatively be described as age-differentiated migration common across ethnic groups: young adult urbanisation and family/older adult suburbanisation with immigration of a similar magnitude to the least and most diverse areas.

Figure 12.4: Dynamics of desegregation

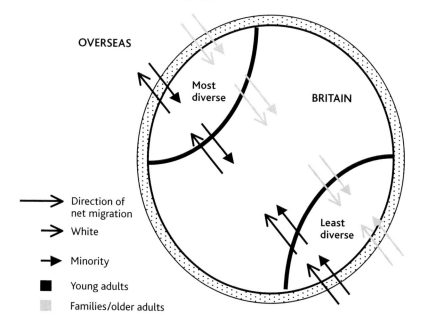

Conclusion

This chapter has analysed UK census data and population estimates to address how ethnic residential segregation has changed over time for different age cohorts, ethnic groups and subnational areas, and to examine the migration dynamics that account for decreased residential segregation. While previous research already highlighted decreasing ethnic segregation over time in England and Wales and important similarities in the age patterns of segregation between ethnic groups (see Sabater, 2010), the new analyses allow us to shed further light on the role of migration in residential desegregation by taking into consideration age-differentiated migration patterns across ethnic groups (Finney and Simpson, 2008).

The analyses in this chapter have found residential segregation between 1991 and 2001 to have decreased for all age cohorts, with the largest decrease in unevenness among young adults. The patterns by age were remarkably similar across ethnic groups, with the exception of the Chinese group that did not experience as great an increase in evenness of young adults as other ethnic groups. Desegregation of young adults was found throughout Britain, although there are examples where this was not the case (such as Black Africans in Southwark and Chinese in Manchester). It has been suggested that immigration of young adults to these districts results in an increase in clustering which offsets the dispersal to elsewhere in Britain.

Dynamics of migration have been shown to explain the desegregation observed. Contrasting internal migration experiences of young adults and other ages, both in terms of the level and direction of movement, have been found, with this age-differentiated migration common to White and non-White populations. Young adults tend to migrate within Britain towards diverse urban areas and are highly mobile, whereas families and older adults demonstrate counter-urbanisation. In terms of residential integration, Whites and non-Whites of young adult and other ages are moving within Britain to the same types of districts, thereby creating ethnic mixing.

International migration generally results in net population gain in the least and most diverse areas of Britain. In the least diverse areas this reinforced the internal gain of families/older adults and replenished young adults lost to elsewhere in Britain. In the most diverse areas immigration replenished loss of families and older adults to elsewhere in Britain. These patterns are consistent for Whites and minorities. Net immigration is of a similar magnitude to the most and least diverse areas, although, for young adults, both White and minority, immigration is greatest to the areas of least minority ethnic concentration. Overall, the findings of this chapter show that the dynamics of ethnic residential desegregation are age-differentiated migration common across ethnic groups – young adult urbanisation and family/older adult suburbanisation.

From this, the conclusion can be drawn that the residential integration of ethnic groups cannot be expected to follow a 'straight line' from urban centres. Rather, the migration geographies are age-differentiated and compounded by ongoing international migration in the most and least diverse areas. The maintenance of an ethnic cluster cannot be assumed to represent ethnic retreat or conflict, as it is likely to be the result of young adult urbanisation, natural growth and replacement immigration. Furthermore, the dynamic maintenance of ethnic clusters is in the context of more general residential dispersal and desegregation.

In understanding the complexities of subnational ethnic group population change, it is necessary to pay attention to different migration experiences at different life stages. Recognising the importance of structural factors such as access to education, training, employment and housing, and life events such as job loss, family formation, childbirth and retirement in driving migration patterns is seen as critically important for assessing changes in ethnic residential segregation across the life course. It may be that commonalities in residential decision-making through the life course transcend differences resulting from ethnicity.

In the study of population dynamics and residential segregation, it also becomes clear that other aspects need to be taken into consideration such as contextual or historical factors. An illustration of this can be found within this book with the work undertaken by Shuttleworth et al, for Northern Ireland, where internal migration appears to have a very small impact on residential segregation in the short run, which is interpreted as a consequence of the underlying geographical structures and the imposing layers of history on population redistribution (see Chapter Nine, this volume).

Measuring the processes that create patterns of ethnic segregation by considering the effects of population size and demographic composition is obviously particularly useful. Within this context, our research is also related to Harris (Chapter Ten, this volume), whose findings suggest that although segregation by ethnicity in London's secondary schools exists, 'there is also little, if any, evidence to suggest those differences are growing, at least not when demographic changes are taken into consideration'. The usefulness of analyses of segregation by ethnicity and age are also found in this book by Östh et al (Chapter Seven, this volume), with a particular focus on residential segregation for middle school-aged children in Sweden.

While age has been shown to be an important component in understanding changing residential segregation, further work could fruitfully examine other elements of time. In particular, is the age-differentiated migration observed here a product of the time period being studied? And to what extent do the migration behaviours of young adults differ generationally from those of their parents and grandparents, and are there specificities to minority ethnic group generational change that may be characteristic of immigrant integration?

Finally, this chapter presents a partial picture in our understandings of ethnic integration: it advances our understanding of the dynamics of desegregation but does not examine what this means socially. Why people decide to move and how they choose their destination is a complex combination of choice and constraint, made by individuals in household and neighbourhood contexts. In order to conclude about ethnic relations, it is necessary to investigate how the motivations behind the migration patterns observed in this chapter are influenced by ethnicity, whether ethnic conflict plays a role, or whether other factors of family, locality and residential aspiration are more dominant in migration decision-making for all ethnic groups.

Acknowledgements

The 2001 Census SARs are provided through the Cathie Marsh Centre for Census and Survey Research (University of Manchester), with the support of the Economic and Social Research Council (ESRC) and the Joint Information Systems Committee (JISC). Use of the 2001 Census CAMS is supported by the Office for National Statistics. Census output is Crown Copyright and all tables containing census data, and the results of analysis, are reproduced with the permission of the Controller of Her Majesty's Stationery Office and the Queen's Printer for Scotland. The authors alone are responsible for the interpretation of the data.

The full population estimates and components of demographic change (births, deaths and net migration) are available from the UK data archive (see www.data-archive.ac.uk) under SN 6043 and SN 6778 respectively. This research was supported by the UK ESRC Understanding Population Trends and Processes (UPTAP) programme (Albert Sabater, Ref PTA-163-27-0002. Nissa Finney, RES-163-27-0011), a University of Manchester Hallsworth Fellowship (Nissa Finney) and the Juan de la Cierva Fellowship Programme of the Ministry of Science and Innovation of Spain (Albert Sabater, Ref JCI-

2009-03757). We are grateful to Ian Plewis and Douglas Massey for helpful comments on earlier drafts of this chapter, and to the editors for their useful insights and suggestions.

Note

[1] For more details on 2001 Census micro-data, including how to access the data, see www.ccsr.ac.uk/sars

References

Alba, R. and Nee, V. (1997) 'Rethinking assimilation theory for a new era of immigration', *International Migration Review*, vol 31, no 4, pp 826-74.

Bailey, A. and Boyle, P. (2004) 'Untying and retying family migration in the New Europe', *Journal of Ethnic and Migration Studies*, vol 30, no 2, pp 229-41.

Bonney, N., McCleery, A. and Forster, E. (1999) 'Migration, marriage and life course: commitment and residential mobility', in P. Boyle and K. Halfacree (eds) *Migration and gender in the developed world*, London: Routledge, pp 136-50.

Burgess, E. (1928) 'Residential segregation in American cities', *Annals of the American Academy of Political and Social Science*, vol 14, pp 105-15.

Cantle, T. (2001) *Community cohesion: a report of the independent review team*, London: Home Office.

Champion, A. (1989) *Counterurbanisation: the changing pace and nature of population deconcentration*, London: Edward Arnold.

Champion, A. (1996) 'Internal migration and ethnicity in Britain', in P. Ratcliffe (ed) *Ethnicity in the 1991 Census, Volume 3, Social geography and ethnicity in Britain: geographical spread, spatial concentration and internal migration*, London: Office for National Statistics/HMSO, pp 135-73.

Champion, A. (2005) 'The counterurbanisation cascade in England and Wales since 1991: the evidence of a new migration dataset', *Belgeo*, vol 1-2, pp 85-101.

Clark, W. and Withers S. (2007) 'Family migration and mobility sequences in the United States: spatial mobility in the context of the life course', *Demographic Research*, vol 17, no 20, pp 591-622.

Dale, A., Lindley, J. and Dex, S. (2006) 'A lifecourse perspective on ethnic differences in women's economic activity in Britain', *European Sociological Review*, vol 22, no 4, pp 459-76.

Dale, A., Shaheen, N., Fieldhouse, E. and Kalra, V. (2002) 'Routes into education and employment for young Pakistani and Bangladeshi women in the UK', *Ethnic and Racial Studies*, vol 25, 942-68.

Dennett, A. and Stillwell, J. (2011) 'A new area classification for understanding internal migration in Britain', *Population Trends*, vol 145, pp 146-71.

de Valk, H. (2007) 'Living arrangements of migrant and Dutch young adults: the family influence disentangled', *Population Studies*, vol 61, no 2, pp 201-17.

de Valk, H. and Billari, F. (2007) 'Living arrangements of migrant and Dutch young adults: the family influence disentangled', *Population Studies*, vol 61, no 2, pp 201-17.

Dorling, D. and Thomas, B. (2004) *People and places: a 2001 census atlas of the UK*, Bristol: Policy Press.

Duncan, O. and Lieberson, S. (1959) 'Ethnic segregation and assimilation', *American Journal of Sociology*, vol 64, no 4, pp 364-74.

Edwards, O. (1972) 'Family composition as a variable in residential succession', *American Journal of Sociology*, vol 77, pp 731-41.

Finney, N. (2011) 'Understanding ethnic differences in migration of young adults within Britain from a lifecourse perspective', *Transactions of the Institute of British Geographers, vol* 36, no 3, pp 455-70.

Finney, N. and Catney, G. (eds) (2012) *Minority internal migration in Europe*, Farnham: Ashgate.

Finney, N. and Champion, A. (2008) *Labour markets, skills and talents: residential migration*, Working Paper, Manchester: *Manchester Independent Economic Review.*

Finney, N. and Simpson, L. (2008) 'Internal migration and ethnic groups: evidence for Britain from the 2001 census', *Population, Space and Place*, vol 14, no 2, pp 63-83.

Finney, N. and Simpson, L. (2009a) *'Sleepwalking to segregation'? Challenging myths about race and migration*, Bristol: Policy Press.

Finney, N. and Simpson, L. (2009b) 'Population dynamics: the roles of natural change and migration in producing the ethnic mosaic', *Journal of Ethnic and Migration Studies*, vol 35, no 10, pp 1707-16.

Flint, J. and Robinson, D. (eds) (2008) *Community cohesion in crisis? New dimensions of diversity and difference*, Bristol: Policy Press.

Fortuijn, J., Musterd, S. and Ostendorf, W. (1998) 'International migration and ethnic segregation: impacts on urban areas', *Urban Studies*, vol 35, pp 367-70.

Geist, C. and McMacus, P. (2008) 'Geographical mobility over the life course: motivations and implications', *Population, Space and Place*, vol 14, pp 283-303.

Johnston, R., Forrest, J. and Poulsen, M. (2002) 'Are there ethnic enclaves/ghettos in English cities?', *Urban Studies*, vol 39, no 4, pp 591-618.

Kalra, V. and Kapoor, N. (2009) 'Interrogating segregation, integration and the community cohesion agenda', *Journal of Ethnic and Migration Studies*, vol 35, no 9, pp 1397–415.

Kaplan, D. and Holloway, S. (1998) *Segregation in cities*, Washington, DC: Association of American Geographers.

Kulu, H. and Milewski, N. (2007) 'Family change and migration in the life course: an introduction', *Demographic Research*, vol 17, no 19, pp 567–90.

Logan, J. (1978) 'Growth, politics and the stratification of places', *American Journal of Sociology*, vol 184, pp 404–16.

McEvoy, D. (2009) 'Ethnic residential segregation in the United Kingdom by age group: the case of Bradford', *Cosmopolitan Civil Societies Journal*, vol 1, no 1, pp 15–38.

Massey, D. and Denton, N. (1988) 'The dimensions of residential segregation', *Social Forces*, vol 67, pp 281–315.

Massey, D., Condran, G. and Denton, N. (1987) 'The effects of residential segregation on Black social and economic wellbeing', *Social Forces*, vol 66, pp 29–56.

Mortimer, J.T. and Shanaham, M.J. (eds) (2004) *Handbook of the life course*, New York: Springer.

Mulder, C.H. (1993) *Migration dynamics: a life course approach*, Amsterdam: Thesis Publishers.

Musterd, S. (2005) 'Social and ethnic segregation in Europe: levels, causes, and effects', *Journal of Urban Affairs*, vol 27, no 3, pp 331–48.

Nazroo, J.Y. (2003) 'The structuring of ethnic inequalities in health: economic position, racial discrimination, and racism', *American Journal of Public Health*, vol 93, no 2, pp 277–84.

Nazroo, J.Y. (2006) 'Ethnicity and old age', in J.A. Vincent, C. Phillipson and M. Downs (eds) *The futures of old age*, London: Sage, pp 66–72.

Noden, P. (2000) 'Rediscovering the impact of marketisation: dimensions of social segregation in England's secondary schools', *Journal of Sociology of Education*, vol 21, pp 372–90.

ONS (Office for National Statistics) (2006) *A guide to comparing 1991 and 2001 Census ethnic group data*, Titchfield: ONS.

Park, R. (1924) *The concept of social distance*, reprinted in *Race and culture: The collected papers of Robert Ezra Park, Vol I*, Glencoe, IL: The Free Press (1950), p 260.

Peach, C. (1996a) 'Good segregation, bad segregation', *Planning Perspectives*, vol 11, pp 379–98.

Peach, C. (1996b) 'Does Britain have ghettos?', *Transactions of the Institute of British Geographers*, vol 21, no 1, pp 216–35.

Peach, C. (2009) 'Slippery segregation, discovering or creating ghettos? Segregation, assimilation and social cohesion', *Journal of Ethnic and Migration Studies*, vol 35, no 9, pp 1381-95.

Phillips, D. (2002) *Movement to opportunity? South Asian relocation in northern cities. End of Award report, ESRC R000238038*, Leeds: School of Geography, University of Leeds.

Phillips, T. (2005) 'After 7/7: sleepwalking to segregation', Speech given at Manchester Council for Community Relations, 22 September (www.humanities.manchester.ac.uk/socialchange/research/social-change/summer-workshops/documents/sleepwalking.pdf).

Phillips, D. (2006) 'Parallel lives? Challenging discourses of British Muslim selfsegregation', *Environment and Planning D: Society and Space*, vol 24, no 1, pp 25-40.

Plane, D.A. and Jurjevich, J.R. (2009) 'Ties that no longer bind? The patterns and repercussions of age-articulated migration', *The Professional Geographer*, vol 61, no 1, pp 4-20.

Ratcliffe, P. with Harrison, M., Hogg, R., Line, B., Phillips, D. and Tomlins, R. (2000) *Breaking down the barriers: improving Asian access to social rented housing*, London: Chartered Institute of Housing.

Rees, P., Wohland, P., Norman, P. and Boden, P. (2011) 'A local analysis of ethnic group population trends and projections for the UK', *Journal of Population Research*, vol 28, pp 149-83.

Robinson, V. (1980) 'Lieberson's isolation index: a case study evaluation', *Area*, vol 12, no 4, pp 307-12.

Rossi, P. (1955) *Why families move: a study of the social psychology of urban residential mobility*, Glencoe, IL: The Free Press.

Rogers, A. and Watkins, J. (1987) 'General versus elderly interstate migration and population redistribution in the United States', *Research on Aging*, vol 9, no 4, pp 483-529.

Rogers, A., Raquillet, R. and Castro, L. (1978) 'Model migration schedules and their applications', *Environment and Planning A*, vol 10, no 5, pp 475-502.

Sabater, A. (2008) 'Estimation of ethnic groups in sub-national areas for analysis of population change, England and Wales, 1991-2001', PhD thesis, Manchester: Centre for Census and Survey Research, University of Manchester.

Sabater, A. (2010) 'Ethnic residential segregation over time and cohorts in England and Wales, 1991-2001', in J. Stillwell, N. Finney and M. Van Ham (eds) *Ethnicity and integration. Understanding population trends and processes*, vol 3, London: Springer.

Sabater, A. and Simpson, L. (2009a) 'Enhancing the population census: a time series for subnational areas with age, sex and ethnic group dimensions in England and Wales, 1991-2001', *Journal of Ethnic and Migration Studies*, vol 35, no 9, pp 1461-77.

Sabater, A. and Simpson, L. (2009b) *Population estimates by single year of age, sex and ethnic group for sub-national areas in England and Wales, 1991-2001* [computer file], Colchester: UK Data Archive [distributor], Study Number (SN) 6043.

Simon, A. (2009) *Calculating ward level internal migration measures using census 2001 data*, Working Paper, London: Thomas Coram Research Unit, Institute of Education.

Simpson, L. (2007) 'Ghettos of the mind: the empirical behaviour of indices of segregation and diversity', *Journal of the Royal Statistical Society A*, vol 170, no 2, pp 405-24.

Simpson, L. and Akinwale, B. (2007) 'Quantifying stability and change in ethnic group', *Journal of Official Statistics*, vol 23, no 2, pp 185-208.

Simpson, L. and Finney, N. (2009) 'Spatial patterns of internal migration: evidence for ethnic groups in Britain', *Population, Space and Place*, vol 15, pp 37-56.

Simpson, L., Cossey, R. and Diamond, I. (1997) '1991 population estimates for areas smaller than Districts', *Population Trends*, vol 90, pp 31-9.

Simpson, L., Finney, N. and Lomax, S. (2008a) *Components of population change: An indirect method for estimating births, deaths and net migration for age, sex, ethnic group and subregional areas of Britain, 1991-2001*, CCSR Working Paper 2008-03, Manchester: University of Manchester.

Simpson, L., Gavalas, V. and Finney, N. (2008b) 'Population dynamics in ethnically diverse towns: the long term implications of immigration', *Urban Studies*, vol 45, no 1, pp 163-83.

Stillwell, J. and Hussain, S. (2008) *Ethnic group migration within Britain during 2000-01: a district level analysis*, Working Paper, Leeds: School of Geography, University of Leeds.

Taeuber, K. and Taeuber, A. (1965), *Negroes in cities: Residential segregation and neighborhood change*, Chicago, IL: Aldine Publishing Company.

van Ham, M. and Feijten, P. (2008) 'Who wants to leave the neighbourhood? The effect of being different from the neighbourhood population on wishes to move', *Environment and Planning A*, vol 40, no 5, pp 1151-70.

Voas, D. and Williamson, P. (2000) 'The scale of dissimilarity: concepts, measurement and an application to socio-economic variation across England and Wales', *Transactions of the Institute of British Geographers*, vol 25, pp 465-81.

Ward, D. (1989) *Poverty, ethnicity and the American city 1840-1925*, Cambridge: Cambridge University Press.

Wingens, M., Windzio, M., de Valk, H. and Aybek, C. (eds) (2011) *A life-course perspective on migration and integration*, Dordrecht: Springer

Wirth, L. (1928) *The ghetto*, Chicago, IL: The University of Chicago Press.

THIRTEEN

A tale of two cities: residential segregation in St Louis and Cincinnati

Sungsoon Hwang

Introduction

Some forms of residential segregation (for example, concentrated poverty) can have negative consequences for social mobility (see Chapters Eleven, Twelve and Fifteen, this volume). They are shown to be associated with, for instance, the achievement gap in education (Vartanian and Gleason, 1999; Card and Rothstein, 2006) and health disparities (Williams and Collins, 2001; Kramer and Hogue, 2009; see also Chapter Fourteen, this volume). Research shows that living in a deprived neighbourhood can have lasting impacts on life chances (Wilson, 1990; see also Chapter Sixteen, this volume). In the US, high school dropout rates are significantly higher in minority neighbourhoods (Orfield et al, 2004). If dropout rates were cut in half, US$45 billion could be saved annually through a decrease in social services and incarceration and an increase in revenue (Bridgeland, 2011). Studies show that 75 per cent of North America's state prison inmates are high school dropouts (Harlow, 2003), and an increasing participation rate of minority students in college to a level the same as that of White students would create at least US$80 billion in new tax revenues (Alliance for Excellent Education, 2003).

In the wake of rising costs of residential segregation, it is important to formulate urban policies that effectively redress the negative effects of segregation. One cannot devise such policies without a good understanding of what causes residential segregation. Yet, processes leading to residential segregation are highly context-dependent. Segregation levels are higher in certain North American cities as compared to other Western cities (Fong, 1996; Musterd, 2005; Johnston et al, 2007). Spatial outcomes of social polarisation vary by cities (Sassen, 1991; Hamnett, 2001; Poulsen et al, 2002;

Maloutas, 2007). External forces (for example, demographic changes) interact with various characteristics of a neighbourhood differently (Megbolugbe et al, 1996). Understanding place-specific processes of residential segregation can also help devise effective 'place-based policies' that consider local characteristics (White House, 2009).

What are the place-specific processes or characteristics that contribute to residential segregation with negative social capital effects? This chapter explores if the structure of the housing market can be one of these place-specific characteristics. In addition, this chapter proposes some methods to answer this question while comparing residential segregation in St Louis and Cincinnati. The two metropolitan areas have gone through similar economic trajectories (they are Rust Belt cities), and have a similar income distribution among social groups (the Gini index is 0.448 for St Louis and 0.447 for Cincinnati). However, they exhibit different spatial patterns of residential segregation – similar residential neighbourhoods are more clustered and differentiated in St Louis than Cincinnati, described in later sections. In addition, they have different levels of school performance – the St Louis School District had an average high school dropout rate of 24.94 per cent in 2005-09, and the Cincinnati School District had 4.61 per cent during the same period, according to the National Center for Education Statistics. This raises a question about context-specific aspects (or different spatialisation) of residential segregation in these two cities.

This research was motivated by several observations made in previous research on residential segregation. First, measurement of residential segregation is not explicitly linked to processes of residential segregation (Duncan and Duncan, 1955). Segregation measures (for example, the index of dissimilarity, *D*) have been developed to describe the degree of segregation rather than explain the process of residential segregation. The arbitrary nature of areal units (that is, residential neighbourhoods) used in computing segregation indices is also a problem (see Chapter Seven, this volume; Wong et al, 1999). Second, researchers often overlook the pivotal role of economic processes that underlie residential segregation. Many factors are at play in shaping residential segregation – namely, residents' preferences, exclusionary zoning and discrimination. To be precise, consumers' preferences interact with other forces, causing population groups to be sorted into different neighbourhoods (Grigsby et al, 1987). Further, varying consumer preferences are increasingly relevant in explaining residential segregation in a pluralistic society (Brown and Chung, 2006). Third, the inherently spatial nature of residential segregation is still under-recognised (Wong, 1997; Reardon et al, 2008; see also Chapters Three,

Four and Nine, this volume), but advances made in spatial statistics and geographic information systems (GIS) present an opportunity to elucidate processes related to residential segregation and housing markets (Anselin, 1998).

In addressing the concerns outlined above, this study draws from the theory of housing economics and on relevant analytical techniques. In particular, hedonic modelling of house prices (Lancaster, 1971; Rosen, 1974) is useful in modelling the heterogeneous housing market. Constructs of housing submarkets (Rothenberg et al, 1991) can be used to examine how those heterogeneous demands for housing are spatially organised. Geographically weighted regression (GWR) (Fotheringham et al, 2001) can aid in revealing the spatial variation of the housing demand within a metropolitan area, and thus help analysts infer local processes that underlie residential sorting and segregation.

In this chapter, we delineate housing submarkets to examine the spatial patterns of residential sorting that hinge on economic processes. We focus on the static analysis of housing submarkets using readily available data and analytical techniques. Then we interpret spatial patterns of residential segregation against findings from housing market analysis and selected archives over the last 60 years in the study areas. In doing so, we explore place-specific processes that might underlie the different spatial patterns of residential segregation in the St Louis and Cincinnati metropolitan areas.

Theoretical framework

Causes of residential segregation

There are three strands of research with regard to what causes residential segregation. The first strand investigates the causes of spatial *sorting*, arguing that residential segregation, viewed as a division of residential space, is caused by preferences involved in residential location choice (Vandell, 1995; Bayer et al, 2004). Residents choose where they live by balancing their preferences for housing space with commuting costs (Alonso, 1964). Quality of public goods affects 'residents voting with their feet' (Tiebout, 1956). Social and natural amenities influence residential location choice (Rosen, 1974). Empirical studies occasionally suggest that households prefer neighbourhoods of similar income level and relatively homogeneous ethnic composition (Clark, 1986; O'Connor et al, 2001). Some recent studies point to the emerging trends toward preference for diverse neighbourhoods, but this seems to be (so far) only as long as residents are not in a minority in the neighbourhood in which they consider living. Prestige and social identity can play a role in residential sorting (Manzi and Smith-Bowers, 2005). This viewpoint focuses on the mechanisms driven by choice.

The second strand of research focuses on what causes spatial *disadvantage*. In this context, it is argued that residential segregation, viewed as a lack of social intermixing in residential space, is caused by discrimination imposed on the socially disadvantaged (Galster, 1988; Charles, 2003). Discrimination is enforced in different forms, which can be explicit or not; this ranges from the Jim Crow Laws, restrictive covenants and discriminatory or predatory lending practices, to neighbourhood stereotyping (Charles, 2003). Legality issues with regard to discrimination have been resolved through a series of court rulings, but the persistence of residential segregation suggests that much work needs to be done in enacting fair housing policies (Carr and Kutty, 2008). This viewpoint focuses on a mechanism shaped by constraints or discrimination.

The third strand of research highlights institutional forces that work in tandem with preferences and constraints discussed earlier. It is argued that government policy and local land use regulations have caused and reinforced residential segregation (Schill and Wachter, 1995; Judd, 1997). The US federal policy that promotes home ownership in suburbs has, according to this argument, effectively subsidised 'White flight' and the urban decay by favouring well-off Whites during the post-war era; this was facilitated by the increase in vehicle ownership and development of the interstate highway system (Muller, 2004). Furthermore, local governing entities use zoning and land use regulations to protect property values and control revenue streams in competition (Gordon, 2008). This land use control of exclusionary type has served to demarcate the division between central cities and suburbs along the racial and class lines in the US. This viewpoint emphasises a mechanism conditioned by political economy.

Residential segregation arises from the interlocking of these complementary forces. The process of residential segregation is mostly rooted in consumer preferences refracted through social, institutional and economic forces (Grigsby et al, 1987; Megbolugbe et al, 1996). Discrimination and institutional forces are important factors affecting residential segregation, but they work in conjunction with economic forces. It is necessary to examine how these forces are at work in unison – this should be considered as a framework for understanding processes of residential segregation. In this regard, the theory of housing submarkets (Grigsby et al, 1987; Rothenberg et al, 1991; Galster, 1996;

Goodman and Thibodeau, 1998; Watkins, 2001) provides alternative perspectives – a more integrative framework centred on economic forces – for conceptualising residential segregation. Below we discuss how this is the case after reviewing the concept of housing submarkets.

Housing submarkets

Residential segregation occurs partly because of the unique characteristics of housing markets. Housing has characteristics distinct from other commodities – namely, heterogeneity, spatial immobility, rigidity and durability. The quality of housing service is derived from a bundle of attributes (for example, housing size, job accessibility, crime, school quality, etc); this is known as the hedonic theory of housing markets (Lancaster, 1971; Rosen, 1974). The combination of those attributes is not easily replicated because housing is at a fixed location. Buying and selling a house is more costly than the transactions of other commodities, and this transaction is sensitive to macroeconomic factors (for example, mortgage rates). Similarly, the business decision to build houses is not readily responsive to demand due to the need to consider uncertainty surrounding return on investment (for example, change in price of raw materials, neighbourhood changes). In addition, housing stocks are relatively durable. An abrupt change is quite unlikely to occur, and neighbourhood characteristics are gradually formed on a remnant of the past. Due to these unique characteristics, the housing market hardly coalesces into a unity. Rather, the housing market is divided into submarkets that are defined sectorally (for example, single family home, condo, apartments) and/or spatially (that is, by neighbourhoods) at various geographic scales (Tu, 1997). Therefore, the housing market can be better viewed as a set of distinct but interrelated submarkets (Galster, 1996).

One can detect a housing submarket given its distinct market mechanism. Residents value specific attributes, and builders cater to that demand within a housing submarket. A market mechanism can be expressed through the preference structure of those segmented residents. The preference structure can be operationalised in terms of hedonic models of house prices (Follain and Jimenez, 1985). Hedonic coefficients represent how residents value attributes specific to a house and its location (that is, its premium). If hedonic coefficients are different across models stratified by housing submarkets, and a segmented model increases prediction accuracy significantly over a pooled model, housing submarkets are considered to exist (Schnare and Struyk, 1976; Bourassa et al, 1999; Watkins, 2001). Due to the distinct market mechanism, housing units that belong to dissimilar housing submarkets are not substitutable (Grigsby et al, 1987; Rothenberg et al, 1991). That is, (prospective) residents would not consider moving to neighbourhoods that are far from meeting their specific needs. Rather, they will consider a set of similar housing submarkets as close substitutes. Non-substitutability is the key to a behavioural definition of housing submarkets.

Important questions still remain: how can housing submarkets be empirically delineated? The field dedicated to delineating housing submarkets is quickly evolving along with advances in GIS and spatial statistics. The set of methods largely consists of (a) a hedonic regression analysis to identify factors that explain variation in housing price, (b) a cluster analysis to delineate homogeneous clusters, and (c) a statistical test to determine the differences among clusters in terms of preference structure. If clusters pass the statistical test, those clusters are confirmed to be housing submarkets (see Watkins, 2001, for detailed description). GWR (Fotheringham et al, 2002) can be used to explore spatial housing submarkets because it can reveal spatially varying relationships between housing price and explanatory variables.

Housing submarkets can be alternatively detected based on sustained housing price differentials across housing submarkets (Maclennan et al, 1987) or a lack of migration among housing submarkets (Jones, 2002) over a certain period of time because housing submarkets result from the inability of the market to resolve price differentials across different locations. In other words, the existence of housing submarkets is attributed to the inefficiency of spatial arbitrage. However, it does not mean that the housing market maintains the status quo in the long term. Rather, the dynamics of the housing market (for example, how neighbourhoods change over time) hinge on the interrelatedness between housing submarkets. External socioeconomic forces (such as the demographic shift, economic restructuring) have a different impact on housing submarkets (Megbolugbe et al, 1996), and this occurs in tandem with institutional forces that are enacted over varying geographic scales (for example, federal mortgage policy, local land use control). For example, professionalisation is likely to engender neighbourhoods as club goods (excludable and non-rivalrous public goods such as non-congested toll roads and golf courses); an influx of immigrants is likely to increase the presence of submarkets that are catered to these immigrants. At first, these changes in one housing submarket have more direct effects on similar submarkets than dissimilar submarkets because similar submarkets are close substitutes. These changes eventually have ripple effects on the entire housing market.

Therefore, housing submarkets can be considered as a framework for understanding the dynamics of neighbourhood change (Grigsby et al, 1987).

Utility of housing submarkets in conceptualising residential segregation

Since housing submarkets are defined at local scales in terms of heterogeneous demand and supply for housing, this allows analysts to examine how residents' relative valuation of those hedonic attributes plays out over geographic space. Housing submarkets provide a framework for theorising residential sorting/segregation in terms of simultaneous operations of multiple factors at play in housing markets. Hedonic modelling (that operationalises heterogeneous housing markets) permits conceptualisation of residential segregation as a multidimensional phenomenon.

Spatial housing submarkets can serve as functionally defined neighbourhoods representing a meaningful unit of analysis for residential segregation; using spatial housing submarkets as a meaningful unit of analysis for residential segregation allows for overcoming the arbitrary nature of areal units used to measure segregation (see Chapter Four, this volume, for a discussion about neighbourhoods and segregation). For example, it would be more informative to examine the extent to which different population groups (for example, income groups, ethnic groups) are represented across housing submarkets rather than across arbitrarily defined neighbourhoods in describing segregation. Further, since housing submarkets are behaviourally defined (that is, non-substitutability), the extent of segregation measured on housing submarkets can be linked to housing choices of different population groups. For instance, the highly uneven distribution of a certain population group across housing submarkets may indicate that this particular group faces constraints in residential location choice. This point is illustrated later.

Residential segregation is often examined without considering the dynamics of neighbourhood change at multiple geographic scales. With housing submarkets as an analytical framework, one can examine how regional external forces interact with local political economic forces across housing submarkets over time, and how such spatial variation plays out in neighbourhood changes and residential segregation of particular population groups. Given the recent development in relevant analytical techniques, the time is ripe to conduct spatial analyses of housing submarkets as an alternative framework for understanding residential segregation. Below I describe spatial patterns of residential segregation through mapping, and re-examine residential segregation structure through a lens of housing submarkets.

Spatial patterns of racial residential segregation in the study areas

St Louis and Cincinnati are located in the southern end of the US Midwestern region (see Figure 13.1). Their population sizes are similar: St Louis metro area has a population of about 2.8 million, and Cincinnati has about 2.1 million as of 2010, using the core-based statistical area (CBSA) as the region definition. They share much economic history with other Rust Belt cities: economic decline during the second half of the 20th century due to the loss of manufacturing jobs, a mainstay of the local economy.

How did the two metro areas fare in terms of racial residential segregation during the era of economic decline? Studies show that racial segregation has steadily decreased over the last 70 years; for instance, the index of dissimilarity, D (measured between Black and White) has decreased from 92.6 in 1940 to 70.7 in 2010 in the St Louis

Figure 13.1: Study areas – St Louis metro area and Cincinnati metro area

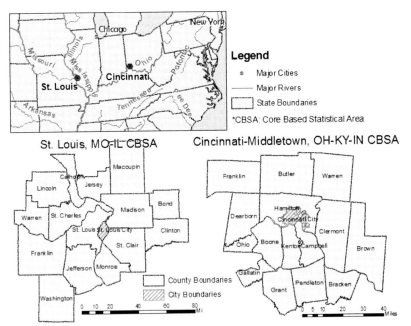

metro area, and from 90.6 to 66.9 in the Cincinnati metro area (Massey and Denton, 1993; Logan and Stults, 2011). Racial segregation in the two metro areas has ranked consistently high at a national scale during much of the 20th century (Massey and Denton, 1993; Iceland et al, 2002). According to the 2010 Census, St Louis ranked 9th, and Cincinnati 12th, among the 50 largest metropolitan areas (Logan and Stults, 2011). If segregation is measured by the isolation index, St Louis ranked 11th, and Cincinnati 23rd in the same study.

The fraction of Blacks at the tract level in the two metro areas is depicted in Figure 13.2. These maps are based on the American Community Survey (ACS) five-year estimates for 2005-09. Blacks are heavily concentrated in and around the central cities of the two metro areas. Tracts in the northern half of St Louis city and east St Louis city (the city in the state of Illinois east of St Louis City) are comprised of nearly 90 per cent Blacks. By contrast, Blacks in Cincinnati city are interspersed with Whites but concentrated in several neighbourhoods. Below I examine the spatial dimensions of racial residential segregation, namely, concentration and clustering at a local scale. The location quotient (LQ) was used to examine the level of concentration (see Figure 13.3), and local Moran's *I* (LI) was used

Figure 13.2: Fraction of Blacks by tracts 2005-09 in study areas

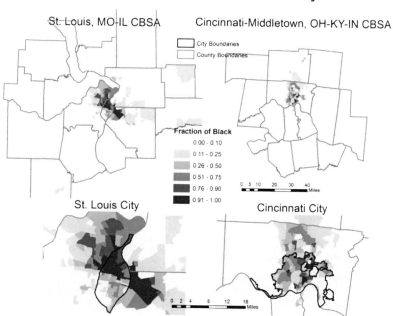

to examine the level of clustering (see Figure 13.4), following Brown
and Chung (2006).

Figure 13.2 suggests that St Louis has higher concentration levels
of Blacks than Cincinnati (as distinct from clustering); this is mainly
because there are more Blacks in the St Louis metro area (18.4 per
cent) than in the Cincinnati metro area (12 per cent). Figure 13.3,
by contrast, indicates that Cincinnati has more tracts with a very
high concentration (for example, LQ greater than five) of Blacks
than St Louis. Figure 13.4 shows spatial clusters of areas with a high
fraction of Blacks marked as HH. HL represents areas with a high
fraction of Blacks surrounded by areas with a low fraction of Blacks,
and LH represents areas with a low fraction of Blacks surrounded by
areas with a high fraction of Blacks. LL represents non–Black clusters.
St Louis exhibits a higher level of clustering (that is, has more large
clusters) of Blacks than Cincinnati. In summary, Cincinnatian Blacks
are highly concentrated in small areas, and in St Louis Blacks are
spread around large residential areas that are geographically adjacent.
Although mapping LI and LQ is useful in revealing the spatial
dimension of residential segregation, mapping LI and LQ considers
spatial distribution of a particular population group over rather

**Figure 13.3: Location quotient of fraction of Blacks in study areas
2005-09**

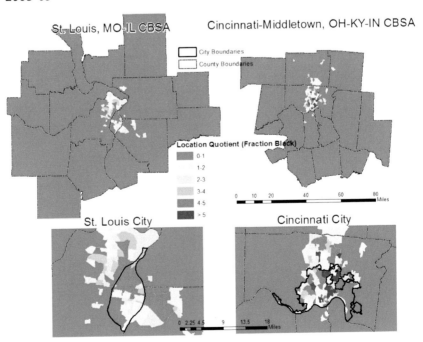

Figure 13.4: Local Moran's *I* of fraction of Blacks in study areas 2005-09

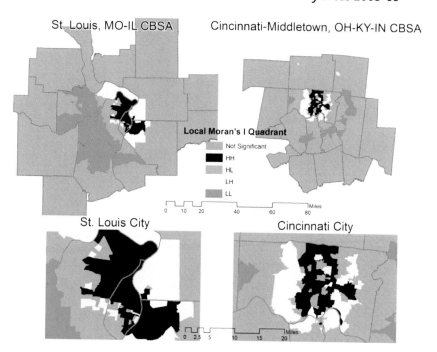

arbitrary areal units (tracts in this case). To examine how population groups are distributed over functionally defined neighbourhoods, it is necessary to delineate housing submarkets spatially, and to assess how groups are distributed across these housing submarkets.

Housing submarkets in the study areas

Delineating housing submarkets

I conducted a hedonic analysis of housing market in the study areas. Hedonic analysis – the process for determining what particular attributes explain variation in housing price, and to what extent if significant – is necessary to identify the underlying dimensions by which a metropolitan area is spatially stratified. Quality of housing (measured as housing price) can be typically modelled in terms of structural characteristics of housing units (for example, age of housing, number of rooms, type of structure such as detached or attached) and neighbourhood characteristics (for example, demographics, school quality). As a result, hedonic analysis allows for defining preferences for housing over those attributes rather than housing itself.

We used the 2005-09 ACS five-year estimates at the tract level for the hedonic analysis. The ACS 2005-09 data pool the population and housing information collected every year in small geographic areas (US Census, 2008). The ACS 2005-09 data are the only available public data that provide a consistent set of up-to-date information relevant to housing market analysis, replacing the long form of the decennial census. Readers should note, however, that house-specific characteristics can be represented in a limited fashion due to spatial aggregation, and sampling errors might invalidate analysis results (Wong and Sun, 2013).

Given ACS data, we consider variables that explain variation in housing prices as listed in Table 13.1. The selection of explanatory variables is guided by common practices of estimating hedonic price functions for housing markets (Adair et al, 1996). Note that variables are focused on aggregate characteristics of neighbourhoods; these variables should be interpreted with caution because they serve as proxy variables. For example, a variable PRBLACK can represent other variables intertwined with race, and PRFMHHWKID can represent other variables correlated with family-oriented environment (for example, school quality) (see Table 13.1).

We conducted factor analysis to identify underlying dimensions across which the housing market is stratified; this is also necessary to treat multicollinearity, to facilitate comparison between two metro areas and to allow for robust GWR analysis. Three distinct factors –

Table 13.1: Explanatory variables of neighbourhood sorting and its principal components

Short name	Description	Factors
PRBLACK	Percentage of Black	Race
PRNHWHITE	Percentage of non-Hispanic White	Race
PRBACHELOR	Percentage of Bachelor's degree	Job skills
PRMANPROF	Percentage of management and professional occupation	Job skills
PRFMHHWKID	Percentage of family household with related people under 18	Life cycle
PFNFHHWOKD	Percentage of non-family household without related people under 18	Life cycle
PRSDETHU	Percentage of a single detached unit (eg, single family home)	Life cycle
MEDYRSTBLT	Median year structure built	Life cycle
PRSERVICE	Percentage of service occupation	Race, job skills
PRNATIVEBR	Percentage of native born	Race, job skills

race, job skills and *life cycle* – are identified as shown in the last column of Table 13.1.

Multiple regression – where median home value was set to the dependent variable, and three factor scores specified as the explanatory variables – reveal that all of *race* (more Whites, less Blacks), *job skills* (more professionals, more college graduates) and *life cycle* (more family with children, less non-family with children) factors are positively associated with house price and are statistically significant. *Job skills* is the single most important factor (with standardised regression coefficient or beta 0.794 for St Louis and 0.653 for Cincinnati), *race* the second (with beta 0.238 and 0.313), and *life cycle* the third (with beta 0.092 and 0.179) in both metro areas. The adjusted R square was 0.694 for St Louis and 0.572 for Cincinnati in these Ordinary Least Squares models based on three (statistically significant) factor scores. Outliers are excluded prior to regression analysis if there is no resident population or the resident is not in the labour force. Mapped regression residuals shows that price in affluent neighbourhoods is consistently under-predicted; this may point to the existence of a 'prestige' premium (that is, residents willing to pay more for prestige) (Manzi and Smith-Bowers, 2005). In general, this finding supports the empirical observation that residential space is sorted simultaneously along the fault line of socioeconomic status, race and life stage.

Housing submarkets are delineated using cluster analysis based on the three factor scores. In other words, homogeneous clusters (as candidates of housing submarkets) are identified in a three-dimensional attribute space – job skills, race and life cycle. A fuzzy *c*-means algorithm (Bezdek, 1981) was applied to the data following Hwang and Thill (2009). Parameters (four clusters with a fuzziness exponent of 1.2) were chosen such that the Xie-Beni index value (Xie and Benie, 1991) is minimised and is amenable to comparison between the two metro areas. Hardened clusters (based on the maximum fuzzy set membership value) were tested for difference in price and the relationship between attributes (job skills, race, life cycle) and housing price. The ANOVA confirms significant price differentials among the four clusters, and regression analysis indicates difference in the hedonic coefficients across clusters.

Housing submarkets in St Louis and Cincinnati

Those four submarkets are labelled as *affluent family (AF)*, *aspiring urbanites (AU)*, *hard-pressed minority (HM)* and *miscellaneous*, respectively, based on overall factor scores. For instance, the AF submarket has high scores in both job skills and life cycle factors. The HM submarket has low scores in both race and job skills factors. The AU submarket has low scores in life cycle, but has moderately high scores in job skills factors. Figures 13.5-13.7 depict a fuzzy set membership value that represents the degree to which tracts belong to the three distinct housing submarkets, that is AF, AU and HM. The fuzzy set membership value ranges from 0 to 1, where 0 means no membership, and 1 means full membership. The higher these values are, the more exclusively the tracts belong to a specified submarket. The medium range of fuzzy set membership values (like 0.5) indicates heterogeneity of tracts (that is, tracts which belong to multiple submarkets). Figure 13.8 shows housing submarkets that are hardened on the basis of the maximum membership.

Similarity and difference in the spatial distribution of housing submarkets can be noted from the figures above. In both metro areas, the AF submarkets are distributed outside of central cities while both HM and AU submarkets are distributed in central cities and inner suburbs. This provides empirical support for the socioeconomic division between central cities and suburbs in other US metropolitan areas (Jargowsky, 2002). A key difference is that the housing submarkets of the St Louis metro area exhibit highly clustered patterns whereas those of Cincinnati are rather dispersed. That is, tracts in the St Louis metro area form large geographic areas that are adjacent to tracts with similar characteristics; conversely, tracts are often not adjacent to tracts with similar characteristics in the Cincinnati metro area, exhibiting rather fragmented spatial patterns of the housing submarkets. The HM submarket is particularly distinct in the St Louis metro area in that it forms one large geographic area in the northern half of the central city (St Louis city) and east St Louis city in Illinois (see Figure 13.8). The spatial division between HM and AU submarkets is rather clear-cut in the St Louis metro area; in contrast, AU submarkets are interspersed with HM submarkets in the Cincinnati metro area.

Residential segregation through a lens of housing submarkets

The figures above show that St Louis has a higher level of residential differentiation (or neighbourhood sorting) than Cincinnati. We compare the price differential between the top quality submarket (AF) and the bottom quality submarket (HM) in the two metro areas, to examine how the individual income distribution was spatially reorganised. The differential was US$118,336 ($98,639 vs $216,975) in the Cincinnati metro area, and US$184,123 ($82,815 vs $266,928)

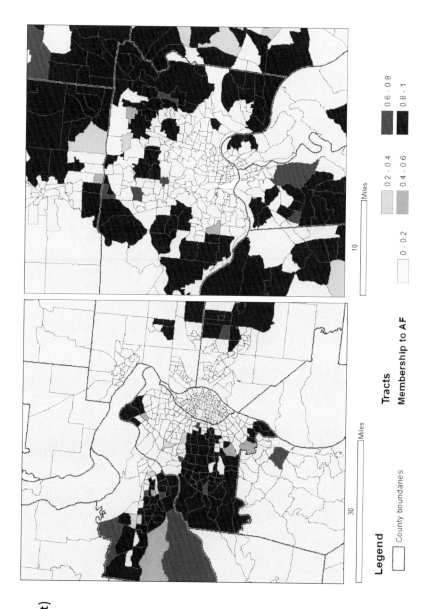

Figure 13.5: *Affluent Family* in St Louis (left) and Cincinnati (right) metropolitan area

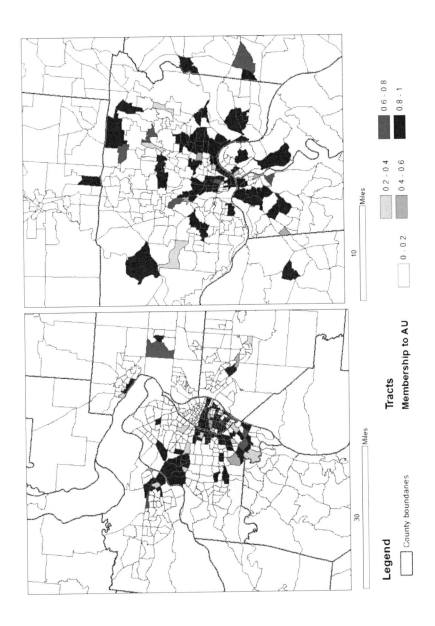

Figure 13.6: *Aspiring Urbanites* in St Louis (left) and Cincinnati metropolitan (right) area

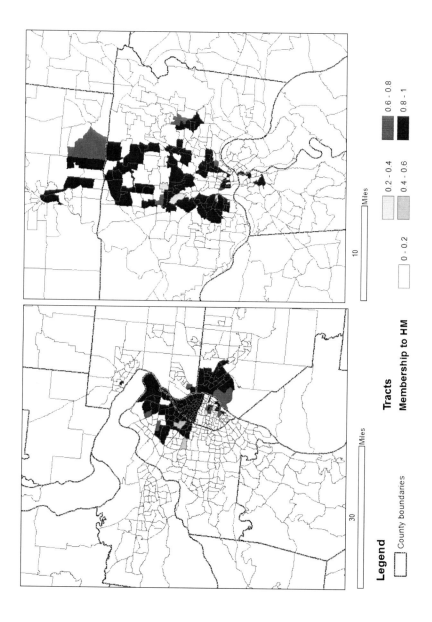

Figure 13.7: *Hard pressed Minority* in St Louis (left) and Cincinnati (right) metropolitan area

Figure 13.8: Hardened housing submarkets in St Louis (left) and Cincinnati (right) metropolitan area

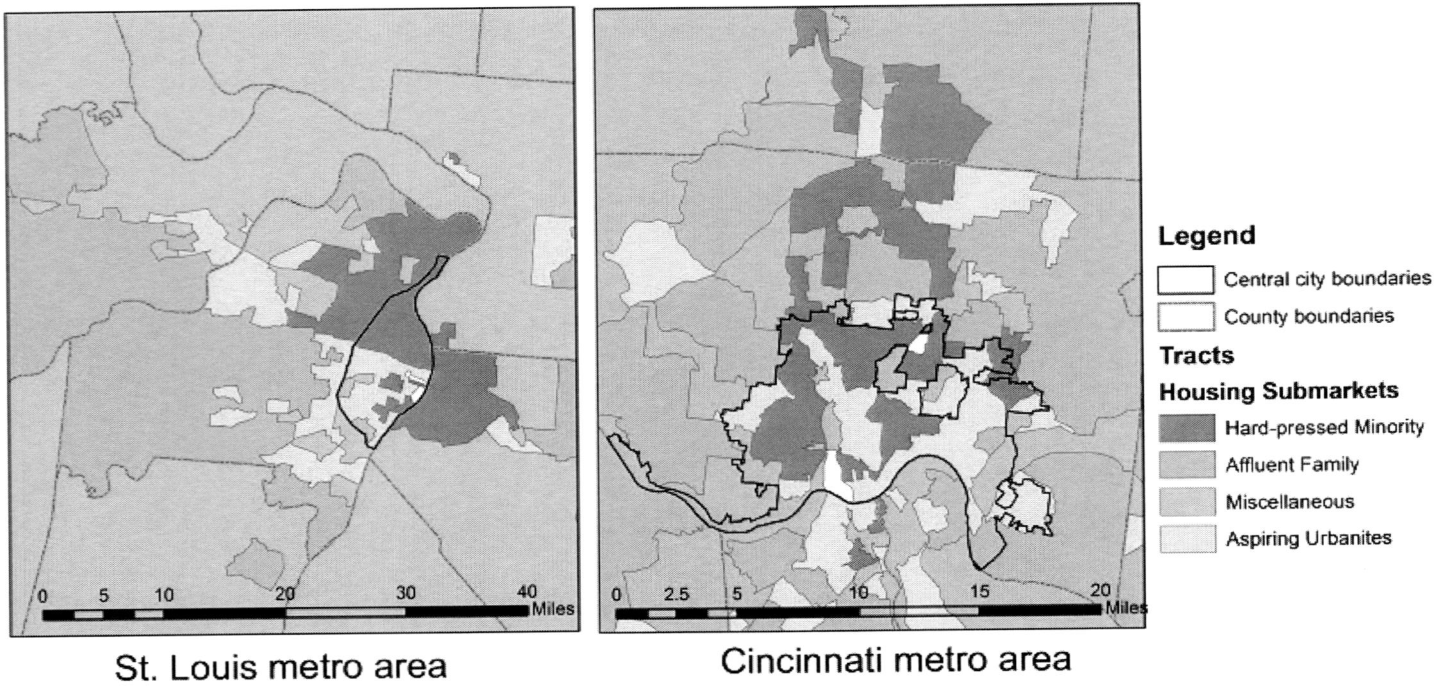
0 5 10 20 30 40 Miles
St. Louis metro area
0 2.5 5 10 15 20 Miles
Cincinnati metro area
Legend
Central city boundaries
County boundaries
Tracts
Housing Submarkets
Hard-pressed Minority
Affluent Family
Miscellaneous
Aspiring Urbanites

in the St Louis metro area, respectively. It may be that St Louis has a higher degree of social polarisation manifested in the residential space compared to Cincinnati. This is an interesting finding given that two metro areas have very similar income distributions among social groups (judging by the Gini index).

We examine how different population groups – low-income groups (LIGs) and Blacks – are represented in different housing submarkets. LIGs, for illustration purposes here, are defined as households with an annual income less than US$15,000 in 2009. If LIGs are unevenly distributed among housing submarkets, this would indicate that they face constrained housing choice among housing submarkets. The extent to which LIGs are represented in each of the housing submarkets is calculated as the number of LIGs multiplied by a fuzzy set membership degree of each tract to different housing submarkets. Table 13.2 shows the extent to which LIGs and Blacks are represented in each of three housing submarkets. Some 8 per cent of LIGs was represented in the AF submarket in the St Louis metro area, and 13 per cent of LIGs was represented in the AF submarket in the Cincinnati metro area. Approximately 29 per cent of LIGs was represented in the HM submarket of St Louis and 26 per cent of LIGs was represented in the HM submarket of Cincinnati. The representation of LIGs in AU submarkets in both metro areas is similar – 22 per cent for St Louis and 21 per cent for Cincinnati.

The distribution of Blacks among housing submarkets shares similarities with the spatial pattern of LIGs. Some 8 per cent of Blacks are represented in the AF submarket of St Louis, and 13 per cent of Blacks are represented in the AF submarket in Cincinnati. The HM submarket accounts for 64 per cent of Blacks in the St Louis metro area, and 58 per cent of Blacks in Cincinnati. Some 13 per cent of Blacks are represented in St Louis' AU submarket, and

Table 13.2: Distribution of low-income groups and Blacks across three spatial housing submarkets

| | Total no of households | Low-income groups | Total | | | % | | |
			AF	HM	AU	AF	HM	AU
St Louis	1,100,246	131,008	10,897	37,590	29,168	8.32	28.69	22.26
Cincinnati	812,007	101,418	12,967	26,666	21,508	12.79	26.29	21.21
	Total population	Black	AF	HM	AU	AF	HM	AU
St Louis	2,803,776	501,659	40,391	319,864	64,716	8.05	63.76	12.90
Cincinnati	2,131,887	247,931	32,704	143,202	42,356	13.19	57.76	17.08

17 per cent of Blacks are represented in Cincinnati's AU submarket. In summary, LIGs and Blacks in the St Louis metro area are more disproportionately represented in the bottom quality housing market than in the Cincinnati metro area. This suggests that LIGs and Blacks are more segregated in the St Louis metro area than in the Cincinnati metro area.

Factors influencing residential segregation in study areas

With GWR, it is possible to examine the spatially varying effects of three underlying factors (job skills, race and life cycle) on house price. The *t*-statistics of the GWR coefficients for the three factor scores are mapped in Figures 13.9-13.11, respectively. Any *t* values less than −1.98 and greater than 1.98 can be interpreted as statistically significant at a 0.05 alpha level. Neighbourhoods with high proportions of skilled workers are positively associated with housing value across most of the St Louis metro area (see Figure 13.9). In contrast, this relationship between job skills and housing value is not as consistent across the Cincinnati metro area as it is across the St Louis metro area. A job skills factor is positively associated with housing value in most areas of St Louis city except for small areas in the north. Contrastingly, the effect of job skills factor is not statistically significant in most areas of Cincinnati city except for Avondale, Walnut Hill and Evanston in Cincinnati city with a significant premium for job skills.

The positive impact of the more Whites and less Blacks on house value is well pronounced in some (but not all) suburbs of the two metro areas (see Figure 13.10). This relationship between race and housing value is, however, not significant in most of the central cities with the exception of several particular areas, namely, Forest Park in St Louis city and Avondale, Walnut Hills and Evanston in Cincinnati city. As the central city is ethnically diverse, a race factor does not necessarily exert a positive influence on housing price across central cities. For example, Forest Park in St Louis city exhibits a positive relationship with a race factor while remaining areas in St Louis city do not. Similarly, Avondale, Walnut Hill and Evanston in Cincinnati city are the only residential areas shown to pay a premium for a race factor.

A *life cycle* factor was influential in the house price-setting process throughout the Cincinnati metro area (see Figure 13.11). In contrast, the positive influence of a *life cycle* factor was largely limited to areas west of St Louis city (Creve Coeur, Olivette, Ladue, Clayton and Richmond Heights), and the southwestern part of St Louis county.

Figure 13.9: *t*-values of GWR coefficients of a *job skills* factor

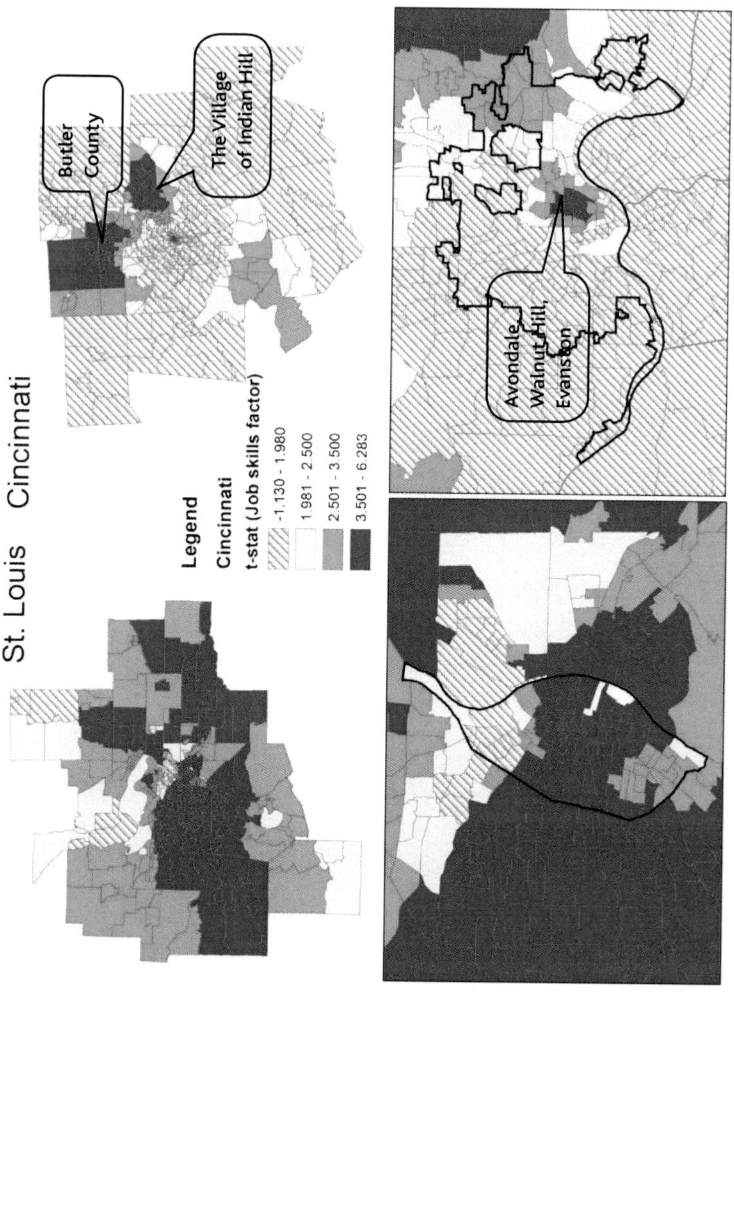

St. Louis   Cincinnati

Butler County

The Village of Indian Hill

Avondale, Walnut Hill, Evanston

Legend

Cincinnati

t-stat (Job skills factor)

-1.130 - 1.980

1.981 - 2.500

2.501 - 3.500

3.501 - 6.283

Figure 13.10: *t*-values of GWR coefficients of a race factor

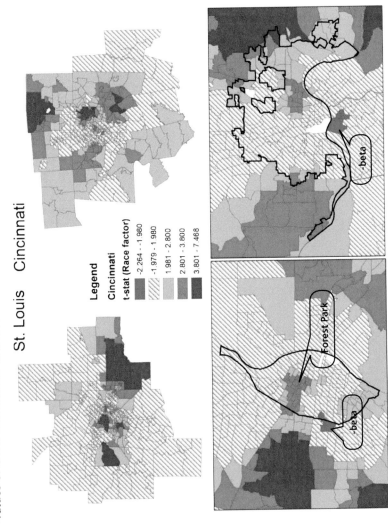

St. Louis   Cincinnati

Legend

Cincinnati
t-stat (Race factor)

-2.264 - -1.980

-1.979 - 1.980

1.981 - 2.800

2.801 - 3.800

3.801 - 7.468

Figure 13.11: *t*-values of GWR coefficients of a *life cycle* factor

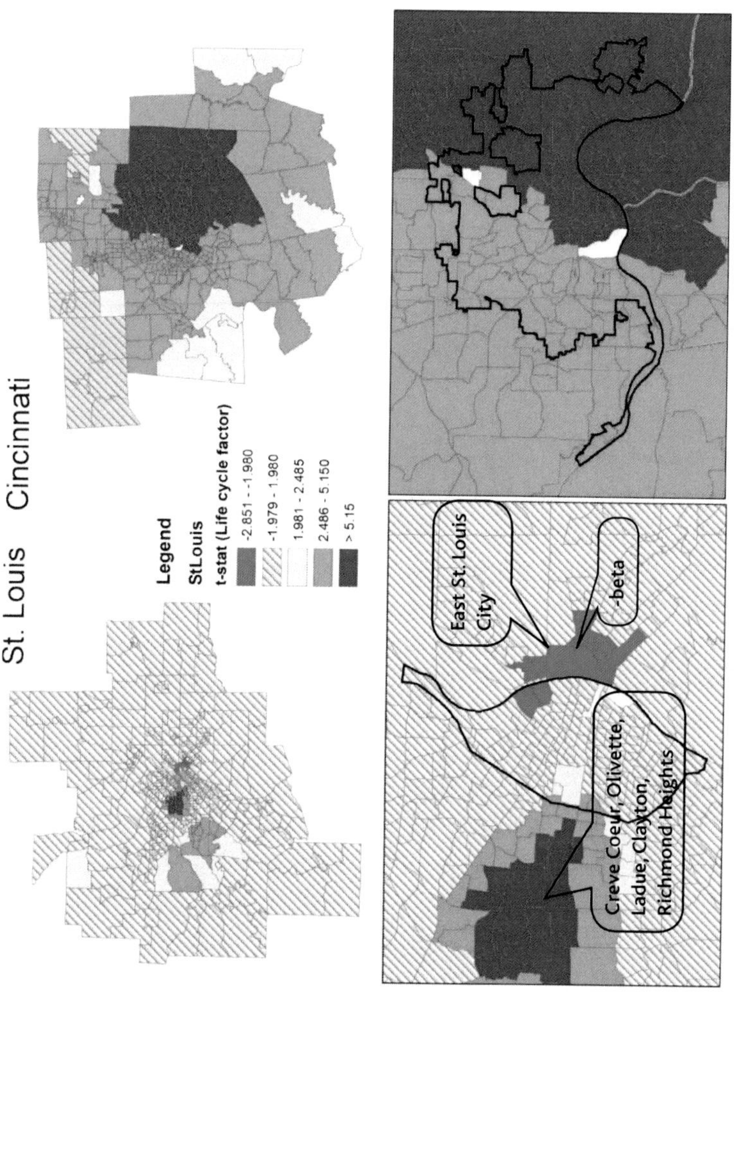

St. Louis   Cincinnati

Legend
StLouis
t-stat (Life cycle factor)
-2.851 - -1.980
-1.979 - 1.980
1.981 - 2.485
2.486 - 5.150
> 5.15

East St. Louis City

-beta

Creve Coeur, Olivette, Ladue, Clayton, Richmond Heights

It appears that political fragmentation (proliferation of independent jurisdiction) has played a role in intensifying spatial segregation in the St Louis metro area. St Louis city was seceded from St Louis county in 1876, and has become an independent city that does not belong to any particular county. Being politically separate entities, municipalities in St Louis county and city government have competed to maximise their tax base while minimising the tax burden. The average number of government employees for each 100,000 residents in the St Louis metro area is 12.5, nearly three times the average (4.4 per 100,000) for the nation's 15 largest metro areas (Gordon, 2008, p 45).

Political fragmentation in the St Louis metro area is particularly well pronounced between St Louis county and St Louis city. Highly uneven distribution of resources between St Louis county and St Louis city can be inferred from residential differentiation organised around St Louis county and St Louis city. Recall that AF was concentrated in St Louis county (Figure 13.5) whereas HM was concentrated in St Louis city (Figure 13.7).

The increase in accessibility brought about by the interstate highway and the possibility of escape from continuing urban decay rendered suburban municipalities economically more attractive to business. In the St Louis metro area, the city's share of regional employment declined from 50.1 to 11.4 per cent while the county's share grew from 21.4 to 40.3 per cent between 1950 and 2000 (Laslo, 2004). With the loss of economic base, the city struggled to keep up with increased demand for social services. The pattern of 'local piracy' was supported by zoning, tax policies and economic development policies (Gordon, 2008). For example, the northern tract of Ladue (population 5,159 in 2010), west of St Louis city, designated so few areas to multi-family homes that median gross rent was US$1,969 in 2005-09. Economic development in the St Louis metro area has not been coordinated among these politically distinct entities. Efforts to reform governments and to bring regionalism have continuously failed. Political fragmentation laid the groundwork for intense competition among local municipalities for revenue streams, and consequently served to align spatial segregation with municipalities (Hill, 1974; Bischoff, 2008).

It is hard to say that Cincinnati is significantly different from St Louis with respect to the intensity and cause of residential segregation. Residential segregation in Cincinnati was caused and reinforced through largely similar mechanisms as in St Louis; this was especially the case in terms of the extent to which discrimination plays a role in maintaining racial segregation (Taylor, 1993), and the manner in which market forces respond to policies (Casey-Leninger, 1993). For example, Indian Hill (with a population of 7,524 and median household income of US$153,667) in the northeast of Cincinnati city zoned 100 per cent of the land as single-family home or agricultural. What makes Cincinnati distinct from St Louis is the relative heterogeneity and spatial fragmentation of the city's housing market. Indeed, Cincinnati city is filled with many census tracts with high-income inequality; for instance, tract 7 has a Gini index of 0.8333, the highest in the nation (Weinberg, 2011). This is actually an indication of social mixing given the fairly small sizes of these tracts. Recall that HM is interspersed with AU in the city (Figure 13.8).

It appears that topography plays a role in residential segregation at a local scale since it can affect building costs, and engender spatial variation in amenities (such as views), thereby acting as a physical barrier among residential blocks. Racial segregation is still high in Cincinnati, and the 'city as a whole' political discourse has not kept up with trends toward more market-oriented governance since the 1960s in other cities (Miller and Tucker, 1990). But it is also noteworthy that Cincinnati has a history of relatively strong civic engagement and a strong metropolitan planning tradition (Fairbanks, 1988; Washington, 2005), although the link between civic engagement and residential segregation is unclear.

Conclusion

This chapter has shown that St Louis has a greater spatial disparity than Cincinnati despite their similar economic histories, socioeconomic characteristics and income distributions among social groups. St Louis exhibits more neighbourhood disparity than that in Cincinnati in terms of the price gaps between top-quality and bottom-quality housing submarkets, and the extent to which the socially disadvantaged are represented across housing submarkets (distinct types of housing in local areas of cities inhabited by residents with a similar demand structure for housing). The poor and Blacks are more disproportionately represented in the bottom-quality submarket in St Louis than in Cincinnati; this indicates that the socially disadvantaged in St Louis face more constraints in their housing choice than those in Cincinnati.

It appears that the constraints in housing choice were shaped by discrimination (for example, neighbourhood stereotyping), and were reinforced by institutional mechanisms (for example, exclusionary zoning). This chapter shows this finding (that is, discrimination and institutional forces constrain housing choice) by interpreting local hedonic regression coefficients in reference to selected archives. St Louis stands out in terms of its unique history of political fragmentation. Proliferation of independent jurisdiction and local land use regulation designed to control revenue streams in St Louis are particularly well pronounced in the clear division of housing submarkets into central cities and suburbs west of those cities. The dilemma of 'desire for growth' despite economic decline has led to intense competition among fragmented governing entities. Intense competition among governing entities works to materialise social polarisation by sorting out resources geographically.

This chapter attempts to demonstrate the potential of spatial analysis of housing submarkets in understanding residential segregation. Housing submarkets provide an alternative perspective for explaining residential segregation. More specifically, mechanisms that drive and constrain housing choice can be examined through a lens of housing submarkets, in conjunction with appropriate analytical techniques. In particular, GWR is useful in exploring localised factors influencing house price, and thus forces leading to residential sorting. For example, GWR helped uncover an artificial homogeneity of St Louis' western suburbs, providing clues to the nature of zoning (exclusion). Spatial analysis of housing submarkets enables analysts to identify what ground-level reality should be investigated by revealing spatial patterns. This chapter is a testament to advance in geographic methods and the potential of geographic methods yet to be realised with respect to segregation studies.

Several limitations of this study can be discussed along with future research. Disaggregate-level data (such as real estate transactions) combined with aggregate data may serve this kind of analysis better than the ACS data partly due to sampling errors in ACS data. This study suggests a link between the degree of residential sorting and negative social capital effects, but it does not establish causality. Further empirical analysis will be needed to examine whether a polarised housing market has any negative impact on school performance as observed in St Louis. It may be worthwhile to further explore the role of political fragmentation and civic engagement in residential segregation. It appears that the processes by which (aspatial) inequality is translated into (spatial) residential segregation are not well understood (Reardon and Bischoff, 2011). This study is an attempt to shed light on this process through a lens of housing submarkets.

Burgeoning urban research and policy issues – neighbourhood effects and mixed income housing, for instance – hinge on the concept of residential segregation in that they are premised on the fact that neighbourhood choice and condition shapes opportunity structure.

Further, research shows the link between residential segregation and housing affordability; local land use control of exclusionary type, one of the mechanisms leading to residential segregation, can make housing unaffordable by limiting housing supply (Quigley and Raphael, 2004; Glaeser and Gyourko, 2008). Given strong policy implications of residential segregation, it is imperative to have sound theories and effective tools conductive to understanding the causes and effects of residential segregation. This chapter calls for attention to spatial economics of housing as theory, and spatial analysis methods as tools for improving our ability to analyse residential segregation.

References

Adair, A.S., Berry, J.N. and McGreal, W.S. (1996) 'Hedonic modelling, housing submarkets and residential valuation', *Journal of Property Research*, vol 13, no 1, pp 67–83.

Alliance for Excellent Education (2003) *Factsheet: The impact of education on: the economy*, Washington, DC: Alliance for Excellent Education.

Alonso, W. (1964) *Location and land use: toward a general theory of land rent*, Cambridge, MA: Harvard University Press.

Anselin, L. (1998) 'GIS research infrastructure for spatial analysis for real estate markets', *Journal of Housing Research*, vol 9, no 1, pp 113–33.

Bayer, P., McMillan, R. and Rueben, K. (2004) 'What drives racial segregation? New evidence using census microdata', *Journal of Urban Economics*, vol 56, no 3, pp 514–35.

Bezdek, J.C. (1981) *Pattern recognition with fuzzy objective function algorithms*, New York: Plenum Press.

Bischoff, K. (2008) 'School district fragmentation and racial residential segregation: how do boundaries matter?', *Urban Affairs Review*, vol 44, no 2, pp 182–217.

Bourassa, S.C., Hamelink, F., Hoesli, M. and MacGregor, B.D. (1999) 'Defining housing submarkets', *Journal of Housing Economics*, vol 8, pp 160–83.

Bridgeland, J. (2011) 'St Louis teachers discuss dropout crisis', Public Broadcasting Service (PBS) (www.pbs.org/newshour/extra/video/blog/2011/11/post_31.html).

Brown, L.A. and Chung, S.-Y. (2006) 'Spatial segregation, segregation indices and the geographic perspective', *Population, Space and Place*, vol 12, pp 125–43.

Card, D. and Rothstein, J. (2006) *Racial segregation and the Black-White test score gap*, NBER Working Paper No 12087, Cambridge, MA: National Bureau of Economic Research.

Carr, J.H. and Kutty, N.K. (eds) (2008) *Segregation: the rising costs for America*, New York and London: Routledge.

Casey-Leninger, C.F. (1993) 'Making the second ghetto in Cincinnati: Avondale, 1925-70', in H.L. Taylor Jr (eds) *Race and the city: work, community and protest in Cincinnati, 1820-1970*, Urbana, IL: University of Illinois Press, pp 232-57.

Charles, C.Z. (2003) 'The dynamics of racial residential segregation', *Annual Review of Sociology*, vol 29, pp 167-207.

Clark, W.A.V. (1986) 'Residential segregation in American cities: a review and interpretation', *Population Research and Policy Review*, vol 5, no 2, pp 95-127.

Duncan, O.D. and Duncan, B. (1955) 'A methodological analysis of segregation indexes', *American Sociological Review*, vol 20, no 2, pp 210-17.

Fairbanks, R.B. (1988) *Making better citizens: housing reform and the community development strategy in Cincinnati, 1890-1960*, Urbana, IL: University of Illinois Press.

Follain, J. and Jimenez, E. (1985) 'Estimating the demand for housing characteristics: a survey and critique', *Regional Science and Urban Economics*, vol 15, pp 77-107.

Fong, E. (1996) 'A comparative perspective on racial residential segregation', *The Sociological Quarterly*, vol 37, no 2, pp 199-226.

Fotheringham, A.S., Brunsdon, C. and Charlton, M. (2002) *Geographically weighted regression: the analysis of spatially varying relationships*, London: John Wiley & Sons.

Galster, G. (1988) 'Residential segregation in American cities: a contrary review', *Population Research and Policy Review*, vol 7, no 2, pp 93-112.

Galster, G. (1996) 'William Grigsby and the analysis of housing sub-markets and filtering', *Urban Studies*, vol 33, no 10, pp 1797-805.

Glaeser, E.L. and Gyourko, J.E. (2008) *Rethinking federal housing policy: how to make housing plentiful and affordable*, Cambridge, MA: AEI Press.

Goodman, A.C. and Thibodeau, T.G. (1998) 'Housing market segmentation', *Journal of Housing Economics*, vol 7, no 2, pp 121-43.

Gordon, C. (2008) *Mapping decline: St Louis and the fate of the American city*, Philadelphia, PA: University of Pennsylvania Press.

Grigsby, W., Baratz, M., Galster, G. and Maclennan, D. (1987) 'The dynamics of neighborhood change and decline', *Progress in Planning*, vol 28, pp 1-76.

Harlow, C.W. (2003) *Education and correctional populations*, Bureau of Justice Statistics Special Report, Washington, DC: US Department of Justice.

Hill, R. (1974) 'Separate and unequal: governmental inequality in the metropolis', *American Political Science Review*, vol 68, no 4, pp 1557-68.

Hamnett, C. (2001) 'Social segregation and social polarization', in R. Paddison (ed) *Handbook of urban studies*, London: Sage, pp 162-76.

Hwang, S. and Thill, J. (2009) 'Delineating urban housing submarkets with fuzzy clustering', *Environment and Planning B*, vol 39, pp 865-82.

Iceland, J., Weinberg, D.H. and Steinmetz, E. (2002) *Racial and ethnic residential segregation in the United States: 1980-2000*, Washington, DC: US Bureau of Census.

Jargowsky, P.A. (2002) 'Sprawl, concentration of poverty, and urban inequality', in G.D. Squires (ed) *Urban sprawl: causes, consequences, and policy responses*, Washington, DC: Urban Institute Press, pp 39-72.

Johnston, R., Poulsen, M. and Forrest, J. (2007) 'The geography of ethnic residential segregation: a comparative study of five countries', *Annals of the Association of American Geographers*, vol 97, no 4, pp 713-38.

Jones, C. (2002) 'The definition of housing market areas and strategic planning', *Urban Studies*, vol 34, pp 549-64.

Judd, D.R. (1997) 'The role of governmental policies in promoting residential segregation in the St Louis metropolitan area', *The Journal of Negro Education*, vol 66, no 3, pp 214-40.

Kramer, M.R. and Hogue, C.R. (2009) 'Is segregation bad for your health?', *Epidemiologic Reviews*, vol 31, no 1, pp 178-94.

Lancaster, K.J. (1971) *Consumer demand: a new approach*, New York: Columbia University Press.

Laslo, D. (2004) 'The past, present, and future of the St Louis labor force', in B. Baybeck and E.T. Jones (eds) *St Louis metromorphosis: past trends and future directions*, St Louis, MO: University of Missouri Press, Table 2, p 72.

Logan, J.R. and Stults, B.J. (2011) *The persistence of segregation in the metropolis: new findings from the 2010 Census*, Census Brief prepared for Project US2010 (www.s4.brown.edu/us2010).

Maclennan, D., Munro, M. and Wood, G. (1987) 'Housing choices and the structure of housing markets', in B. Turner, J. Kemeny and L.J. Lundqvist (eds) *Between state and market: housing in the post-industrial era*, Stockholm: Almqvist & Wiksell International, pp 26-52.

Maloutas, T. (2007) 'Segregation, social polarization and immigration in Athens during the 1990s: theoretical expectations and contextual difference', *International Journal of Urban and Regional Research*, vol 31, no 4, pp 733-58.

Manzi, T. and Smith-Bowers, B. (2005) 'Gated communities as club goods: segregation or social cohesion', *Housing Studies*, vol 20, no 2, pp 345-59.

Massey, D. and Denton, N. (1993) *American apartheid: segregation and the making of the underclass*, Cambridge, MA: Harvard University Press.

Megbolugbe, I.F., Hoek-Smit, M.C. and Linneman, P.D. (1996) 'Understanding neighborhood dynamics: a review of the contributions of Williams G. Grigsby', *Urban Studies*, vol 33, no 10, pp 1779-95.

Miller, Z.L. and Tucker, B. (1990) 'The new urban politics: planning and development in Cincinnati, 1954-1988', in R.M. Bernard (ed) *Snow belt cities: metropolitan politics in the northeast and midwest since World War II*, Bloomington, IN: Indiana University Press, pp 91-108.

Muller, P. (2004) 'Transportation and urban form: stages in the spatial evolution of the American metropolis', in S. Hanson and G. Giuliano (eds) *The geography of urban transportation*, New York: Guilford Press, pp 59-85.

Musterd, S. (2005) 'Social and ethnic segregation in Europe: levels, causes, and effects', *Journal of Urban Affairs*, vol 27, no 3, pp 331-48.

O'Connor, A., Tilly, C. and Bobo, L.D. (2001) *Urban inequality: evidence from four cities*, New York: Russell Sage Foundation.

Orfield, G., Losen, D., Wald, J. and Swanson, C.B. (2004) *Losing our future: how minority youth are being left behind by the graduation rate crisis*, Cambridge, MA: The Civil Rights Project at Harvard University [Contributors: Advocates for Children of New York, The Civil Society Institute].

Poulsen, M., Forrest, J. and Johnston, R. (2002) 'From modern to post-modern? Contemporary ethnic residential segregation in four US metropolitan areas', *Cities*, vol 19, no 3, pp 161-72.

Quigley, J.M. and Raphael, S. (2004) 'Is housing unaffordable? Why isn't it more affordable?', *The Journal of Economic Perspectives*, vol 18, issue 1, pp 191-214.

Reardon, S.F. and Bischoff, K. (2011) 'Income inequality and income segregation', *American Journal of Sociology*, vol 116, issue 4, pp 1092-153.

Reardon, S.F., Matthews, S.A., O'Sullivan, D., Lee, B.A., Firebaugh, G., Farrell, C.R. and Bischoff, K. (2008) 'The geographic scale of metropolitan racial segregation', *Demography*, vol 45, issue 3, pp 489-514.

Rosen, S. (1974) 'Hedonic prices and implicit markets: product differentiation in pure competition', *Journal of Political Economy*, vol 82, pp 34-55.

Rothenberg, J., Galster, G.C., Butler, R.V. and Pitkin, J. (1991) *The maze of urban housing markets: theory, evidence, and policy*, Chicago, IL and London: University of Chicago Press.

Sassen, S. (1991) *The global city: New York, London, Tokyo*, Princeton, NJ: Princeton University Press.

Schill, M.H. and Wachter, S.M. (1995) 'Housing market constraints and spatial stratification by income and race', *House Policy Debate*, vol 6, no 1, pp 141-67.

Schnare, A. and Struyk, R. (1976) 'Segmentation in urban housing submarkets', *Journal of Urban Economics*, vol 3, pp 146-66.

Taylor, R.B. (1993) 'City building, public policy, the rise of the industrial city, and Black ghetto-slum formation in Cincinnati, 1850-1940', in H.L. Taylor Jr (ed) *Race and the city: work, community and protest in Cincinnati, 1820-1970*, Urbana, IL: University of Illinois Press, pp 156-92.

Tiebout, C.M. (1956) 'A pure theory of local expenditures', *The Journal of Political Economy*, vol 64, no 5, pp 416-24.

Tu, Y. (1997) 'The local housing sub-market structure and its properties', *Urban Studies,* vol 34, no 2, pp 337-53.

US Census (2008) *A compass for understanding and using American community survey data: what general data users need to know* (www.census.gov/acs/www/Downloads/handbooks/ACSGeneralHandbook.pdf).

Vandell, K.D. (1995) 'Market factors affecting spatial heterogeneity among urban neighborhoods', *Housing Policy Debate*, vol 6, no 1, pp 103-39.

Vartanian, T.P. and Gleason, P.M. (1999) 'Do neighborhood conditions affect high school dropout and college graduation rates?', *Journal of Socio-Economics*, vol 28, no 1, pp 21-41.

Washington, M. (2005) 'The stirrings of the modern civil rights movement in Cincinnati, Ohio, 1943-1953', in J. Theoharis and K. Woodard (eds) *Groundwork: local Black freedom movements in America*, New York and London: New York University Press, pp 215-34.

Watkins, C.A. (2001) 'The definition and identification of housing submarkets', *Environment and Planning A*, vol 33, pp 2235-53.

Weinberg, D.H. (2011) *US neighborhood income inequality in the 2005-2009 period*, Washington, DC: US Bureau of the Census.

White House (2009) 'Developing effective place-based policies for the FY 2011 budget' (www.whitehouse.gov/sites/default/files/omb/assets/memoranda_fy2009/m09-28.pdf).

Williams, D.R. and Collins, C. (2001) 'Racial residential segregation: a fundamental cause of racial disparities in health', *Public Health Reports*, vol 116, no 5, pp 404-16.

Wilson, W.J. (1990) *The truly disadvantaged: the inner city, the underclass, and public policy*, Chicago, IL: University of Chicago Press.

Wong, D.W.S. (1997) 'Spatial dependency of segregation indices', *The Canadian Geographer*, vol 41, no 2, pp 128-36.

Wong, D.W.S. and Sun, M. (2013) 'Handling data quality information of survey data in GIS: a case of using the American Community Survey data', *Spatial Demography*, vol 1, no 1, pp 3-16.

Wong, D.W.S., Lasus, H. and Falk, R.F. (1999) 'Exploring the variability of segregation index D with scale and zonal systems: an analysis of thirty US cities', *Environment and Planning A*, vol 31, pp 507-22.

Xie, X.L. and Beni, G. (1991) 'A validity measure for fuzzy clustering', *IEEE Transactions on Pattern Analysis and Machine Intelligence*, vol 13, pp 841-7.

OUTCOMES

FOURTEEN

'Religious' concentration and health outcomes in Northern Ireland

Gemma Catney

Introduction

After over 30 years of intense sectarian–related violence and sustained tensions between Catholics and Protestants, Northern Ireland can, in some senses, be described as a 'post-conflict' society. The more peaceful political context of recent years has altered the perceptions and lived realities of many residents of Northern Ireland, and has developed alongside changes in the socioeconomic environment; violence and other expressions of sectarian conflict have greatly reduced, and cities such as Belfast have seen a dramatic rise in levels of economic investment and development. Residential segregation is decreasing, and there is evidence of changing attitudes towards living in communities of a mixed residential composition and increasing tolerance between groups (Catney, 2008).

However, 'religious' population clustering remains marked; Shuttleworth and Lloyd's (2009a) study, making use of the Northern Ireland Census-based grid square resource, found that, in 2001, some 66 per cent of Protestants lived in areas that were 75 per cent or more Protestant, while 59 per cent of Catholics lived in areas that were 75 per cent or more Catholic. Evidence for the distinct geography of residential concentration in Northern Ireland dates as far back as the 17th century (see, for example, Jones, 1960; Boal, 1996; Hepburn, 1996; Bardon, 2005), but the recent period which saw the most significant changes to the intensity of residential segregation began in the late 1960s, at the onset of a sustained and widespread period of civil disturbances and violence, known colloquially as 'The Troubles'. The mass population movements of people which took place during this time, when there was considerable migration of individuals and households, either by choice or by force, to areas where they were in a 'religious' majority, are well-known for their role in increasing residential segregation across Northern Ireland (Compton and Power,

1986; Darby, 1986; Cormack and Osborne, 1994; Compton, 1995; Doherty and Poole, 1997, 2000). The amplified potential for violence at the interfaces during this time led to the erection of peace walls (Shirlow and Murtagh, 2006). While this period of extreme conflict and violence has now largely subsided, many residents of Northern Ireland are still living in areas dominated by their 'own' religious group. Social rented housing provided by the Northern Ireland Housing Executive is segregated into distinct Catholic and Protestant areas (Shuttleworth and Lloyd, 2007, 2009b). Despite increasing social interactions between the two communities, sectarian violence and tensions between the two groups still remain in some areas (Shirlow and Murtagh, 2006; Bryan et al, 2009). Relatively little is known about the impact this socio-political environment has on the health and wellbeing of the population of Northern Ireland.

The next section draws on the literature on segregation and health with an ethnic/racial group dimension. This literature is considerably more developed than equivalent research for Northern Ireland, and provides a useful means by which to consider the impact of segregation on health, and potential mechanisms behind these outcomes. The nature of segregation by religion in Northern Ireland is rather different to that of ethnic group or ethno-religious clustering observed in other places, such as, for example, the rest of the UK, the US, or parts of mainland Europe (see Catney et al, 2011; Finney and Catney, 2012); segregation in Northern Ireland developed as a result of intense inter-community tension, and this context therefore differs to the processes by which ethnic group segregation may occur. (Note that compared to the rest of the UK, Northern Ireland is home to a very small minority ethnic population [NISRA, 2013], with considerably lower levels of immigration, established foreign-born populations or UK-born second-generation minorities.) Yet there are some important similarities between religious concentration in Northern Ireland and ethnic group concentrations elsewhere; initial immigrant clustering in 'settlement' or 'gateway' areas is associated with a mixture of positive and negative causes, the former including practicalities such as well-developed supportive networks and specialised religious or cultural facilities, the latter including housing discrimination, and/or as a means of protection from hostility such as racism (Peach, 1996; Phillips 1998, 2006). The maintenance of concentrated pockets of Catholics or Protestants is partly associated with ties to community and certain locales and the maintenance of social and familial networks, but also with a lack of choice in the (social) housing market, and with fear of intolerance (Catney, 2008).

After this review, a brief outline of the current state of knowledge on Northern Ireland segregation and health follows, before an introduction to the data and methods used to explore this theme. After reporting the results, the impact of 'religious' concentration on health in Northern Ireland is discussed.

Residential segregation and (ill)health

While an individual's health may be affected by one or many personal circumstances (for example, genetics, deprivation) and lifestyle choices, the residential environment is also known to have an impact on the physical and mental health of its inhabitants. The relationship between health and the *physical* (including built) environment is well-known – access to green spaces and clean air, sufficient opportunities for exercise and the means to eat healthily, are just some attributes that might promote better health (Srinivasan et al, 2003; Gordon-Larsen et al, 2006). However, the *social* environment is also recognised as playing an important role in affecting health (Macintyre et al, 1993).

Numerous studies have explored how ethnic residential segregation affects health outcomes. Examples of some of this (dominantly US-based) literature include the effect of segregation on weight status in adults (Chang, 2006); the spread (and containment from the rest of the population) of infectious diseases such as tuberculosis (Acevedo-Garcia, 2000); poor mental health, such as anxiety and depression (Lee, 2009); all-cause and cardiovascular disease mortality rates (Fang et al, 1998); increased mortality risk (Jackson et al, 2000); and poor self-rated health (Subramanian et al, 2005). In attempting to explain the relationship between segregation and various health outcomes, some research has pointed towards the physical proximity of groups in, for example, urban clusters, or, importantly, the fact that areas of high co-ethnic density may be more socioeconomically deprived (Williams and Collins, 2001). For some health outcomes, it is the sociocultural context that has an impact on health – the negative impacts on mental health, such as stress, of residing in an area with unequal opportunities and exposure to discrimination (see Kramer and Hogue, 2009, and Williams and Collins, 2001, for useful reviews of the mechanisms of how segregation may affect health status). The effect of being in a minority or majority within a larger population is a central theme in some of this research. Many studies on ethnic disparities in health and healthcare have shown the health status of minority populations to be worse than the majority (usually White) population (Charatz-Litt, 1992; Nickens, 1995; Bollini and Siem,

1995; Nazroo, 1998), although the impacts are diverse between and within ethnic groups. In their US study, Fang et al (1998), for example, found that individuals in the White ethnic group in a dominantly White neighbourhood benefited from their majority 'status'; however, those identifying as Black, especially those in older age groups in majority White areas, had higher mortality rates than their peers in predominantly Black neighbourhoods, despite their higher socioeconomic status. The literature points to several mechanisms by which being in a minority can have a negative effect on one's health. Exploring ethnic inequalities in health, Nazroo (1998), Williams and Collins (2001) and Williams and Jackson (2005) highlight a number of possible ways in which minority ethnic groups might be more likely to have poor health. These include, although not exclusively, ecological effects (the geographical concentration of minority ethnic groups in particular, often disadvantaged, locales), socioeconomic deprivation and material disadvantage (as an outcome of discrimination and inequalities), and social exclusion (for example, from the rest of society, and a weak position in the social hierarchy). Residential location *per se* may have a detrimental effect on health when it is associated with higher levels of deprivation and unequal access to favourable economic and housing opportunities; this is more likely to affect minority populations who tend to be clustered in areas with these characteristics (Williams and Collins, 2001). Karlsen and Nazroo (2002) demonstrated the detrimental effects of racism on the health of minority ethnic populations (see also Gee, 2002); related to this, they argue that racism (and consequently poor health) contributes to the concentration of groups in unsatisfactory housing, disadvantaged geographical areas and inferior labour market opportunities, further acting to distinguish these groups as 'others'. Bécares et al (2012) discuss the impact that racial stereotyping can have on health outcomes in their cross-national study of Caribbean individuals in the US and UK. While mainly from an economic perspective, Wilkinson (1996) also highlights the detrimental impact on health that comes from the stigmatisation of disadvantaged groups.

However, there is substantial evidence to suggest that residing in an area of greater minority ethnic concentration has a *positive* impact on health (Smaje, 1995), providing high levels of social support and social capital, the maintenance of ethnic identity and understanding (Nazroo, 1998), and the reduction of exposure to racial discrimination (Halpern and Nazroo, 2000). This 'protective', 'empowering' or 'buffering' effect has associated health benefits (Beaudoin, 2009; Kramer and Hogue, 2009), as demonstrated for some immigrant groups in Grady and McLafferty's (2007) study of birth weights of infants to women in New York City.

Of particular interest in this chapter is what effect a minority or majority 'religious status' may have on health outcomes in Northern Ireland. While borrowing from hypotheses in the ethnicity literature, on which most work on this theme has concentrated, the focus here is on Catholics and Protestants in Northern Ireland – subcategories of the population based on religion rather than ethnic group.

Health in the context of the Northern Ireland conflict

A special issue in *Social Science & Medicine* (2010, vol 70, no 1) focused on the complex relationship between conflict, violence and health in several countries and regions, calling for further development in interdisciplinary research on physical and mental wellbeing and conflict (Panter-Brick, 2010). In the case of Northern Ireland specifically, some research has indicated that the violence and stress associated with The Troubles has had an impact on both *physical* health (for example, through physical injury; see Hamilton et al, 2003) and *mental* health (including an increased risk of psychological morbidity; see O'Reilly and Stevenson, 2003), not only during the main period of conflict, but with more enduring negative consequences (for a review, see French, 2009).

Comparatively little is known about the effect of the Northern Ireland conflict and, more specifically, the residential separation of Protestants and Catholics, on health outcomes. The only study to date to explore directly the relationship between segregation and health in Northern Ireland used ecological data on hospital activity and prescribing costs to assess how the residential patterns of Catholics and Protestants may affect health outcomes (French, 2009). It was found that segregation explained variations in prescribing costs for anxiety and depression after controlling for socioeconomic disadvantage, but did not help to explain variations in costs of acute and elderly care (French, 2009). Certainly, the relationship between ill health and inter-communal tension is not straightforward. There is evidence that population clustering can be associated with strong inter-community links and communal cohesion, which can have a positive impact on health outcomes. However, the more beneficial outcomes which come from residential clustering (for example, well-developed social networks and support mechanisms) may not be felt when the form of residential concentration is also associated with a history of violence and tension; clustering in this context may be the outcome of social barriers, such as fear and intolerance, and institutional barriers through segregated social housing practices, rather than the more positive reasons for co-group concentration – a shared cultural or religious heritage and practice, for example (Boal, 1981; Peach, 1996, 2000).

Adding to this complexity is the possibility that the impact of segregation on health (positive or negative) might affect different subpopulations in different ways; some research on ethnic inequalities in health has suggested that minority populations do less well in health terms than the majority, while other studies show the reverse. How does this play out in Northern Ireland, for Catholic/Protestant differences? In Northern Ireland, Catholics comprise a minority of the population, although it is a large minority, and the proportion of Catholics and Protestants is much more similar to each other than any minority ethnic group is to the majority White British ethnic group in Britain. Of interest here is the *local* proportion of the population; definitions of minority or majority here relate to an individual's specific residential area. This research aims to test the association between 'minority status' and health status, and if this holds for each of the two main religious groups. The study makes use of individual-level data derived from the 2001 Northern Ireland Census of Population to explore this relationship, while adjusting for other socioeconomic and demographic factors known to be associated with variations in health.

Data

The Northern Ireland Mortality Study (NIMS) is an exercise in data linkage comprising two sets of routinely collected data: information taken from the 2001 Census returns for the whole population of Northern Ireland, and deaths occurring to this population for subsequent years. The Northern Ireland Statistics and Research Agency (NISRA) maintains this anonymised dataset in a 'safe setting' at its headquarters in Belfast. (See O'Reilly et al, 2012, for a detailed description of the data.)

This analysis is concerned with the two communities that make up the majority of the population in Northern Ireland, namely, Protestants and Catholics. The assignment of 'religious affiliation' was determined by two questions included in the 2001 Census form – the first on current religious affiliation – and a supplementary question, to be answered if the respondent did not have a current affiliation, asking the community background the person had been brought up in. This is used to assign a 'religion' for the 14 per cent of respondents who said they did not have a current religious affiliation.

Determining if an individual resided in an area with a minority or majority of their own religious group was based on percentages of Catholics and Protestants, hereafter referred to as 'concentration'. This is defined here by five categories of (rounded) percentage Catholic in a given super output area (SOA) (average population just under 2,000 individuals): <=10 per cent, 10-29 per cent, 30-69 per cent, 70-89 per cent and >=90 per cent. Given that nearly all individuals resident in Northern Ireland in 2001 identified themselves as either Catholic or Protestant in the census, highly concentrated areas are defined as areas with <=10 per cent or >=90 per cent Catholic (equating respectively to approximately >=90 per cent or <=10 per cent Protestant). Using the composite variable of religion and community background, in this NIMS dataset, the Catholic population represents 43.4 per cent of the Northern Ireland population, and Protestants 53.3 per cent. Those with an 'Other' religion or no religion/community background are not included in the analysis.

The NIMS provides individual-level data with cross-tabulations of an extensive number of socio-demographic and economic variables. Demographic factors (age, sex and marital status) known to influence health outcomes were included for analysis. A three-fold indicator determining the level of population density – urban (settlements with greater than 75,000 people), intermediate (between 2,500 and 75,000) and rural (less than 2,500) – was included to determine the level of urbanness. Four indicators normally associated with the assessment of socioeconomic status were used in the analysis: household tenure and property value,[1] household access to a car, education and the National Statistics socioeconomic classification (hereafter NS-SEC; see Rose and Pevalin, 2002). As well as these individual-level variables, potential effects of deprivation at the area level were also explored. For this, the income deprivation domain of the 2005 Northern Ireland multiple deprivation measure (NIMDM) (NISRA, 2005) was used to calculate areas of least to most income-deprived, derived from the cumulative population divided into quintiles. The 2005 NIMDM income domain is based on 2003 data; while this presents a slight mismatch when used in conjunction with 2001 Census data, this set of scores is closest temporally to 2001.

Health outcomes and methodology

Two health outcomes are explored in the analyses: the first measure is general health in the previous year, where respondents of the census were asked 'Over the last 12 months would you say your health has on the whole been...', with tick box responses provided as 'good', 'fairly good' or 'not good'. The latter two categories were combined into one for the purposes of this analysis. The only other measure of health in the census comes from a question on the presence or absence of a limiting long-term illness (LLTI), regarded primarily as an indicator of physical health. General health is more useful for this study given that it is seen as reflective of both physical and mental wellbeing. The ability of self-reported health to predict subsequent mortality and morbidity is well demonstrated globally (Idler and Benyamini, 1997). However, it should be noted that some of the literature remains sceptical about the reliability of self-reported health outcomes (see, for example, Jylhä et al, 1998; Beckett et al, 2000), and some regional and subpopulation variations have been shown in the UK (Young et al, 2010). Subramanian et al (2005) provide an example of an analysis of the effects of residential concentration on self-rated health in their study of US metropolitan areas.

All-cause mortality was used as an additional health-related outcome for all deaths that occurred between mid-2001 and 2007 to the census-enumerated population. Fang et al (1998) explored the impact of 'segregation' (defined by a percentage threshold) between White and Black individuals in New York City on all-cause and cardiovascular disease mortality, and argued that being in a minority in one's area of residence had a negative effect on health, as measured by mortality risk. They concluded from their study that '... segregation influences mortality, independent of other relevant socioeconomic and demographic characteristics' (Fang et al, 1998, p 476). Collins and Williams (1999) measured social isolation of Black from White individuals in US cities, finding that in areas with high levels of segregation, isolation was positively associated with mortality risk. Jackson et al (2000) demonstrated the increase in risk of all-cause mortality with higher levels of residential segregation (as measured by proportion in a census tract and using the US National Longitudinal Mortality Study in the US).

Logistic regression was used to determine the factors influencing variation in self-reported health (good = 0, fair/not good = 1). Analysis was restricted to those aged 25 to 74 at the 2001 Census and living in private households. The upper age restriction was necessitated because neither NS-SEC nor education is coded for those aged 75 years or older at the census, and the lower age bound was set because at 25 years an individual's educational attainment trajectory is likely to have reached its completion for most people. Using this population, and with the same independent variables as the logistic modelling, a Cox proportional hazards model was fitted to explore the characteristics that influence variation in survival rates, and how this relates to community background concentration.[2]

Context

Of the 799,319 people in the NIMS project-specific dataset, almost half (48.6 per cent) lived in areas comprising either 90 per cent or above Catholics or 90 per cent or more Protestants; only 21.0 per cent lived in areas with between 30 and 69 per cent Catholics. For context, Figure 14.1 shows percentage Catholic by community background at SOA level as a proportion of the total population (note that an equivalent ward-level map is provided in Chapter Four, this volume). As is well known, there is a distinct geography to the residential distribution of Catholics (and therefore Protestants) in Northern Ireland. The broad east–west differential of a greater proportion of

Figure 14.1: Spatial distribution of Catholics (by community background), as a proportion of the total population in Northern Ireland, at Super Output Area Level, 2001

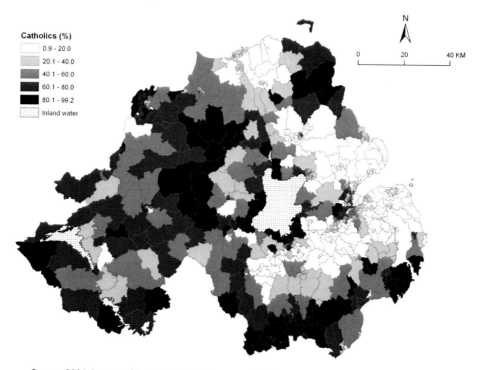

Source: 2001 Census, Table KS007b. Author's own calculations.

Catholics in the west of Northern Ireland and a smaller percentage in the east is also mirrored for Belfast. For reference, a map of the counties of Northern Ireland and the location of the Belfast Urban Area (BUA) in the east is provided in Chapter Four, this volume.

Descriptive statistics provide insight into the composition of the area types used in the analysis, and these can be are summarised as follows. Most of those in the more highly concentrated areas consist of urban dwellers, although over one-third (37.5 per cent) of Protestants and Catholics in the 70-89 per cent Catholic areas live in rural areas. Areas that are more mixed by religion tend to be more evenly divided across the urban–rural spectrum. Areas that have the most religious mixing tend to be home to the most affluent residents, whether measured using access to a car, social renting, absence of educational qualifications or working in routine occupations. However, as a general rule, people in predominantly Catholic areas tend to be more disadvantaged socioeconomically than their peers in predominantly Protestant areas, for a given level of residential concentration. For example, while the proportion of people in the most professional forms of employment (taken from the NS-SEC variable introduced earlier) is lower in areas of highest religious concentration (and likewise, rises for those in routine occupations), it is the most Catholic areas that contain the fewest in professional occupations and the most in 'routine' forms of employment. By far the largest proportion (11.7 per cent) of those not working are in the most concentrated Catholic areas. Similarly, in terms of economic activity, fewer employed and more unemployed people (aged 25-74) can be found in the most Catholic areas (for example, 46.9 per cent were employed, compared with a range of 56.8 to 63.7 per cent in the other area types). The proportion of those with a degree are lowest in the most concentrated areas, although more so for the areas of 90 per cent or above Catholics. These predominantly Catholic areas also fare worst for other education levels, and have the highest proportion with no qualifications (54.7 per cent, compared with 49.1 per cent for predominantly Protestant areas). Even with their younger population structure, residents in predominantly Catholic areas reported poorer levels of general health (43.8 per cent with poor health, compared to 39.1 per cent in predominantly Protestant areas).

More specifically, what are the socioeconomic profiles of individuals according to their religion/community background and area of residence? Catholics outside predominantly Catholic areas are more likely to be employed, belong to a professional class, own their home and have access to a car. Protestants in the most Catholic areas are more likely than their Catholic neighbours in these areas to have a degree, be employed, have a professional occupation, own an expensive house and have access to two or more cars. Unemployment and permanent sickness rates are higher for Catholics in areas with higher proportions of Catholics. Taking these socioeconomic variables as an indicator of 'affluence', not only are Catholics in the most Protestant areas more affluent than their Catholic peers in the most Catholic areas, but they also tend to be more affluent than their Protestant neighbours in these Protestant areas. Whereas Catholics in the most Protestant areas are clearly more affluent than those in the most Catholic areas, the differences for Protestants in these areas are less clear-cut. The most affluent Protestants are found in less concentrated areas. Protestants in the most Catholic areas are more deprived than their peers in the less Catholic areas, but less deprived than Catholic co-residents.

General health and concentration

The logistic regression modelling results are reported in Table 14.1. The outcome variable is poor general health. While just under 70 per cent of the total NIMS population reported good general health, this figure was slightly lower for the NIMS sample used in the analyses (which includes only 25- to 74-year-olds), at just over 60 per cent, for both Catholics and Protestants. Model 1 (a and b) controls for area concentration (percentage Catholic), age in five-year bands, sex and marital status. Socioeconomic status (SES) of the individual and the urban/rural character and deprivation quintiles of area of residence are then added for Model 2 (a and b). Males and females are presented together as testing indicated that there was no significant interaction between sex and Catholic concentration. Age is included but not reported, and shows the expected higher (statistically significant) likelihood of poor health for older than younger age groups. The results have been stratified by community background for two reasons; (1) as this allows the potential effect of being a minority to be explored for both groups separately; and (2) because there are thought to be differences in how the two groups perceive and report their health (O'Reilly and Rosato, 2010).

The relationship between demographic and socioeconomic characteristics and self-reported health shows no surprises. Females are more likely to report poor general health than males, which, unlike the poorer health of those who are not married, is persistent after controlling for socioeconomic background. Each indicator of SES makes a significant contribution in the fully adjusted models (with the exception of the 'unclassified' NS-SEC class for

Table 14.1: Relationship between the likelihood of reporting general health 'fair/not good' in the preceding 12 months and area of residence according to community background (higher values show higher likelihood of having fair/not good health)

	Community background Catholic		Community background Protestant	
	Model 1a	Model 2a	Model 1b	Model 2b
SEX				
Male (ref.)	1.00	1.00	1.00	1.00
Female	1.15*** (1.13, 1.17)	1.15*** (1.13, 1.17)	1.20*** (1.18, 1.21)	1.17*** (1.15, 1.18)
MARITAL STATUS				
Married (ref.)	1.00	1.00	1.00	1.00
Never married	1.34*** (1.31, 1.36)	0.98 (0.96, 1.00)	1.31*** (1.29, 1.34)	0.91*** (0.89, 0.93)
Separated/divorced/widowed	1.88*** (1.84, 1.93)	1.20*** (1.17, 1.22)	1.73*** (1.70, 1.76)	1.07*** (1.05, 1.09)
CONCENTRATION (% CATHOLIC)				
≤10	0.95* (0.91, 0.99)	1.02 (0.97, 1.07)	1.16*** (1.15, 1.18)	1.02** (1.01, 1.04)
10-29	0.90*** (0.88, 0.93)	0.94*** (0.91, 0.98)	0.95*** (0.94, 0.97)	0.98* (0.96, 1.00)
30-69 (ref.)	1.00	1.00	1.00	1.00
70-89	1.16*** (1.14, 1.19)	1.00 (0.98, 1.03)	1.13*** (1.09, 1.17)	1.04* (1.00, 1.08)
≥90	1.50*** (1.47, 1.53)	1.04*** (1.01, 1.06)	1.37*** (1.28, 1.46)	1.11*** (1.03, 1.19)
SOCIAL CLASS (NS-SEC)				
Professional (higher/lower managerial) (ref.)		1.00		1.00
Intermediate		1.11*** (1.09, 1.14)		1.13*** (1.11, 1.15)
Routine		1.26*** (1.22, 1.29)		1.25*** (1.23, 1.28)
Not working		1.41*** (1.37, 1.46)		1.53*** (1.47, 1.58)
Unclassified		0.85** (0.76, 0.96)		1.02 (0.90, 1.16)
EDUCATIONAL ATTAINMENT				
Degree (ref.)		1.00		1.00
A-level		1.33*** (1.27, 1.38)		1.22*** (1.18, 1.27)
O-level		1.37*** (1.33, 1.41)		1.31*** (1.28, 1.34)
None		1.90*** (1.84, 1.96)		1.72*** (1.68, 1.77)

(continued)

Table 14.1: Relationship between the likelihood of reporting general health 'fair/not good' in the preceding 12 months and area of residence according to community background (higher values show higher likelihood of having fair/not good health) (contd.)

	Community background Catholic		Community background Protestant	
	Model 1a	Model 2a	Model 1b	Model 2b
HOUSING TENURE				
≥£200,000 (ref.)		1.00		1.00
£150,000–199,999		1.19*** (1.14, 1.24)		1.21*** (1.18, 1.24)
£100,000–149,999		1.35*** (1.30, 1.40)		1.35*** (1.32, 1.39)
£75,000–99,999		1.49*** (1.43, 1.55)		1.52*** (1.47, 1.56)
≤£75,000		1.50*** (1.43, 1.56)		1.62*** (1.57, 1.67)
Private renter		1.97*** (1.88, 2.06)		1.92*** (1.85, 1.99)
Social renter		2.50*** (2.40, 2.61)		2.68*** (2.60, 2.78)
CAR ACCESS				
≥2 cars (ref.)		1.00		1.00
1 car		1.33*** (1.30, 1.35)		1.35*** (1.33, 1.37)
No car		1.65*** (1.60, 1.69)		1.76*** (1.72, 1.81)
SETTLEMENT BAND				
Urban (ref.)		1.00		1.00
Intermediate		0.96*** (0.94, 0.98)		0.91*** (0.90, 0.93)
Rural		0.99 (0.97, 1.01)		0.96*** (0.94, 0.97)
INCOME QUINTILES				
1 Least deprived (ref.)		1.00		1.00
2		1.08*** (1.04, 1.12)		1.05*** (1.03, 1.07)
3		1.10*** (1.06, 1.14)		1.09*** (1.07, 1.12)
4		1.18*** (1.14, 1.22)		1.15*** (1.12, 1.17)
5 Most deprived		1.24*** (1.20, 1.29)		1.18*** (1.15, 1.22)

Notes: Age in five-year bands is also included in all models (not shown). Data represent odds ratios (95% confidence intervals) from separate logistic regression models.
$***p<0.001$; $**p<0.01$; $*p<0.05$.

Source: NIMS. Author's own calculations.

Protestants). Marked gradients are seen for all the indicators of SES. For example, more professional forms of employment are associated with better health, and lower levels of educational attainment equate to poorer health. Car ownership and more expensive owner-occupied housing relate to lower likelihoods of reporting poor general health. Strong gradients are observed for area-based deprivation, where the likelihood of poor general health increases for areas with a greater proportion of low-income residents. Individuals in urban areas have a higher likelihood of reporting poor general health than those in rural areas.

Table 14.1 also shows the variation in general health across concentration quintiles, with the areas of most mixing by religion (that is, 30-69 per cent Catholic) acting as the reference category. For Catholics (Model 1a), likelihood of ill health is lowest in areas with a higher proportion of Protestants (that is, less than 30 per cent Catholic), and then the likelihood of reporting poor general health is greater for each category of increasing Catholic percentages. Catholics in areas comprising a 90 per cent or above Catholic residential composition were considerably more likely to be in poor health than Catholics in the more mixed reference category (odds ratio 1.50; 95 per cent confidence intervals [CI] 1.47, 1.53). With further adjustment for socioeconomic characteristics at the individual and area level (note the reduction in significance for some concentration categories) and the urban/rural character of area of residence (Model 1b), this excess of reported poor health was reduced to 4 per cent (odds ratio 1.04; 95 per cent CI 1.01, 1.06), but a 'U-shaped' relationship between health and community background composition was apparent (the likelihood of poorer health is slightly higher for greater concentrations of Catholics or Protestants – that is, at either ends of the percentage Catholic spectrum), with Catholics in areas of 10-29 per cent Catholics demonstrating the best health.

The separate models for Protestants (Models 1b and 2b) show essentially the same pattern as for Catholics, although the U-shaped relationship between health and greatest concentration shown in Model 1b is more evident than in Model 2b. With further adjustment for socioeconomic and area factors (Model 2b; again, some reduction in significance for concentration categories is apparent) the excess levels of poor health in the most concentrated areas is attenuated – the difference between the most Protestant and reference areas (<=10 per cent Catholic and 30-69 per cent Catholic) has reduced, although Protestants in the most Catholic areas (90 per cent and over) were still more likely to complain of poor health than their peers in the reference category (30-69 per cent Catholic); odds ratio 1.11 (95 per cent CI 1.03, 1.19). Again, Protestants in areas with 10-29 per cent Catholic were slightly, although significantly, more likely to have the best levels of health (odds ratio 0.98; 95 per cent CI 0.96, 1.00).

Mortality and concentration

A further health outcome is explored through all-cause mortality. Some 24,500 deaths occurred to NIMS sample members in the project-specific dataset, after exclusions (for example, only those in the age range 25-74, and only Catholics and Protestants), in roughly equal proportions of Catholics and Protestants. The results of the fully adjusted Cox proportional hazards models are presented in Table 14.2. Variables included in Models 3a and 3b are identical to those in Models 1b and 2b: concentration (percentage Catholic), age (not reported), sex, marital status, individual and area-level SES and area settlement type. The general health variable from the logistic regression modelling is also included here. Females had a lower risk of mortality than males, and marriage was shown to have a protective effect. NS-SEC categories revealed some non-statistically significant results, but an overall gradient of increased mortality risk for lower occupational classes; a roughly similar finding can be seen for educational attainment. Other measures of SES (car access and housing tenure) had a similar impact on risk of death (an increased risk with lower SES). The effect of area-level deprivation on mortality risk was a somewhat mixed picture, and there was not a significant effect for most categories. Level of area urbanness showed lower mortality risk in less urban areas, but these figures were not significant for Protestants.

Models only controlling for age, sex and marital status (not shown) had significant results for nearly all categories of concentration, but in the fully adjusted models (3a and 3b, Table 14.2), Catholic concentration was not significant for any category but the most Protestant areas, in Model 3a only (showing risk of death to be higher in the least Catholic areas). Interestingly, likewise, area-level deprivation shows just one significant effect, despite being a useful predictor of poor health (Models 1b and 2b). It is therefore difficult to ascribe too much weight to these results; concentration, in this study, appears not to have a significant effect on mortality risk. As discussed later in the chapter, certain causes of death may be more strongly related to concentration than all-cause mortality.

Table 14.2: Relationship between mortality risk and area of residence according to community background

	Community background Catholic	Community background Protestant
	Model 3a	Model 3b
SEX		
Male (ref.)	1.00	1.00
Female	0.58*** (0.56, 0.61)	0.54*** (0.53, 0.56)
MARITAL STATUS		
Married (ref.)	1.00	1.00
Never married	1.23*** (1.16, 1.31)	1.27*** (1.20, 1.33)
Separated/divorced/widowed	1.21*** (1.15, 1.27)	1.13*** (1.09, 1.18)
CONCENTRATION (% CATHOLIC)		
≤10	1.21** (1.06, 1.37)	0.99 (0.94, 1.04)
10-29	1.08 (0.98, 1.18)	0.99 (0.94, 1.04)
30-69 (ref.)	1.00	1.00
70-89	1.02 (0.96, 1.09)	0.93 (0.85, 1.02)
≥90	1.06 (1.00, 1.13)	1.06 (0.90, 1.24)
SOCIAL CLASS (NS-SEC)		
Professional (higher/lower managerial) (ref.)	1.00	1.00
Intermediate	1.02 (0.95, 1.09)	1.03 (0.98, 1.08)
Routine	1.03 (0.96, 1.11)	1.05* (1.00, 1.11)
Not working	1.20*** (1.11, 1.31)	1.23*** (1.14, 1.32)
Unclassified	0.76 (0.36, 1.60)	0.54 (0.20, 1.45)
EDUCATIONAL ATTAINMENT		
Degree (ref.)	1.00	1.00
A-level	1.04 (0.88, 1.24)	1.08 (0.95, 1.22)
O-level	1.17** (1.05, 1.30)	1.04 (0.97, 1.13)
None	1.25*** (1.13, 1.38)	1.06 (0.99, 1.14)
HOUSING TENURE		
≥£200, 000 (ref.)	1.00	1.00
£150,000–199,999	1.05 (0.92, 1.21)	1.02 (0.94, 1.11)
£100,000–149,999	1.07 (0.94, 1.20)	1.08* (1.00, 1.17)
£75,000–£99,999	1.16* (1.03, 1.32)	1.26*** (1.16, 1.37)
≤£75,000	1.16* (1.02, 1.33)	1.26*** (1.15, 1.37)
Private renter	1.15 (0.99, 1.33)	1.25*** (1.13, 1.38)
Social renter	1.47*** (1.30, 1.68)	1.59*** (1.45, 1.73)
CAR ACCESS		
≥2 cars (ref.)	1.00	1.00
1 car	1.14*** (1.07, 1.21)	1.12*** (1.07, 1.17)
No car	1.38*** (1.28, 1.48)	1.39*** (1.31, 1.48)

(continued)

Table 14.2: Relationship between mortality risk and area of residence according to community background (continued)

	Community background Catholic	Community background Protestant
	Model 3a	Model 3b
GENERAL HEALTH		
Good (ref.)	1.00	1.00
Fair/not good	2.22*** (2.11, 2.34)	2.38*** (2.29, 2.47)
SETTLEMENT BAND		
Urban (ref.)	1.00	1.00
Intermediate	0.94* (0.89, 0.99)	0.97 (0.94, 1.01)
Rural	0.85*** (0.80, 0.91)	0.98 (0.93, 1.03)
INCOME QUINTILES		
1 Least deprived (ref.)	1.00	1.00
2	1.00 (0.90, 1.12)	1.02 (0.97, 1.08)
3	1.05 (0.94, 1.18)	1.01 (0.96, 1.07)
4	1.01 (0.90, 1.12)	1.05 (0.99, 1.11)
5 Most deprived	1.03 (0.92, 1.16)	1.08* (1.02, 1.16)

Notes: Age in five-year bands is also included in all models (not shown). Data represent hazards ratios (95% CI) from separate Cox proportional hazards models.
$***p<0.001; **p<0.01; *p<0.05$.

Source: NIMS. Author's own calculations.

Discussion and conclusion

The aim of this chapter was to explore whether the health of people in Northern Ireland varied systematically according to the religious composition of the area in which they lived. We know from the literature on ethnic inequalities in health that a combination of residential concentration in deprived locales, socioeconomic position and social status can have a negative effect on the health of minority ethnic populations (Nazroo, 1998; Williams and Collins, 2001), but that residential concentration has also been shown to provide social and community support conducive to better health (Smaje, 1995; Beaudoin, 2009; Kramer and Hogue, 2009). From the literature, and given the recent history of socio-political conflict and sectarianism in Northern Ireland, it might be expected that having a religious affiliation which is a minority in one's residential area would, all other things being equal, have been associated with poorer health status. Likewise, it might be expected that residing in an area in which one is in a religious majority might have a protective effect on health. However, the current analysis shows a rather mixed picture in terms of these potential outcomes.

In the fully adjusted models (Models 1b and 2b), with the exception of areas of 10-29 per cent Catholics, the likelihood of having poor health was highest in more concentrated than mixed areas (30-69 per cent Catholic), for both Catholic and Protestant residents in these areas. A 'U-shaped' relationship between concentration levels and health was apparent (that is, higher likelihoods of reporting poor general health in more concentrated Catholic and Protestant areas). However, differences in health status were relatively minimal for all area types. In general, mixed areas were more 'healthy' for both groups, although areas of 10-29 per cent Catholic (that is, a slight Protestant majority but not the most Protestant areas [<=10 per cent Catholic]), faired best in health terms, for both Catholics and Protestants.

Catholics with the best health were found in areas with a Protestant majority (10-29 per cent Catholic), and Catholics in areas with a 90 per cent and above Protestant composition (<=10 per cent Catholic concentration) had a similar higher likelihood of poor health to their peers in the most Catholic areas. For neither Catholics nor Protestants is there evidence of a systematic 'minority or majority effect' on general health; for both groups, the most concentrated areas of Catholics and Protestants saw an increased likelihood of reporting poor health. As for Catholics, Protestant general health was best in areas with 10-29 per cent Catholics, and there was no evidence of health advantage when the proportions of Protestants increased further than this. As with Catholics, the highest likelihood of reporting poor general health could be found in areas of highest Catholic concentration. This was more marked for Protestants than Catholics in the fully adjusted models, but their slightly higher risk of poor health in majority Protestant areas and less in mixed (30-69 per cent Catholic) areas does not support the hypothesis that minority 'status' predicts poor health.

The overall similarity of the relationship between health and areas with a given Catholic composition for *both* Catholics *and* Protestants is an important observation, and suggests effects that are independent of the resident's community background. This similarity between areas despite the community background of its residents deserves some further consideration.

The absence of better levels of health in the most highly concentrated areas may be because the negative effects of living in what might be perceived as a 'closed system', with limited opportunities (in the labour market, housing, etc) and with higher levels of inter-communal tension with neighbouring areas, outweighs any positive effects such as increased social capital, which is known to be associated with improved mental health (Kawachi et al, 1999). Grady and McLafferty (2007) helpfully distinguish the differences between ethnic density and residential segregation in the context of health studies, the former being a voluntary process, while the latter an outcome of constraints to choice. The effects observed here are not, however, very marked, and while there is some evidence of poorer health in the more concentrated areas, this is not overwhelming.

The apparently distinct behaviour of areas of the same Catholic concentration on health for both Catholics and Protestants suggests that the area effects may represent unexplained residual confounding (Becher, 1992) because the census-based variables included in the analysis do not capture all aspects of poverty affecting individuals in concentrated Catholic areas (regardless of their religion, or of affluence in the areas with 10-29 per cent Catholics). Long-term inequalities in access to the labour market, both geographic and demographic, may be important, and there is ample literature demonstrating the association between unemployment and poor health (Moser, 1984; Morris et al, 1994; Wadsworth et al, 1999; Bartley and Plewis, 2002; Marmot et al, 2006; Dorling, 2009; Bambra, 2010). There is a disproportionate concentration of worklessness in predominantly Catholic areas with, for example, one in six living in such areas at the time of the census defined as 'permanently sick'. Economic activity was not, however, included as an explanatory variable in the regressions because of the very high correlation between poor self-reported health and some categories, such as permanently sick, which would lead to over-adjustment in the models.

The contribution of selective migration is likely to be considerable for, as the review by Kramer and Hogue (2009) suggests, the effects of segregation cannot easily be separated from the factors which gave rise to these divisions. As the authors note:

> ... one challenge in conceptualising segregation is that its social and health-relevant effects are often described in terms of the *process* of segregation – a series of forces that differentially allot individuals into residential environments and economic opportunities on the basis of race [in this case, religion/community background] – as opposed to the *condition or state* of segregation, which is the description of spatial residential patterns at a point in time. Many studies essentially estimate the degree to which measuring the *state* approximates what we believe the *process* to be. (Kramer and Hogue, 2009, p 180)

Certainly, given the nature of the sectarian conflict in Northern Ireland throughout The Troubles, increased residential separation became a significant phenomenon, as people sought safety and refuge among their own community (Compton and Power, 1986; Darby, 1986; Doherty and Poole, 1997). Although additional area effects may be required to explain the poorer levels of health in the more Catholic areas, selective migration might explain the slightly better health among Catholics in the areas of 10-29 per cent Catholics, and is suggested by the increasing affluence of Catholics in more Protestant areas. There has been a growth of a Catholic middle class in Northern Ireland since the early 1990s, which has facilitated upward geographical mobility into predominantly Protestant areas which could previously not have been afforded: 'Catholics entering new occupations are moving into areas which are geographically separate from the bulk of the Catholic population in the BUA [Belfast Urban Area]' (Cormack and Osborne, 1994, p 83; see also Cebulla and Smyth, 1995). In-depth interviews with internal (within Northern Ireland) migrants by Catney (2008) demonstrated how this expansion by the Catholic community, particularly recent university graduates, into traditionally predominantly Protestant (affluent) areas, is continuing. As noted earlier with reference to the descriptive statistics, Catholics in the most Protestant areas tend to be more socioeconomically advantaged than Catholics in the most Catholic areas, and indeed more advantaged than Protestants living in these predominantly Protestant areas. It has been shown that migrants who move from more to less deprived areas tend to be healthier than those who move in the opposite direction and that, in turn, leads to a less healthy residualised population in deprived areas (see, for example, Norman et al, 2005 and Connolly and O'Reilly, 2007). Given the relationship between poor health and deprivation and the fact that segregated areas in Northern Ireland tend to be less affluent, selective out-migration helps to explain the increased likelihood of reporting poor health in more concentrated areas. The most Protestant areas (<=10 per cent Catholic) will be subject to similar persistent unequal access to labour opportunities to the most concentrated Catholic areas, and thus it is these more affluent majority Protestant areas (10-29 per cent Catholic) that are subject to this 'healthy' selective in-migration.

The results for all-cause mortality show a significant effect for concentration levels only for the most Protestant areas, for Catholic individuals. In terms of mortality, Catholics fare worse in areas in which they are a minority; their risk of dying is highest in areas with the lowest proportion of Catholics. The lack of significance in the mortality results could suggest that mortality risk is not well predicted by level of religious concentration in an individual's neighbourhood. This effect may differ if the health outcome were to be made less general, to explore cause-specific mortality, as discussed below.

There are several limitations with the present analysis that could be considered in further research. Some possible explanations for the differences found for general health status between Catholic and Protestant areas have been offered. However, there may be unmeasured effects operating in the most Catholic areas which have not been fully controlled for, that require further study: are the socioeconomic measures, for example, capturing all facets of deprivation? The measurement of health used in the study also has some limitations, such as the reliability of self-reported health measurement, as discussed earlier, and the facets of health which this indicator actually measures. Community dynamics may be more likely to have an impact on some aspects of ill health than others. Mental health, for example, might be expected to be affected by the support (or lack of it) that might come from the presence (or absence) of being in a majority status. As stated by Fang et al (1998), segregation may have a stronger or weaker relationship with different causes of death; those that relate to genetics and/or family history may be expected to be less important in studies of this kind when compared to reasons for mortality that are associated with one's social and/or physical environments. Likewise, many causes of death are known to be associated with age, and while age is controlled for in this study, this cannot in itself fully account for the higher risk of mortality from certain causes. An obvious extension to this work, therefore, would be to examine cause–specific mortality. Another area for further consideration relates to the measurement of concentration used here. Further work is needed to explore how residential segregation as measured using indices of unevenness and exposure, for example, rather than concentration, affects health status in Northern Ireland. While measuring population concentration through percentage membership of a given group was appropriate for this research, employing these other measures might help capture other aspects of the social environment that may have an impact on health. Likewise, it could be argued that the geographical areas used to report the data are not representative of 'true' communities or neighbourhoods, and therefore do not provide an effective means of measuring community interactions. Lloyd et al (Chapter Four, this volume) demonstrate the importance of considering inter-neighbourhood interaction in segregation research and Kearns and

Parkinson (2001) discuss the meaning and problems of defining neighbourhoods. The modifiable areal unit problem (MAUP) may have affected these specific findings; some of the SOAs which are labelled as majority Catholic may contain pockets of Protestant areas, and this may have an impact on these results (see Chapters Five and Seven, this volume; see also Lloyd, 2012, for studies that highlight the importance and impact of scale on segregation). Further research should also consider the process of selective migration discussed (see Jackson et al, 2000, for an allied argument). An update of this work once the outputs from the 2011 Census are linked to the NIMS (not available at the time of writing) will be invaluable in understanding how the relationship between health and segregation may have changed during a time of further decreasing segregation in the 2000s.

In policy terms, while the present study finds no evidence that population concentration *per se* has a negative impact on one's health, the specific dynamics of 'unhealthy' areas deserve further attention; in particular, policy makers would do well to consider what factors are important and which processes are in operation in these areas affecting the health status of its residents.

Acknowledgements

Sincere thanks to Michael Rosato of the NILS-RSU (Research Support Unit) for helpful contributions to earlier versions of this chapter. A much earlier version of this work was presented at a special session on segregation at the 2010 Annual Meeting of the Association of American Geographers (Washington, DC), and the author wishes to thank the delegates at the session for their helpful feedback. Sincere thanks also to the organisers of the session, who are also the editors of this book, for their comments and advice. Dermot O'Reilly's involvement with an earlier draft is acknowledged. The help provided by the staff of the Northern Ireland Mortality Study (NIMS) and the NILS Research Support Unit is acknowledged. The NIMS is funded by the Health and Social Care Research and Development Division of the Public Health Agency (HSC R&D Division) and NISRA. The NILS-RSU is funded by the Economic and Social Research Council (ESRC) and the Northern Ireland Government. The author alone is responsible for the interpretation of the data and any views or opinions presented are solely those of the author and do not necessarily represent those of NISRA/NIMS.

Notes

[1] Property value data are linked to the NIMS from the Land and Property Services for Northern Ireland database.

[2] Note that some individuals will have moved from their 2001 SOA origin, or have changed their socioeconomic status, by the time they die.

References

Acevedo-Garcia, D. (2000) 'Residential segregation and the epidemiology of infectious diseases', *Social Science & Medicine* vol 51, no 8, pp 1143-61.

Bambra, C. (2010) 'Yesterday once more? Unemployment and health in the 21st century', *Journal of Epidemiology and Community Health*, vol 64, pp 213-15.

Bardon, J. (2005) *A history of Ulster*, Belfast: Blackstaff Press.

Bartley, M. and Plewis, I. (2002) 'Accumulated labour market disadvantage and limiting long-term illness: data from the 1971-1991 ONS Longitudinal Study', *International Journal of Epidemiology*, vol 31, no 2, pp 336-41.

Beaudoin, C.E. (2009) 'Bonding and bridging neighborliness: an individual-level study in the context of health', *Social Science & Medicine*, vol 68, no 12, pp 2129-36.

Bécares, L., Nazroo, J., Jackson, J. and Heuvelman, H. (2012) 'Ethnic density effects on health and experienced racism among Caribbean people in the US and England: a cross-national comparison', *Social Science & Medicine*, vol 75, no 12, pp 2107-15.

Becher, H. (1992) 'The concept of residual confounding in regression models and some applications', *Statistics in Medicine*, vol 11, no 13, pp 1747-58.

Beckett, M., Weinstein, M., Goldman, N. and Yu-Hsuan (2000) 'Do health interview surveys yield reliable data on chronic illness among older respondents?', *American Journal of Epidemiology*, vol 151, no 3, pp 315-23.

Boal, F.W. (1981) 'Ethnic residential segregation, ethnic mixing and resource conflict: a study in Belfast, Northern Ireland', in C. Peach, V. Robinson and S. Smith (eds) *Ethnic segregation in cities*, London: Croom Helm, pp 235-51.

Boal, F.W. (1996) 'Integration and division: sharing and segregating in Belfast', *Planning Practice and Research*, vol 11, no 2, pp 151-8.

Bollini, P. and Siem, H. (1995) 'No real progress towards equity: health of migrants and ethnic minorities on the eve of the year 2000', *Social Science & Medicine*, vol 41, no 6, pp 819-28.

Bryan, D., Stevenson, C. and Gillespie, G. (2009) *Flags monitoring project: interim report covering 2008 with comparative figures from 2007 and 2006*, Belfast: Office of the First Minister and Deputy First Minister.

Catney, G. (2008) 'Internal migration, community background and residential segregation in Northern Ireland', Unpublished PhD thesis, Belfast: School of Geography, Archaeology and Palaeoecology, Queen's University Belfast.

Catney, G., Finney, N. and Twigg, L. (2011) 'Diversity and the complexities of ethnic integration in the UK: guest editors' introduction', *Journal of Intercultural Studies*, vol 32, no 2, pp 107-14.

Cebulla, A. and Smyth, J. (1995) 'Industrial collapse and post-Fordist overdetermination of Belfast', in P. Shirlow (ed) *Development Ireland: contemporary issues*, London: Pluto Press, pp 81-93.

Chang, V.W. (2006) 'Racial residential segregation and weight status among US adults', *Social Science & Medicine*, vol 63, no 3, pp 1289-303.

Charatz-Litt, C. (1992) 'A chronicle of racism: the effects of the white medical community on black health', *Journal of the National Medical Association*, vol 84, no 8, pp 717-25.

Collins, C.A. and Williams, D.R. (1999) 'Segregation and mortality: the deadly effects of racism?' *Sociological Forum*, vol 14, no 3, pp 495-523.

Compton, P.A. (1995) *Demographic review Northern Ireland 1995*, Belfast: Northern Ireland Economic Development Office.

Compton, P.A. and Power, J.P. (1986) 'Estimates of the religious composition of Northern Ireland local government districts in 1981 and change in the geographical pattern of religious composition between 1971 and 1981', *The Economic and Social Review*, vol 17, no 2, pp 87-105.

Connolly, S. and O'Reilly, D. (2007) 'The contribution of migration to changes in the distribution of health over time: five-year follow-up study in Northern Ireland', *Social Science & Medicine*, vol 65, no 6, pp 1004-11.

Cormack, R.J. and Osborne, R.D. (1994) 'The evolution of a Catholic middle class', in A. Guelke (ed) *New perspectives on the Northern Ireland conflict*, Aldershot: Avebury, pp 65-85.

Darby, J. (1986) *Intimidation and the control of conflict in Northern Ireland*, Dublin: Gill and Macmillan.

Dorling, D. (2009) 'Unemployment and health', *British Medical Journal*, vol 338, pp b829.

Doherty, P. and Poole, M.A. (1997) 'Ethnic residential segregation in Belfast, Northern Ireland, 1971-1991', *The Geographical Review*, vol 87, no 4, pp 520-36.

Doherty, P. and Poole, M. (2000) 'Living apart in Belfast: residential segregation in a context of ethnic conflict', in F.W. Boal (ed) *Ethnicity and housing: accommodating differences*, Aldershot: Ashgate, pp 179-89.

Fang, J., Madhavan, S., Bosworth, W. and Alderman, M.H. (1998) 'Residential segregation and mortality in New York City', *Social Science & Medicine*, vol 47, no 4, pp 469-76.

Finney, N. and Catney, G. (eds) (2012) *Minority internal migration in Europe*, Farnham: Ashgate.

French, D. (2009) 'Residential segregation and health in Northern Ireland', *Health and Place*, vol 15, no 3, pp 888-96.

Gee, G.C. (2002) 'A multilevel analysis of the relationship between institutional and individual racial discrimination and health status', *American Journal of Public Health*, vol 92, no 4, pp 615-23.

Gordon-Larsen, P., Nelson, M.C., Page, P. and Popkin, B.M. (2006) 'Inequality in the built environment underlies key health disparities in physical activity and obesity', *Pediatrics*, vol 117, no 2, pp 417-24.

Grady, S.C. and McLafferty, S. (2007) 'Segregation, nativity, and health: reproductive health inequalities for immigrant and native-born black women in New York City', *Urban Geography*, vol 28, no 4, pp 377-97.

Halpern, D. and Nazroo, J.Y. (2000) 'The ethnic density effect: results from a national community survey of England and Wales', *International Journal of Social Psychiatry*, vol 46, no 1, pp 34–46.

Hamilton, J., Byrne, J. and Jarman, N. (2003) *A review of health and social care needs of victims and survivors of the Northern Ireland conflict*, (NI) Eastern Health and Social Services Board (unpublished).

Hepburn, A.C. (1996) *A past apart: studies in the history of Catholic Belfast, 1850-1950*, Belfast: Ulster Historical Foundation.

Idler, E. and Benyamini, Y. (1997) 'Self-rated health and mortality: a review of twenty-seven community studies', *Journal of Health and Social Behavior*, vol 38, pp 21-37.

Jackson, S.A., Anderson, R.T., Johnson, N.J. and Sorlie, P.D. (2000) 'The relation of residential segregation to all-cause mortality: a study in black and white', *American Journal of Public Health*, vol 90, no 4, pp 615-17.

Jones, E. (1960) *A social geography of Belfast*, Oxford: Oxford University Press.

Jylhä, M., Guralnik, J.M., Ferrucci, L., Jokela, J. and Heikkinen, E. (1998) 'Is self-rated health comparable across cultures and genders?', *The Journals of Gerontology, Series B: Social Sciences*, vol 53B, no 3, pp S144-52.

Karlsen, S. and Nazroo, J.Y. (2002) 'Relation between racial discrimination, social class, and health among ethnic minority groups', *American Journal of Public Health*, vol 92, no 4, pp 624-31.

Kawachi, I., Kennedy, B.P. and Glass, R. (1999) 'Social capital and self-rated health: a contextual analysis', *American Journal of Public Health*, vol 89, no 8, pp 1187-93.

Kearns, A. and Parkinson, M. (2001) 'The significance of neighbourhood', *Urban Studies*, vol 38, no 12, pp 2103-10.

Kramer, M.R. and Hogue, C.R. (2009) 'Is segregation bad for your health?', *Epidemiological Reviews*, vol 31, no 1, pp 178-94.

Lee, M.-A. (2009) 'Neighborhood residential segregation and mental health: a multilevel analysis on Hispanic Americans in Chicago', *Social Science & Medicine*, vol 68, no 11, pp 1975-84.

Lloyd, C.D. (2012) 'Analysing the spatial scale of population concentrations by religion in Northern Ireland using global and local variograms', *International Journal of Geographical Information Science*, vol 26, no 1, pp 57-73.

Macintyre, S., Maciver, S. and Sooman, A. (1993) 'Area, class and health: should we be focusing on places or people?', *Journal of Social Policy*, vol 22, no 2, pp 213-34.

Marmot, M., Wilkinson, R.G., Bartley M., Ferrie, J. and Montgomery, S.M. (2006) 'Health and labour market disadvantage: unemployment, non-employment, and job insecurity', in M. Marmot and R.G. Wilkinson (eds) *Social determinants of health*, Oxford: Oxford University Press, pp 78-96.

Morris, J.K., Cook, D.G. and Shaper, A.G. (1994) 'Loss of employment and mortality', *British Medical Journal*, vol 308, pp 1135-9.

Moser, K., Fox, J. and Jones, D. (1984). 'Unemployment and mortality in the OPCS Longitudinal Study', *Lancet*, vol ii, pp 1324-9.

Nazroo, J. (1998) 'Genetic, cultural or socio-economic vulnerability? Explaining ethnic inequalities in health', *Sociology of Health and Illness*, vol 20, no 5, pp 710-30.

Nickens, H.W. (1995) 'Race/ethnicity as a factor in health and health care: the role of race/ethnicity and social class in minority health status', *Health Services Research*, vol 30, no 1 (pt 2), pp 151-62.

NISRA (Northern Ireland Statistics and Research Agency) (2005) *Northern Ireland multiple deprivation measure 2005*, Belfast: NISRA, Crown Copyright.

NISRA (2013) *Statistics Bulletin. Census 2011: detailed characteristics for Northern Ireland on health, religion and national identity*, Belfast: NISRA (www.nisra.gov.uk/Census/detailedcharacteristics_stats_bulletin_2011.pdf).

Norman, P., Paul, B. and Rees, P. (2005) 'Selective migration, health and deprivation: a longitudinal analysis', *Social Science & Medicine*, vol 60, pp 2755-71.

O'Reilly, D. and Stevenson, M. (2003) 'Mental health in Northern Ireland: have "The Troubles" made it worse?', *Journal of Epidemiology and Community Health*, vol 57, pp 488-92.

O'Reilly, D. and Rosato, M. (2010) 'Dissonances in self-reported health and mortality across denominational groups in Northern Ireland', *Social Science & Medicine*, vol 71, no 5, pp 1011-7.

O'Reilly, D., Rosato, M., Catney, G., Johnston, F. and Brolly, M. (2012) 'Cohort description: the Northern Ireland Longitudinal Study (NILS)', *International Journal of Epidemiology*, vol 41, no 3, pp 634-41.

Panter-Brick, C. (2010) 'Conflict, violence and health: setting a new interdisciplinary agenda', *Social Science & Medicine*, vol 70, no 1, pp 1-6.

Peach, C. (1996) 'Good segregation, bad segregation', *Planning Perspectives*, vol 11, no 4, pp 379-98.

Peach, C. (2000) 'The consequences of segregation', in F.W. Boal (ed) *Ethnicity and housing: accommodating differences*, Aldershot: Ashgate, pp 10-23.

Phillips, D. (1998) 'Black minority ethnic concentration, segregation and dispersal in Britain', *Urban Studies*, vol 35, no 10, pp 1681-702.

Phillips, D. (2006) 'Parallel lives? Challenging discourses of British Muslim self-segregation', *Environment and Planning D*, vol 24, no 1, pp 25-40.

Rose, D. and Pevalin, D. (eds) (2002) *A researcher's guide to the National Statistics socio-economic classification*, London: Sage.

Shirlow, P. and Murtagh B. (2006) *Belfast: segregation, violence and the city*, London: Pluto Press.

Shuttleworth, I.G. and Lloyd, C.D. (2007) *Mapping segregation in Belfast: Northern Ireland Housing Executive estates*, Belfast: Northern Ireland Housing Executive.

Shuttleworth, I.G. and Lloyd, C.D. (2009a) 'Are Northern Ireland's communities dividing? Evidence from geographically consistent Census of Population data, 1971-2001', *Environment and Planning A*, vol 41, pp 213-29.

Shuttleworth, I.G. and Lloyd, C.D. (2009b) *Mapping segregation in Northern Ireland: Northern Ireland housing estates outside Belfast*, Belfast: Northern Ireland Housing Executive.

Smaje, C. (1995) 'Ethnic residential concentration and health: evidence for a positive effect?', *Policy & Politics*, vol 23, no 3, pp 251-69.

Subramanian, S.V., Acevedo-Garcia, D. and Osypuk, T.L. (2005) 'Racial residential segregation and geographic heterogeneity in black/white disparity in poor self-rated health in the US: a multilevel statistical analysis', *Social Science & Medicine*, vol 60, no 8, pp 1667-79.

Srinivasan, S., O'Fallon, L.R. and Dearry, A. (2003) 'Creating healthy communities, healthy homes, healthy people: initiating a research agenda on the built environment and public health', *American Journal of Public* Health, vol 93, no 9, pp 1446-50.

Wadsworth, M.E.J., Montgomery, S.M. and Bartley, M.J. (1999) 'The persisting effect of unemployment on health and social well-being in men early in working life', *Social Science & Medicine*, vol 48, no 10, pp 1491-9.

Williams, D.R. and Collins, C. (2001) 'Racial residential segregation: a fundamental cause of racial disparities in health', *Public Health Reports*, vol 116, no 5, pp 404-16.

Williams, D.R. and Jackson, P.B. (2005) 'Social sources of racial disparities in health', *Health Affairs*, vol 24, no 2, pp 325-34.

Wilkinson, R.G. (1996) *Unhealthy societies: the afflictions of inequality*, London: Routledge.

Young, H., Grundy, E., O'Reilly, D. and Boyle, P. (2010) 'Self-rated health and mortality in the UK: results from the first comparative analysis of the England and Wales, Scotland, and Northern Ireland Longitudinal Studies', *Population Trends*, vol 139, pp 11-36.

FIFTEEN

Class segregation

Danny Dorling

Introduction

This chapter concentrates on the causes, outcomes and implications of social and geographical segregation by class, using the example of how social geography has changed in Britain since around 1968, and putting these changes into a wider geographical and historical context. (Northern Ireland is not included for numerous reasons, not least because it has a special and very different recent history of segregation.)

Here I argue that the antecedents of the current growth in class segregation in Britain can be seen as early as the mid-1960s especially in voting records from around that time onwards. Figure 15.4, below, shows the first tiny increase in this form of segregation to have occurred in 1964. Compared to 1960s racial segregation and rioting in the US, what was happening in the UK was almost imperceptible change, but it was slow and steady change in one particular direction. By the end of the 1970s economic polarisation was following that earlier rise in political segregation. This led to rising social polarisation, seen most clearly in rising spatial segregation between tenures and within the British housing market during the 1980s. The same occurred in the US. Poorer areas became residualised, while in rich areas house prices began to soar upwards, stumbled briefly in 1989, and then took off again.

During the 1990s wealth inequalities continued to grow, and next came consequential and huge rises in health inequalities. In the UK, this is what increasing class segregation resulted in. In the US, race may have been more important. In mainland Europe no similar great rises in segregation were measured, and in some rich nations, processes of equalisation were taking place during this same period (Dorling, 2012). In the UK for a few years in the early 2000s, it looked as if the rising segregation might be ending, but that again was just a stumble. The overall outcome has been increasingly 'different strokes for different folks' growing up in different neighbourhoods.

In Britain, and it can also be argued in the US, the implications of this rising segregation have been a growth in ignorance across the board: ignorance of poverty for the rich, ignorance by the poor of the true value of riches held by the few, and more and more people seeing themselves as average, while fewer *are* near to average. But that could be about to end, not with a bang, but with the hiss of wealth slowly but surely escaping out the value of assets, which themselves depend on segregation for their value: housing and land.

The geography of class segregation

To be segregated is to be separated for part of the time. There are many ways in which such separation is possible, but it must always involve physical separation at some point to be geographical segregation. Boys can be segregated from girls in separate schools, even if it is almost impossible for them not to mix in families (Fuller et al, 2005). Servants and the upper classes can be segregated between floors of a country house, even if they must mix in that house for the service to occur. If people are completely segregated, between living in Myanmar and Thailand, for example, then they may be considered not as segregated, but as simply living in completely separate areas. For another example of where separation is not segregation: men on Mount Athos are not segregated from women, they are completely separated – no women are ever allowed on to the land of Mount Athos (see della Dora, 2011).

Conversely, people who are taught together at school and who play together out of school are only segregated into different families, not castes or classes. Segregation is about mixing only part of the time, enough for the lack of mixing the rest of the time to be of lasting importance. In very mixed neighbourhoods children play after school with other children outside of their families. Here, there is even less segregation than in areas where almost all children do not go to the nearest school to their home. The same can be true if adults from otherwise different social groups mix in workplaces, but also during recreation outside of work, on holiday or through where they shop. Segregation tends to be least at the start and end of life. In Sheffield, UK, there is only one maternity unit where almost all babies are born, and one city mortuary for any bodies to be held where anyone who has not been in the care of a doctor is taken.

The time during which people are segregated can be very long, and the amount of mixing that occurs can be very slight, but still enough for the segregation to be evident. People have only to mix ever so slightly to know that they are segregated. For example, people can spend almost all of their childhood living in areas where other people (*not* like them) do *not* live. They might only occasionally come across someone from a different social class, for instance, when a dignitary visits their estate, or they go to the doctor's. Alternatively, the farm labourers on the country estate of a very rich child might be the poorest of people that child ever sees, she rarely mixes with them, but she knows she is different because she sees them and occasionally hears them talking. While these two are extreme examples, it is worth asking much more generally just how differentiated lives in Britain and similar countries are today (Wilson and Keil, 2008). In the US, race plays a larger part again. This further complicates the pictures of geographical segregation. Elsewhere, one religious group may see itself as above another, even if it is not always economically more prosperous.

Britain (excluding Northern Ireland) is useful to study because social class is so much more important than most other factors such as race or religion. Figure 15.1 (below) makes one attempt to show just how much the norms of British society alter by where people in Britain live. It is based on 2001 Census data. When the 2011 Census is released it will be possible to determine the extent to which the polarisation shown in Figure 15.1 has risen or fallen. Later in this chapter the changes since the 1971 Census, and from a little before even that time, are discussed. For now, Figure 15.1 divides the country into 1,282 areas of equal population size and colours each area by one of 15 shades. The shading of the areas is done according to what is normal in each place. The two extreme places are described below: first, the worst-off place, and then the best-off, and then the average place. In each case the number of disadvantages and then advantages are counted up using the following numerals in brackets: (1), (2) ... to (7). That is why these seven numbers appear oddly placed in brackets in each of the next three paragraphs – you need to count them up. You have to count to appreciate the depths of segregation.

In the worst-off places in Britain, *most* (1) infants live in a family where there is no car, and that is the case for all children living in these areas under the age of five. *Most* (2) children of school age live in families with almost no spare wealth, they would inherit almost nothing if their parents were to die, and this is the case for the majority of children in all the streets around them – it is simply normal. Here (3) *less than* a fifth of young adults will go to university, often as few as one in ten. If they go, they will rarely return. Of those adults who work (4), *the majority* work in a job that is described as either unskilled or semi-skilled. Often these jobs require a great deal of skill, for instance, making lunch for 200 youngsters at a school, but this is given the understated title 'dinner lady', with an equally understated pay packet, belying the skill required in the job. Between the ages of 40 and 59 in these areas (and also for people much older and younger), *most* (5) people live in housing owned by the council or a housing association and rent. Between the ages of 60 to 74, *most* (6) describe their health as poor, because it is poor. *Most* (7) die under the age of 80. All the areas where all seven of these conditions are true are coloured darkest red.

In contrast to the most disadvantaged areas just described, in the many areas coloured darkest blue, the very opposite is most often the case. If you are reading this chapter – and you are British – you are likely to have grown up in the kind of place about to be described, a very unusual place, but one where what is nationally unusual is locally usual. If you are not British the same still applies, unless you are from a very equal country such as Norway, Japan, Denmark or the Netherlands, places where we can guess so much less about you from just knowing within that country where you come from.

In the best-off places in Britain *most* (1) infants live in a family where there are two or more cars and that is the case for all children living in these areas under the age of five. Most parents can almost always just hop in the car with their toddler. *Most* (2) children of school age in this type of area live in families with so much spare wealth that they would each inherit £54,000 and usually a lot more, if their parents were to die. This is the case for the majority of children in all the streets around them – it is simply normal to be rich here. Here (3) *more than* 40 per cent of young adults will go to university by age 19, often almost all go by age 30, especially the young women. When they go they then tend to move to London before returning to areas like these to have their own children. Of those adults who work (4) *the majority* work in a job that is grandly described as professional or management. Inflated salaries at the top end of the labour market means that some workers are overvalued. Many of those in the professions and management are seen, for instance, as receiving good remuneration for talking tough about 'leadership' over long paid-for lunches in an expenses-paid culture. In contrast, many workers whose jobs demand considerable skills, responsibility and commitment are undervalued and are not understood as possessing skills. *All* work requires some degree of skill, but what is currently labelled as highly skilled and low skilled may in future be seen as rather arbitrary. Between the ages of 40 and 59 in these areas, and much older and younger, *most* (5) people are living in homes they by now own outright – they hold property. Between the ages of 60 to 74, *most* (6) describe their health as good, because it is

Figure 15.1: Social class residential segregation in Britain, all ages, 2001

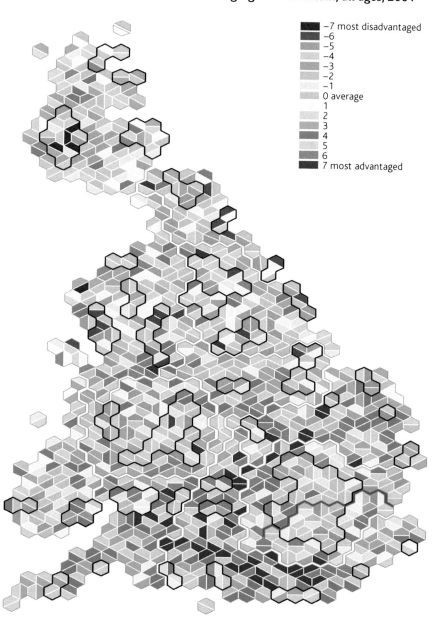

Note: This is a cartogram showing every parliamentary constituency in Britain as a hexagon with roughly similar populations and hence sizes. The divisions within each constituency are also shown by dividing each in half and colouring the two halves separately.

Source: Dorling (2011)

good. *Most* (7) die well over the age of 83, the women often in their nineties. All these areas where all seven of these conditions is true are coloured darkest blue.

So what is it to be 'normal', to live in a 'normal' area? Well, there is nothing normal about being normal in a highly class-segregated society. Most people are not normal but it *is* normal to be either better-off than average or worst-off – polarisation is the norm. Should you want to check whether the neighbourhood you live in is normal, then ask around and ensure that: (1) *most* children live in a family that has just one car; (2) *most* children of school age live in families with a little spare wealth so that average inheritances on sudden death of both parents would be £20,000-54,000 – here, (3) *between* a fifth and two-fifths of young adults will go to university. Of those adults who work (4) *the majority* work in a job that is described in a 'levelling' way as either skilled manual or lower professional. Between the ages of 40 and 59 in these areas, (5) *most* people are renting privately and after that, the next largest group are paying a mortgage. Between the ages of 60 to 74, (6) *most* describe their health as fair. The average life expectancy (7) *is* around 80, 81 or 82 in all of these areas, although individuals in these areas are, of course, more varied in exactly when they die. Where all seven of these conditions is true, those areas are coloured grey. If you happen to be British and this fits your area and you also fit these boundaries, you are very unusual – you are normal. If you are not British, ask someone you know where they come from in Britain, and whether it mattered in terms of who they are now.

Figure 15.1 is a map of the spatial manifestation of growing social class segregation. In countries where car use is determined much more by need than by wealth, car users are more often found in the countryside, not among the affluent. In a highly class-segregated society you have access to many cars if you have much money. Your home has many rooms if you have much money, not if you have many people who need to sleep there. In Figure 15.1, each hexagon is a Westminster parliamentary constituency. These are the areas used to elect Members of Parliament (MPs). Each has been placed in the map so as to be as close to its original neighbours as possible. Each is also split in half along a line that best divides the poorer half of each constituency from its richer half. Often these two sides of each area will be quite similar. When that is the case the two halves tend to be coloured the same shade. However, sometimes there are great differences within a parliamentary constituency and this mapping technique helps to reveal some of that, as well as give the more populous cities the space they deserve in the overall impression gained.

Next, in Figure 15.2, is a non-geographical image of British society. All but one of the figures in this chapter are taken from the book, *Fair play*, which allows me to avoid having to go into details about the sources or give many references to data and explanations of the statistics behind the figures. If you want to know more, go to the source. Carry on reading here if you want to hear an argument not interrupted by too much detail. So let's consider this particular image of British society, and ask how we got here.

Is this image fair, is it true, and are only half the population normal? Well, the figure for a quarter being poor and a tenth being very poor is very commonly quoted. About a quarter of people, especially children, do not have what most people consider as essentials. They are unable to afford to take a holiday once a year, unless they stay at a family (such as grandparents') or friend's home. However, the image shown in Figure 15.2 is not based on actual numbers; it is more indicative than empirical, but it may well ring true. That is because just as about a quarter of us are poor (and rising), and a tenth of us are very poor (and rising rapidly), so, too, about a quarter of us are asset rich (and today will be much more so if we brought a home in the South East or London before 2005) and about a tenth are exclusively rich.

Figure 15.2: Social class financial segregation in Britain, 2011

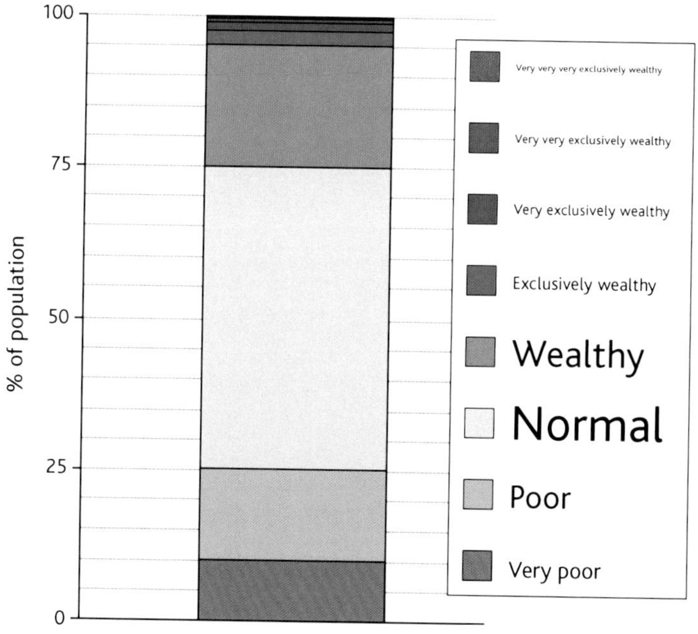

Source: Dorling (2011, p 162)

The statistics just quoted can simply be read off the chart below – Figure 15.3 is based on actual data rather than being schematic. But whether the numbers are based on reams of survey data, or are just how an academic says they see the world as being, the extent to which you believe the pictures you are about to be presented with might well depend as much on what you bring to this chapter as on what is within it. That is because, in a highly divided class system, we all tend to have quite different but often firmly held views.

As inequality has risen in Britain, it has closed down much of the concern for others. One newspaper headline writer got it spot on in 2008: 'As the middle classes feel the pain of comparison with the super-rich, we lose all enthusiasm for the common good' (Russell, 2008). Then, in late 2011 it was revealed, using data from the British Social Attitudes Survey, that as British class segregation rose further: 'Private education perpetuates a form of "social apartheid" and has given rise to a political class drawn from a "segregated elite" that does not understand or share the views of most people, the annual British Social Attitudes Survey warns on Wednesday' (Ramesh, 2011). When the differences between people's life chances were falling, from the 1920s through to the late 1970s, these apartheid attitudes became less chilling. Only the last decade of these falls is shown in Figure 15.3 below.

The poor in Figure 15.3 are people excluded from the norms of society, with 'excluded' being as defined by the majority of the population. The exclusively rich are also defined in this way. The asset rich have substantial monies. If they were to drop dead today they would be liable for inheritance tax. In fact, less than a third of them ever pay that tax as they tend to spend most of their assets before death. In contrast the 'core poor' will hardly ever have held assets of any value. They are people seen as poor whether their assets, income or their own views are taken into account. They are poor by any definition.

How did we come to be so divided and why did the arrows shown in Figure 15.3 start to separate from 1980 onwards? One suggestion is that the separation in living standards followed another separation – an economic separation in life chances – and that separation itself followed a separation of beliefs and prejudices. Figure 15.4, shown next, provides data that back up this point.

To understand Figure 15.4 you need to know that the Conservative (Tory) Party is Britain's most successful political party, the party that has held office the most times since 1920, and the one that has not much changed its identity. You also need to understand that a segregation index measures how geographically concentrated a group

Figure 15.3: Changes in financial segregation in Britain 1968-2005

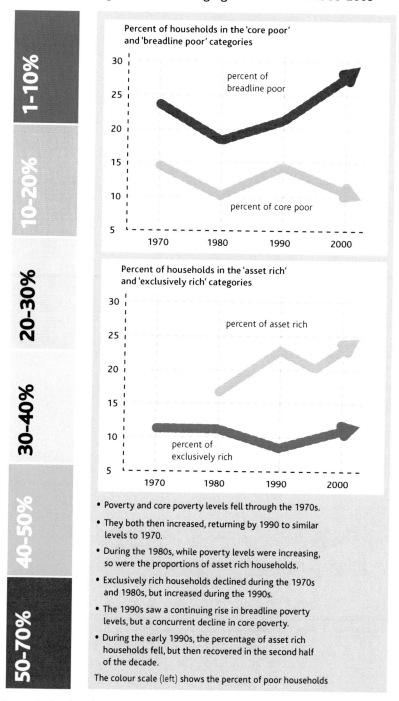

Percent of households in the 'core poor' and 'breadline poor' categories

Percent of households in the 'asset rich' and 'exclusively rich' categories

1-10%

10-20%

20-30%

30-40%

40-50%

50-70%

- Poverty and core poverty levels fell through the 1970s.

- They both then increased, returning by 1990 to similar levels to 1970.

- During the 1980s, while poverty levels were increasing, so were the proportions of asset rich households.

- Exclusively rich households declined during the 1970s and 1980s, but increased during the 1990s.

- The 1990s saw a continuing rise in breadline poverty levels, but a concurrent decline in core poverty.

- During the early 1990s, the percentage of asset rich households fell, but then recovered in the second half of the decade.

The colour scale (left) shows the percent of poor households

Source: Dorling (2011)

is, irrespective of how large that group is. Were Tory voters spread in the same way as the rest of the voters, so as to be found in equal proportion in every area of the country, the index would be 0 per cent. Were they all to be found in areas exclusively occupied by them (that is, other areas occupied exclusively by other groups), then the index would be 100 per cent. The index is the proportion that would have to move to other areas to spread the Tory voters around in the same way as the other voters. The areas used here are Westminster parliamentary constituencies, the smallest areas for which votes are revealed.

Figure 15.4 shows the minimum number of Tory voters who have to be moved between parliamentary constituencies for an equal number to be allocated to every area. It is a segregation index. Tory segregation was at an all-time high in the strange 'Khaki Election' of 1918.[1] That segregation rate then fell, stumbling upwards only slightly in 1935 before falling again, right through to 1959. Where one lived in Britain mattered less and less for how one voted, but then something changed.

In 1963 Bob Dylan's worldwide hit 'Blowin' in the Wind' was released, and became one of the theme tunes of the American Civil Rights Movement. However, and in hindsight, things were blowing in another direction than that which Dylan imagined, in both the US

Figure 15.4: The segregation of political belief by area in Britain 1981-2010

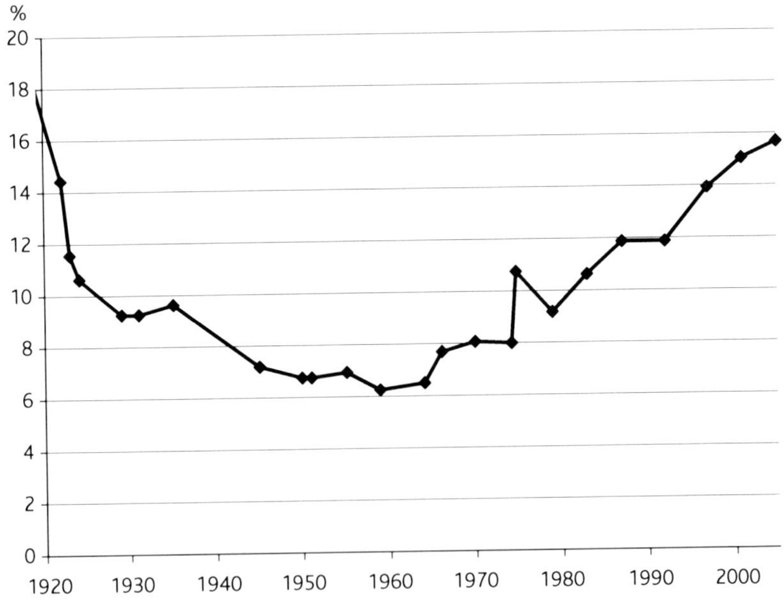

Source: Dorling, D. (2006)

and the UK. In 1964 there was a tiny rise in Tory voting segregation. It jumped up two years later in 1966, jumped again in October 1974, fell back with Margaret Thatcher's landslide in 1979, but then rose and rose and rose. South East England became progressively more and more Conservative as the rest of Britain went the other way. That political polarisation began before the other forms of polarisation we can measure by diverging health outcomes or rising economic inequalities. And it is hard not to think it is important that these events occurred in this order.

Class segregation can rise as other forms of segregation fall. Civil rights were won in Britain as well as in the US from the mid-1960s onwards. Partly to try to mitigate some of the shame of imposing greater immigration controls Race Relations Acts of Parliament were passed to try and ensure greater fair play. More importantly, societal attitudes changed from extreme racism being very normal in the 1970s to it being a social gaff to be obviously racist by the 2000s.

Table 15.1, below, illustrates how *class* is many times more important than *race* in influencing one set of life chances, the chance of any individual child entering medical school. Someone from Social Class I (professional) parents is $6.76/0.28 = 24$ times more likely to go to medical school than someone whose parents are unskilled. Someone who is Black and of Social Class I has $6.20/4.93 = 25.8$ per cent higher chance than someone who is White. There are, of course, far fewer Social Class I Black children. Class differences are almost 100 times higher than race differences, as 24 times is 2,500 per cent.

The class segregation involved in access to higher education is huge, with these multiples of thousands of percentages at the extremes. In contrast, the geographical inequalities can appear much less, as shown in Figure 15.5 below. However, this figure includes everyone going to university, not just those going to medical school, and it also includes everyone from every class, not just the two extremes. The metropolitan North, the Black Country (an area of the English West Midlands north and west of Birmingham and south and east of Wolverhampton), the East End of London (within area 38 shown in the figure) and the Norfolk coast fair worse, while the golden bowl of the North Western Home Countries (including Buckinghamshire, Hertfordshire, Berkshire and Surrey), coupled with parts of Cheshire and North Yorkshire, fare best. Underlying the map in Figure 15.5 are class differences in educational chances, but also other effects, such as a low number of immigrants harming overall chances for particular areas. Immigrants tend to have more 'get up and go', and so areas such as London do better despite more poverty at its heart.

Table 15.1: An example of segregation by race and class in Britain: medical school admissions

Standardised admission ratios for UK medical schools 2000

Ethnic group	% of UK population	% of all school admissions	Selection ratio*	% of admissions from social classes I and II	Standardised admission ratio by social class+						
					Overall	I	II	III non-manual	III manual	IV	V
Asian	4.2	25.5	0.55	60.5	6.07	41.73	5.41	3.83	3.29	3.56	5.15
Bangladeshi	0.5	0.9	0.40	48.0	1.80	9.82	1.27	1.89	NC	1.93	6.00
Indian	1.7	13.8	0.63	74.0	8.12	72.32	7.96	3.17	4.68	2.78	0.18
Pakistani	1.3	4.5	0.62	39.0	3.46	NC	5.29	3.71	2.71	2.25	3.08
Chinese	0.3	2.0	0.45	68.0	6.67	54.55	6.01	NC	9.02	2.86	NC
Other	0.4	4.3	0.51	73.6	10.75	127.05	3.63	6.96	NC	4.76	NC
Black	2.0	1.9	0.36	82.8	0.95	6.20	1.75	0.16	0.64	0.07	NC
African	0.9	1.4	0.34	70.0	1.56	12.25	1.63	0.24	1.83	0.37	NC
Caribbean	1.0	0.3	0.44	78.3	0.30	0.78	0.75	0.10	0.25	NC	NC
Other	0.1	0.2	0.39	100.0	2.00	18.18	3.92	NC	NC	NC	NC
White	92.2	67.6	0.52	79.5	0.73	4.93	1.22	0.27	0.32	0.13	0.05
Other	0.6	3.0	0.6	72.6	5.00	53.64	2.67	2.38	4.71	1.21	NC
Not known	0.2	2.0	0.40	NA	10.00	9.82	1.27	1.89	NC	1.93	6.00
Total	100.0	100.0	0.63	72.5	1.00	6.76	1.38	0.41	0.42	0.28	0.20

*Selection ratio = admissions as a proportion of applications.
+Some ratios are high as the ratios are based on very small denominators.
NA = Data not available. NC = Not calculable because there were no pupils in this subgroup.

Source: Dorling (2011, p 124)

Figure 15.5 contains both a normal map showing the rate at which people aged 18 and 19 go to university from each county in England, and a population cartogram, inset, of the same areas showing the same rates, but with the circles drawn in proportion to population, not land area. A relatively small area in population terms, such as North Yorkshire (area number 6) is over-emphasised on the normal map.

The large majority of those going to university from each area shown in Figure 15.5 are middle class before they go. Almost all are middle class once they have gone, although many continue to identify with working-class origins long after having passed through the middle class-making machine – that is the modern university.

Figure 15.5: The English geography of class segregation in education, 2005

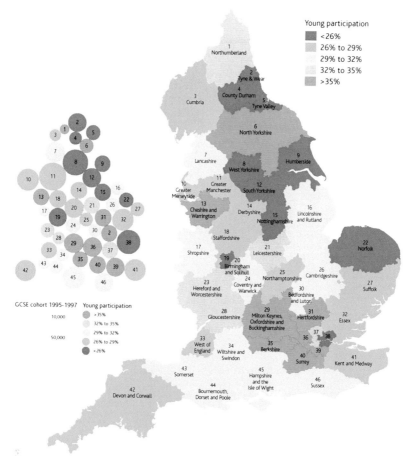

Source: Dorling (2011, p 143)

Before taking too seriously the idea that universities provide social class changing opportunities, it is worth noting that, on average, from the poorest 20 per cent of wards in the country, only 4 children out of a class of 30 used to go to university. The New Labour government did improve that statistic, by a (deceptively) massive 25 per cent. That rise appears high in per cent terms but is small in absolute effect, because it amounted to only 1 extra child in each class of 30 children from poorer areas going to university by the time Labour left power. They invested a huge amount of money across the country's schools, some of which did improve the services provided to children in those schools in the worse-off areas. They started an Educational Maintenance Allowance scheme, much more of which found its way to those areas, and helped young people stay on at school at ages 16 and 17. Most importantly they encouraged universities to become less discriminating to working-class children.

As a result, by 2010, instead of 4 out of 30 children from the poorest fifth of areas going to university, 5 out of 30 went. Although a 25 per cent increase on a low number is not necessarily a huge influx, New Labour claim this as one of their greatest achievements (Dorling, 2011, p 147). It certainly angered some people on the political right who thought that too many of these children were being allowed into universities. The right-wing press was often claimed that 'dumbing down' was occurring. Only in a country as socially divided as the UK could the provision of an additional university place for the 5th most able child in a class of 30 children be seen as dumbing down. But before becoming too caught up in these slight changes in slight chances, it is worth sitting back and considering how the UK compares to other countries when it comes to income inequality, social mobility and educational mobility.

Figure 15.6 provides a summary that essentially implies that the UK has a very rigid class structure, high income inequality and little mobility between income groups, but that all this is not the fault of its education systems (the education system actually provides more mobility than that in Norway or Germany). It is just that children in Britain start off far more unequal in the first place, and the education system can, in general, only do a little to alleviate that. The axis labelled 'income immobility' in the figure is a measure of social mobility that compares how easy it is to predict the income of an adult from that of their parents when their parents were the same age. Brazil has the lowest social mobility and Denmark the highest.

The rigidity of the UK class system is thus comparable to the rigidity of society in the US. Social mobility is even lower and income

Figure 15.6: Social mobility, income inequality and education mobility, selected countries, 2008-9

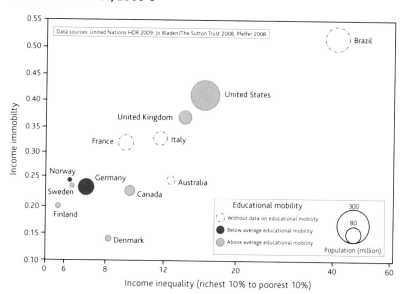

Source: Dorling (2011, p 158)

inequality even higher in the US than in the UK. Because in the dim and distant past (about 150 years ago and more) these inequalities were much lower in the US for people who were not slaves or their children a myth of opportunity emerged in the US which has remained. This was also substantiated by the US being an actual destination of great upwards mobility for people emigrating from Europe at the time, and for a few decades later. The US high school system, a largely comprehensive and nationalised state education system, also helps maintain a sense of some fairness in a land of very low opportunities. However, what Figure 15.6 also shows is that in comparison to the only non-rich world country shown, opportunities for more equality in income and social mobility are far higher in the US than in Brazil.

Worldwide income inequalities have been growing, creating a new kind of global class divide. This is illustrated in Figure 15.7 which shows how, compared to world average household income, incomes in first Europe and then North America and then Japan pulled away and upwards, leaving the Near East, South America and Eastern Europe behind the average. In recent decades the Far East and China have seen average incomes rise to join this average group, leaving Northern and South-eastern Africa behind, areas joined by a rising but previously more impoverished India (made relatively much poorer from 1800 onwards with colonialism and continuing to rise). Central Africa continues to plummet in relation to the world average, incomes falling to a tenth of that average by the turn of the millennium, in contrast to nearer 10 times the average in the most affluent places.

One trend worth pointing out in Figure 15.7 is the lost decade for the Japanese at the very end of the period (the big dip in the line for Japan). This has now become two lost decades, and it looks as if North America and Europe may also be about to lose decades. In terms of worldwide class/income divides this is a reduction in global inequality. The extent to which the world is currently unequal in terms of income distribution is illustrated in Figures 15.8a and 15.8b below.

These global inequalities are now having a great effect on class segregation within Britain. As the income gap between continents and regions has grown over time, for instance, between Greater India (India defined according to its 1900 old borders) and Western Europe, people migrating into Western Europe from many parts of the Indian subcontinent would, on average, find themselves entering British society at a lower and lower initial entry point. In contrast, as North America rose from being well below the global average income-earning economy in 1600, surpassing Western Europe in the 1850s, immigrants to Britain from the US from then on would tend to enter far higher up in the British class hierarchy. The greatest concentration

Figure 15.7: Rising and then falling income inequalities, all countries, 1200-2000

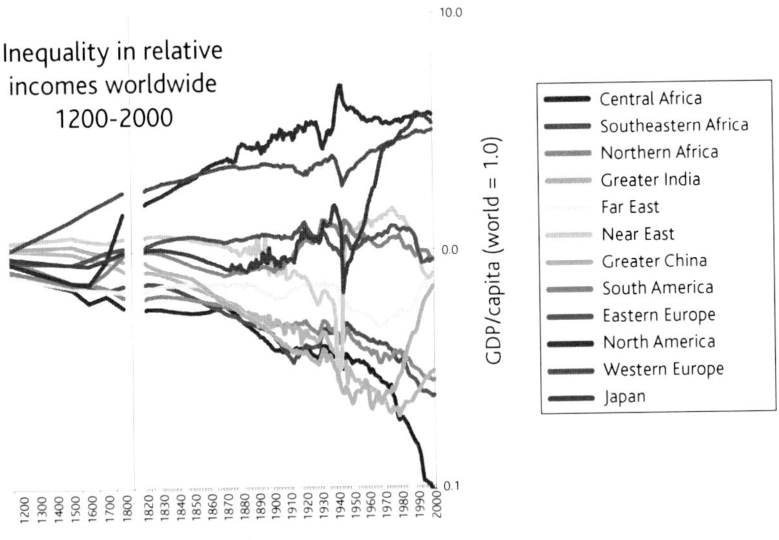

Source: Dorling (2011, p 323)

of American-born children in Britain is now found around Hyde Park and Mayfair in London. Figures 15.8a and 15.8b illustrate why the relationships between particular groups of people entering Britain from particular countries tend to be as they are.

There is great inequality within many countries, and so just because someone arrives from one particular country, this does not directly imply that they are either rich or poor, but in aggregate, different immigrant groups tend to be slotted into the class structure at particular points because of these (until recently) growing global divides. The two figures that make up Figure 15.8 (a and b) are both population cartograms. Each country is drawn with its area made to be proportional to the values being mapped.

The world is hugely unequal, and that inequality has been growing for centuries. As a result, just three areas dominate the cartogram of global GDP: North America, Western Europe and Japan/China. These countries form the three circles of wealth in Figure 15.8a above. The particular kind of class segregation found within Britain today is as a result of its position on the edge of one of those circles. Poorer countries tend to have far greater inequalities.

Figure 15.8b shows the world shaped by poverty, in this case poverty as revealed through the numbers of people who are undernourished. Inequalities in most of the countries drawn large here tend to be far greater than those found within the richer countries. Income inequalities between people are found to be lowest in Cuba and China (note that the data were for 2002) and highest in South Africa and Brazil. The most unequal of the rich countries can also be seen in the map of undernourishment as millions are still going hungry in the US. Compare Eastern Europe to the UK to see one reason why there has been migration into the lower parts of the British class hierarchy from Eastern Europe in recent years. And look at how Eastern Europe has fared economically since 1989 (see Figure 15.7).

It takes a greatly divided world for immigration status to become so linked to class at the top and bottom of the class scale, but it also takes the country into which immigrants are entering to be highly divided for there to be extra places at the bottom and top of that scale to be populated. Figure 15.9 shows how the proportion of all income received by the best-off 1 per cent in Britain fell from 1918 through to 1979 and then rose relentlessly. The best-off 1% took a greater and greater share of national income almost every year from 1979 through to 2014 by which time their share had both risen to 15% and was rising faster than in any earlier year according to HMR estimates. After paying tax, about a third of their income, their share of total national

Figure 15.8a: Inequality in wealth, international, GDP, 2002

Source: Dorling (2011, p 135)

Figure 15.8b: Inequality in food international, undernourishment, 2002

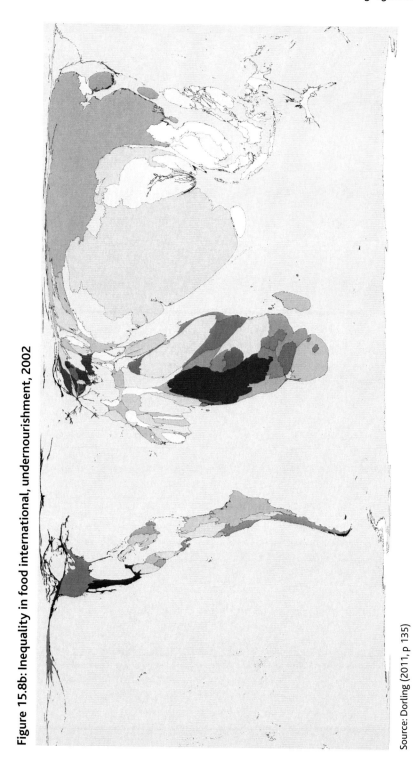

Source: Dorling (2011, p 135)

Figure 15.9: Inequality in income in Britain, top 1%, 1918-2011

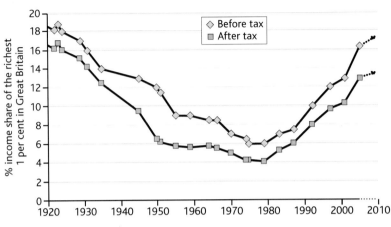

Source: Dorling (2011, p 70)

income rose from 8.2% in 2012-13 to 9.8% in 2013-14 (Wintour 2014). Note that Figure 15.9 is based on a different data series which considers inequalities between households which are greater still. It fell like this in most countries, but then only rose as high again in a few countries, particularly in the UK and US. In the UK it is currently rising rapidly back to its 1918 peak as average incomes are falling in relation to inflation and incomes at the top are continuing to climb rapidly. Taxation now mutes the inequalities a little, but it in the past it was used to mute them far more. Today the highest earning 1% of individuals pay about a third of all their income in tax reducing their tax-home share from around 15% to just under 10%. Income tax rates were much higher for most of the period when income inequalities were falling. High taxation of very high incomes helped deter greed.

Guardian journalist and former newspaper editor Peter Wilby asked the obvious question about all this in May 2011:

> Why aren't we more angry? Why isn't blood running, metaphorically at least, in the streets? Evidence of how the rich prosper while everyone else struggles with inflation, public spending cuts and static wages arrives almost daily. The Institute for Fiscal Studies reports that last year incomes among the top 1% grew at the fastest rate in a decade. According to the Sunday Times Rich List, the top 1,000 are £60.2bn better off this year than in 2010, bringing their collective wealth close to the record pre-recession levels. (Wilby, 2011)

He concluded:

> This generation of the middle classes has internalised the values of individualist aspiration, as zealously propagated by Tony Blair as by Margaret Thatcher. It does not look to the application of social justice to improve its lot. It expects to rely on its own efforts to get ahead and, crucially, to maintain its position. As psychologists will tell you, fear of loss is more powerful than the prospect of gain. The struggling middle classes look down more anxiously than they look up, particularly in recession and sluggish recovery. Polls show they dislike high income inequalities but are lukewarm about redistribution. They worry that they are unlikely to benefit and may even lose from it; and worse still, those below them will be pulled up sufficiently to threaten their status. This is exactly the mindset in the US, where individualist values are more deeply embedded. Americans accepted tax cuts for the rich with equanimity. Better to let the rich keep their money, they calculated, than to have it benefit economic and social inferiors.

In other affluent countries people think in different ways to the British who have become habituated to high levels of inequality over a long time. If you were born after 1989 then you have known nothing else. Figure 15.10 shows how abruptly inequalities rose in Britain during the 1980s.

Figure 15.10: Inequality in income in Britain, GINI, 1961-2008

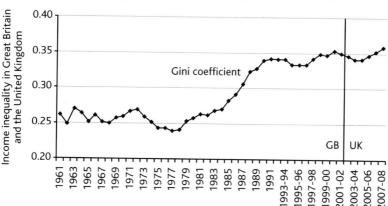

Source: Dorling (2011, p 69)

High income inequality means high and rising inequalities in wealth and growing poverty, but poverty for other people if you do not live in poor areas. As the rich become more and more segregated from the poor in Britain rising poverty affects their daily lives less and less. This is easily illustrated if the fortunes of people living in the seats of 1997 Labour Cabinet ministers are compared to the fortunes of those living in the seats of the then Conservative Shadow Cabinet. Labour was traditionally the political party of the poor in Britain and the Conservatives were the party of the rich. For every 100 people who were poor in 1991 in those Conservative strong holds, 197 were poor in traditional Labour areas. That rose to 201 by 2001.

Much more dramatic was the move away of wealth from Labour areas between 1991 and 2001. For every 100 people who were wealthy in Conservative areas in 1991, 29 were wealthy in Labour areas. That fell to 22 by 2001. All this is shown in Table 15.2, as are the numbers of intermediate areas. Labour came to power in the face of high and rising inequalities, including those measured by income and wealth, and hence, growing class segregation. Initially it muted slightly the previous Conservative administration's celebration of inequality, partly because its ministers were still finding their feet and sorting out trouble-makers from among the back benches. Labour policies on education did reduce gaps a little, but in general they allowed division to continue to grow, and the spatial outcomes reflect that (see Figure 15.11).

As areas become more segregated between rich and poor, as people with better health in poorer areas leave, as those whose lives suddenly take a turn for the worse in more affluent areas also have to leave because the living has become so expensive, class and place begin to conflate. Income, wealth and location all tend to convey the same meanings. You can begin to tell more and more about who someone is, and how much money they had to get there, from their postcode.

Sorting postcodes by poverty rate, or in the case of Table 15.3 below, wards by poverty rate, can be used to reveal all kinds of macro-trends, even among the rarest of outcomes. In this case the growing national murder rate is shown to have become more and more concentrated within the poorest areas of Britain over time. Growing class segregation means a return to Victorian inequalities where murder is relatively common in what were called slum areas, but hardly known among the gentry. Although most things in life in Britain are far better than they were in Victorian times, murder rates have returned to what they were then. This is despite it being illegal to carry weapons now. Firearms could be legally carried then!

Table 15.2: Class residential segregation in Britain, 1997-2005 (%)

Constituencies grouped by the political post held by the MP elected for each seat immediately after the 1997 General Election	Cabinet Minister	Government Minister (non-Cabinet)	Government Backbench	Non-Tory Opposition (Lib Dem/PC/SNP)	Conservative Backbench	Conservative Shadow Cabinet
Breadline poor latest estimates (at time of publication this was 2001)	201	178	133	127	103	100
Breadline poor 1991 estimates	197	173	127	125	101	100
Asset wealthy latest estimates (at time of publication this was 2001)	22	26	61	84	107	100
Asset wealthy 1991 estimates	29	39	76	94	119	100

Source: Dorling (2011, p 20)

Figure 15.11: Inequality in health in Britain, mortality, 1999-2008

Difference between best and worst districts by life expectancy (years):

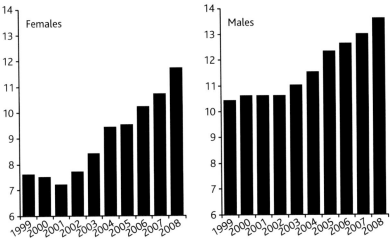

Source: Dorling (2011, p 71)

Table 15.3: Inequality in crime in Britain, murder ratios, 1981-2000

Standardised morality ratios (SMRs) for murder in Britain, by ward poverty, 1981-2000

Area	1981-85	1986-90	1991-95	1996-2000	% change
Least poor	54	59	55	50	−4
Decile 9	67	65	67	60	−7
Decile 8	62	69	68	66	4
Decile 7	74	85	72	81	7
Decile 6	79	77	83	88	9
Decile 5	95	95	95	103	8
Decile 4	112	122	125	130	18
Decile 3	119	130	148	147	28
Decile 2	151	166	191	185	34
Poorest	243	261	271	282	39
Extreme ratio	4.50	4.42	4.89	5.68	

Note: expected values are based on 1981-85 national rates (100 is the national average)

Source: Dorling (2011, p 20)

Many murders are conducted in the heat of the moment with very little premeditation, but allowing class divides to continue to grow and for people to become more and more segregated as a result will increase rates of violence overall (Dorling et al, 2008). Some might think that

that violence increases mainly in places some distance from them, but generally, more unequal societies become nastier and more brutal places to live and compete in no matter where any one individual lives.

Almost all affluent societies in the word are less class-ridden than Britain. The segregation of people by social class in Britain is so acute that we tend to think of it as normal. Just as a White American in 1950s Mississippi might have thought it normal to eat in a Whites-only café and to sit at the front of the bus and never socialise with Black Americans so, in class-segregated Britain, we are increasingly tending to 'stick to our own'. We have schools for our social class, universities for our social class (or no university), jobs for our social class, housing estates, holidays, clothes, hobbies, even jokes for one social class and not another. And all this is becoming more and more established, but it is also becoming more noticed and resented by many.

In Japan, over the course of the last 20 years, housing and land prices have been falling every year (Allen, 2011; Nakaya, 2011). Close to the heart of the British class system is land and the wealth stored in housing. At one point recently, half of all personal wealth in Britain was held in the form of housing equity, but only by the minority who own property or the shrinking group who were purchasing it. That proportion has now fallen as, outside of London and the South East, housing and land values have been falling. When the property bubble finally bursts it tends, as the Japanese experiences have shown, to carry on deflating year after year. If we come together in future in Britain, it is more likely to be with a long, slow, hissing sound, as the land and housing markets gradually lose momentum, rather than with a bang. It is possible to imagine one can hear that noise beginning today, but to be sure that class segregation is reducing, wait until there is any evident sign of the value of property in London falling, and those falls being sustained; at present there is precious little sign of that.

Notes

[1] The 1918 general election was known the khaki elections, due to the importance of demobilised soldiers, often still in uniform. A very large number of Liberal and Tory MPs stood on the same 'ticket'. They were literally issued a coupon by Lloyd George and the Conservative leader Bonar Law as candidates who had agreed to support the pair and hence Conservative voting may have appeared more segregated than it was as Conservatives could choose to vote for a coupon Liberal in many areas rather than a Conservative without a ticket or one unlikely to win locally. Almost a hundred years later the Conservative and Liberal party are again in coalition.

References

Allen, K. (2011) 'Will UK property prices weather a new recession?', *The Guardian*. London, 9 October.

Della Dora, V. (2011) *Imagining Mount Athos*, Virginia: University of Virginia Press.

Dorling, D. (2006) 'Class alignment renewal', *The Journal of Labour Politics*, vol 14, no 1, pp 8-19 (www.dannydorling.org/?page_id=1240).

Dorling, D. (2008) 'Prime suspect: murder in Britain', in D. Dorling, D. Gordon, P. Hillyard, C., Pantazis, S., Pemberton and S. Tombs (eds) *Criminal obsessions: Why harm matters more than crime*, 2nd edn, London: Centre for Crime and Justice Studies.

Dorling, D. (2011) *Fair play: a Daniel Dorling reader on social justice*, Bristol: Policy Press.

Dorling, D. (2012) *The no-nonsense guide to equality*, Oxford: New Internationalist.

Fuller, A., V. Beck, et al. (2005) *Employers, young people and gender segregation*. EOC Working Paper Series (number 28). London, Equal Opportunities Commission.

Nakaya, T. (2011) Personal communication. And see: http://tochi.mlit.go.jp/english/land/01-02_21k.pdf. See page 25 headed by 'Nationwide accumulated land price changes'.

Ramesh, R. (2011) 'Private schools fuel division in society, politics and pay, says study', *The Guardian*. London, 7 December.

Russell, J. (2008). 'Inequality is closing down our concern for others: As the middle classes feel the pain of comparison with the super-rich, we lose all enthusiasm for the common good', *The Guardian*. London, 18 January.

Wilby, P. (2011). 'Anxiety keeps the super-rich safe from middle-class rage', *Guardian*, London, 18 May.

Wilson, D. and Keil, R. (2008) 'The real creative class', *Social and Cultural Geography*, vol 9, no 8, pp 841-47.

Wintour, P. (2014) 'Labour reveals tax data showing UK economic growth "only helps top 1%"', the *Guardian*, 13 May (http://www.theguardian.com/politics/2014/may/13/labour-tax-data-shows-growth-helps-top-1-percent).

SIXTEEN

Exploring socioeconomic characteristics of ethnically divided neighbourhoods

Kenneth N. French

Introduction

Large US cities are generally ethnically diverse and may have high levels of ethnic residential segregation (see Chapter Six, this volume, for context). What are the socioeconomic impacts for those living in these ethnically segregated neighbourhoods? Do separate living spaces equate to equal living spaces for all ethnic groups in a city? The goal of this chapter is to investigate the consequences of living in segregated neighbourhoods in Milwaukee, Wisconsin, the second most segregated American city in 2000 (Glaeser et al, 2001, 8). The research will identify where ethnic groups live and analyse the social effects of these spatial distributions. In terms of social impacts, various socioeconomic variables (for example, income levels and public school reading scores) are analysed and compared to the ethnic residential patterns. Socioeconomic variables are statistically summarised for the most segregated African American, Hispanic and White neighbourhoods. The results of the chapter may help to determine if there is a connection between social inequality and spatial inequality in an American urban landscape.

Impacts of ethnic residential segregation

As Peach (1996) noted, there is 'good' and 'bad' segregation, where people may live in segregated areas that have formed for either positive or negative reasons. Ethnic residential segregation can be seen as 'a process that victimizes some groups while liberating others' (Kaplan and Woodhouse, 2004, p 583). Ethnic group members may feel 'liberated' by living and working in an ethnic neighbourhood where they do not face constant discrimination. Historically, many immigrants who came to America clustered into ethnic enclaves. This 'good' segregation of ethnic enclaves provided new arrivals, with 'social support and a semblance of the old world now lost to them' (Mayadas and Segal, 2000, p 208). The ethnically segregated generate social contacts, preserve ethnic culture, offer support to group members and create ethnic businesses (van Kempen and Özüekren, 1998). Ethnically segregated neighbourhoods may have provided economic opportunities in the development and growth of ethnic businesses. For example, if ordinary restaurants do not provide certain ethnic dishes, then there would be the possibility of the establishment of an ethnic restaurant to satisfy an unmet demand. This restaurant might then serve both the local ethnic community and people in the wider metro area. Overall, there have been few studies on the positive consequences of ethnic residential segregation (Varady, 2005; Yuan, 2008).

In general, 'bad' segregation was associated with a place that had poorer quality of life outcomes (for example, poor education, high poverty, high infant mortality rates and high unemployment rates). These ethnically segregated neighbourhoods were associated with high crime rates, poor health (Ellen, 2000; Kawachi and Berkman, 2003) and areas of social vices, and were places that housed the most downtrodden in American society. Segregated areas may be subject to a 'spatial mismatch' (Kain, 1968), in which job opportunities are not highly accessible. In another study, Mouw (2002) found that residential and network segregation in African Americans led to employment segregation between African Americans and Whites. This lack of access to jobs (and good quality jobs in particular) is likely a reason for the differences in socioeconomic status among ethnic groups (de Souza Briggs, 2005, p 34). While previous research has indicated both advantages and disadvantages of living in segregated neighbourhoods, refined estimates of the actual impacts (for example, disparities in income, educational attainment levels) have usually been missing from the literature. This chapter tries to fill some of the remaining gaps by studying the consequences of ethnic residential segregation (for example, by matching ethnic distributions with locations of educational attainment and poverty). By investigating the influences of segregation, researchers can better understand whether living in an ethnic neighbourhood has a positive or negative impact on its residents.

Quality of life

At the abstract level, segregation affects the quality of life of residents in the neighbourhoods (see Chapter Thirteen, this volume). However, the term 'quality of life' does not have a universally accepted definition, and thus has a diversity of meanings (Dissart and Deller, 2000; Randall and Morton, 2003). Depending on how researchers define and operationalise 'quality of life', the results from analyses can vary from one study to the next. Hirschman (1989) stated that opinions regarding the issue of quality of life are subjective. Adding a geographic dimension of scale can also affect the results of quality of life studies, as there may be differences in measurements of the quality of life for individuals, neighbourhoods, cities, states and nations. Given the various definitions and contexts of 'quality of life', education and income are often related to the concept.

Haring et al (1984) considered the question of whether educational attainment had an influence on subjective wellbeing, and were able to determine that educational attainment is positively linked to subjective wellbeing. They also found that a person's subjective wellbeing is more influenced by their occupational status than by income. Reynolds and Ross (1998) found that people with higher levels of education not only experience better physical and mental health, but also have lower levels of morbidity, disability and mortality. Education improves wellbeing by providing better access to full-time work and fulfilling employment, which leads to better psychological and physical health, and to less economic hardship. In a random sample postal survey of 2,000 residents in West Virginia, Bukenya et al (2003) found that quality of life satisfaction increased with higher income and education status. Friedman and Rosenbaum (2001) found that people with a higher education or income can choose to locate themselves in places that reflect their position in society, usually in the suburbs. Poor people with little education are 'forced' to live in locations that are less than ideal, which leads to the key question in this research: does educational attainment relate to the ethnic make-up of residential neighbourhoods in Milwaukee?

Research regarding the effects of income on a person's quality of life has provided mixed results. Bukenya et al (2003) found that the quality of life of West Virginians increased with income and decreased with higher unemployment. In a cross-national study, Easterly (1999) compared per capita income and quality of life between many nations. The data on income levels were for 1960, 1970, 1980 and 1990, with 81 indicators on the quality of life, categorised in seven areas: individual rights, war, education, health, transport, class and gender, and 'bads' (for example, pollution, suicide rates and crime rates). The results of the analysis indicated that 61 of the 81 quality of life indicators have significantly positive relations with income, while only 12 of the 81 indicators are negatively related to income. In general, these findings related to economic theory, which 'suggest[s] that individuals with higher incomes are more likely to be satisfied with life and have better health' (Bukenya et al, 2003, p 289).

Socioeconomic characteristics, such as educational attainment and income levels, can be operationalised as indicators of quality of life. This chapter explores how ethnic residential segregation varies according to education and income in Milwaukee. Are certain ethnic group members 'better off' in terms of per capita income than other ethnic group members? Do these patterns vary by residential location? Does this indicate 'good' or 'bad' segregation? These questions can be answered by analysing the consequences of living in segregation in Milwaukee.

Analysing the impacts of living in segregation

The first part of this section describes the study area and measurement of current segregation patterns in Milwaukee. The second part cartographically analyses the geographic distribution of economic and educational factors in Milwaukee. The third part investigates correlations between ethnic patterns and socioeconomic characteristics. Using previous research as a guide, the fourth part undertakes comparisons of socioeconomic characteristics between ethnically concentrated neighbourhoods. The fifth part cartographically analyses school quality. The sixth part deals with ethnic businesses and their locations. The last part of the research investigates the cultural landscape of the ethnically concentrated areas. The overall objective of this chapter is to assess the impacts, as measured by socioeconomic indicators and as reflected by social institutions, of living in ethnically divided neighbourhoods in the city of Milwaukee.

Study area

According to the 2000 US Census, the population of Milwaukee (Milwaukee and Waukesha counties) was about 1.3 million. The US Census-defined racial and ethnic categories analysed in this chapter were: non-Hispanic White, non-Hispanic African American and Hispanic. The 'non-Hispanic' terminology of each category was dropped for semantic reasons, so that 'White' in this chapter actually represents 'non-Hispanic White'. The ethnic make-up of Milwaukee predominately consists of African Americans (17.9 per cent), Hispanics (7.1 per cent) and White (70.9 per cent). Most African Americans in Milwaukee reside in neighbourhoods northwest of the downtown area (see Figure 16.1); Hispanic residential concentrations are located southwest of downtown (see Figure 16.2); and Whites (see Figure 16.3) mostly live along the scenic north shore of Lake Michigan and western suburbs of Waukesha County.

The Civil Rights history of Milwaukee in the 1960s, consisting of a contested open housing campaign to desegregate the White suburbs, indicates tense relations between ethnic groups (Gurda, 1999; Jones, 2010). Currently, Milwaukee has some of the highest ethnic residential segregation levels in the US. The index of dissimilarity (*D*) at the census tract level between Whites and African Americans is 81.9, between Whites and Hispanics it is 59.2 and between African Americans and Hispanics it is 78.9. The cartographic and statistical analyses reveal Milwaukee to be highly ethnically segregated, which may have an impact on the socioeconomic characteristics of ethnic group members living in segregated areas.

Socioeconomic consequences

Mapping the spatial distributions of selected socioeconomic variables can reveal areas of advantage or disadvantage for Milwaukee in 2000. The maps of various economic and education variables indicate the extent of spatial disparities in the city. These distributions can then be spatially associated with ethnic residential distributions to see whether certain ethnic groups have higher or lower qualities of life.

A map of median household income (see Figure 16.4) reveals that the western suburbs of Milwaukee were wealthier than neighbourhoods near downtown. The exceptions were the rich neighbourhoods along the north shore of Lake Michigan. Conversely, the poorer neighbourhoods with the lowest median household incomes were located in the eastern sections of the city. None of the neighbourhoods with a median household income below US$25,000 were located in the western suburbs of Waukesha County.

In terms of educational attainment levels, the majority of the Bachelor's degree-educated people in Milwaukee lived in the western suburbs and north shore neighbourhoods (see Figure 16.5). Conversely, the neighbourhoods with the lowest proportions of people having a Bachelor's degree (under 10.0 per cent) were located in the

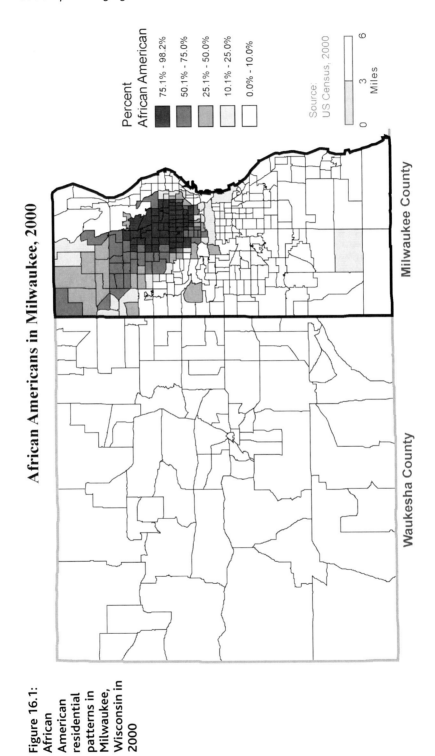

Figure 16.1:
African
American
residential
patterns in
Milwaukee,
Wisconsin in
2000

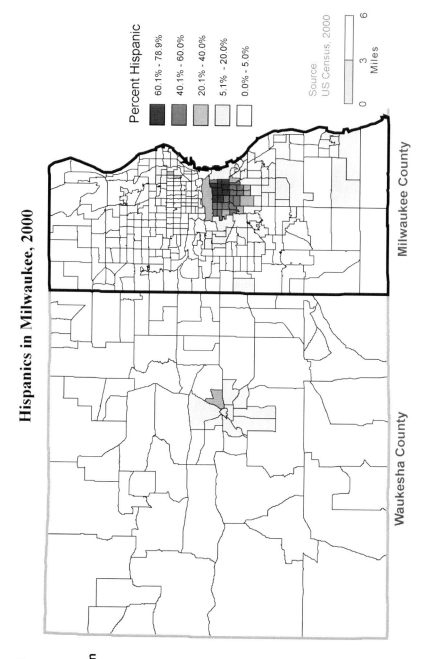

Figure 16.2:
Hispanic
residential
patterns in
Milwaukee,
Wisconsin in
2000

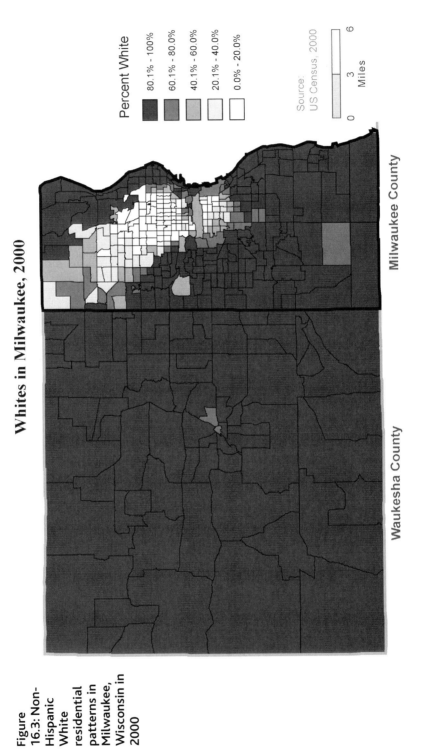

Figure
16.3: Non-
Hispanic
White
residential
patterns in
Milwaukee,
Wisconsin in
2000

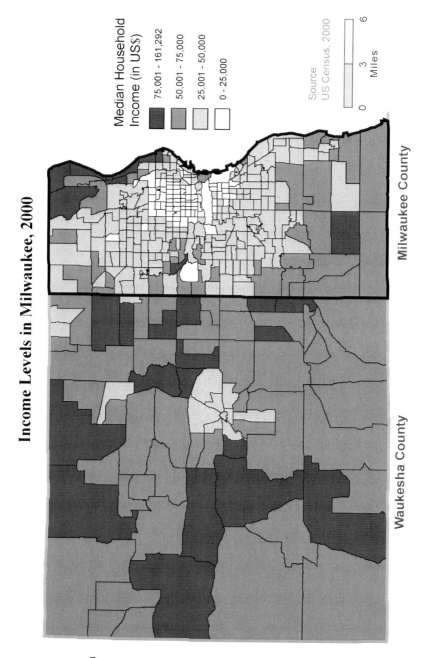

Figure 16.4: Median household income in Milwaukee, Wisconsin in 2000

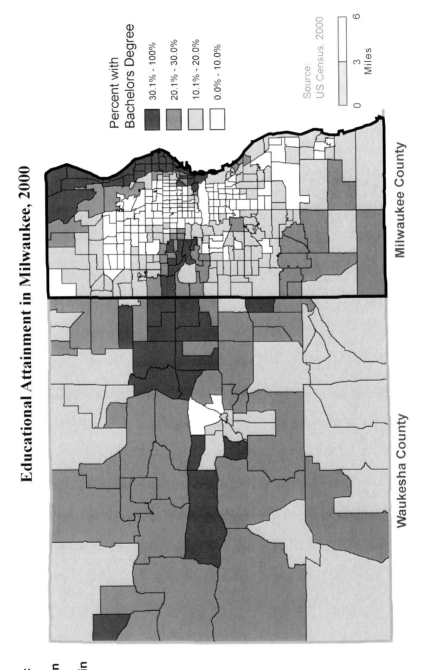

Figure 16.5:
Bachelor's
education in
Milwaukee,
Wisconsin in
2000

inner-city sections of Milwaukee. The highest proportions of people over 25 with less than a ninth grade education were located in the neighbourhoods southwest of downtown Milwaukee. A possible reason for the low educational attainment in these tracts was that they contain immigrants who entered the US as young adults and who did not have the same educational chances as those born in the US. The neighbourhoods with the highest proportions of people with only a high school degree, or high school equivalency, were found mainly northwest and southwest of the downtown area. Other areas that also had a higher proportion of only high school-educated people were located in the rural parts of Waukesha County in the west. These likely were neighbourhoods of the rural working class, as many people with only a high school education do not work in the white-collar jobs that tend to pay more. Some neighbourhoods with the lowest proportions of only high school-educated people were found in the western rural-suburban fringes of Milwaukee.

Overall, there were differences in the spatial distributions of socioeconomic variables in Milwaukee. The neighbourhoods with the lowest income were generally located in the inner-city neighbourhoods of Milwaukee. The areas with the higher proportions of high educational attainment were mainly located in the western suburbs of Milwaukee. Mapping socioeconomic variables in Milwaukee revealed spatial inequalities with differences in the locational patterns of education and income. In fact, there appears to be a strong spatial association between ethnic distributions and several socioeconomic variables in Milwaukee.

Ethnic and socioeconomic comparisons in Milwaukee

Statistical analyses were performed to explore the strength of correlations (Pearson's *r*)[1] between ethnic group percentages and socioeconomic variables. Ethnic percentages, in which higher percentages were used as a proxy for segregation, were correlated with several educational attainment levels (see Table 16.1). There was a strong positive relationship (0.673) between percentage White and percentage with a Bachelor's degree. A strong inverse relationship (−0.540) was evident between the percentage African American and percentage with a Bachelor's degree. As the percentages of African Americans increased in the neighbourhoods, there was a decrease in the percentage with a Bachelor's degree. The relationship between the percentage of Hispanics and the percentage of the population with only a ninth grade education is very strong (0.764). Overall,

Table 16.1: Pearson's correlation coefficients (*r*) between ethnic percentages and educational attainment in Milwaukee

	% with only a ninth grade education	% with only a high school degree	% with a Bachelor's degree
Percentage White	−0.581	−0.117	0.673
Percentage African American	0.250	0.120	−0.540
Percentage Hispanic	0.764	0.031	−0.354

neighbourhoods with a higher percentage of Whites tend to have higher educational attainment. Conversely, the higher African American or Hispanic percentages in an area are strongly related to poorer educational outcomes.

The correlations between ethnic percentages and income levels in Milwaukee were also very strong (see Table 16.2). The strong inverse relationship between percentage White and percentage in poverty was clear (−0.803); as the neighourhoods' White percentage increased, the percentage of people in that neighbourhood living in poverty decreased. The opposite was true for African Americas, as the correlation between percentage African American and percentage in poverty displayed a strong positive relationship (0.709). Neighbourhoods with higher percentages of African Americans had higher poverty levels. The correlation coefficients between percentage Hispanic and various economic variables were weak-to-moderate in strength.

Problems of ecological inference in using neighbourhood-wide data (census tracts) generalised to all people in an area are a concern. If an ethnically mixed neighbourhood has high poverty levels, does this indicate that every ethnic group member has a high poverty rate, or do certain groups have higher levels than others? To make inferences on the socioeconomic levels for ethnic group members, ethnic–specific data (for example, Hispanic per capita income) must be analysed.

There were weak-to-moderate correlations between a neighbourhood's ethnic percentage and ethnic–specific educational

Table 16.2: Pearson's correlation coefficients (*r*) between ethnic percentages and income variables in Milwaukee

	Median household income (US$)	Per capita income (US$)	% in poverty
Percentage White	0.687	0.714	−0.803
Percentage African American	−0.570	−0.582	0.709
Percentage Hispanic	−0.284	−0.334	0.237

attainment characteristics (see Table 16.3). As a neighbourhood's percentage of Whites increased, there was an increase in the percentage of Whites with a Bachelor's degree (0.458). Conversely, a moderate negative relationship (−0.330) was evident between percentage White and percentage of Whites with only a ninth grade education. A weak inverse relationship between percentage African American and percentage of African American with a Bachelor's degree was found (−0.235). This hints that, as the percentage of African Americans in a neighbourhood decreases, the percentage of African Americans in those neighourhoods with a Bachelor's degree increases. The relationship (0.381) between percentage Hispanic and percentage of Hispanics with only a ninth grade education was moderate (0.381). This would indicate poor educational attainment levels for Hispanics living in more segregated Hispanic areas.

In terms of ethnic-specific economic characteristics, there were several moderate correlations with ethnic percentages (see Table 16.4). The correlation between percentage White and White median household income levels were strongly positive (0.596). Living in a highly concentrated White neighbourhood related to Whites having higher income levels and lower poverty levels. For African Americans, there was a moderate-strength inverse relationship between percentage African American and African American median household income (−0.340). The correlation values suggest to a certain degree that

Table 16.3: Pearson's correlation coefficients (*r*) between ethnic percentages and ethnic-specific educational variables in Milwaukee

Hispanic areas	Ethnic % with only a ninth grade education	Ethnic % with only a high school degree	Ethnic % with a Bachelor's degree
Percentage White	−0.330	−0.148	0.458
Percentage African American	0.170	0.091	−0.235
Percentage Hispanic	0.381	−0.051	−0.179

Table 16.4: Pearson's correlation coefficients (*r*) between ethnic percentages and ethnic-specific income variables in Milwaukee

	Ethnic median household income (US$)	Ethnic per capita income (US$)	Ethnic % in poverty
Percentage White	0.596	0.540	−0.513
Percentage African American	−0.340	−0.192	0.306
Percentage Hispanic	−0.228	−0.244	0.218

African Americans living in more segregated African American neighbourhoods have lower income levels and higher poverty. Correlations between percentage Hispanic and Hispanic economic characteristics were weak.

Overall, Whites living in White-concentrated Milwaukee neighbourhoods tend to have better educational attainment and economic levels. African Americans and Hispanics, in general, tend to have lower socioeconomic statuses, especially those living in segregated areas. In fact, African Americans living in neighbourhoods with fewer African Americans had higher median household incomes than African Americans in segregated areas. The correlation coefficients indicate that living in segregated neighbourhoods may benefit some groups over others. A more geographically focused exploration – comparing socioeconomic variables within ethnically concentrated neighbourhoods – would allow this to be interrogated further.

Comparing ethnically concentrated neighbourhoods

What are the impacts for ethnic groups living in residentially segregated neighbourhoods? Contrasting the socioeconomic characteristics of neighbourhoods by ethnic make-up can reveal differing patterns. Before comparing socioeconomic data between ethnic groups, ethnically concentrated neighbourhoods had to be defined. An 'ethnic neighbourhood' was defined by selecting the 15 census tracts that had the highest population proportions for each ethnic group. To guard against rural bias, only census tracts with over a population density of 1,000 people per square mile were selected; the 1995 US Census defines an urbanised area as having at least 1,000 people per square mile. For example, the top 15 census tracts with the highest percentages of African Americans were identified to create 'African American' residential areas. Quotations are used here since not all residents in these neighbourhoods were African American, and the 'African American' neighbourhood could house people of different racial ethnic backgrounds. Nonetheless, the process of selecting the top 15 census tracts was also used to generate 'White' and 'Hispanic' neighbourhoods.

As mentioned earlier, the highest concentration of African American neighbourhoods was northwest of downtown, and the highest concentration of Hispanic neighbourhoods was southwest of the central business district. The White-concentrated neighbourhoods in the city were scattered in the western suburbs and the north shore. After selecting the top 15 census tracts with the highest proportions of each ethnic group, the data for these 15 tracts were averaged to facilitate the comparisons between each ethnically concentrated area. The neighbourhood averages for ethnic-specific characteristics (for example, percentage of African Americans with a Bachelor's degree) were compiled for each ethnic area. The analysis indicates, for example, the average percentage of Hispanics, African Americans and Whites living in poverty within their respective segregated neighbourhoods.

The results of averaging the data for each ethnically concentrated neighbourhood can be divided into educational and economic categories. Educational attainment differs among ethnic groups in the ethnically concentrated neighbourhoods (see Table 16.5). Hispanics in the 'Hispanic' neighbourhoods had the highest proportion of population (42.5 per cent) with less than a ninth grade education. On average, roughly one-third of African Americans in the 'African American' neighbourhood had only a high school degree or high school equivalency, the highest average for any racial ethnic group. On average, 28.9 per cent of Whites achieved a Bachelor's degree, which was 15 times the proportion of Hispanics earning a Bachelor's degree. Overall, there were stark contrasts in educational attainment between each ethnically segregated neighbourhood that can have an impact on the future quality of life of the residents.

In Milwaukee, economic differences between ethnic groups in their respective neighbourhoods in 2000 were immense (see Table 16.6). Comparing the averages of household income revealed that Whites (US$67,158) in the 'White' neighbourhoods have almost more than four times the average income of African Americans (US$18,001) in the 'African American' neighbourhoods. A similar pattern was found in the averages of per capita income, with Whites (US$34,175) having higher per capita incomes than African Americans (US$9,580) and Hispanics (US$7,910) in their respective neighbourhoods. The average poverty levels for each 'ethnic' neighbourhood indicated that the poorest groups were African Americans (43.1 per cent) and Hispanics (35.5 per cent) in their particular neighbourhoods. These numbers

Table 16.5: Averages of educational attainment for each 'ethnic' neighbourhood in Milwaukee in 2000

Ethnic neighbourhood	Ethnic % with only a ninth grade education	Ethnic % with only a high school degree	Ethnic % with a Bachelor's degree
'White'	2.6	22.9	28.9
'African American'	10.8	31.5	2.6
'Hispanic'	42.5	18.6	1.9

Table 16.6: Averages of economic characteristics for each 'ethnic' neighbourhood in Milwaukee in 2000

Ethnic neighbourhood	Ethnic median household income (US$)	Ethnic per capita income (US$)	Ethnic % in poverty
'White'	67,158	34,175	2.2
'African American'	18,001	9,580	43.1
'Hispanic'	25,540	7,910	35.5

were 16 to 19 times greater than the average White percentage living in poverty (2.2 per cent) in the 'White' neighbourhoods. The consequences of living in ethnically concentrated neighbourhoods benefit some ethnic groups, but not others.

The analysis above indicates that African Americans in the 'African American' neighbourhoods have low economic levels (for example, highest poverty level) and less education attainment characteristics. Hispanics living in the 'Hispanic' neighbourhoods had low per capita income levels and the highest proportion with only a ninth grade education. For some African Americans and Hispanics living in segregated neighbourhoods, due to the aforementioned social inequalities, it may be difficult to move up the social ladder.

Whites in the 'White' neighbourhoods have the best quality of life characteristics: highest income levels and very high educational attainment. The segregated White neighbourhoods seemed to provide Whites in these areas with better social amenities. In comparison, minority ethnic groups living in their segregated spaces did not have such favourable socioeconomic characteristics. This analysis did well in summarising socioeconomic differences by segregated areas, yet there may be other variables that also relate to 'good' or 'bad' segregation, but have not been examined.

School quality

One way to decrease the gap in social inequality between minority ethnic groups and Whites would be through education. Better educated students, for all ethnic groups, have more opportunities to increase their socioeconomic status that in turn may relate to achieving higher paying jobs and better quality of life characteristics. The following discusses how public school quality is related to ethnic residential segregation in Milwaukee, Wisconsin.

Data from the Wisconsin Department of Education Report Card for 2000, based on the standardised reading comprehension tests administered to third graders in all 248 public schools in the study area, placed third graders into advanced, proficient, basic and minimal categories. While several variables can affect school quality (for example, school funding and teacher experience), the percentage of students reaching the advanced reading level is used as a proxy for school quality (see Figure 16.6). The public schools with less than 10 per cent of their students achieving the advanced reading level were northwest and southwest of downtown Milwaukee. Several schools in Waukesha County and the north shore neighbourhoods had a higher proportion of students reaching the advanced reading category. A few inner-city neighbourhoods also had students performing very well.

The overall patterns reveal that public school quality in Milwaukee tends to be better in neighbourhoods with higher proportions of Whites. However, school quality is generally worse for schools located in African American and Hispanic neighbourhoods. Due to the poorer quality schools in certain ethnically concentrated areas, it is probably difficult for African American and Hispanic children to 'get ahead' in the future and to overcome the obstacles of social inequality found in American society.

Ethnically owned businesses in Milwaukee

Analysing ethnic residential patterns focuses on segregation at 'night', when people are away from work. Another aspect of segregation involves where people work and how this relates to where people live. If members of an ethnic group tend to live near their places of work (and in segregated areas), then there would be fewer chances of workplace interactions with people with a different racial ethnic background. However, a positive aspect of ethnically segregated areas would be the creation of ethnic enclaves (through ethnic businesses), which not only cater to the needs of ethnic group members but can also benefit the entire city. For example, ethnic restaurants may generally serve members of that ethnic group, but they can also provide everyone in the city with the opportunity to experience ethnic-specific dishes. Cities can promote their ethnic enclaves as tourist destinations, in which ethnic diversity can be celebrated. The locations of ethnically owned businesses could be related to the existence of ethnic residential enclaves in Milwaukee, in that if ethnic-owned businesses were scattered throughout the city, then no ethnic business enclaves would exist. If the majority of businesses were geographically concentrated, then there would be evidence of the existence of ethnic business enclaves. It is important to map ethnically owned businesses to

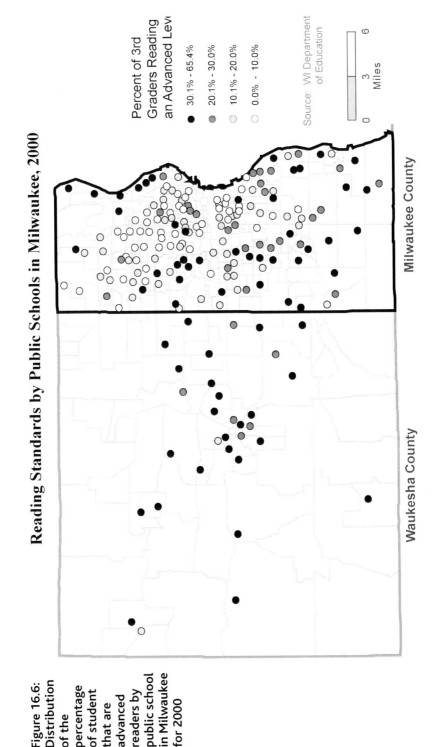

Reading Standards by Public Schools in Milwaukee, 2000

Percent of 3rd
Graders Reading
an Advanced Level

● 30.1% - 65.4%
● 20.1% - 30.0%
○ 10.1% - 20.0%
○ 0.0% - 10.0%

Source: WI Department
of Education

0   3   6
Miles

Milwaukee County

Waukesha County

Figure 16.6:
Distribution
of the
percentage
of student
that are
advanced
readers by
public school
in Milwaukee
for 2000

examine whether employment locations are concentrated in ethnically segregated residential neighbourhoods.

Data from the *2000 directory of minority-owned firms* provided by the Wisconsin Department of Commerce list minority-certified businesses in Milwaukee. The category of 'minority' in the business directory includes businesses that are owned by women and minority ethnic groups. The women-owned businesses were kept in the analysis dataset, since a woman owner could also be associated with a minority ethnic group. Given that the dataset does not just include minority ethnic groups, caution was used when interpreting the results. The main drawback of this dataset was that ethnicity is inferred and self-identified by the business owners.

The methodology to show the geographic distribution of ethnically owned businesses involved the geocoding of addresses for each business in a geographic information system (GIS), and the mapping of the 627 business establishments. Then Hispanic-owned businesses were drawn from this database by using the surname of the owner. For example, business owners with the surnames of 'Gonzales' or 'Lopez' were categorised as Hispanic. The same could not be done for African Americans, as African American surnames are difficult to identify. Minority ethnic-owned businesses can then be compared to the ethnically concentrated neighbourhoods mentioned earlier in this chapter.

Hispanic-owned businesses were mainly located southwest of downtown Milwaukee (see Figure 16.7). Very few Hispanic-owned firms were located in the western suburbs of Waukesha County or the northern inner city neighbourhoods. Hispanic businesses were located along prominent thoroughfares: historic Mitchell Avenue, National Avenue and South 16th Street (renamed Cesar E. Chavez Drive in this ethnic enclave). The urban landscape in the Hispanic-concentrated neighbourhoods is filled with bilingual signage irrespective of whether the firm is Hispanic-owned or not. El Rey, a large grocery store and restaurant, provides residents in the area with imported Mexican products and Mexican cuisine. A positive impact of segregation in Milwaukee is the clustering of Hispanic businesses in the 'Hispanic' neighbourhoods.

Cultural landscape

Most of this chapter's research on the impacts of living in segregated Milwaukee areas indicates negative consequences for minority ethnic groups. However, are there other non-socioeconomic data that may indicate 'good' segregation? A sense of place and community pride can be seen in the cultural landscape of many segregated neighbourhoods.

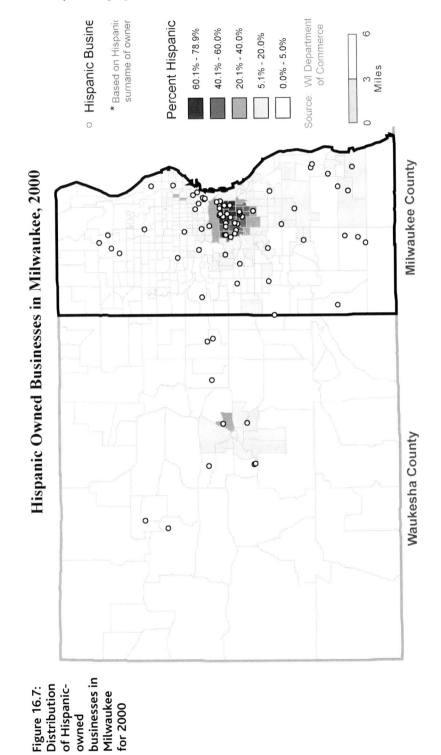

Figure 16.7:
Distribution
of Hispanic-
owned
businesses in
Milwaukee
for 2000

The urban landscape of African American-concentrated areas indicates the honouring of several prominent African Americans. North Third Street was renamed Dr Martin Luther King Drive and is the location of several murals honouring local and national African Americans. African American heritage is also displayed in Milwaukee's Juneteenth celebration and parade on 19 June (see Figure 16.8). Juneteenth is a popular African American festival that started in the state of Texas and signifies the ending of slavery in America (Donovan and de Bres, 2006, p 379). An estimated 100,000 people attended the Juneteenth festivities in Milwaukee.

A 'windshield' survey of the Hispanic-concentrated neighbourhoods of Milwaukee illustrates similar cultural pride in urban space. As North 16th Street crosses into the Hispanic areas it changes to Cesar E. Chavez Drive in honour of the prominent labour activist from Arizona. One of the murals in this segregated neighbourhood depicts Cesar Chavez (see Figure 16.9), Jesus Salas (founder of Wisconsin's agricultural labour union) and Aztec iconography. The Aztec pyramid and calendar indicate the strong Mexican American presence in this part of Milwaukee. The Hispanic ethnic enclave is famous for its Cinco de Mayo (5 May) event, which celebrates a Mexican militia

Figure 16.8: Juneteenth celebration in 2011 on Dr Martin Luther King Drive in Milwaukee

Photo taken by author

Figure 16.9: Small section of a mural celebrating Hispanics. The image represents Cesar Chavez and is located on Cesar Chavez Drive in Milwaukee

Photo taken by author

victory over French troops in 1862. All of the ethnic festivals, while geared to specific ethnic group members, are open for all Milwaukee residents to attend.

Discussion

Milwaukee is residentially divided by race and ethnicity. Is the segregation in Milwaukee 'good' or 'bad'? A comparison of the characteristics of ethnically concentrated neighbourhoods reveals several social inequalities. Whites living in the 'White' neighbourhoods had higher educational attainment and income levels, while African Americans and Hispanics living in their respective segregated neighbourhoods had lower educational attainment and income levels. In terms of school quality, the higher proportion of students who were reading at an advanced level was located in suburban elementary schools. For African Americans and Hispanics living in segregated Milwaukee neighbourhoods, these results indicate 'bad' segregation. A positive impact of ethnic segregation for Hispanics in Milwaukee was the development of ethnic business enclaves. These Hispanic-owned firms have the possibility of serving both the local ethnic community and people in the wider metro area. The cultural landscape of the African American and Hispanic neighbourhoods indicates a strong sense of community. Ethnic murals and celebrations reflect a sense of pride in one's ethnic group and ethnic neighbourhoods.

This Milwaukee case study on the impacts of segregation merely touches on the link between social inequality and spatial inequality. Future research could investigate social capital and other criteria to understand the strength of a segregated community. Urban scholars could analyse more socioeconomic variables (for example, health quality, housing quality and crime rates) in respect to living in segregation. Scholars and policy makers should also try to answer a question that the results of this chapter suggest: what can be done to alleviate some of the negative impacts of living in segregation? Geographers should do more than measure, map or analyse the impacts of segregation – attempts should be made to offer solutions to problems that arise from residential ethnic segregation.

Note

[1] We understand that the significance of correlation coefficient is inflated due to the likely presence of spatial autocorrelation. Nonetheless, these coefficient values provide us with some general ideas of correlation levels.

References

Bukenya, J., Gebremedhin, T. and Schaeffer, P. (2003) 'Analysis of rural quality of life and health: a spatial approach', *Economic Development Quarterly*, vol 17, pp 280-93.

de Souza Briggs, X. (2005) *The geography of opportunity: race and housing choice in metropolitan America*, Washington, DC: Brookings Institution Press.

Dissart, J. and Deller, S. (2000) 'Quality of life in the planning literature', *Journal of Planning Literature*, vol 15, pp 135-46.

Donovan, A. and de Bres, K. (2006) 'Foods of freedom: Juneteenth as a culinary tourist attraction', *Tourism Review International*, vol 9, pp 379-89.

Easterly, W. (1999) *Life during growth*, Washington, DC: The World Bank (http://econ.worldbank.org/external/default/main?pagePK=64165259&theSitePK=469372&piPK=64165421&menuPK=64166093&entityID=000094946_99060201522485).

Ellen, I. (2000) 'Is segregation bad for your health? The case of low birth weight', *Brookings-Wharton Papers on Urban Affairs*, pp 203-29.

Friedman, S. and Rosenbaum, E. (2001) 'Differences in the locational attainment of immigrant and native-born households with children in New York City', *Demography*, vol 38, pp 337-48.

Glaeser, E., Vigdor, J. and Sanford, T. (2001) *Racial segregation in the 2000 Census: promising news*, Washington, DC: Brookings Institution.

Gurda, J. (1999) *The making of Milwaukee*, Milwaukee, WI: Milwaukee County Historical Society Press.

Haring, M.J., Stock, W.A., Okun, M.A. and Witter, R.A. (1984) 'Education and subjective well-being: a meta-analysis', *Educational Evaluation and Policy Analysis*, vol 6, pp 165-73.

Hirschman, A.O. (1989) 'Having opinions – one of the elements of well-being', *The American Economic Review*, vol 79, pp 75-9.

Jones, P. (2010) *The Selma of the north: Civil rights insurgency in Milwaukee*, Cambridge, MA: Harvard University Press.

Kain, J. (1968) 'Housing segregation, negro employment, and metropolitan decentralization', *Quarterly Journal of Economics*, vol 82, pp 175-97.

Kaplan, D. and Woodhouse, K. (2005) 'Research in ethnic segregation II: measurements, categories, and meanings', *Urban Geography*, vol 26, pp 737-45.

Kawachi, I. and Berkman, L. (2003) *Neighborhoods and health*, Oxford, NY: Oxford University Press.

Mayadas, N. and Segal, U. (2000) 'Refugees in the 1990s: a US perspective', in P. Balgopal (ed) *Social work practice with immigrants and refugees*, New York: Columbia University Press.

Mouw, T. (2002) 'Are Black workers missing the connection? The effect of spatial distance and employee referrals on interfirm racial segregation', *Demography*, vol 39, pp 507-28.

Peach, C. (1996) 'Good segregation, bad segregation', *Planning Perspectives*, vol 11, pp 379-98.

Randall, J. and Morton, P. (2003) 'Quality of life in Saskatoon 1991 and 1996: a geographic perspective', *Urban Geography*, vol 24, pp 691-722.

Reynolds, J.R. and Ross, C.E. (1998) 'Social stratification and health: education's benefit beyond economic status and social origins', *Social Problems*, vol 45, pp 221-47.

US Census (1995) 'Urban and rural definitions' (www.census.gov/population/censusdata/urdef.txt).

van Kempen, R. and Özüekren, A. (1998) 'Ethnic segregation in cities: new forms and explanations in a dynamic world', *Urban Studies*, vol 35, pp 1631-56.

Varady, D. (2005) *Desegregating the city: ghettos, enclaves, and inequality*, Albany, NY: State University of New York.

Yuan, A. (2008) 'Racial composition of neighborhood and emotional well-being', *Sociological Spectrum*, vol 28, pp 105-29.

SEVENTEEN

Conclusion: possible future agendas and summary thoughts

Christopher D. Lloyd, Ian G. Shuttleworth
and David W.S. Wong

Introduction

The lesson that segregation matters is continually reinforced by events in the real world, including the recent Swedish riots in May 2013 and the English riots in August 2011. In each case, the root causes of the trouble were initially attributed to segregation and its close relative, social inequality. To a large extent, therefore, this book and the importance of its subject matter speak for themselves. The purpose of this concluding chapter is thus not to look backward and to elaborate on each chapter, but instead to look forward by drawing together the various contributions and by distilling their key points to suggest a broad research agenda on the theme of segregation. Although taking this type of overview is problematic (for instance, others may have very different visions), our aim is to stimulate debate about some future directions for further work. There are four broad avenues that occur from our reading of the book; these are *measuring and capturing segregation, understanding processes, making comparisons* and *understanding outcomes*. Although the emphasis is on measurement or methodological issues, the four broad avenues together pose challenges and opportunities for segregation researchers, and we argue that this book is well placed to begin such a stock-taking exercise as it brings together international contributions dealing with segregation in countries including Sweden, the UK and the US, draws on a range of different types of data, as well as different methodologies. These agendas for the future build on the themes that have been the focus for the book, and the interrelated trinity of concepts, data and methods are of key importance in understanding research to date, and how it may develop in the future.

Measuring and capturing segregation

There have been considerable advances in the past decade in how segregation is measured that have taken the field beyond the status quo of traditional census-based analyses of segregation. Historically, these have used population counts aggregated for fixed spatial output units that have been provided by national statistical bodies. In the UK context, for example, typical units that have often been used have been wards and in the US, tracts or block groups. By default, given the reliance on census data, the focus of concern has been the population 'at home', captured at its place of residence as it would be during the night. Many analyses use global indices that provide general summaries of population distributions, and there has always been considerable methodological debate about the most appropriate ways to measure segregation with, for example, different dimensions of segregation such as evenness and exposure being suggested (Massey and Denton, 1988), as well as arguments about the most sensible indicators to use in the earlier well-known 'index wars'. In a number of ways, however, a wider range of data, techniques and approaches have re-opened the field.

One strand of research has continued using aggregated population counts across spatial units but has sought to give geography a more central place by experimenting with measures that are sensitive to spatial variations in segregation within study areas, that deal with population patterning and that try to escape from the confines imposed by fixed statistical output geographies (Wong, 1993; Reardon and O'Sullivan, 2004). Several chapters in the book advance this tradition, showing new ways in which to analyse aggregate census data, and to tease out the complexities of spatial scale and form. Lloyd et al (Chapter Four) illustrate one possible method by which to measure interaction between zones. Their approach is used to construct neighbourhoods and so to derive better segregation measures than would be available using standard aspatial segregation measures that are constrained to population output geography boundaries. This is done through the use of spatial interaction data, in this case, one-year migration, which is used to weight attribute data with places with high levels of interaction given greater weights. Wong (Chapter Three) also deals with a similar theme by considering spatial proximity that can be used in the calculation of segregation indices by capturing the spatial distance between ethnic groups using the example of Washington, DC.

Both these approaches try to deal directly or indirectly with the modifiable areal unit problem (MAUP). This means that not only are the indices partially an artefact of the shape and the size of the units used, but also that the units are not necessarily socially meaningful (for example, as neighbourhoods), and also that they are impossible to use as a robust basis for cross-national comparison as it is difficult to compare 'like with like' (a theme to which we return later).

Another response to these statistical problems of boundaries, geographies and spatial units is to avoid the use of aggregate data altogether, or to produce and use data not tabulated according to traditional census geographies. This diminishes the problem of MAUP and facilitates the appropriate spatial delimitation of areas for segregation analysis, although it does not completely avoid it. Several chapters (Chapters Five, Seven, Ten and Eleven) in the book therefore explore the use of non-standard individual-level administrative or population register data. They are likely to be of particular interest to UK readers given the stated intention that the 2011 UK Census will be the last in its traditional form, with mooted replacements including better use of linked administrative data, a large-scale population survey or some combination of these two options. Using historical census data from selected US cities, Páez et al (Chapter Five) show how segregation can be evaluated using a new spatial association measure at the individual and very small-area spatial scale. This method could be extended to contemporary problems where individual-level micro-data are available. In the same vein, Östh et al (Chapter Seven) demonstrate the use of Swedish population registry data in another generalisable approach in which attribute data, coded to 100m cells, can be aggregated across bespoke population neighbourhoods to produce a variety of population and segregation statistics. This reduces the impact of MAUP because the analysis is not restricted to fixed and previously defined statistical units, but the question still remains, in both this contribution and that of Páez et al, of what is the most suitable spatial level for analysis in terms of social meaning. The direction of travel across many countries is likely to be towards the greater availability of individual-level micro-data, whether it is sourced from traditional censuses or from administrative sources, but from wherever the data come, one challenge for segregation researchers will be to modify existing segregation measures or to create others to accommodate different data types (Wong and Shaw, 2011).

The use of administrative data has drawbacks – for instance, some of the individual and household attributes recorded in a census are not found in the same form in administrative data sources – but it also sometimes has advantages. These lie in the different information that is captured by administrative systems and the greater frequency by which data are updated – both issues to which we return when looking at *processes*. Both of these advantages are apparent in the chapters of van Ham and Manley (Chapter Eleven), and of Harris (Chapter Ten). Harris uses administrative data on education to provide insights into the movements of pupils between schools in Greater London and the ways in which segregation patterns have evolved over time. This would be impossible to do in this way using standard census-based approaches to residential segregation, although it should be acknowledged that census data is a useful context for any study of this nature. Van Ham and Manley use administrative data on house letting in the UK to consider residential choice and the factors which decide who gets allocated to which house.

The use of these administrative data on education and housing take the analysis of segregation beyond the customary focus on residential segregation (in effect, the static resident population on census night). This points the way towards considering segregation not just in residential terms, but also across different domains of activity such as work, leisure and education (Wong and Shaw, 2011). There is a clear need to do this. There is a growing interest in populations, and their interactions, at different times of the day, and a strong realisation that there is more to segregation than place of residence. The changing data environment in which more data become available, whether from administrative sources or traditional censuses or not, will very likely lead to the ability to consider populations on a near 24/7 basis. Some administrative data, such as those on education, already permit a wider perspective than just place of residence, and the greater linkage of administrative data and the wider availability of individual micro-data will expand the scope for analysis. To these data can be added those which are being created by the private sector or in the 'electronic mist' that is increasingly the accompaniment to everyday life in much of Europe and North America. Here there is a focus on 'big data' and mining the traces left by social internet media and mobile phones using commercial data. These can be used to trace populations and to geocode individuals to quite precise times and places (in a relative sense). These are as yet emerging trends, and further work is needed to develop the means to analyse segregation using these data. Traditional measures – for example, the index of dissimilarity – are unlikely to be sufficient, and a fresh look is needed to explore how best to summarise and capture these details so they can be used in segregation studies.

New data sources and new methods provide opportunities to measure and to conceptualise segregation. However, the requirement to measure and to conceptualise segregation in new ways is not driven by data and methodological developments alone. Chapters by Johnston et al (Chapter Two) and Wright et al (Chapter Six) advocate the need for new thinking about how segregation is conceptualised and measured because of social change and multiculturalism. Johnston et al argue that the advent of multiculturalism and multiethnic cities has outdated conventional ways of thinking about and measuring segregation that were often predicated on the Black/White divide in US cities during the 20th century. Now, it is suggested, the focus of segregation studies should be on understanding how urban mosaics evolve, measuring diversity and capturing local variations. Similar forces are acknowledged by Wright et al who remark on the growth of multiethnic metropolitan areas and the creation of new diverse neighbourhood types that now overlay older geographies of segregation. They highlight, using US Census data, the decline in the number of White-only tracts in cities, and growing patterns of urban diversity, although they argue that 'White flight' remains an issue.

In the measurement of segregation, the chapters in this book have highlighted the importance of new social concepts in understanding changing societies and the need to look across other activity domains (other than the residential). The contribution of new data sources to help to cope with other types of segregation, for example, in education, has been noted, as have advances in methods to aid researchers in coping with the spatial complexities of population data and the ways in which it is represented using official geographies. In the future, it is likely that segregation researchers will extend existing methods but develop new ones as well. This is probable because of the rapidly evolving data environment more generally, but especially in the US and the UK, where changes in the availability of traditional census data and its augmentation by new sources will mean that some analyses formerly done will be difficult, whereas new opportunities will arise. An example of relatively simple analysis that could be done previously but is no longer easy to do is to include socioeconomic and housing variables based on decennial census data in segregation studies, as the 2010 Census in the US stopped collecting socioeconomic and housing information. Chief among new opportunities are those that will enable 'big data' to throw light on 24/7 populations if new analytical tools can be found and applied.

Understanding processes

Most research views segregation as a pattern. This is not surprising given that most of this research has been based on cross-sectional census data that freeze a population at one moment in time. Such an approach makes it difficult to understand how segregation patterns have changed through time given just a starting point, say in 2001, and an end point, for example, in 2011. Overall changes can be observed and measured (assuming that the difficulty of the analysis is not multiplied by different official statistical geographies at each date that make it impossible to compare like-with-like – see the later discussion of *comparisons*), but there is no reliable way to estimate, even in the best case, whether most of the changes occurred towards the start or the end of the period, nor what demographic forces drove them. It is also difficult, if not impossible, to estimate the demographic components of population (births, deaths and migration), and the extent to which they serve to redistribute populations and thereby lead to changes in segregation, let alone the motives for population change. However, there is a public interest in understanding how and why segregation has changed through time. This has been matched by an academic appreciation of the need to understand more about population dynamics (Simpson, 2007), and how they drive changes in segregation levels.

This research agenda, focused on dynamics and processes, has in the past been difficult to approach. However, the creation of non-standard census data outputs and the production and release of linked administrative data have gone some way towards providing the resources for this understanding of dynamics. Several chapters in the book speak to this research agenda. Shuttleworth et al (Chapter Nine) assess how far internal migration within Northern Ireland since 2001 has redistributed the population by religion and thereby changed levels of segregation. The data used for this were from the Northern Ireland Longitudinal Study (NILS), based on a 28 per cent sample of the Northern Ireland population. The large sample size makes it possible to examine safely change for quite small geographies. In principle, the Swedish population register, as used by Östh et al (Chapter Seven), could be used in the same way, and could be extended, like the NILS, to consider the impact of births and deaths as well as internal migration (as measured by address changes) on the changing geography of population. The level of disaggregation, particularly in terms of time and place, seen in the Harris (Chapter Ten) and van Ham and Manley (Chapter Eleven) chapters, also permits a detailed analysis of segregation processes and patterns for, respectively, education and housing. The challenges in using data of these kinds are three-fold and reside in gaining access to the data, analysing often large-scale and complex datasets, and maintaining public trust by using the data responsibly. Despite the desirability of using large longitudinal datasets to follow population groups through time, it is possible to research process using more conventional sources. In this respect, the chapters by Sabater and Finney (Chapter Twelve) and Hwang (Chapter Thirteen) that use, respectively, UK and US Census data, are interesting. Sabater and Finney make the point well that segregation is a process with a significant life cycle element while Hwang considers processes across different housing submarkets in US cities to create ethnic segregation.

One immediate challenge for segregation researchers will be to make better use of emerging longitudinal datasets to get a better grasp of local population dynamics. This will demand the acquisition and use of unfamiliar methods (although these are ready and waiting, as they are already commonly used in other fields of social and health research) to cope with modelling events, lapses and duration. The contribution of social scientists who have worked on segregation will be to bring a clearer understanding of space, geographical variation and the complexity of the concept of the neighbourhood. However, there are other opportunities which arise from two more distant sets of challenges, one quantitative and one qualitative.

To understand better the dynamics of segregation, particularly with regard to residential choice, there is room to revive and to expand the corpus of work that was undertaken using the Schelling Model (Schelling, 1969) as its bedrock. Agent-based simulation models, with the benefits of additional computing power, can be made much more realistic, taking as their starting points in real urban geographies rather than the random distributions that are usual. Furthermore, they could use real behavioural parameters derived from the analysis of micro-data. These would be a better guide as they represent actual behaviour rather than the intentions and aspirations taken from surveys that in many cases are not translated into reality. Moreover, this type of approach would permit estimates of the behaviour of different types of people in different kinds of place, thus enhancing the value of micro-simulation as a method to assess selected 'what if' scenarios. It is easy to imagine several of these – what would be the effects on segregation if 10 per cent of people moved every year rather than 5 per cent and the median distance moved increased from 3km to 4km? How might residential behaviour and migratory change in a population alter if the proportion of people with degree or higher qualifications increased from 15 to 40 per cent? Coupling this with some appreciation of how residential choice interacted with the structures imposed by already-existing population geographies will likely allow our collective understanding of segregation processes to grow.

The second challenge is qualitative and concerns the need to widen segregation studies beyond their usual current boundaries, and also beyond the parameters set by the majority of the chapters in this book. Our understanding of process will always be, to some degree, incomplete if we lack information on perceptions and motivations, and how they influence people's behaviour across a wide range of everyday activities and choices. But these qualitative accounts, often drawn from small samples, run the risk of emphasising the unique at the expense of the general, whereas the usual quantitative analyses of segregation are good at capturing the general but are much weaker at understanding the details and behaviours which shape local patterns. Using quantitative or qualitative methods is not an either/or choice, although it is sometimes portrayed and understood as such. In fact, however, there is considerable merit in combining quantitative and qualitative methods in a mixed-methods approach to segregation to take advantage of the strengths of both. Qualitative insights, for example, would add much to quantitative analyses of residential and school choice.

The process and the dynamics that shape all aspects of segregation are thus likely to gain importance in future research agendas. One focus will be quantitative and will probably take advantage of newly available longitudinal databases, survey information and administrative data. This will require greater expertise in a wider range of quantitative methods than currently, and it might also be expected that new measures of segregation and interaction will be required to cope with dynamic change. A second focus will be on considering process in the depth that is possible using carefully designed qualitative studies of localities and population groups to throw light on behaviour, choices, decisions and how these are constrained. The art will be in bringing these two macro-approaches together, and this might be done through the development and extension of existing agent-based modelling frameworks.

Making comparisons

The need to make comparisons between places and times is something of a holy grail in segregation research. In principle, it is highly desirable to make comparisons between different times (is segregation greater now than in the past?) and between places (is city X more segregated than city Y?). In practice, however, this is more difficult than might be expected, for two major reasons. First, the well-known problems associated with the dynamics of spatial units sometimes make it difficult to compare segregation for the same places through time – wards, for example, in the UK, change shape, size and numbers between censuses; approaches to areal interpolation offer possible solutions. Making comparisons between places is even more complex since the spatial units used to represent population data are not even the same and can vary markedly in shape, spatial size and population size. It is difficult, for example, to make meaningful comparisons between US and UK cities because of the different geographies used to produce outputs from the respective national censuses. Moreover, problems with making international comparisons arise from the variations in what is collected by national statistical systems. Many census-based systems, for instance, ask questions about ethnicity, whereas other population data systems, for example, the Swedish population register, record information on country of birth (see Chapter Seven, this volume). Thus, even if the problems associated with spatial units were to be overcome, there would still be conceptual problems arising from the meaning of the data that have been collected. Thus, although comparative studies of segregation are desirable from the perspectives of public understanding of society, and academic research agendas, their feasibility is questionable. However, several contributions to the book suggest ways in which these problems can be partially surmounted and some progress made towards the goal of comparative studies of segregation.

The chapter by Mateos (Chapter Eight) is of key importance to this comparative agenda as it engages directly with the conceptual basis that underlies the collection of ethnicity (or allied) data in national data systems spanning Australia, Canada, Mexico, the US, Japan, South Korea, Israel, Australia, New Zealand and a range of 10 European countries. This understanding of the social and conceptual meaning of statistics is vital as the first building block towards rigorous cross-national research. Other chapters, most notably those by Östh et al (Chapter Seven) and Páez et al (Chapter Five), but also Wong (Chapter Three), suggest possible methods, if individual-level or highly spatially disaggregated data are available, to overcome, at least partially, the problems of incompatible spatial units. The contribution of new methods does not end with these chapters, however, as further insights can be gained from geostatistical approaches and a better understanding of how official output geographies interact with the spatial structure of population (see, for example, Shuttleworth et al, 2011; Cockings et al, 2013).

The development of ways to make reasonable and reliable comparisons of segregation through time, and between different places, is unlikely to be straightforward or easy. But it is something worth attempting, and the book begins to sketch out how this task might be begun. It is therefore probable that this will be a theme for fruitful research engagement in the next decade. Besides the technical challenges, however, there are intellectual challenges about the most appropriate contexts for comparative segregation work. Does it make sense, for instance, to compare London and Helsinki, or the English city of Bradford and Los Angeles? Clearly, this depends on the questions to which answers are being sought, but these in turn depend on a wider understanding of the political, economic and social contexts of various cities and the countries they are located in. This will certainly be an area that requires more thought.

Understanding outcomes

We made the case earlier that the importance of segregation was self-evident given political events on the streets of European cities. However, it is worthwhile reflecting more broadly on the implications of segregation and inequality since these ideas (and empirical contributions relating to them) are relevant to several major fault lines in advanced societies. In the realm of economics there are discussions around the subjects of egalitarianism, the role of market forces, social inequality and the part played by segregation in shaping life chances via access to social and economic resources. It has been pointed out that inequality and social exclusion, issues that are closely related to segregation, are harmful to everyone in society in the 'spirit level' argument (see Wilkinson and Pickett, 2010). On the other hand, there are those who are far more accepting of the spatial and social inequalities that seem to be spreading in many European societies as the price that has to be paid for economic growth and the necessary drawing back of the role of the state. In the domain of politics and culture, there are continual debates about the merits or otherwise of multiculturalism, social integration and diversity. Arguments centre over whether immigration and the growth of segregated communities are 'good' or 'bad' things, and whether integration with the norms of the host society should be encouraged or even forced. Research on segregation and its outcomes speaks to all these concerns, and given the centrality of these and similar debates in popular and political discourses, it is highly likely that this research agenda, on the outcomes and implications of segregation, will increase in importance in the next decade.

Two contributions, those of Catney (Chapter Fourteen) and Dorling (Chapter Fifteen), address the questions of the outcomes and implications of segregation. The chapter by Catney operates at a local level and has a specific focus, probing the question whether segregation has a positive or a negative impact on health. It contributes to the literature about whether segregation is 'good' or 'bad' in terms of outcomes for minorities. This is a complex area – segregation can have positive outcomes in some circumstances because mutual support from people living close to each other can provide 'bonding social capital'. On the other hand, it can also act to have negative consequences because segregation may lead to isolation from a wider range of social opportunities and information networks (a shortage of 'bridging social capital'). The balance between the negative and positive outcomes of segregation at this more micro-scale is thus finely balanced, and the way that the balance tips may depend on local circumstances and the groups in question. The work of Dorling is very much at a more macro-level, dealing with nations, regions and international trends, and starkly sketches the inequalities arising from social segregation. These limit life chances, restrict access to educational opportunities and then limit employment chances later in life. Equity and an egalitarian society are often seen as essential ingredients in ensuring long-lasting social peace. If this argument is correct, then the persistence and growth of socioeconomic inequalities is a bellwether for stormy times ahead. French (Chapter Sixteen) takes a citywide focus and considers the impacts of living in segregated neighbourhoods for those living in Milwaukee, Wisconsin. The chapter shows how the experience of particular ethnic groups may differ markedly in terms of educational attainment and income levels, with lower levels of both for African Americans and Hispanic neighbourhoods than White neighbourhoods. As well as outcomes that may be associated with 'bad' segregation, French also identifies benefits for some groups in being part of an 'ethnic neighbourhood', and this serves as a reminder that the term 'segregation' should not automatically be seen in a negative light.

Since debates about egalitarianism and multiculturalism show no signs of going away, it is probable that there will be growing interest in the next decade in understanding more about segregation by ethnicity and social class across multiple spatial scales. Much of the research effort will go into documenting how segregation matters at various spatial scales since to develop a convincing argument, a considerable weight of empirical evidence is needed. But the research programme will require more than the amassing of facts (even though these are needed). It will also likely need greater amounts of evidence on how segregation matters, and the processes by which it shapes life chances and access to economic and social resources whether by ethnicity, immigrant status, age or social class. However, this research work will come to nothing in practice unless there is a will and a way to engage with the public and politicians and to disseminate the results of the work in an accessible and understandable way. Securing this engagement might prove to be the most daunting challenge.

Final remarks

While this edited volume was intended to be as inclusive and comprehensive as practically possible, and the broad avenues through which we organise the volume cover most general aspects relevant to segregation studies, a clear deficiency of the volume is its uneven geographical coverage. This is inevitable given reasons of space, timing and linguistic competence. The editors and most contributing authors primarily have access to English-language literature, and thus literatures written in other languages are not considered. Similarly, conceptual and empirical discussions have been restricted mostly to the developed world (the US, UK and Europe). Clearly, segregation in the African, Asian and Latin American continents has not been addressed, and the nature and landscape of segregation in those places are also somewhat different from areas we have covered. To take one national example, many segregation studies in China (mostly published in Chinese) have focused on racial-ethnic differences, but only in selected western parts of the country where minorities are more prominent. More recent Chinese studies also consider segregation between population groups classified by income, occupation or housing characteristics so as to address the societal changes associated with economic reform. Due to the massive rural–urban migration to the large cities and coastal manufacturing zones of China during the past two decades or so, some studies have also investigated segregation between immigrants and local people. However, the majority of the Chinese studies are aspatial in nature, employing the popular index of dissimilarity and the location quotient. The social context of segregation in even this one national example is very different from that seen in North America and Europe, and these differences are multiplied if nations and societies across the other continents are also considered and different statistical systems and data systems are added to the mix. A meaningful survey of segregation across the world is thus far beyond the scope of this volume. However, segregation is and is likely to remain a major issue across South America (Arcand and D'Hombres, 2004, provide a Brazilian example), Africa (see Christopher, 2001, for an example in South Africa) and Asia (perhaps in ways that we cannot fully imagine, given our perspective), and a major challenge for the future might be to improve our understanding of these societies working with academics based in these countries. In this regard, some of the techniques and approaches suggested in this book might be translatable across the world, data permitting.

Within a European and North American context, it might seem to be self-evident that research on segregation in all its guises is important and interesting. There seem to be many research opportunities opening up that are driven by new data and new methods, and the research that is being conducted on segregation across the academic community appears to deal with topics that are of considerable public interest. But, while we think this, are these opinions general, and are others even aware of our collective work? In many cases, the answer is probably 'no' to both these questions, and our work has little impact beyond an academic readership. 'Impact' is a much over-used word in the UK higher education system at this time, and the mere sight of it is enough (understandably) to raise hackles in many cases. However, there is a real rationale behind it that is often lost in all the managerial speak that is beloved of research councils and academic managers, and that is to contribute to wider social debates and discussions. It is therefore perhaps up to us (the academic community collectively) to make sure that our research is disseminated and our voices are heard when we have something to contribute. It is therefore hoped that this book, in its own small way, makes a contribution to this process and begins a wider discussion.

References

Arcand, J.-L. and D'Hombres, B. (2004) 'Racial discrimination in the Brazilian labour market: wage, employment and segregation effects', *Journal of International Development*, vol 16, pp 1053-66.

Christopher, A. J. (2001) 'Urban segregation in post-apartheid South Africa', *Urban Studies*, vol 38, pp 449-66.

Cockings, S., Harfoot, A., Martin, D. and Hornby, D. (2013) 'Getting the foundations right: spatial building blocks for official population statistics', *Environment and Planning A*, vol 45, pp 1403-20.

Massey, D.S. and Denton, N.A. (1988) 'The dimensions of residential segregation', *Social Forces*, vol 67, pp 281-315.

Reardon, S.F. and O'Sullivan, D. (2004) 'Measures of spatial segregation', *Sociological Methodology*, vol 34, pp 121-62.

Schelling, T. (1969) 'Models of segregation', *The American Economic Review*, vol 59, pp 488-93.

Shuttleworth, I., Lloyd, C.D., Martin, D. (2011) 'Exploring the implications of changing census output geographies for the measurement of residential segregation: the example of Northern Ireland 1991-2001', *Journal of the Royal Statistical Society, Series A*, vol 174, no 1, pp 1-16.

Simpson, L. (2007) 'Ghettos of the mind: the empirical behaviour of indices of segregation and diversity', *Journal of the Royal Statistical Society A*, vol 170, no 2, pp 405-24.

Wilkinson, R. and Pickett, K. (2010) *The spirit level: Why equality is better for everyone*, London: Penguin.

Wong, D.W.S. (1993) 'Spatial indices of segregation', *Urban Studies*, vol 30, pp 559-72.

Wong, D.W.S. and Shaw, S.-L. (2011) 'Measuring segregation: an activity-space approach', *Journal of Geographical Systems*, vol 13, no 2, 127-45.

INDEX

Note: The following abbreviations have been used – *f* = figure; *n* = note; *t* = table. Page numbers in italics indicate photographs